ARUBA

ROSALIE KLEIN

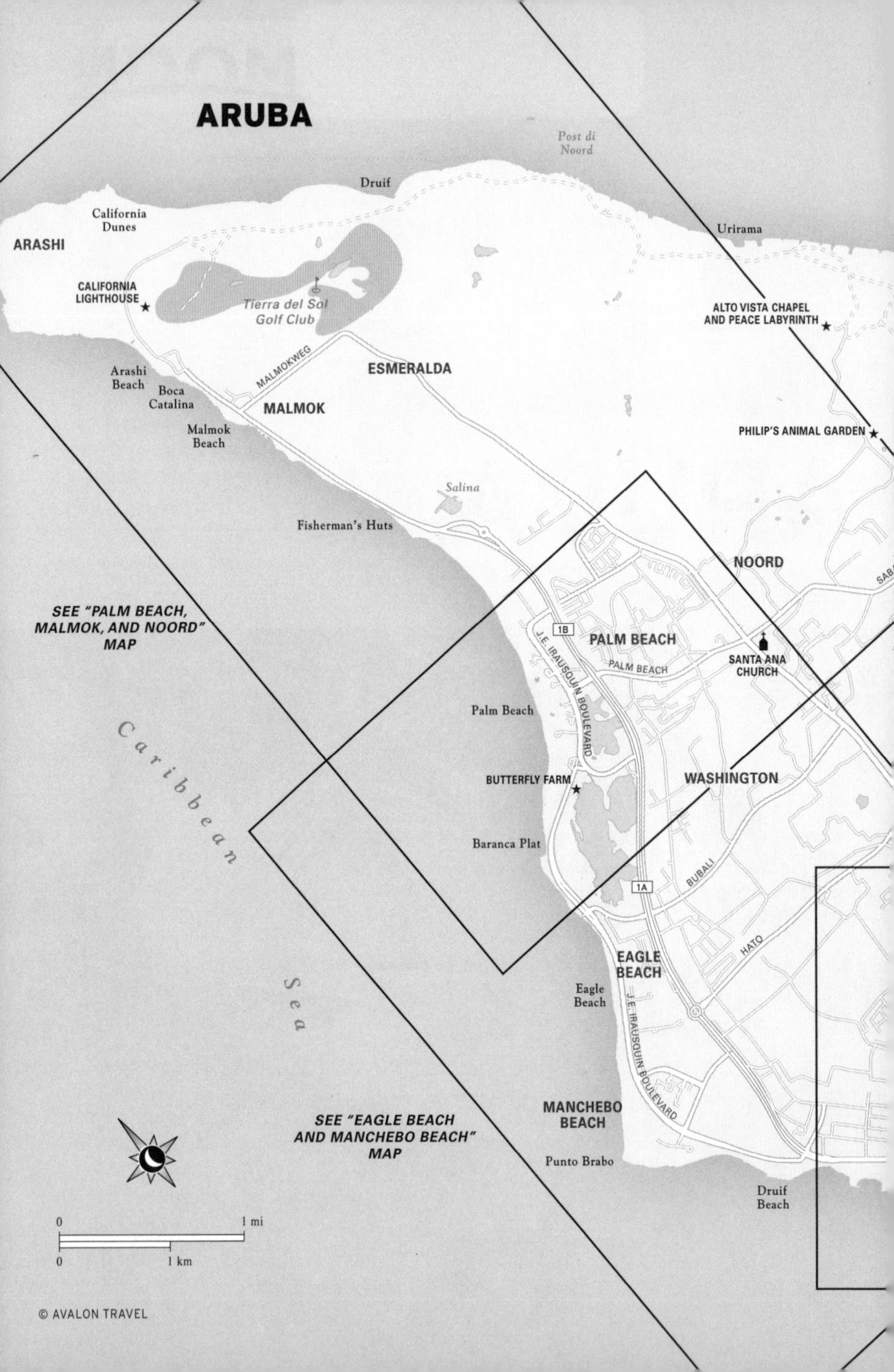
ARUBA
Post di Noord
Druif
California Dunes
ARASHI
Urirama
CALIFORNIA LIGHTHOUSE
Tierra del Sol Golf Club
ALTO VISTA CHAPEL AND PEACE LABYRINTH
MALMOKWEG
ESMERALDA
Arashi Beach
Boca Catalina
MALMOK
Malmok Beach
PHILIP'S ANIMAL GARDEN
Salina
Fisherman's Huts
NOORD
SEE "PALM BEACH, MALMOK, AND NOORD" MAP
1B
PALM BEACH
J.E. IRAUSQUIN BOULEVARD
PALM BEACH
SANTA ANA CHURCH
Palm Beach
Caribbean
BUTTERFLY FARM
WASHINGTON
Baranca Plat
1A
BUBALI
HATO
EAGLE BEACH
Eagle Beach
Sea
J.E. IRAUSQUIN BOULEVARD
MANCHEBO BEACH
SEE "EAGLE BEACH AND MANCHEBO BEACH" MAP
Punto Brabo
Druif Beach
0
1 mi
0
1 km
© AVALON TRAVEL

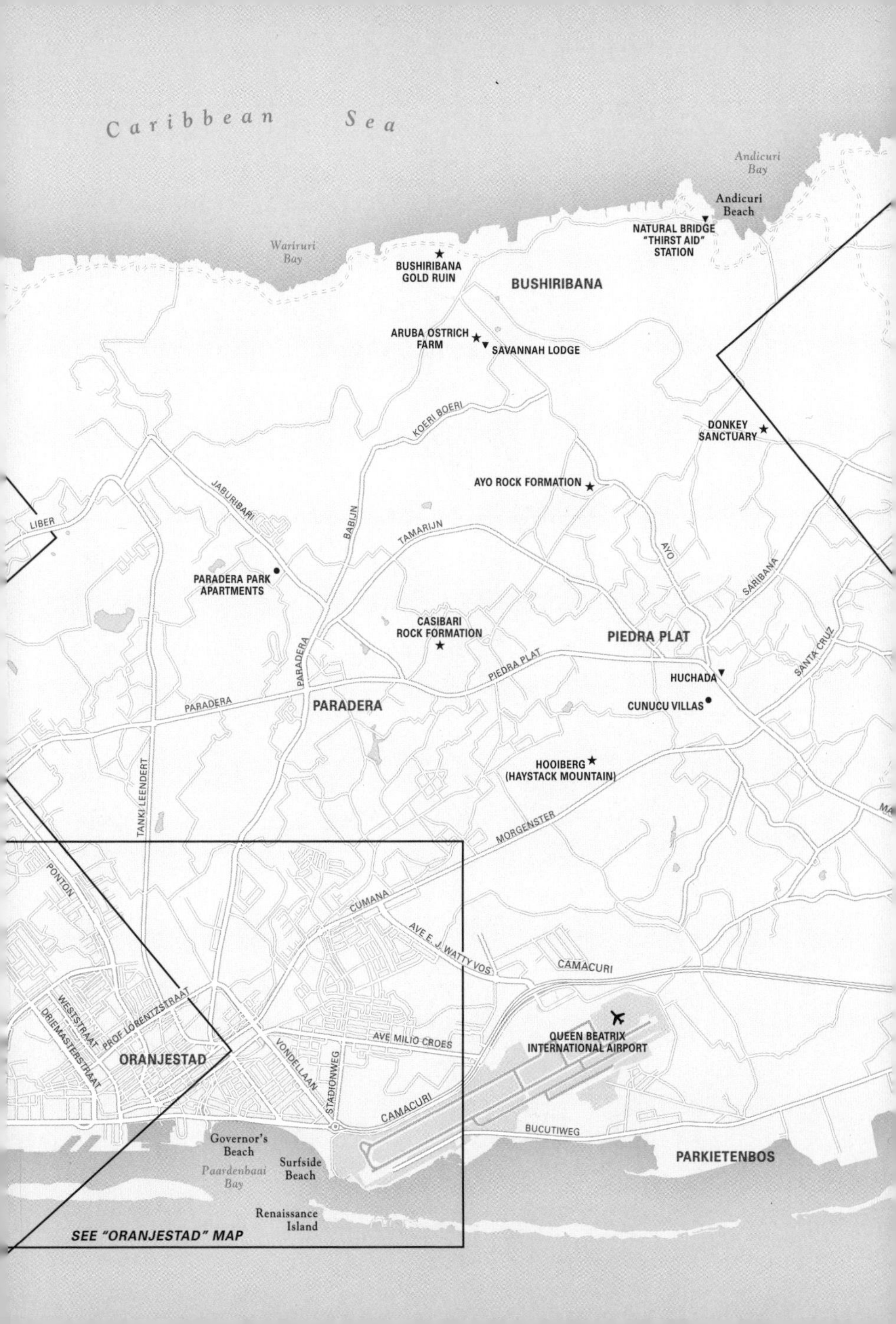

Caribbean Sea

Andicuri Bay

Andicuri Beach

NATURAL BRIDGE

"THIRST AID" STATION

Wariruri Bay

BUSHIRIBANA GOLD RUIN

BUSHIRIBANA

ARUBA OSTRICH FARM

SAVANNAH LODGE

KOERI BOERI

DONKEY SANCTUARY

JABURIBARI

AYO ROCK FORMATION

LIBER

BABIJN

TAMARIJN

AYO

PARADERA PARK APARTMENTS

SARIBANA

CASIBARI ROCK FORMATION

PIEDRA PLAT

PARADERA

SANTA CRUZ

PIEDRA PLAT

HUCHADA

PARADERA

PARADERA

CUNUCU VILLAS

HOOIBERG (HAYSTACK MOUNTAIN)

TANKI LEENDERT

MORGENSTER

PONTON

CUMANA

AVE E. J. WATTY VOS

CAMACURI

WESTSTRAAT

PROF LORENTZSTRAAT

DRIEMASTERSTRAAT

QUEEN BEATRIX INTERNATIONAL AIRPORT

AVE MILIO CROES

ORANJESTAD

VONDELLAAN

STADIONWEG

CAMACURI

BUCUTIWEG

Governor's Beach

Paardenbaai Bay

Surfside Beach

PARKIETENBOS

Renaissance Island

SEE "ORANJESTAD" MAP

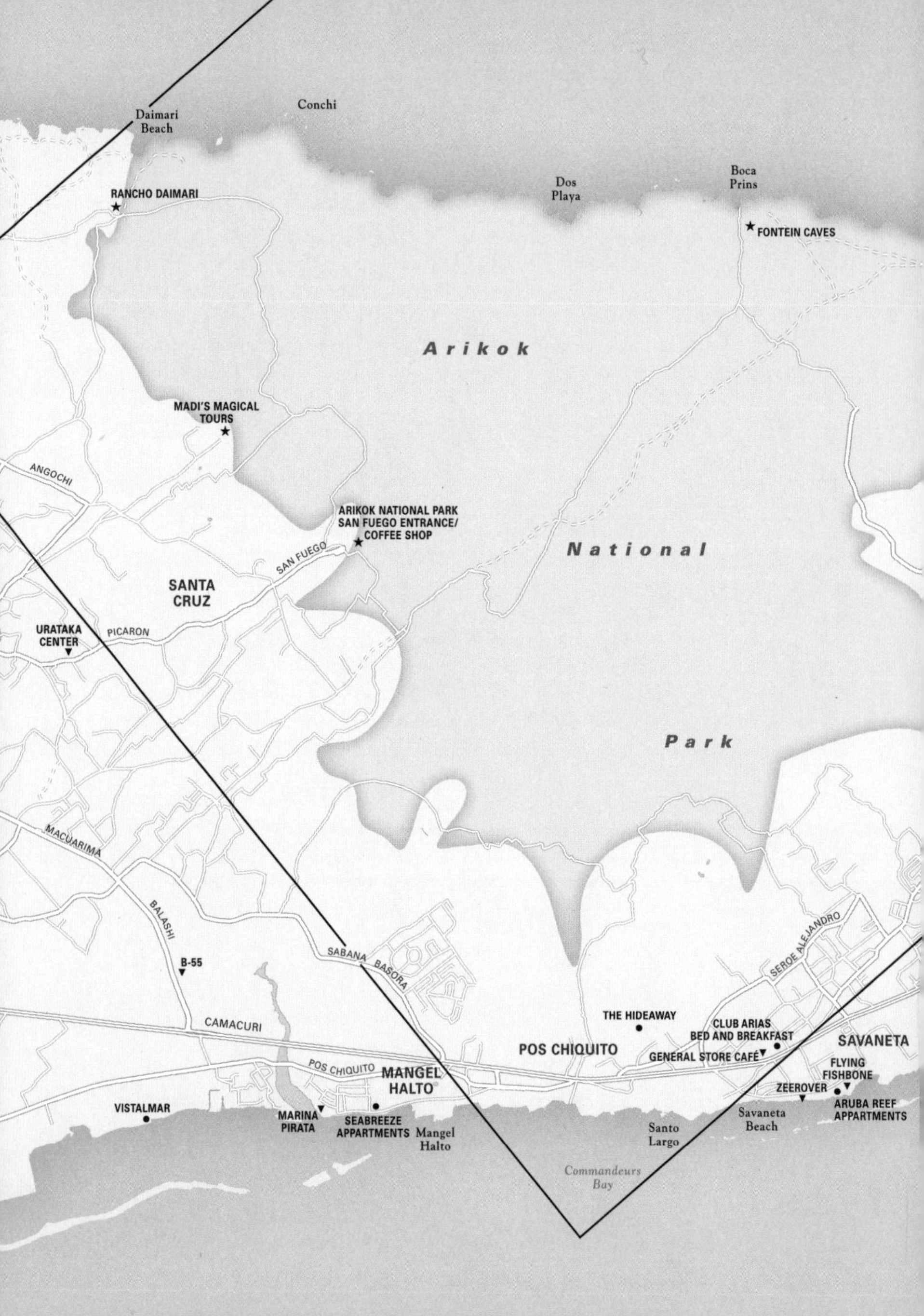

Conchi
Daimari Beach
RANCHO DAIMARI
Dos Playa
Boca Prins
FONTEIN CAVES
Arikok
National
Park
MADI'S MAGICAL TOURS
ANGOCHI
ARIKOK NATIONAL PARK SAN FUEGO ENTRANCE/ COFFEE SHOP
SAN FUEGO
SANTA CRUZ
URATAKA CENTER
PICARON
MACUARIMA
BALASHI
B-55
SABANA
BASORA
SEROE ALEJANDRO
CAMACURI
THE HIDEAWAY
CLUB ARIAS BED AND BREAKFAST
POS CHIQUITO
GENERAL STORE CAFÉ
SAVANETA
FLYING FISHBONE
POS CHIQUITO
MANGEL HALTO
ZEEROVER
ARUBA REEF APPARTMENTS
VISTALMAR
MARINA PIRATA
SEABREEZE APPARTMENTS
Mangel Halto
Santo Largo
Savaneta Beach
Commandeurs Bay

ARUBA (CONTINUED)
SEE "ARIKOK NATIONAL PARK" MAP (P. 85)
Caribbean Sea
QUADIKAKIRI CAVES
Rincon Bay
Grapefield Beach
Boca Grande
SABANA LODO
Bachelor's Beach
WEG FONTEIN
WEG SEROE BLANCO
SERO GRANDI
LOURDES GROTTO/ SEROE PRETO CITY OF LIGHTS
BRASIL
PALISIAWEG
SEROE COLORADO
COSTA RIBA
FORTHEUVEL STRAAT
ESSO HEIGHTS
LAGO HEIGHTS
LAGOVILLE
CAYA JOSE GEERMAN
PASTOR HENDRIK STRAAT
ESSOVILLE
WEG BRASIL
CHARLIE'S BAR
SEROE COLORADO
Roger's Beach
Baby Beach
San Nicolas Bay
RUM REEF BAR
JADS DIVE SHOP
PASTOR HENDRIK STRAAT
SAN NICOLAS
ROYAL DUTCH MARINE CAMP
Caribbean Sea
0
1 mi
0
1 km
© AVALON TRAVEL

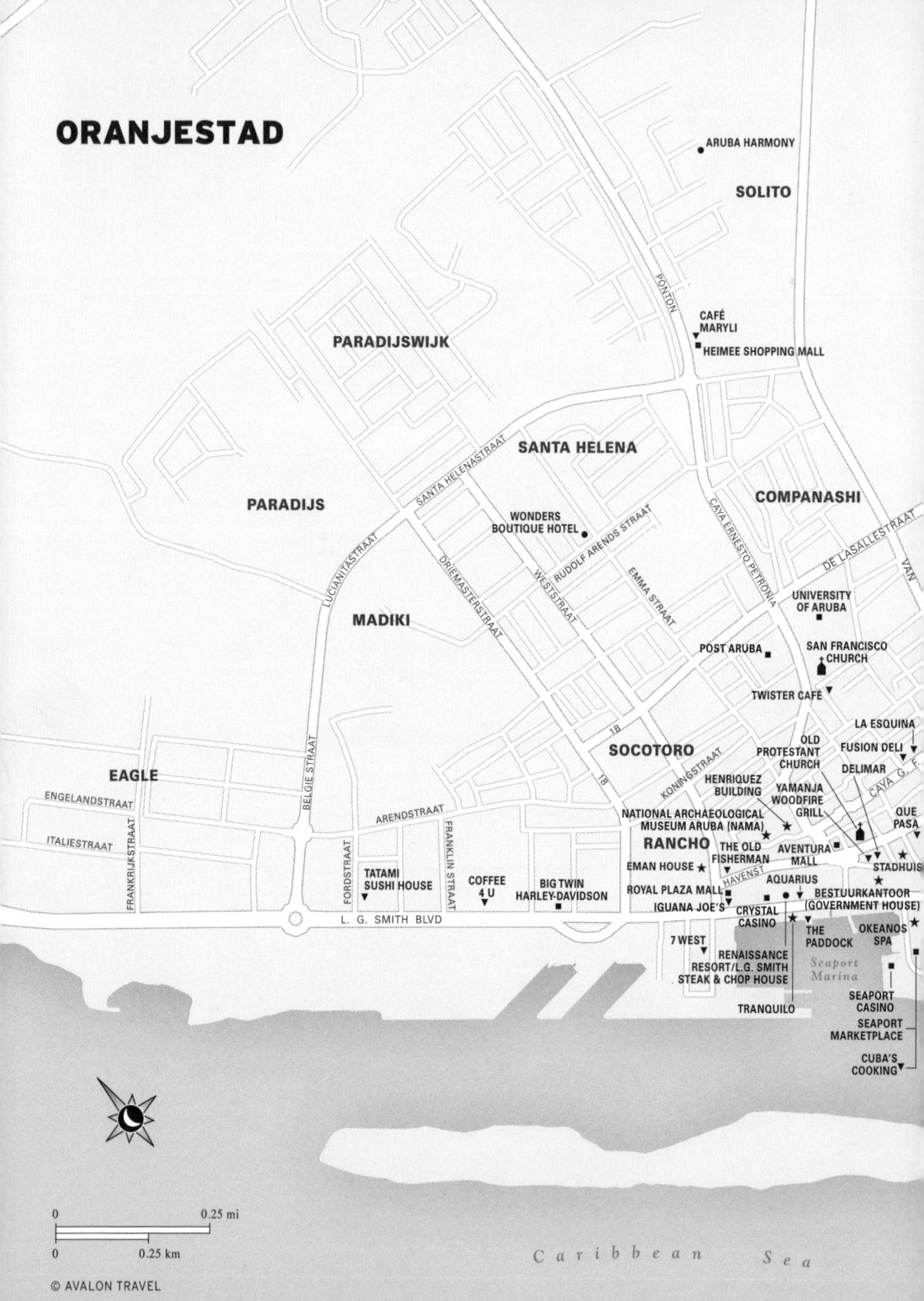
ORANJESTAD
ARUBA HARMONY
SOLITO
PONTON
CAFÉ MARYLI
HEIMEE SHOPPING MALL
PARADIJSWIJK
SANTA HELENA
SANTA HELENASTRAAT
PARADIJS
COMPANASHI
WONDERS BOUTIQUE HOTEL
RUDOLF ARENDS STRAAT
CAYA ERNESTO PETRONIA
DE LASALLESTRAAT
VAN
LUCIANITASTRAAT
DRIEMASTERSTRAAT
WESTSTRAAT
EMMA STRAAT
UNIVERSITY OF ARUBA
MADIKI
POST ARUBA
SAN FRANCISCO CHURCH
TWISTER CAFÉ
1B
LA ESQUINA
SOCOTORO
OLD PROTESTANT CHURCH
FUSION DELI
EAGLE
BELGIE STRAAT
KONINGSTRAAT
DELIMAR
CAYA G. F.
HENRIQUEZ BUILDING
YAMANJA WOODFIRE GRILL
ENGELANDSTRAAT
ARENDSTRAAT
NATIONAL ARCHAEOLOGICAL MUSEUM ARUBA (NAMA)
QUE PASA
ITALIESTRAAT
FRANKRIJKSTRAAT
FORDSTRAAT
FRANKLIN STRAAT
RANCHO
THE OLD FISHERMAN
AVENTURA MALL
EMAN HOUSE
STADHUIS
HAVENST
TATAMI SUSHI HOUSE
COFFEE 4 U
BIG TWIN HARLEY-DAVIDSON
ROYAL PLAZA MALL
AQUARIUS
BESTUURKANTOOR (GOVERNMENT HOUSE)
IGUANA JOE'S
CRYSTAL CASINO
L. G. SMITH BLVD
THE PADDOCK
OKEANOS SPA
7 WEST
RENAISSANCE RESORT/L.G. SMITH STEAK & CHOP HOUSE
Seaport Marina
SEAPORT CASINO
TRANQUILO
SEAPORT MARKETPLACE
CUBA'S COOKING
0
0.25 mi
0
0.25 km
Caribbean Sea

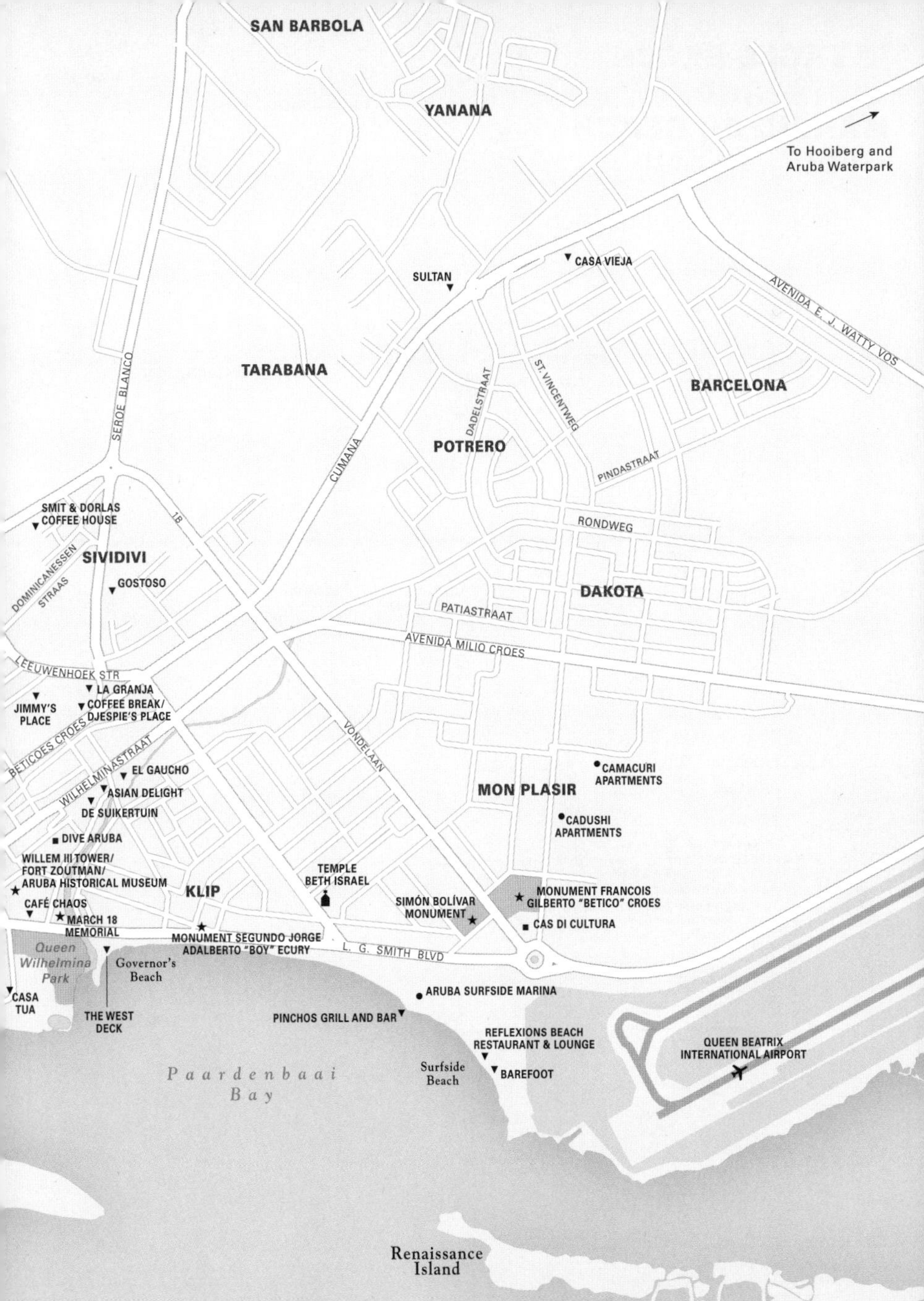

SAN BARBOLA
YANANA
To Hooiberg and
Aruba Waterpark
CASA VIEJA
SULTAN
AVENIDA E. J. WATTY VOS
TARABANA
BARCELONA
DADELSTRAAT
ST. VINCENTWEG
SEROE BLANCO
POTRERO
CUMANA
PINDASTRAAT
SMIT & DORLAS
COFFEE HOUSE
18
RONDWEG
SIVIDIVI
DOMINICANESSEN
STRAAS
GOSTOSO
DAKOTA
PATIASTRAAT
AVENIDA MILIO CROES
LEEUWENHOEK STR
LA GRANJA
JIMMY'S
PLACE
COFFEE BREAK/
DJESPIE'S PLACE
BETICOES CROES
VONDELAAN
WILHELMINASTRAAT
EL GAUCHO
CAMACURI
APARTMENTS
ASIAN DELIGHT
MON PLASIR
DE SUIKERTUIN
CADUSHI
APARTMENTS
DIVE ARUBA
WILLEM III TOWER/
FORT ZOUTMAN/
ARUBA HISTORICAL MUSEUM
TEMPLE
BETH ISRAEL
KLIP
MONUMENT FRANCOIS
GILBERTO "BETICO" CROES
CAFÉ CHAOS
SIMÓN BOLÍVAR
MONUMENT
MARCH 18
MEMORIAL
CAS DI CULTURA
MONUMENT SEGUNDO JORGE
ADALBERTO "BOY" ECURY
L. G. SMITH BLVD
Queen
Wilhelmina
Park
Governor's
Beach
CASA
TUA
ARUBA SURFSIDE MARINA
THE WEST
DECK
PINCHOS GRILL AND BAR
REFLEXIONS BEACH
RESTAURANT & LOUNGE
QUEEN BEATRIX
INTERNATIONAL AIRPORT
Surfside
Beach
BAREFOOT
Paardenbaai
Bay
Renaissance
Island

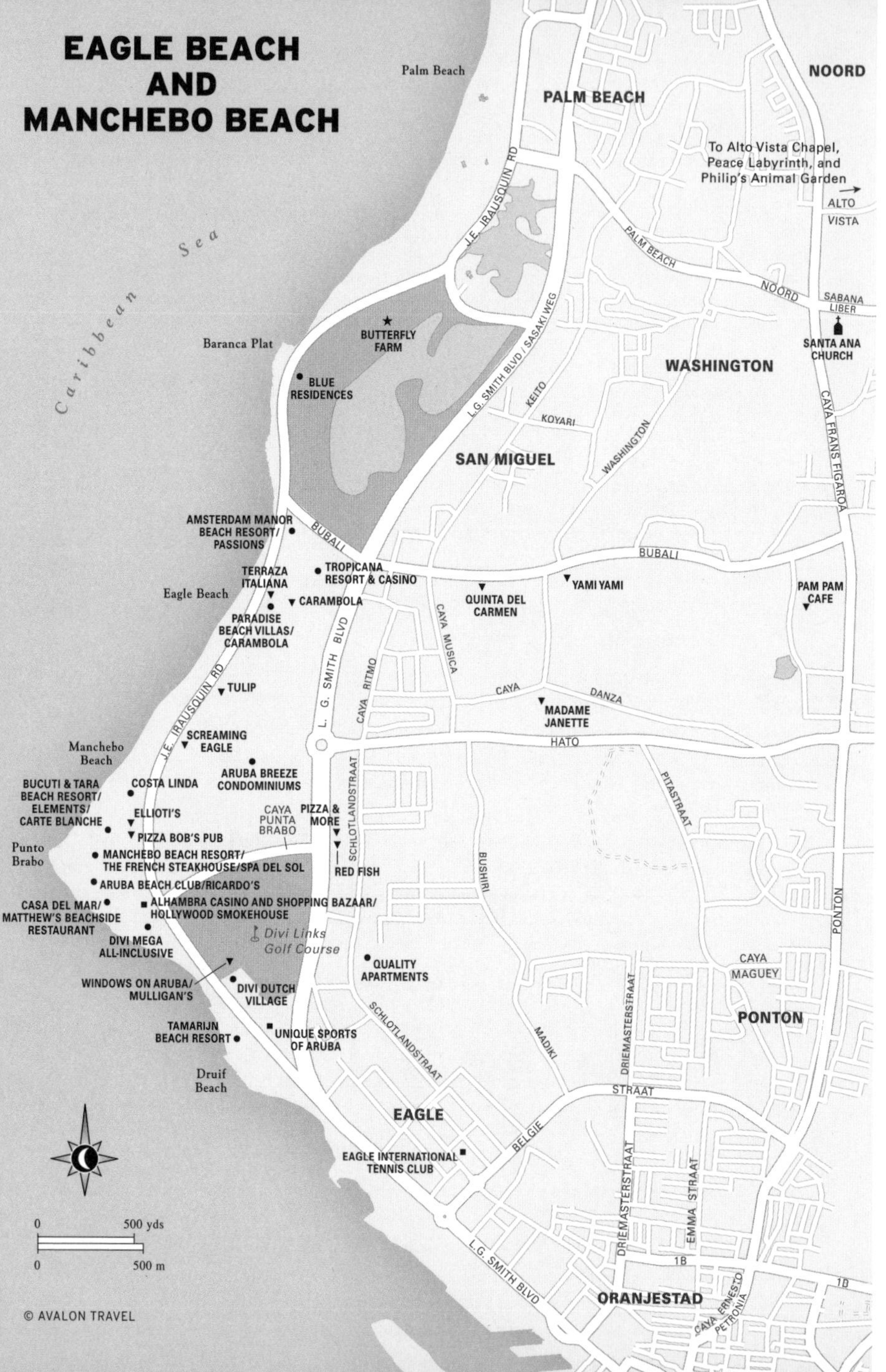
EAGLE BEACH AND MANCHEBO BEACH
Palm Beach
NOORD
PALM BEACH
To Alto Vista Chapel, Peace Labyrinth, and Philip's Animal Garden
ALTO VISTA
J.E. IRAUSQUIN RD
PALM BEACH
NOORD
SABANA LIBER
Caribbean Sea
BUTTERFLY FARM
SANTA ANA CHURCH
Baranca Plat
L.G. SMITH BLVD / SASAKI WEG
WASHINGTON
BLUE RESIDENCES
KEITO
KOYARI
WASHINGTON
CAYA FRANS FIGAROA
SAN MIGUEL
AMSTERDAM MANOR BEACH RESORT/ PASSIONS
BUBALI
BUBALI
TERRAZA ITALIANA
TROPICANA RESORT & CASINO
Eagle Beach
CARAMBOLA
QUINTA DEL CARMEN
YAMI YAMI
PAM PAM CAFE
PARADISE BEACH VILLAS/ CARAMBOLA
CAYA MUSICA
CAYA RITMO
L. G. SMITH BLVD
J.E. IRAUSQUIN RD
TULIP
CAYA
DANZA
MADAME JANETTE
SCREAMING EAGLE
Manchebo Beach
HATO
ARUBA BREEZE CONDOMINIUMS
BUCUTI & TARA BEACH RESORT/ ELEMENTS/ CARTE BLANCHE
COSTA LINDA
ELLIOTI'S
PIZZA BOB'S PUB
CAYA PUNTA BRABO
PIZZA & MORE
SCHLOTLANDSTRAAT
PITASTRAAT
Punto Brabo
MANCHEBO BEACH RESORT/ THE FRENCH STEAKHOUSE/SPA DEL SOL
RED FISH
BUSHIRI
ARUBA BEACH CLUB/RICARDO'S
CASA DEL MAR/ MATTHEW'S BEACHSIDE RESTAURANT
ALHAMBRA CASINO AND SHOPPING BAZAAR/ HOLLYWOOD SMOKEHOUSE
DIVI MEGA ALL-INCLUSIVE
Divi Links Golf Course
PONTON
QUALITY APARTMENTS
CAYA MAGUEY
WINDOWS ON ARUBA/ MULLIGAN'S
DIVI DUTCH VILLAGE
DRIEMASTERSTRAAT
PONTON
MADIKI
TAMARIJN BEACH RESORT
UNIQUE SPORTS OF ARUBA
SCHLOTLANDSTRAAT
Druif Beach
STRAAT
EAGLE
BELGIE
EAGLE INTERNATIONAL TENNIS CLUB
DRIEMASTERSTRAAT
EMMA STRAAT
0
500 yds
0
500 m
L.G. SMITH BLVD
1B
1B
ORANJESTAD
CAYA ERNESTO PETRONIA

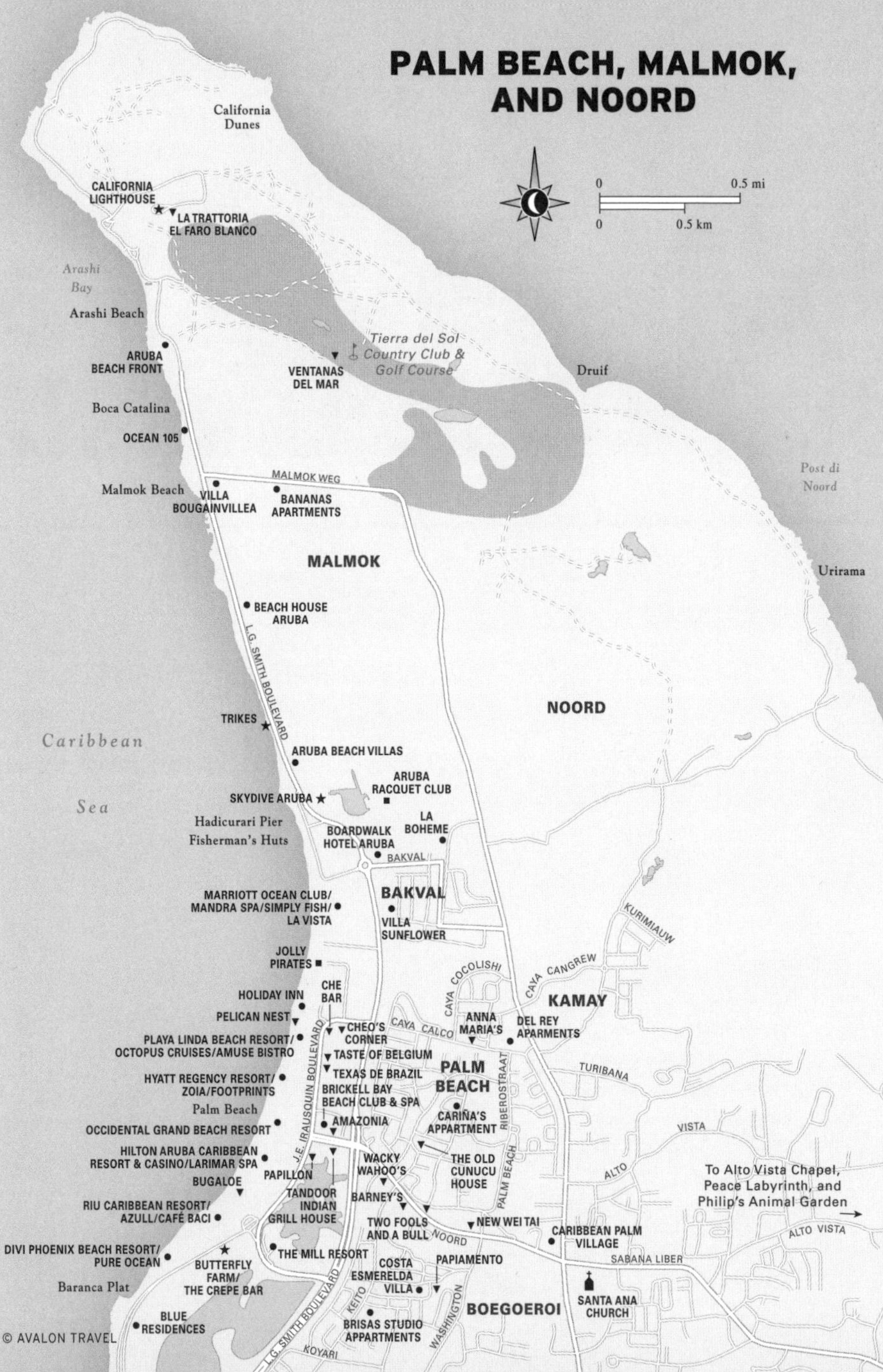

PALM BEACH, MALMOK, AND NOORD
0
0.5 mi
0
0.5 km
California Dunes
CALIFORNIA LIGHTHOUSE
LA TRATTORIA EL FARO BLANCO
Arashi Bay
Arashi Beach
ARUBA BEACH FRONT
VENTANAS DEL MAR
Tierra del Sol Country Club & Golf Course
Druif
Boca Catalina
OCEAN 105
MALMOK WEG
Malmok Beach
VILLA BOUGAINVILLEA
BANANAS APARTMENTS
Post di Noord
MALMOK
Urirama
BEACH HOUSE ARUBA
L.G. SMITH BOULEVARD
NOORD
TRIKES
Caribbean
ARUBA BEACH VILLAS
ARUBA RACQUET CLUB
SKYDIVE ARUBA
Sea
Hadicurari Pier
Fisherman's Huts
BOARDWALK HOTEL ARUBA
LA BOHEME
BAKVAL
MARRIOTT OCEAN CLUB/ MANDRA SPA/SIMPLY FISH/ LA VISTA
BAKVAL
VILLA SUNFLOWER
KURIMIAUW
JOLLY PIRATES
CAYA COCOLISHI
CAYA CANGREW
HOLIDAY INN
CHE BAR
KAMAY
PELICAN NEST
CHEO'S CORNER
CAYA CALCO
ANNA MARIA'S
DEL REY APARMENTS
PLAYA LINDA BEACH RESORT/ OCTOPUS CRUISES/AMUSE BISTRO
TASTE OF BELGIUM
PALM BEACH
RIBEROSTRAAT
TURIBANA
HYATT REGENCY RESORT/ ZOIA/FOOTPRINTS
TEXAS DE BRAZIL
BRICKELL BAY BEACH CLUB & SPA
Palm Beach
J.E. IRAUSQUIN BOULEVARD
CARIÑA'S APPARTMENT
OCCIDENTAL GRAND BEACH RESORT
AMAZONIA
VISTA
HILTON ARUBA CARIBBEAN RESORT & CASINO/LARIMAR SPA
WACKY WAHOO'S
THE OLD CUNUCU HOUSE
PALM BEACH
ALTO
PAPILLON
To Alto Vista Chapel, Peace Labyrinth, and Philip's Animal Garden
BUGALOE
TANDOOR INDIAN GRILL HOUSE
BARNEY'S
RIU CARIBBEAN RESORT/ AZULL/CAFÉ BACI
TWO FOOLS AND A BULL
NEW WEI TAI
NOORD
CARIBBEAN PALM VILLAGE
ALTO VISTA
DIVI PHOENIX BEACH RESORT/ PURE OCEAN
BUTTERFLY FARM/ THE CREPE BAR
THE MILL RESORT
COSTA ESMERELDA VILLA
PAPIAMENTO
SABANA LIBER
Baranca Plat
KEITO
WASHINGTON
BOEGOEROI
SANTA ANA CHURCH
BLUE RESIDENCES
BRISAS STUDIO APPARTMENTS
L.G. SMITH BOULEVARD
KOYARI

Contents

DISCOVER

Aruba

Peek out the window when coming in for a landing on Aruba. You'll be struck by the contrast between the intense blue of the Caribbean Sea and the snowy white of the beaches. "Aruba is right next door to heaven," is how one longtime visitor describes it.

Some of the most stunning beaches in the Caribbean line the west coast of the island, with turquoise waters as calm as any lake. Here you'll find Palm Beach, a parade of resorts strung over one mile, each at least 10 stories tall. At Eagle Beach and adjacent Manchebo Beach, smaller and more intimate resorts stretch to the outskirts of the main town of Oranjestad. These tourist areas offer a wealth of easily accessible activities, eateries, casinos, and shopping.

But a visit to Aruba is not complete without exploring beyond the hotels and restaurants. From Palm Beach, turn a corner at the Westpunt going north and a lunar landscape of coral rock and pillow basalt greets your eyes, while spume from the crashing waves surges high, carving the rock into fantastical shapes. Adventure awaits in every direction, from Arikok National Park, a nature preserve that showcases incredible geological formations and native species, to

Clockwise from top left: art deco water tower in Oranjestad; a trupial bird; a Carnival dancer; diving into the ocean; a colorful tour bus; relaxing at Renaissance Island.

Conchi (Natural Pool), a dramatic spot for swimming and snorkeling created by cooled lava rock. And even further, there are the caves, dunes, and *bocas* (coves) on the eastern end of the island near San Nicolas.

The best part about Aruba is that there's little divide between island dwellers and tourists. It is an extension of the ease among the locals themselves. Don't be surprised to find a table of islanders sitting right next to you at a resort restaurant or casino any night of the week. This congenial relationship with vacationers has made Aruba the most popular repeat destination in the Caribbean.

Aruba can be a tranquil respite from the hustle and bustle of everyday existence, or each day can offer an exciting discovery of nature, island culture, or a new sport on land, sea, or in the air. The richness and variety of this "One Happy Island" can fulfill the vacation needs of honeymooners, singles, families, and adventurers. It is a place where modern luxury and the rugged landscape exist side by side. Your Aruban vacation can embrace either or both—the choice is yours.

Clockwise from top left: Turk's cap cactus; a tall ship in Oranjestad Harbor; a vibrant tropical flower; the California Lighthouse.

Planning Your Trip

Where to Go

Aruba measures only 186.5 square kilometers (72 square mi), merely a speck on a map of the Caribbean. A single major road, **1A,** allows visitors to drive from the **California Lighthouse** on its northwest point to **Baby Beach** at the extreme southeast tip. An ordinary rental car will suffice for traveling to these easily accessible sights, but if you're planning to take in the more rural spots on the island such as **Natural Pool** or **Andicuri Beach,** a 4x4 will serve you much better and significantly enhance the experience. Allow at least a day for touring the main sights; two if you wish to see everything. Organized tours will give you a good introduction to the island and a lay of the land, but there is much to see beyond their limited schedule.

If you plan to stay in the major hotels in **Eagle/Manchebo Beach** and **Palm Beach** and travel no farther than **Oranjestad,** then **Arubus,** the public mass transit system, is the way to go. Nearly every hotel has a bus stop directly in front or nearby that will take you to the main terminal in town. Service is frequent and the transports are modern, clean, and comfortable.

Oranjestad

Aruba's capital offers visitors a taste of **authentic island life.** Playa, as it is also known, boasts quaint side streets interwoven with major shopping avenues. Right next to **malls with designer shops,** the town residents are still living in **homes from the 18th century.** Aruba's history and culture are on display here in museums such as the **National Archaeological Museum Aruba (NAMA)** or the **Aruba Historical**

Oranjestad

a cooling dip on the north coast

Museum. Wind down your day with **superb dining** and **casino play.**

Oranjestad also features a harbor filled with **deep-sea fishing** boats; the major **Renaissance Resort;** and many attractive **guesthouses.** Some local beaches like **Surfside and Druif** are practically deserted during the week and fill up with islanders on weekends.

Eagle Beach and Manchebo Beach

This resort area offers a **tranquil getaway.** Miles of beaches are shaded by large copses of sea grape. There are many spots where, at certain times of the day, a visitor can settle down, look around, and not see a soul.

The apartment-style resorts here are **well suited to families.** The **Divi Links golf course** is surrounded by a beautiful resort so golfers can roll out of bed to an early tee time. Organized activities for kids, such as arts and crafts, scavenger hunts, pool games, and contests, keep the whole family happy. Close proximity to Oranjestad allows history buffs and shoppers **easy access to museums and designer stores.**

Palm Beach, Malmok, and Noord

Palm Beach is one of the most popular places on the island for **lounging on the beach** and **nightlife.** Restaurants, casinos, and clubs sit next door to **glamorous resorts.** It is the center of every water activity imaginable. **Sailing, snorkeling, scuba diving** off the *Antilla* shipwreck, **tubing, deep-sea fishing, parasailing, windsurfing,** and ***Seaworld Explorer*** are all here. Family fun is close by at the exhilarating **Butterfly Farm** and **Philip's Animal Garden.**

North Coast

The dramatic, craggy north coast sharply contrasts Aruba's tranquil western shores. Follow the **spectacular coast trail** in a 4x4 or ATV to find **secluded coves for surfing.** Off-road adventurers enjoy traversing the **Aruban outback** for a trip back in time. **Horseback tours** provided by stables such as **Rancho Daimari,** weave through the dramatic coastal formations. Befriend a giant bird at the **Aruba Ostrich Farm** or do some **rock climbing at Ayo** and explore the **Bushiribana Gold Ruin.**

The **Tierra Del Sol Country Club and Golf**

Course, featuring one of the most challenging courses in the world, borders the coastal road. A beacon to the northwest point, the **California Lighthouse** can be visited by car and on **mountain bike and Segway tours.**

Santa Cruz, Paradera, and Piedra Plat

Aruba's inland residential areas of Santa Cruz, Paradera, and Piedra Plat are home to interesting **rock formations, native architecture,** and **inexpensive guesthouses,** all allowing visitors to immerse themselves in authentic island life. Santa Cruz borders Aruba's national park protecting indigenous flora and fauna.

Hikers find just what they love on the trails of **Arikok National Park.** Make the trek to Aruba's highest point, **Seroe Jamanota,** or visit **Conchi (Natural Pool)** within the preserve. Conchi is the best example of the dramatic lava rock formations on Aruba. This is horseback riding and ATV country. Easy **spelunking** can be found in **Quadikakiri and Fontein Caves** on the far side of the park. Meet local fauna at the **Donkey Sanctuary** or go **rock climbing** among formations at **Casibari.** Collectors can sift through **antiques at Rococo Plaza** in Paradera.

horses at Conchi (Natural Pool) in Arikok National Park

San Nicolas, Savaneta, and Pos Chiquito

The unspoiled and **secluded coves** of Aruba's eastern end are favorite spots for **kitesurfers, sunbathers,** and **snorkelers.** The south side is known for **pristine beaches** with stunning turquoise seas. A barrier reef following the coast is home to some of the island's **best scuba spots.**

Meet and interact with islanders at **authentic local fish restaurants** along the shore. The weekly **Carubbian Festival** is a multicultural mix of regional food, entertainment, and authentic handicrafts, all rolled into a lively street fair in San Nicolas. On the outskirts of the town is the spiritually atmospheric **Lourdes Grotto.**

When to Go

Unlike many resort destinations at more northern latitudes, Aruba has the advantage of eternal summer with little change between the seasons. The most expensive **peak travel time** is **December 15-April 15.** This is also when the island is the most crowded.

In **September** and **early October** room rates are lowest. Visitors can waltz into any restaurant without a reservation and enjoy a deserted beach. Other surprisingly quiet times to escape the cold and the crowds are the 10 days before Christmas and the week after New Year's.

The spectacular pageantry of **Carnival** dominates Aruba from the first weekend in January until Ash Wednesday. The last two weeks in particular are filled with parades and musical events.

Before You Go

Passports, Visas, and Vaccinations

Valid, current passports are required for visitors from the **United States** and **Canada.** Aruban immigration requires that officials see a **return ticket** upon arrival. An Embarkation-Disembarkation form, or **ED-Card,** will be issued to visitors on the plane prior to arrival to fill in and give to Aruban immigration. You keep a section of this during your stay; be sure to have it ready to return to local immigration officials when you depart.

Nationals of most countries are required to have a visa to enter Aruba. Exemptions are made for the United States, Canada, the European Union and territories (the Schengen Territory), United Kingdom, Ireland, and Colombian and Jamaican nationals coming from the United States with valid residence permits or U.S. visas.

Transportation

Aruba's **Reina Beatrix International Airport** receives regular commercial flights daily from the United States and Canada. Several **cruise ship lines** include Oranjestad Harbor on their agenda.

Once on the island, visitors will find ample, if pricey **taxis.** It is easy to rent **mopeds, cars,** and **jeeps,** or rent or arrange minibuses to chauffeur around large groups. Some are equipped for people with disabilities. None of the major hotels provide shuttle service to and from the airport, so taxis are the most common means of transfer. A strip mall of **car rental agencies** is just outside the airport arrivals terminal. The **public bus system, Arubus,** also services major resorts and all residential areas. Buses stop frequently in front of all hotels to take visitors to Oranjestad. For touring, readily available options are **ATVs, 4x4s, Segways,** and Harley-Davidson **motorcycles.** For visits over major holiday weeks make car rental reservations well in advance. If you are planning to spend most of your week relaxing on the beach, it is not really necessary to rent a car because nightlife and diverse dining options are within easy walking distance of most major resorts.

Carnival dancers

the Butterfly Farm

The Best of Aruba

Aruba's principal attractions are its gorgeous beaches and azure waters. Still, it is worth it to travel beyond the beaches to explore the unique topography of the island and its culture. Main tourist areas offer a myriad of choices for dining and nightlife, but you will also find excellent eateries in less-trafficked places. Free musical entertainment can be had at several venues. The most stunning show, however, is the colorful sunset along Aruba's western shore. Hotel beach bars and independent lounges offer happy hour prices while you enjoy this spectacle, which can segue into a romantic dinner right on the beach.

Day 1

After you have settled into your accommodations, run down to the beach to savor the sunset while taking advantage of happy hour. Look for 2-for-1 cocktails at most hotel bars and cafés nearby. If you're staying in the Palm Beach area, try **Bugaloe** at the end of the **De Palm Pier.** If you're staying in the Manchebo Beach area, enjoy a gourmet fresh fish entrée beachside at **Ricardo's** in the **Aruba Beach Club.**

After hours, take in some free live music at Palm Beach's **Arawak Gardens, Fusion Wine and Piano Bar** in the **Alhambra Shopping Bazaar,** or at the bandstand by the water at the **Renaissance Marketplace** in Oranjestad. If it's a weekend, find a great band and fun crowd at **Café Chaos** across the street from Renaissance Marketplace or at **South Beach Lounge** in Palm Beach.

Day 2

If it is a Sunday, check out the luxurious brunch at **Windows on Aruba** at the **Divi Links.** Enjoy an exhilarating morning stroll or jog along the paths parallel to Eagle Beach or following the shore from the Marriott to Malmok. If you prefer, refresh your chi instead with some yoga on the beach at the **Manchebo Beach Resort.** For a true introduction to pampering and relaxation, **Okeanos Spa** will take you out to **Renaissance Island** for a treatment in their private cove.

If it's not a Sunday, or you're hungry for lunch, head over to the **Butterfly Farm** in Palm Beach for your first real outing; it won't be your last visit.

Butterflies are most active in the mornings. Enjoy some refreshing, light crepes at the cute **Crepe Bar,** attached to the farm.

Those eager to learn to snorkel or dive should join a sailing and snorkeling tour. Dive operators like **Unique Sports of Aruba** will have you exploring under the water in a few short hours. Quick morning courses allow novices to dive at one of the easier, shallower dive sites around the west coast, or snorkelers can enjoy a trip to the ***Antilla*** **shipwreck** and **Arashi Beach.**

Share a romantic dinner on the beach at **Elements** at the **Bucuti & Tara Beach Resort,** or book a private sail and dinner for two on the ***Tranquilo.*** Afterwards, stroll along the Palm Beach promenade for some souvenir shopping. Stay until late to party at **Señor Frog's.**

Day 3

Catch a bus to **Oranjestad** for the day. Explore the landmark buildings that house the **National Archaeological Museum Aruba (NAMA)** and the **Aruba Historical Museum** located within **Fort Zoutman.**

Check out a charming lunch spot with a view of the harbor at **The Paddock,** or meet island movers and shakers at their favorite power lunch restaurant **Aquarius.** Break up the day by indulging in an underwater adventure on the ***Atlantis*** **submarine.**

For dinner, savor the gourmet cuisine at celebrated **L.G. Smith's Steak & Chop House** or a romantic meal on the water at **Pinchos Grill and Bar.**

Day 4

Today, get away from both beach and town and do some touring with **Madi's Magical Tours,** a highly personalized, unique safari tour with a dawn trip to **Conchi (Natural Pool)** on the north coast. From there, Madi can take you on an outback adventure lasting all or part of a day.

You can also choose to rent a 4x4 to tour on your own: Start the day by watching the sunrise from the **California Lighthouse.** From there you can head down the north coast road or make your way back to Noord and take in such sights as **Alto Vista Chapel, Philip's Animal Garden,** and **Santa Ana Church.** If venturing farther along the coast in a four-wheel drive, follow the

Santa Ana Church

the Aruba Ostrich Farm

gravel road to the **Bushiribana Gold Ruin** and the **Aruba Ostrich Farm.** After scrambling around the **Ayo Rock Formation,** explore the countryside even further on horseback with **Gold Mine Ranch.**

Unwind from an exhausting day of touring with a sunset "toes in the sand" dinner at **Footprints** at the Hyatt.

Day 5

Enjoy a day of hiking or horseback riding in **Arikok National Park** and the caves and coves beyond. A hearty but inexpensive breakfast of *arepas* can be had at **Cheo's Corner** in **Paseo Herencia Shopping Mall** in Palm Beach before you venture out into the wilds. Paved roads within the park allow exploration by car, or park rangers will guide you through various hiking paths, such as **Cunucu Arikok Trail,** or to the summit of **Seroe Jamanota.** A trek to **Conchi (Natural Pool)** will take up a morning or nearly the entire day. Enjoy a lunch of authentic Aruban cuisine at **Urataka Center** on the road leading to the park. Call **Rancho Daimari** if you'd prefer to take the tour on horseback.

If you booked a reservation online months in advance, you can savor a gourmet dinner at **Carte Blanche,** in the **Bucuti & Tara Beach Resort.** This is a long, full, and entertaining evening of socializing with the chef while watching him prepare a delicious dinner.

Day 6

Try one of Oranjestad's many early morning eateries, such as **Smit & Dorlas Coffee House.** Drive to **San Nicolas** to soak in the scenery of "Sunrise City" and experience a real Caribbean town. Take a dip at **Baby Beach** or **Roger's Beach,** two of the most beautiful inlets on Aruba. You can also set up diving or snorkeling trips in this area with **JADS Dive Shop.**

On the way back from San Nicolas, stop at **Zeerover** in **Savaneta** for fresh fish island-style, or **B-55,** next to the old drive-in theater on the main highway, for good pizza and a beautiful view. From either of these eateries you can easily stop at **Mangel Halto** for a relaxing swim.

For a full day of water fun, families can skip the excursion in favor of the **Aruba Waterpark** off the Oranjestad-Santa Cruz road. They have a nice kitchen featuring local cuisine and barbecue.

Returning from the south side of the island takes you past the **Orange Mall** on the Sasaki Highway, which houses **Red Fish** restaurant, an affordably priced haven for fresh-caught fish and island cuisine.

Day 7

Dig into a buffet breakfast at **La Vista** within **Marriott Aruba Resort & Stellaris Casino** to fuel up for windsurfing or kitesurfing lessons with **Aruba Active Vacations.** For a real thrill, try **Skydive Aruba** in the field across the road from the windsurfing center. Scuba is a no-no less than 24 hours before departure, but sailing and snorkeling are always an option. Try something really different by exploring the south shore with **Aruba Kayak Adventures,** which includes lunch, or opt for a customized surfing tour with **Aruba Surf School.**

In the evening hours you can pick up some last-minute souvenirs and explore the hot spots at **Arawak Gardens.** It is also a good time to give in and buy that pair of earrings that caught your fancy at **Gemstones International** on the Palm Beach strip or go back for one of the exquisite handcrafted accessories at **Caribbean Queen** in Palm Beach Plaza. Combine shopping with some island history and culture while enjoying the ***Waltzing Waters*** at **Paseo Herencia Shopping Mall.** Finish the day at **Señor Frog's** in Palm Beach for tasty Mexican food, giant drinks, and the most entertaining staff on the island.

Local Culture

Islanders love to share their culture and traditions with visitors, particularly around holidays and during Carnival season.

MUSEUMS

National Archaeological Museum Aruba (page 74)

A number of archaeological digs have resulted in a huge collection of ceramics and artifacts linked to the inhabitants of Aruba from prehistoric times. The museum mixes original colonial architecture with a new, special environment, housing exhibits that are entertaining and very hands-on.

Aruba Historical Museum (page 75)

Situated in the landmark Fort Zoutman, the museum provides an overview of the cultural development of the island from prehistoric through colonial and modern times. Antiques and artifacts recreate landmark moments in colonial history and the ways islanders survived by fishing and producing aloe.

Paseo Herencia Shopping Mall

FESTIVALS AND EVENTS

Carnival (page 135)

Considered the premier manifestation of Aruban artistry and creativity, Carnival season includes spectacular parades and original music. Lasting five to nine weeks, it takes place early January-Ash Wednesday and flaunts island culture at its loudest and most jubilant.

Carubbian Festival (page 134)

If you can't be on Aruba for Carnival, the weekly Carubbian Festival in San Nicolas is the next best thing. The festival is held every Thursday all year long. Tickets include transportation from resorts to the east end of Aruba and come with vouchers for the festival's authentic island and regional cooking.

Bon Bini Festival (page 134)

Put on every Tuesday evening within Fort Zoutman in Oranjestad, the Bon Bini Festival provides a taste of Carnival, with a focus on folkloric dance, music, and traditions.

Caribbean Sea Jazz Festival (page 138)

The last weekend in September means two nights of local, regional, and international artists performing innovative, interpretive music. Concert tickets are a bargain, and audience numbers are a fraction of those in mega-stadiums, resulting in an intimate musical experience.

Paseo Herencia Shopping Mall Cultural Shows (page 134)

Six nights a week, Paseo Herencia in Palm Beach hosts a free cultural show beginning at 8pm. Each night highlights some aspect of local folkloric or modern dance and music. The programs are an entertaining introduction to island traditions, and the mall is conveniently situated near all Palm Beach resorts.

Betico Day (page 135)

January 25 is the birthday of one of Aruba's most celebrated statesmen: Gilberto Francois "Betico" Croes. A lengthy show in Plaza Betico Croes behind the Cas di Cultura is accompanied by food and handicrafts.

Himno y Bandera Day (page 135)

Celebrating Aruban independence means a flurry of festivities, often for days prior to the actual date of March 18. There is a street fair, a national show, and wonderful handicrafts for sale.

Best Water Sports

Sailing and Snorkeling Cruises

OCTOPUS CRUISES (PAGE 50)

As the only tour boat in Aruba without a motor, *Octopus* offers a truly authentic sailing experience. Snorkeling stops start at easy, placid sites, where the fish flock to swimmers in search of snacks. One of the most impressive wrecks in all the Caribbean, the *Antilla,* is one snorkel stop when conditions permit.

TRANQUILO (PAGE 50)

Enjoy "toes in the water" sailing on the beautiful ketch *Tranquilo,* which tours Aruba's south side snorkel sites. This is one of the few boats that runs all-day trips—and the only one offering the personal expertise and congenial presence of Captain Anthony and his family.

Scuba Diving

UNIQUE SPORTS OF ARUBA (PAGE 52)

Unique Sports of Aruba provides daily morning lessons for complete novices and regularly scheduled tours for experienced, certified divers. The instructors and divemasters are friendly and capable.

DIVE ARUBA (PAGE 52)

Personal service, customized to experience and ability, is the Dive Aruba trademark. Veteran divemaster Clive Paula takes experienced, certified divers to out-of-the-way sites.

Windsurfing, Kitesurfing, and Surfing

ARUBA ACTIVE VACATIONS (PAGE 56)

Develop a windsurfing obsession with the congenial instructors at Aruba Active Vacations, one of the best outfitters on the island. Find them at Fisherman's Huts, just north of the Ritz-Carlton Resort in Palm Beach. They have a large inventory of equipment designed for surfers of all abilities.

Snorkeling is a kid-friendly pastime.

cruising the coastline

ARUBA SURF SCHOOL (PAGE 56)

Instructor Dennis Martinez is passionate about surfing. He also customizes his lessons at Aruba Surf School to his students' ability and experience and scouts out the best surf on any given day.

Parasailing, Tubing, Banana Boats, and Waverunners

NATIVE DIVERS WATERSPORTS (PAGE 57)

Native Divers Watersports pays strong attention to safety while providing a fun time for the whole family. It's easy to arrange the water activity of your choice, from a banana boat ride to parasailing.

FUN FOR EVERYONE (PAGE 57)

Conveniently located in front of the Riu Palace Resort, Fun for Everyone has four boats for tubing, parasailing, and banana boat rides. They take banana passengers on a complete tour of the northwest coastline all the way to the Westpunt.

Deep-Sea Fishing

The principal departure points for fishing boats are Oranjestad Harbor and Hadicurari Pier, at the north end of Palm Beach. Crews clean your catch and take it to a recommended restaurant to have it prepared for your dinner.

DRIFTWOOD FISHING CHARTERS (PAGE 55)

Driftwood is named after the owner's popular seafood restaurant, where they will happily cook up your catch. Captain Herby has a passion for the sport. And since he has to provide the catch of the day for the restaurant's dinner menu, he's highly motivated to find the fish!

MELINA CHARTERS (PAGE 56)

Melina departs from Hadicurari Pier, conveniently close to the Palm Beach resorts. Captain Piet is a very amiable host, with a love of the sport and a keen knowledge of the best fishing grounds.

Best Bets for the Budget-Conscious

Beach House Aruba

ACCOMMODATIONS

Sunflower Villas (page 179)

The vibrant art of the hostess adorns every aspect of this cozy guesthouse in Bakval. This peaceful home offers close proximity to Palm Beach as well as the opportunity to learn the art of mosaic.

Beach House Aruba (page 177)

Right on the water and on the outskirts of Palm Beach, the friendly hosts at this delightful guesthouse are central to its charm. Convenience, great prices, and a casual atmosphere give this house a real island feel.

Costa Esmeralda (page 178)

These charming and contemporary studios, suites, and duplex town houses are close to Palm Beach action and excellent dining.

Seabreeze Apartments (page 186)

A very charming complex of studio apartments just minutes from Mangel Halto Beach, Seabreeze offers a real escape from the Palm Beach crowds.

EATS

Cuminda criollo (local cuisine) is admittedly a bit heavy on the starches and fried foods, but you will always go home full, without walloping your wallet. A safe bet for health-conscious yet affordable dining is to stick to fresh-caught local fish and stews.

Casa Vieja (page 98)

The most authentic of Colombian restaurants on Aruba, Casa Vieja on the eastern outskirts of Oranjestad serves up huge mixed-meat platters. Eat and drink like royalty for pennies.

Zeerover (page 122)

Everyone's favorite place for fresh fish and shrimp, Zeerover is basically a glorified fish shack right on the water in Savaneta. Dine on the dock or under the canopy with ice-cold beers, pool tables, and TVs showing the latest soccer matches.

Pizza & More (page 109)

The owner/chef hails from Italy and the restaurant is conveniently located in Orange Mall, near the Machebo Beach resorts. It has a dedicated clientele for a good reason: the best pizza on Aruba for rock-bottom prices. There are also fine pasta dishes and delicious homemade soups in addition to pizza.

Terrazza Italiana (page 109)

Enjoy a romantic meal on this terraced restaurant within the Paradise Beach Villas. Centrally located, Terrazza Italiana offers spectacular views and great pizza and pasta without the usual high prices.

ENTERTAINMENT

Renaissance Marketplace (page 149)

The bandstand at the waterside in Renaissance Marketplace in Oranjestad features various bands. You'll be treated to classic rock, folk, pop, latin, reggae, mellow, or metal, depending on who's playing.

Arawak Gardens (page 132)

Singers and musicians take the stage in a centralized gazebo at Arawak Gardens in Palm Beach. Five different restaurant terraces allow patrons to linger over dinner or drinks in this amiable alfresco setting.

Aruba Reef Apartments

Romantic Rendezvous

Accommodations

ARUBA REEF APARTMENTS (PAGE 185)

Book the ultimate island fantasy: These waterside apartments offer seclusion and a private beach to make honeymooners (or honeymooners at heart) feel like they are the only two people in world.

Spas

OKEANOS SPA (PAGE 68)

Ease tired muscles and relieve stress with a massage at the Okeanos annex on Renaissance Island. Couples can have a full morning or afternoon session in their private cove, with a stunning view of the sea and absolute privacy.

ZOIA (PAGE 69)

Within the Hyatt Regency Resort in Palm Beach, ZoiA has a special room for couples with a giant bath and a private terrace with a beautiful view.

Cruises

RED SAIL SPORTS DINNER CRUISE (PAGE 54)

Sample an elegant dinner with wine and a champagne toast, while cruising the coast and watching the sun set.

TRANQUILO (PAGE 50)

Aside from day trips, the *Tranquilo* also offers a catered dinner with champagne for two on a sunset trip.

Sunsets

HILTON ARUBA CARIBBEAN RESORT & CASINO (PAGE 181)

With one of the longest stretches of sand in Palm Beach, the Hilton has plenty of room to offer a tranquil, private spot. This is the most reasonably priced of all the private beach dinners.

PUNTO BRABO (PAGE 37)

This wide stretch of beach north of the Costa Linda Resort is filled with large clusters of sea grape and greenery offering plenty of private spots to cuddle up and watch the sunset.

Punto Brabo

Eats

LA TRATTORIA EL FARO BLANCO (PAGE 119)

Next to the California Lighthouse, La Trattoria El Faro Blanco offers the most spectacular sunset view from a charming terrace overlooking the entire northwest coast.

PINCHOS GRILL AND BAR (PAGE 94)

Sitting right on the water at Surfside Beach, Pinchos was specifically designed to stoke romantic embers. Couches and hammocks for two are just made for cuddling while savoring the sunset and a delectable meal.

ZEEROVER (PAGE 122)

Though this is a family restaurant, tables out on the dock of this waterside spot offer an escape from the crowd. Enjoy the fresh seafood, casual atmosphere, and stunning view of the sunset.

Explore the Outback

Exploring Aruba's wilds is an interesting proposition, especially when trying to follow directions or looking for road signs, which are in short supply. Ensure an enjoyable, frustration-free day filled with all the must-see sights by taking a tour with an enthusiastic and knowledgeable guide.

Safari Tours

MADI'S MAGICAL TOURS (PAGE 60)

One of the most unique ways to tour Aruba's outback is with guide extraordinaire Madi. She leads small, personal, and customized trips infused with her native charm.

MADAGASCAR ARUBA ADVENTURE (PAGE 60)

Madagascar is also a small tour operator with a very friendly guide. Tours usually end up longer than scheduled, as host and guide Alfredo does not hurry passengers past the most interesting sights just to meet a schedule.

Motorcycle, All-Terrain Vehicle, and Trike Tours

Fun and funky modes of transport make getting to the tour sights as exciting as the destinations themselves.

Family Fun

Aruba Waterpark

WALTZING WATERS (PAGE 134)

The free *Waltzing Waters* show in the Paseo Herencia Shopping Mall goes on four times nightly on the half-hour, 7:30pm-10:30pm.

DREAM BOWL (PAGE 129)

At the Palm Beach Plaza Mall, Dream Bowl offers six lanes with neon-glowing gutters and balls, complemented by arcade games, air hockey, and foosball tables.

BUTTERFLY FARM (PAGE 78)

The Butterfly Farm amazes kids and adults with an entertaining introduction to the beautiful world of these exotic insects.

DONKEY SANCTUARY (PAGE 83)

Enjoy a hands-on session with the residents of Aruba's wild donkey population in Bringamosa. The staff allows children to share in the animals' care.

ARUBA OSTRICH FARM (PAGE 81)

An encounter with the world's largest birds at the Ostrich Farm in Matividiri is informative, fun, and always suprising.

PHILIP'S ANIMAL GARDEN (PAGE 79)

Become intimately acquainted with exotic animals that have been saved from neglect at this not-for-profit refuge.

SURFSIDE BEACH (PAGE 35)

With a shoreline sheltered by a barrier reef, Surfside Beach has extremely quiet, shallow waters. The adjacent restaurant sports a kiddie pool and provides service on the beach.

BABY BEACH (PAGE 43)

The breakwaters at Baby Beach create a tranquil lagoon rimmed with a circle of soft sand. Public *palapas* are scattered along the shore for shade. Vendors rent beach chairs and sell snacks.

PALM BEACH (PAGE 38)

Wave action is negligible here and the shallow seas are ideal for youngsters. It's also close to all the resorts, beach toys, refreshments, and bathrooms.

ARUBA WATERPARK (PAGE 53)

Eminently affordable, this collection of slides ranges from kiddie to killer. It also has a great place for lunch. There is a playground too for a change of pace.

Explore the Bushiribana Gold Ruin on an ATV tour.

BIG TWIN HARLEY-DAVIDSON (PAGE 61)

The thrill of zipping along island roads on these giant motorbikes from the Harley-Davidson franchise in Oranjestad, as well as their ability to traverse some of the worst trails, provides one of the best touring experiences.

TRIKES (PAGE 61)

The ultimate car-motorcycle-ATV hybrid, trikes allow passengers and drivers complete comfort while touring in style. Trikes can cover tough terrain, and heads will turn wherever you go.

Horseback Tours

Aruba's principal mode of transport from colonial times is still one of the best ways to explore off the beaten track.

RANCHO DAIMARI (PAGE 63)

Ideally located on the north shore close to some of the most dramatic coastal trails, Rancho Daimari picks up and returns guests to their resort by van. Two-hour trips focus on Daimari Beach, Dos Playa, and Conchi (Natural Pool).

GOLD MINE RANCH (PAGE 63)

Riding enthusiasts encounter alternate trails and sights within Arikok National Park on the menu of Gold Mine Ranch. Guides take riders to sites along the coast or inland.

Hiking Trails

Arikok National Park is Aruba's hiking center, where trails have been groomed, timed, and measured for degree of difficulty. Rangers are on hand to lead groups for a nominal fee.

CUNUCU ARIKOK TRAIL (PAGE 64)

This popular trail is about two hours round-trip from the park visitor center. It offers a chance to study endemic flora and fauna along with a genuinely restored landmark farmhouse.

NATURAL POOL TRAIL (PAGE 66)

The all-day journey of the Natural Pool Trail takes hikers directly to Conchi and past Dos Playa beach on the way back. Find forest trails, dramatic rock formations along the coastline, and secluded beaches for a cooling swim.

SEROE JAMANOTA TRAIL (PAGE 64)

Aruba's highest point, Seroe Jamanota, offers two access routes: Reaching the summit can be a relaxing morning stroll or a hard-core adventure. Either way, the reward is stunning vistas.

Beaches

Look for ★ to find recommended beaches.

Highlights

★ **Renaissance Island:** This tranquil island offers both family-friendly and adults-only beaches. It also has nice snorkeling, a spa, a restaurant, and friendly flamingos. The island is privately owned by the Renaissance Resort; guests have unlimited access and nonguests can purchase a day pass (page 35).

★ **Eagle Beach:** Eagle Beach is one of the best beaches on the island and offers many of the same amenities as Palm Beach—only with fewer people and slightly bigger waves (page 37).

★ **Palm Beach:** Aruba's principal playground has every manner of amenity and activity available within a few steps of your beach lounge. It also has the quietest waters of the long beachfronts (page 38).

★ **Baranca Plat:** You'll enjoy calm waters, snowy white sands, and the feeling of having a special place in the sun all to yourself at this cozy little cove, a short walk from the big resorts. (page 39).

★ **Fisherman's Huts:** Relax among the dunes and take in the colorful sails and parachute kites speeding across the water at this windsurfing beach (page 39).

★ **California Dunes:** This expansive area is scenic and private—great for long walks and topless sunbathing (page 40).

★ **Andicuri Beach:** Dramatic terraces of limestone formations surround this secluded beach. The wave action here is perfect for body surfing (page 41).

★ **Black Stone Beach:** The natural rock bridges at this beach make for beautiful photo ops. The beach is named for the lava stones found along the shore (page 41).

★ **Baby Beach and Roger's Beach:** Two of Aruba's most beautiful beaches are within the remains of the old Lago Colony. Both have manmade lagoons great for swimming, surrounded by long stretches of white sands, and bordered by greenery and carved stone cliffs (page 43).

Caribbean islands are usually synonymous with beautiful beaches, but veteran travelers will tell you that Aruba's are exceptional. Aruba has been hailed as one of the top beach destinations in the world. The soft, snowy white sands (a composition of coral and shells crushed into a fine powder over eons) and the breathtaking blue waters make sunbathing, beachcombing, and swimming popular pastimes here. Although the temperature is consistently warm, Aruba's beaches are never too hot for a barefoot stroll, even at noon.

Palm Beach and Eagle Beach are the most raved about beaches on the island, with fine accommodations along their shores. The long, uninterrupted miles of sand are the main attraction for both visitors and developers. Unquestionably, the nature of Aruba's beaches has dictated the degree of development of resort areas, as well as their character. It was long ago decided that Palm Beach offered the "best beachfront," though, of course, vacationers who return to Manchebo Beach and Eagle Beach year after year are confident that they're staying at the best.

Along Palm Beach the shallow water extends almost a half mile from the shore with negligible wave action. Many consider this ideal for families with very young children. The extremely shallow, still water is perfect for a baby's first encounter with the sea. Swimming areas are well-marked, patrolled, and maintained.

Eagle Beach is not quite as maintained and patrolled as Palm Beach, but all the resorts in Aruba take responsibility for the safety of their beachfront. As more resorts crop up along Eagle Beach, more cordoned-off swim sections can be expected.

There is stronger wave action at Eagle Beach, and particularly Manchebo Beach, due to the bottom suddenly dropping off very close to shore. The current at Punto Brabo, where the southern shore meets west and various currents collide, also contributes to bigger waves. This makes it very popular with surfers and bodyboarders. Other great spots favored for bodyboarding or waveboarding are Andicuri, Dos Playa, and Urirama, all on Aruba's north coast, where heavy winds from the northeast result in strong waves.

Previous: Malmok Beach; Flamingo Beach on Renaissance Island. **Above:** Eagle Beach.

Oranjestad

Oranjestad's beaches are artificial, carved out from the harbor and created by dumping sand in the early 1950s. Before that, it was strictly a harbor area. Jetties have established some very calm coves and small stretches of beachfront.

DRUIF BEACH

The relatively wide, public **Druif Beach** (J. E. Irausquin Blvd. at the western outskirts of the town) is an extension of the beachfront from the Tamarijn Beach Resort. It provides a great deal of greenery, shade trees, and areas cleared for small campfires or setting up grills. You will most likely find islanders here on the weekends making a day of it with their families. The water is very shallow and quiet, which makes it a nice spot for small children to play in the waves. A minor cautionary note: If you are planning to lay out a towel on the grass, please check for and avoid some patches of plants with rather nasty and tenacious thistles that are common during the dry season.

Directly across the road from the beach are two supermarkets with bathrooms and snack and drink options. Behind them is Ling & Sons, a supermarket with a café offering fresh smoothies, sandwiches, and a salad bar.

GOVERNOR'S BEACH

Just past the Renaissance complex is a bridge over a lagoon that divides Oranjestad's commercial area from the residential neighborhoods. This headland is informally named **Governor's Beach** (L. G. Smith Blvd. by Lagoonweg, on the east side of Wilhelmina Park) because it sits directly across from what has traditionally been the residence of Aruba's governor. It has some thatched *palapas* for shade, a bathroom, and a boardwalk. Overlooking the waterfront is a charming restaurant called West Deck. In the middle of the beach is a striking monument dedicated to local fishers lost at sea. The area marks the beginning of a long stretch of narrow beach extending all the way east along L. G. Smith Boulevard to Surfside, ending at the beginning of the airport runways, interspersed with limestone terraces.

All of this L. G. Smith beachfront is exceptionally quiet and shallow, which is good for little ones. There are lots of shade trees along the shore masking the area from L. G. Smith

Governor's Beach

Free Use of All Beaches

By law, all of Aruba's beaches are public within 20 meters (65 ft.) of the waterline. This includes all beaches running along Palm Beach and Eagle Beach, no matter what resort is situated there. Blue pillars signal the dividing line. This rule was reaffirmed by Aruba's ministers of tourism and infrastructure in 2010.

No resort personnel can prevent anyone from sitting on the public beach of their choice, though they can ask you not to use the lounges belonging to the resorts reserved for guests. Interlopers are usually detected by their towels. The *palapas* or "chikies," the little thatched huts placed along the shore for shade are another matter, about which there is some debate.

Thatched *palapas* are built on the beach and maintained by the resorts. According to law, if they are on the public section of the beach, then technically they are available to anyone, without fee for usage. Anyone can place a beach towel on the sand to bask in the sun, or under a *palapa* for shade, as long as they are within 20 meters of the waterline.

Exceptions are De Palm Island and Renaissance Island; their owners do have the right to limit access. Homes that are situated on the water, such as in Malmok or Savaneta, have to abide by the same 20-meter rule. Homeowners cannot claim the entire shorefront as their own.

This practice insures Aruba's beaches belong to the Aruban people and all island guests. It is only fair that islanders should not be prohibited from enjoying the natural assets that are their heritage. Beaches are a way of life for Aruban people, accessible at all hours. They do not have opening and closing times. Beaches also do not require beach tags or usage fees; they are always free for all.

Boulevard and its busy traffic. Many locals also come to this beach to set out on their boats or Jet Skis.

SURFSIDE

In front of the Talk of the Town Resort is the Plaza Turismo, the main plaza of the first section of the **Linear Park** (entrance is around the side of the plaza between the airport and Reflexions, at the east end of L. G. Smith Blvd.). The miles of dirt paths bordering L. G. Smith Boulevard have been manicured with jogging and biking lanes, gardens, and periodically placed bathrooms and open-air showers. This area, and its beachfront, has had a number of incarnations but is still most commonly referred to as **Surfside.**

The beach is a wide curving cove of white sand and very quiet waters. This is often where sailboats go for safe harbor when the western shore turns rough. Since this beach is popular with the local European crowd, you may encounter some topless sunbathers.

All the conveniences you will need for a luxurious day at the beach are here: a nice restaurant, bar, small pool on the terrace, and superb service at your beach lounge.

The chic **Reflexions Lounge** (L. G. Smith Blvd. 1A, 297/582-0153, www.beach-aruba.com, 10am-10pm daily) features a shaded interior dining room that opens out to the sea and a sunny terrace. Food and drink service is also available to sunbathers.

★ RENAISSANCE ISLAND

Guests at the Renaissance Resort have unlimited access to **Renaissance Island** (300 meters [328 yd] off Aruba's south shore, just north of the airport, 800/421-8188 or 297/583-6000, www.marriott.com, access is only by boat, day pass for nonguests $99), one of Aruba's nicest beaches. There are two sections connected by boardwalks, with mangroves and palm trees providing privacy.

Flamingo Beach, on the western side, is adults only. Since it is secluded, topless sunbathing is allowed. The flamingos that gives the beach its name keep guests entertained and are quite tame.

The eastern half of Renaissance Island offers a large sweep of beach outfitted for families. The tranquil lagoon is perfect for introducing toddlers to the sea. There are also a snack bar, volleyball court, and a dock for paddleboats.

Water taxies to the island leave from two locations about every 15 minutes. One departure point is in the lobby of the Marina Tower of the Renaissance Resort, the other is next to the harbor heliport.

Day passes for nonguests include lunch at the very charming Papagayo restaurant, a drink, beach towels, and use of the tennis court. The day pass also allows a choice of one activity: Visitors can snorkel, kayak, or toodle around on a paddleboat.

Okeanos Spa (297/583-6000, www.okeanosspaaruba.com) has an outlet adjacent to Flamingo Beach called The Cove. Purchasing a massage at this spa also gives you access to the island, but no other amenities.

Eagle Beach and Manchebo Beach

These two shore areas that border the southwestern curve of Aruba combined are renowned as one of the longest uninterrupted beachfronts in the Caribbean. The full stretch has not been fully developed—although there is rapid development of condominium complexes taking over Eagle Beach—and there are still quite a few areas that remain deserted throughout the day. Large clusters of greenery offer both privacy and shade.

These beaches are an important nesting area for local and visiting sea turtles from early spring through late autumn. During turtle season, there is the distinct possibility of seeing a giant leatherback lay her eggs or new hatchlings struggling to the sea. The local foundation TurtugAruba keeps an eye on these events and takes steps to protect them from disruption, and visitors are asked to report any turtle activity to them.

MANCHEBO BEACH

The wide expanse of **Manchebo Beach,** on the southwestern point of the island, is lined with smaller resorts that provide sunbathers with plenty of space. Unlike at some of the larger hotels, you will not feel crowded or packed together. Holiday weeks are busy everywhere, but here, one can still enjoy the feeling of an isolated island getaway.

Most of the shorefront resorts are only two stories high, and there are accommodation options directly on the beach. The smaller resorts have a well-established European clientele, but

Manchebo Beach is never crowded.

the timeshare beaches are primarily occupied by visitors from North and Latin America.

PUNTO BRABO

Huge, old sea grape trees stand sentinel along the shore just where Manchebo and Eagle Beaches meet at **Punto Brabo or "Rough Point"** (access via the south lane of J. E. Irausquin Blvd.), a very wide beach that fronts the Bucuti and Costa Linda Resorts. At this southwest curve of the island currents intertwine and the sea bottom drops off close to shore. The beach is a stunning expanse of brilliant white sands.

Those who choose to stay in this area often mention how much they enjoy the great wave action for body surfing and playing in the waves. Care should be taken with very young children here.

The green areas offer shelter and plenty of secluded spots to string up a hammock or set up a grill—which islanders will frequently do on the weekends. There is ample parking just north of Costa Linda Resort.

★ EAGLE BEACH

The sea is quiet on **Eagle Beach** (J. E. Irausquin Blvd. btwn. La Quinta Beach Resort and the north end of Amsterdam Manor Beach Resort), which is practically deserted for long stretches. The far northern edge is marked by Aruba's famous twin fofoti trees. This duo of a rare species makes a popular photo site.

Since the resorts along the beach are all across the street, the wide shorefront of soft, white sugar sands is sparsely populated with vacationers. Many guests often prefer to stay around the beautiful pool decks of their resorts, rather than on the beach itself. However, on weekends, it is quite busy with island residents. The past scarcity of resorts has left Eagle Beach unofficially designated as a "local" beach, with parking areas along the shore. It is not unusual to find families or groups camping here. During Easter vacation, called Semana Santa, the beach is filled from one end to the other with tents and islanders enjoying the holiday.

However, resorts do have a presence on the sand now. The La Cabana and Amsterdam Manor hotels have set up beach bars for refreshments at the northern end of Eagle Beach. Some condos along this stretch have erected *palapas* for shade. Resorts have amenities along the shore for their patrons, such as lounges or shaded structures. The casual passerby can often find unused and unattended *palapas* and lounges on the beach. Snack wagons are set up for business during the day for a bite to eat around the lunch hour.

Eagle Beach

Water Safety Around the Shore

Before the tourism boom, the beach- and shorefronts were vast and the population was small. Easygoing islanders rarely gave much thought to cordoning off swim areas. But as the number of resorts grew, each resort started taking on the responsibility of marking off a protected area of the sea for the safety of its guests.

Currently, the swim area markers are maintained by a dedicated enterprise contracting with the hotels. Swimmers should avoid sitting on or clinging to swim barrier ropes at all times. Although the ropes are cleaned regularly, soft corals also regularly begin to grow on the underwater ropes. These can sting and cause a very irritating rash. If you do accidentally run into them, try a topical steroid to relieve the pain and itching.

The Coast Guard has placed a line of buoys beyond the swim areas in Palm Beach to designate a "no wake" zone where fast boat traffic is prohibited. Those crossing the zone while ferrying passengers to larger boats are required to maintain slower speeds to avoid creating a large wake. Swimmers and snorkelers should avoid the areas beyond the swim zone because of the frequent boat traffic.

All commercial boat operators are now required to take courses and obtain at least a "small boat license" showing they have learned safety procedures and the "rules of the road." The government has also initiated a program to station trained lifeguards in the towers along the beach which had stood unoccupied for decades.

Aruba's offshore breezes are delightfully cooling. This wind is one of the reasons the waters fronting Palm Beach are so quiet. The drawback is that they tend to blow objects out to sea—including beach balls, lightweight floats, and other fun water toys. The gentle wave motion generated on the water's surface by these breezes is often not noticeable but still steadily moving away from the shore. Keep a close eye on youngsters in swim rings and lightweight floats.

Also take care not to fall asleep on a float; it is not unheard of for people to wake up far from land. Most float and small craft operators keep a small rescue boat handy for just such events. But even if you don't float away, falling asleep in the middle of the giant sun reflector that is the Caribbean Sea may prove very distressing. It is no fun being stuck in a hotel room with a sunburn.

Scuba divers are trained to never dive alone. This commonsense rule is wise for almost anyone indulging in water activities on the sea. Don't go off by yourself to snorkel in areas you are unfamiliar with. Take a buddy and inform friends or family where you are going and a reasonable range of when you expect to be back. Dive operators and snorkel charters can provide buddies and will keep an eye on patrons. They are experienced in handling distressing situations on the sea. If you are trying a water activity for the first time, having supervision is always a good idea.

Palm Beach, Malmok, and Noord

One of the most famous beaches in the world, Aruba's Palm Beach offers lakelike waters and every convenience imaginable. This is the center and departure point for 90 percent of all water activities on the island. Except for the all-inclusive resorts of Riu Palace, Riu Antillean, and Occidental Grand, the beach hotels welcome passersby to their beachfront restaurants, shops, and bars. Clean, modern bathrooms are always close at hand.

★ PALM BEACH

Palm Beach (from south of the Divi Phoenix Resort to the north end of the Holiday Inn) is Aruba's principal playground, which also makes it a busy and often crowded place. This is a perfect spot to make friends and socialize. But for visitors looking for seclusion and privacy, it is not ideal.

The waters here are the calmest of all of Aruba's large beaches, making it a favorite area for families with little ones, ideal for their first introduction to the sea. Palm Beach is truly one of the "dream beaches" of the world, a seeming endless stretch of soft white sands and gentle, clear surf.

★ BARANCA PLAT

Just south of Palm Beach is a small cove called **Baranca Plat or "Flat Stone"** (turn off on the water side where the road divider begins on J. E. Irausquin Blvd., just north of the Blue Condo complex). Here you will find seclusion among the sea grape trees, with all the conveniences of Palm Beach only a five-minute walk away. It is a tranquil, conveniently located option for a break from the more heavily populated beaches.

The surrounding jetties produce very quiet waters and no waves. The shallow water makes it an excellent spot for little children to splash and play without being buffeted about. Pelicans and gulls often fill the jetties and make for an entertaining show.

No signs mark this beach. You'll know it by a platform where waverunners are tethered. It is just minutes south of the main resorts and directly across from Blue Residences.

★ FISHERMAN'S HUTS

North of Palm Beach, beyond the Ritz-Carlton, is the windsurfing and kitesurfing capital of Aruba with number of operations teaching both sports, as well as places for refreshments and shade. This long stretch called **Fisherman's Huts** (L. G. Smith Blvd. across from Bakval) is named for tiny beachside domiciles passed down by fishing families through the generations. The name remains but the huts are gone: They were removed to make way for a new resort. The beach is very popular with islanders. You can spend your days watching the colorful sails whipping through the waves and the aerial acrobatics of the kitesurfers.

Beach access is clearly marked with a sign on L. G. Smith Boulevard, and there is ample parking.

BOCA CATALINA

Bordered by limestone formations, **Boca Catalina** (L. G. Smith Blvd. 501 and 2a/2b Rd., Malmokweg) offers some very nice snorkeling. The beach area is not large, but the water is very quiet and ideal for all ages. Boca

Outcroppings bordering Boca Catalina beach provide interesting snorkeling.

Catalina is also a popular place for larger sailboats to stop during their charter runs.

The road to get here ends at the south end of the final cluster of waterfront homes. There is a wooden stairway entry at the northern point. Though bordered by the luxurious homes of Malmok, the beach is public. There are some shaded tables, but no public facilities. There is limited parking and it can get very busy with islanders on the weekends.

MALMOK BEACH

Malmok Beach (L.G. Smith Blvd north of Fishermen's Huts) is a very short stretch of beach that fronts some of the guest houses along the Malmok strip, south of Boca Catalina. It is marked by the remains of a ship sticking out close to the water. Most of it is quite rocky, interspersed with a few sandy areas. Entry to the sea here is also lined with rocks and the water is very shallow for some distance out to sea.

The ocean is very busy with windsurfers and kitesurfers whizzing by frequently. Care is advised when swimming here; it is better for simply sunbathing. The rocky formations that abut the beach are also very popular with local fishermen, so snorkelers should watch out for fishing line and hooks, and just stick to the beach areas.

ARASHI BEACH

The last beachfront house of Malmok ends at the start of serene **Arashi Beach** (L. G. Smith Blvd., north of the waterfront homes), an area that has been tailored to accommodate the public. A manicured, spacious parking lot with chemical toilets and shaded tables and benches for picnics is adjacent to the beach. Every day a colorful wagon selling snacks and snow cones sets up for business here.

There are several thatched *palapas* on the beach maintained by the government. It is usually crowded with locals on the weekends; many islanders take advantage of its amenities for birthday parties and events.

The southern section of the shallow cove is quieter than the northern side, where the waves tend to break with more force.

North Coast

Many coves are scattered along Aruba's north shore. A good number are suitable as a beach break while touring the Aruban outback, though swimming is usually not recommended. Riptides are rampant here and can pull swimmers out to sea. Body surfing is generally not recommended due to the heavy waves, though some very fit athletes do indulge in it. Keep in mind there are no lifeguards, and any help would have to come from far away. Children should be kept out of these waters.

★ CALIFORNIA DUNES

A long, rolling area of Sahara-like dunes, generally referred to as the **California Dunes** (from the turnoff from the west point and paved road, follow the start of a gravel road along the north coast to the base of the lighthouse), is rather pretty, and a nice change of scenery from other shorelines. The dunes follow the coast for about a mile in line with the mount of the lighthouse and end in some rough shores not really suitable for swimming. In the past it was a popular place for nude sunbathing, and there are still a few isolated areas offering shelter for those that care to indulge. If nude sunbathing isn't for you, enjoy a nice nature walk.

DRUIF AND URIRAMA BEACHES

On the nameless north coast road are **Druif and Urirama Beaches** (Druif is about 2 km (1.24 mi) past the California Dunes; Urirama is another 2 km past Druif). Aside from waveboarders, these beaches attract anglers who have built shacks of driftwood on the sand. Here they can clean their fish and seek shelter from the sun. Islanders picnic here, but swimming is not good for the uninitiated. However, the dramatic photo ops of rugged seas crashing into the shore and the surrounding cliffs are worth the trip.

★ ANDICURI BEACH

Andicuri Beach (follow the winding road leading directly to the sea via the left fork from Ayo Rock Formation) is a wide, pristine beach flanked by dramatic limestone formations. It offers large waves fun for body surfing. Good swimmers will enjoy the surf, but it may be a bit much for children. The scenery around the beach is quite dramatic, with stark, almost petrified trees.

Andicuri is only accessible with an off-road vehicle. Getting here is a scenic journey in itself.

★ BLACK STONE BEACH

From Andicuri Beach a gravel road along the coast leads to **Black Stone Beach** (1.5 km [0.9 mi] past Andicuri Beach), where a very dramatic rock formation sits at the juncture of two natural bridges carved out of the cliffs. Where the sea meets the shore, the land is covered with the lava pebbles for which the beach is named. These were formed millions of years ago from magma bubbling up in deep-sea beds. The magma quickly cooled and fragmented, and the constant wearing away by waves has made them smooth.

It is a fun climb down to the shoreline and easy enough for youngsters. Waves crash against the shore with great force here; this is definitely not an area for swimming.

DAIMARI BEACH

One of the best ways to get to the very large, secluded **Daimari Beach** area with two separate coves divided by cliffs is on a horseback riding tour with **Rancho Daimari** (J. E. Irausquin Blvd. 382 A, 297/586-6284,

The California Dunes have plenty of private places.

www.arubaranchodaimari.com, 8am and 2pm daily, $78). The Natural Pool itinerary includes galloping through the coves of Daimari Beach. The beaches can also be accessed via the Natural Pool Trail in Arikok National Park. Once on the trail, continue north past the Natural Pool for about half a kilometer to reach the beach. While parts of the cove have calm waters that little ones can enjoy, most of the beach is better for body surfing. The entire area covers about 100 meters (109 yd.) of surf, and conditions vary depending on the wind and time of year.

DOS PLAYA

Dos Playa are dual coves divided by rock formations, hence the name. Featuring rolling dunes and nice waves, this is a favorite spot for local bodyboarders, but it is not recommended for children, and care should be taken if you are not a strong swimmer.

Located within Arikok National Park, Dos Playa is also a popular hiking tour destination (Rooi Tambu Trail, length 5.5 km (3.4 mi), 2-3 hrs round-trip from park welcome center via Mira Lamar pass).

To get here by car, follow the Mira Lamar pass gravel road and signs pointing to Dos Playa through the park for four kilometers (2.5 mi) to the crest of a hill, where you will see the beach below. From here it is a five-minute walk to the beach proper.

BOCA PRINS

Boca Prins is an enormous cove with a wide beach circled by limestone terraces and outcroppings. Quite secluded, it can be accessed through Arikok National Park (via Rooi Prins Trail ending at Phantage, 5.5 km [3.4 mi] from the visitor center), not far from the caves on the eastern end of the island.

By car you can travel to the beach via Mira Lamar pass. The path, a sand road that parallels the hiking route to the shore, is marked by signs. It is a nice place to take a break and grab a cold drink from the little snack bar across the road.

The sea at Boca Prins is deceptive, and there are some treacherous riptides. Take care not to go out too far from shore if taking a dip.

Andicuri Beach

San Nicolas, Savaneta, and Pos Chiquito

The eastern and southern coasts feature quiet beaches and excellent swimming for all ages. The southern side is rimmed by protective sandbars and reefs, assuring calm waters and some very nice snorkeling.

★ BABY BEACH AND ROGER'S BEACH

Two of Aruba's loveliest beaches are within the former Lago Colony. A paved road leads through the colony to the island's eastern tip, forking at the Rum Reef Bar. To the left is the entrance to Baby Beach. To the right is Roger's Beach, named for Captain Robert Rogers who convinced oil company executives to choose Aruba as the place to build their Caribbean refinery.

Baby Beach is considered a prime swimming destination. The artificial lagoon inside the breakwaters is perfectly still, very shallow, and ideal for young children, hence the name. There is a long, clean circle of white beach surrounding the water, with cliffs of greenery rising up to the Lago housing above. Though it is popular with a number of tours, it is sufficiently expansive to provide several quiet areas for a more private sunbathing session or swim. The area is very popular with islanders on the weekends and a favorite camping spot during holidays.

The area boasts some stunning reefs beyond the breakwater, but the seas that far out are quite dangerous. The best of the reef is a few hundred yards from shore. Close in, there is a wide barrier of stag- and elkhorn coral that sometimes breaks the surface. It is easy for the uninitiated snorkeler to get lost and trapped within. Coral scrapes are painful and get infected easily. When snorkeling, be watchful not to drift out past the breakwater. Unfortunately, there is little to see within that limit. It is better to arrange

Baby Beach

Easter Week Camping

A time-honored way to celebrate Semana Santa on Aruba is to pack up the family and take to the beach. Islanders set up temporary homes on the shore in anything from pup tents to elaborately outfitted trailers powered by generators. The latter are frequently air-conditioned, with full-size refrigerators and giant plasma screens. First-time visitors are often under the mistaken impression that this is how islanders live.

Islanders devoted to camping sometimes relocate on the beach other weeks of the year. During summer vacation, Christmas, or the first week in October (an important school break), camping is quite popular. However, Easter week is when local beaches are certain to get very crowded.

This creates traffic snarls at Eagle Beach and Arashi Beach, two favored campsites on the west side of Aruba. Baby Beach and Roger's Beach will be lined with camping tents and trailers. Parking around these areas becomes much more difficult.

Naturally, with more campers there is also more trash. The government puts out chemical toilets and extra waste bins to reduce the impact on beach areas. Ecologically minded organizations along with the local waste removal company Ecotech have made inroads on the litter situation. A contest for the cleanest campsite at the end of the week yields great rewards, from cash prizes to weekend stays at major resorts. The community draws together to see that everyone has a fun and clean camping holiday.

being taken to the reef by **JADS Dive Shop** (Seroe Colorado 245E, 297/584-6070, http://jadsaruba.com).

Roger's Beach, right next door, is generally ignored by visitors because it stands in the shadow of the refinery. That is a mistake: It is a clean, beautiful beach, with shallow waters and snowy sands. It provides an equally ideal swimming area for little ones, with far less traffic than Baby Beach. A few picturesque native fishing boats are moored at the docks that occupy the eastern end of the cove.

BOCA GRANDE

The name "Large Mouth," tells you something about this big cove off the northeastern shore. It has a very nice semicircle of soft white sand and makes a nice spot for working on a tan while watching the colorful kites as surfers jump the waves and do tricks. Take the same route as you would for Baby Beach to get to **Boca Grande** (drive through San Nicolas heading east past all the settlements and out toward the former Lago Colony). You will be able to spot it from the large red anchor that marks the entry to Lago Colony. On weekends, it fills up with kitesurfers whipping across the water, which is somewhat prohibitive for swimmers.

SAVANETA BEACH

A road running parallel to the main highway between Oranjestad and San Nicolas follows the southern shoreline. This allows access to the southside beaches, such as **Savaneta Beach.** To get to the beaches, visitors must cross little wooden bridges placed periodically over the water pipes from WEB, Aruba's water production plant. Follow the main highway (1A) past the Pos Chiquito rotunda and continue on to Savaneta; then turn right at the gas station and head toward the water. Turn at the first right, which is a paved road. When you are 200 meters (0.15 mi) past the turn, take a left over a cement crossing over the pipes. The area along the shore is dotted with dense mangrove clusters, limestone outcroppings, and a secluded stretch of snowy, white sand. This beach has quiet, crystal clear waters, nice snorkeling, and is generally ignored, except by the residents of the neighborhood.

MANGEL HALTO

The sheltered beach of **Mangel Halto** in Pos Chiquito features a series of connected coves with a barrier reef not far from shore. For the best swimming experience, pass through a

Mangel Halto

break in the mangroves at the far right of the main beach. Beyond is an expansive swimming area that starts very shallow, standing depth, but then suddenly drops into a deep bowl, before going shallow again.

When the waters are low, the mangrove roots actually make a tunnel to some even more secluded beaches beyond the main area. They are not always accessible when the tides are high. Since these are thick mangrove clusters, make sure to fully coat yourself in mosquito repellent if you are planning to spend much time here.

Shaded tables and *palapas* are available for a relaxing beach day.

To get to Mangel Halto, turn toward the ocean at the Balashi traffic light on Highway 1A. Go to the end of the road, which ends in a T-intersection and Aruba's water and power plant. Turn left and cross the small bridge over Spaanslagoen. Turn right at the second road past the bridge, where there is a sign for Marina Pirata. Follow this road to the very end and turn left. The beach entrance is clearly marked 500 meters farther along the road bordering the sea, Spaanslagoenweg.

Recreation

Aruba is a playground for all ages. Clear, tropical waters and a lush marine environment are perfect for scuba diving, snorkeling, and every other water sport. Resorts and independent venues host excellent facilities for tennis and golf. Arikok National Park provides a range of hiking and biking options. The best part is that the constant, reliable climate lets visitors enjoy their favorite activities in any season.

There are several ways to explore the island on land, sea, and even in the air. Tour companies offer a head-spinning number of options for discovering the Aruba outback and major sights. Entrepreneurial islanders are always on the lookout for original and interesting ways to show off their beloved homeland. In addition to bus and safari tours, there are trikes (motorcycle-car hybrids), Harley-Davidson treks, all-terrain vehicles, and horseback riding tours. For those who feel the journey should be as exciting as the destination, try a 4x4 "safari" adventure, with a guide or on your own. Tour guides can provide fascinating and knowledgeable commentary, while assuring you'll get to see all those hard-to-find spots. As with snorkeling and diving, it is always advisable to explore a new area with an experienced guide in order to get the lay of the land.

Aruba's steady trade winds provide wonderful sailing weather. Experienced sailors can rent Sunfish sailboats and two-person cats for cruising the coast. Charter boats ply the waters for morning or afternoon snorkeling trips or sunset sails daily.

Scuba companies start their day with novice resort courses that allow students to safely explore the exhilarating underwater landscape in only a few hours. These fully tested programs are endorsed and standardized by international dive organizations.

Other athletic pastimes to try are windsurfing and kitesurfing. Aruba is considered one of the world's top destinations for both. If there is any way to play in the waves, the island has it—usually within a few steps from most major resorts.

Aruban waters have also been declared

Previous: tubing at sea; exploring the outback on horse. **Above:** a hiking path in Arikok National Park.

Look for ★ to find recommended recreation.

Highlights

★ **Octopus Cruises:** Enjoy smooth sailing on a wide, three-hulled sailboat. Snorkel stops include the *Antilla* shipwreck. The crew is known for their patient instruction, great lunches, and rum punch (page 50).

★ ***Tranquilo:*** For sailing fanatics who enjoy the thrill of leaning into the wind, the all-day trips on the *Tranquilo* deliver. Travel to a secluded reef on Aruba's south side for excellent snorkeling opportunities (page 50).

★ **JADS Dive Shop:** The only dive operator working out of the Baby Beach area, JADS offers safe diving to one of Aruba's most vibrant reefs. Serious divers interested in the unusual will find it here (page 52).

★ **Unique Sports of Aruba:** This reliable and respected dive shop in the Palm Beach area offers a diverse range of water activities (page 52).

★ **Madi's Magical Tours:** Don't just take a tour, go tripping with Madi! Her friendly personality makes her small group tours one of the best ways to see what Aruba's outback has to offer (page 60).

★ **Big Twin Harley-Davidson:** Indulge your *Easy Rider* fantasy with a guided tour on your own Harley (page 61).

★ **Trikes:** These motorcycle-car hybrids are one of the most popular and fun ways to tour the island (page 61).

★ **Rancho Daimari:** Outback adventures are even more enjoyable on horseback, one of the best ways to get to Conchi and Daimari Beach. Experienced riders can opt for a gallop on the beach (page 63).

★ **Skydive Aruba:** One of the most thrilling and adventurous ways to see Aruba is by taking a skydiving trip with an experienced instructor (page 63).

★ **Okeanos Spa:** This is the only spa that offers access to Renaissance Island, which is absolutely the most romantic spot for a couple's massage. It's the ultimate vacation indulgence (page 68).

"marlin country" by officials of the annual international billfishing tournaments. Deep-sea fishing is available as full- or half-day trips, and boats depart from several convenient locations.

Golfers will be delighted to find two vastly different courses close to the major resort areas. Both employ veteran pros and offer helpful clinics. Aruba's gusty winds are an interesting challenge; with a tailwind, some golfers report record drives.

From sumptuous to simple, Aruba's day spas offer a menu of treatments to relax the body and restore the spirit. Vacation time is the right time to sample these services, even if the most strenuous thing you do is walk back and forth from your beach lounge to the beach bar.

A principal reason veteran visitors give for returning to Aruba again and again is "whatever you like to do, day or night, Aruba has it all." Vacationers can spend their time lazing on the beach, or they can get busy from morning to sunset enjoying a favorite activity or learning a new one. Whether you choose to tour the coastline by sailboat, explore the underwater environment, or visit popular tourist sites, you will find reasonably priced services accommodating individuals and any size family or group.

Water Activities

Seeing the tropical marine environment for the first time, whether snorkeling or on a scuba dive, has literally changed lives. It can elicit eco-conservation attitudes or, at the very least, the dedication to an invigorating and fascinating pastime. Snorkeling trips, as well as other water tours, are easily arranged through independent booking agents right on the beaches in front of most resorts.

SNORKEL SITES

Aruban waters provide a large variety of dive and snorkel sites. Aside from reef areas, there are quite a few wrecks, some purposely placed, such as the Jane Sea and the Sonesta Planes. These soon become havens for schools of fish. Some dive operations have mapped out 39 dive spots around Aruba, though many are not accessible or appropriate for the casual vacation diver. The most commonly visited sites are popular for a good reason: Calm waters assure a safe, enjoyable adventure for divers with limited experience. Those with years of diving expertise should look to some of the smaller, private operators for diving beyond the norm. They can provide custom trips to remoter locations. Aruba has a few appealing offshore snorkeling sites along the west coast, not far from Palm Beach.

It is always advisable to snorkel with a buddy, and that's a required practice for scuba divers. Renting an inflatable snorkel vest is also advisable when snorkeling on your own.

BOCA CATALINA

Bordering Boca Catalina (north of Palm Beach on the west coast, close to Malmokweg), the coastline is a coral wall rampant with a variety of sealife. This is a good spot for offshore snorkeling, with no need to swim far to enjoy the schools of grunts, copperheads, and silversides that shelter under the limestone outcroppings. There are two entry points, but the most interesting sealife can be found at the entry where steps have been carved into the stone. This is just where the houses on the water side begin. Swim north or south of this point.

MANGEL HALTO

Aruba's south side has an extensive reef formation bordering the mangrove reefs along Pos Chiquito, the midpoint of the island. The inner lagoon has some sealife, but a sandy bottom. It is enclosed by an extensive outcropping of elkhorn and staghorn coral. The areas facing into the lagoon provide interesting snorkeling. Traveling through the reef to the outer areas and the drop-off reefs is best done with an experienced guide who knows the route, as it requires snaking through sharp coral that skims the surface.

SNORKELING CRUISES

★ OCTOPUS CRUISES

One of the most experienced sailing outfitters on Aruba, **Octopus Cruises** (Borancana 12, departs from Playa Linda beach, 297/593-3739, www.octopusaruba.com, 9am-12:30pm Wed.-Fri., 1:30pm-4pm Mon.-Fri., and 5pm-7pm Tues. and Thurs., $37.50-52.50) has a 40-foot trimaran sailboat. This is an authentic, tranquil sailing experience with Captain Jethro, one of the few fully certified sailors on the island. It is the only boat on Aruba without a motor, running strictly on sail power. They limit the number of passengers to 22 per trip, to assure comfort and personal attention.

Jethro has been sailing Aruba's waters for decades; he loves the sailor's life. His crew is particularly patient and thorough with instructions for novice snorkelers. Fish are accustomed to their daily visits and do not shy away from snorkelers.

Morning trips include a continental breakfast with mimosas and two snorkel stops, including the *Antilla* shipwreck. The buffet lunch features a fresh salad and make-your-own hoagies, with a wide array of exotic tropical fruits. Shorter afternoon trips are mostly spent snorkeling, but offer a snack of their famous Dutch cheese baguettes and fresh fruit. Relaxing sunset sails feature cocktails and snacks, but no snorkel stops. An open bar is included for all trips.

★ *TRANQUILO*

The all-day trips on the 43-foot ***Tranquilo*** (Alto Vista 34K, departs from Renaissance Harbor, 297/594-2173, www.tranquiloaruba.com, 10am-3pm Tues., Thurs., and Fri., $85) have long been a family affair made popular decades ago by Captain Mike, a local sailing legend. His son Anthony has kept up the tradition and is passing the love of the sea and sailing on to the next generation.

Best known as offering the only regularly scheduled full-day trips to Aruba's south side, the *Tranquilo* gives visitors authentic toes-in-the-water moments at some of the windier points along the coast. The single keel affords heeling well into the wind and a real sailor's adventure on the water.

The snorkel spot is an attractive reef that is part of the Mangel Halto formation, affectionately referred to as "Mike's Reef." A platform on one of the sandbanks facilitates entry and exit. The *Tranquilo* has a regular clientele who come back each year for the famous Dutch pea soup that Anthony's mom, Celia, makes for lunch. *Tranquilo* also offers a Romantic Dinner for Two tour ($475), which includes a champagne toast, wine, and a customized menu arranged in advance via email.

JOLLY PIRATES

With a name like **Jolly Pirates** (J. E. Irausquin Blvd. 230, 297/586-8107, www.jolly-pirates.com, 9am-1pm, 2pm-5pm, and 5:30pm-7:30pm daily, $32-60) the mood is already set for these popular trips on picturesque, old-styled wooden schooners. Captain Harold and his lively crew have a reputation for doing their best to deliver on those expectations. The ships are also famous for their rope swing.

Trips depart from the Hadicurari Pier by MooMba Beach, where they maintain their headquarters and logo shop. Jolly Pirates runs two stylish ships, each taking a maximum of 65 passengers. Morning trips include snorkeling, barbecue lunch, an open bar, and fresh fruit; afternoon snorkel trips and sunset sails offer the bar only.

DIVING

Snorkeling is an easy and quick way to explore the marine environment. But to really study the reef and wrecks in detail, visitors should learn how to scuba dive.

PADI-certified (Professional Association

of Diving Instructors) dive shops are plentiful on Aruba, with most along the Palm Beach boardwalk. Some go beyond just SCUBA (self-contained underwater breathing apparatus) lessons, and offer sailing trips with SNUBA (surface nexus underwater breathing apparatus). With scuba, each diver has his or her own breathing unit. SNUBA deploys what is known in the diving community as a "hookah." Four divers are attached to one tank, which floats on the surface. This allows them to submerge to a maximum of about 6 meters (20 ft.) under the water. Since the tank of air is shared, time underwater is also quite limited. SNUBA divers still have to get some instruction and learn a few scuba techniques.

Resort courses, devised and approved by PADI, provide enough background information and preliminary training for novices to perform a shallow, heavily supervised dive. The actual use of scuba equipment is not very complicated or difficult to learn. Becoming a fully certified diver involves training to plan and perform dives without supervision, and that requires much more background knowledge. So you can learn enough in a resort course to get a taste of the sport. The ideal conditions of Aruba's tropical marine environment make the island the perfect place for an introduction to what may become a lifelong interest.

Full certification courses are offered by all the certified dive shops. They cover an intense four days of classes, pool sessions, and dives, and meet PADI requirements. It is essential to contact a dive shop prior to your trip to arrange a class since all the lectures, pool work, tests, and dives that would normally be conducted over a five-week period are compressed into a few days. Be prepared to commit nearly the entire day, each day, to complete the course.

Certifying organizations also allow for the option of doing the class and pool work over several weeks in the United States or Canada and then traveling to an exotic destination to fulfill the dive requirements in a more desirable location. Proof that this class and pool work was successfully completed must be in hand before Aruban dive shops can administer the, usually four, qualifying dives. The dives are underwater exercises and tests that must be passed satisfactorily. All PADI-affiliated dive shops on Aruba offer a package price for this service and should be contacted prior to arrival, with all paperwork in order.

Night Diving

Aruba is the perfect place for certified divers who have never enjoyed the exhilaration of night diving. As beautiful as the underwater world is during the day, once night has fallen, a rarely seen environment is exposed. Nocturnal sealife comes out to play, unveiling new mysteries of the deep.

The deeper a diver descends during the day, the more color is lost. Bright corals and fish take on a bluish cast. The bright lights used at night reveal in a way that can never be seen during the day the actual brilliant hues of sponges and corals. The stunning colors of various creatures that come out to feed are amazing. Diurnal fish actually get sleepy at night, so they are not so quick to dart away.

The most daunting aspect for novice night divers is keeping oriented to the dive boat or entry point. In pitch-black waters, particularly over an extensive reef area, divers can get quite confused. For this reason, the *Antilla* is a superb choice for an inaugural nocturnal dive. It is a huge object, the dive is not too deep, and it offers an enormous diversity of sealife within a limited area. Following its structure orients you as to where you are and where the dive boat is tied on. The assurance of the dive boat being close by allows night divers to relax and enjoy this fascinating experience.

Divers who have been considering giving night diving a try will never have a better opportunity. Aruba's warm waters and the comfortable air temperatures make for a pleasant night dive experience.

A signed form from a doctor confirming the diver's fitness for the sport is also required.

Pregnant women and individuals with chronic conditions requiring daily medication, such as diabetes, high blood pressure, heart disease, asthma, epilepsy, or having had recent major surgery, are usually not eligible for any of these activities. A bad cold or congestion will also disqualify you since this can result in serious damage to the sinuses or eardrums. As much as you might want to still try diving, be sure to inform the operators of any possible prohibitive conditions, and listen to them when they tell you no.

★ JADS DIVE SHOP

The only dive shop within Lago Colony and next to Baby Beach, **JADS** (Seroe Colorado 245E, 297/584-6070, http://jadsaruba.com, resort course $99, full certification $425) offers the best way to dive some of Aruba's most stunning reefs. No other dive operator has the advantage of this location, with boats taking divers out to remoter spots on the east side in record time. Patrons will find this PADI facility very conscientious and the staff personable and informative. Even though JADS is located on the far end of the island from major resort areas, they also do hotel pickup and return.

DIVE ARUBA

One of the island's most experienced PADI Open Water instructors, Clive Paula operates **Dive Aruba** (Williamstraat 8, 297/582-7337, www.divearuba.com, Mon.-Sat., dives and classes by appointment, resort course $85, full certification $425). He runs a small, very personalized operation out of Oranjestad, taking out only seven divers at a time. Dive trips are geared to certified divers, so if you are seeking a novice resort course, it is important to book ahead. Departing from the town harbor, his superfast boat can assure quick access to remoter and unusual sites. Trips include hotel pickup and return. This is the only dive operation with the added perk of obtaining a very cool "Dive with Clive" souvenir T-shirt.

★ UNIQUE SPORTS OF ARUBA

One of the most respected PADI-certified scuba shops in Palm Beach is **Unique Sports of Aruba** (J. E. Irausquin Blvd. 81, between RIU and Hilton Resorts, 297/586-0096, www.uniquesportsaruba.com, resort courses 9:30am Mon.-Sat. $105, PADI certification $475, National Geographic $125 extra, SNUBA $55), the exclusive island agent for SNUBA. It is also a National Geographic Dive facility, with specialty courses including two additional dives. These offer eco-awareness dive training, with particular attention to techniques that ensure no harm comes to the marine environment. A NITROX-enriched air diving course is also on the menu.

Unique Sports of Aruba runs sailing and snorkeling trips on a Cruzencat catamaran, which also feature SNUBA sessions. For those who feel more comfortable walking into the water, there are alternative trips twice daily that allow divers to enter offshore at Arashi. These private sessions are for 2-4 divers. The desk is also an agent for small craft activities, such as waverunners and tubing.

ARUBA WATERSPORTS CENTER

Between the Hilton and Occidental Resorts is **Aruba Watersports Center** (J. E. Irausquin Boulevard 81b, 297/586-6613, www.arubawatersportcenter.com, 9am-5pm daily, resort course Mon.-Sat. $95, open water $425, bicycle rental $25), a reliable family operation offering diving and all small craft activities, plus Sunfish and Beachcat boat rentals. There are two PADI-certified instructors, very capable and personable, simply known as J.T. and Jake. The complex also offers a shop on the boardwalk for beachwear and sundries. It's a good place to pick up watertight beach boxes, sunblock, and other minor items.

UNDERWATER TOURS

You don't have to get wet to enjoy Aruba's amazing underwater environment. Family-oriented excursions provide a memorable experience for all ages and nonswimmers.

Family Fun at Aruba Waterpark

The affordable **Aruba Waterpark** (Hooiberg z/n, 297/585-0060, www.arubavacationpark.com, 11am-6pm Tues.-Sun., $11 adults, $8 children) houses a great collection of slides for all ages. There are slow, steady, and shallow slides for young ones and daredevil drops for the "take no prisoners" teenagers. Lifeguards are on duty. The high slides were ingeniously designed with a gradual nature walk to the top, rather than an exhausting climb up steep stairs.

The park boasts a serviceable and inexpensive restaurant with a continually changing menu. The standard fare of barbecue and hamburgers is always available, but the chef also cooks up a variety of local dishes.

Planted in the midst of the Aruba countryside, with stunning views of the surrounding landscape, the waterpark is inland. It is not that hard to find: Just head for the Hooiberg and follow the signs.

ATLANTIS SUBMARINES AND *SEAWORLD EXPLORER*

Two of the most unusual transports for touring the marine landscape are the ***Atlantis* Submarines** and ***Seaworld Explorer*** (L. G. Smith Blvd., toll-free 800/609-7374, 297/582-4545 DePalm office will connect you, www.depalmtours.com; *Atlantis:* 11am daily, 90 minutes $105 adults, $79 children, under 4 not allowed; *Seaworld Explorer:* 11am daily, $44 adults, $29 children). *Atlantis* takes passengers past drop-off reefs and a few small wrecks on the south side, reaching depths of 46 meters (150 ft.). Passengers look out portholes that line the sides of the sub. This is thrilling for one side of the submarine, but there is little to see but the sandy bottom on the other. After the sub turns, the other side gets to see the interesting stuff. The impossible-to-miss ticket office and logo retail shop at Oranjestad Harbor is the embarkation point.

Seaworld Explorer is a semi-submarine: the top half stays above the surface. The underwater portion has wide all-around picture windows for a panoramic view. It departs from the De Palm Pier in Palm Beach, taking passengers over the *Antilla* shipwreck and west-side reef areas. If you begin to feel a little claustrophobic down below, you can go up top to enjoy the wide-open vista of the coastline.

SEA TREK

Sea Trek (L. G. Smith Blvd. 142, 297/582-4545, www.depalmtours.com, $49 adults, $36 children) uses hard hat helmets like divers of old, but with space-age design. This allows nonswimmers to actually walk on the ocean floor, tethered to the surface. This adventure is only available at **De Palm Island** (Balashi z/n, 297/585-4799, www.depalmtours.com, 9am-6pm daily, $99 adults, $69 children, with round-trip transport by bus) and not included in the price of a day on the island. No special training is required. As a bonus, personnel will film you during the trek, and you may choose to purchase the DVD as a souvenir.

SAILING

Families and groups with diverse tastes will particularly appreciate the many large catamarans and trimarans common to Aruba. They have a stability that guarantees smooth sailing in heavy winds. Their wider breadth also makes it easier to move about and stretch out. Day trips are geared to pleasing all passengers, with snorkel stops, instruction, equipment, light meals, and beverages included. Guests have the option of exploring the reefs or simply relaxing on board and working on their tan.

Palm Beach has the greatest concentration of water activities, including sailboat departures. Three large piers provide boarding and debarkation points for most trips. Pier operators are large water sports companies that offer a diversity of services, and they usually have a few sailboats. They also have contracts with visiting cruise ships, resulting in days when the trips are not available to independent bookings.

An alternative to these larger companies are smaller, owner-operated boats, which provide good value and a dedication to the craft. The love of sailing is often passed down through the generations, and captains who run their own boats, whether for sailing or deep-sea fishing, are dedicated to the art. The atmosphere on these boat trips can feel like spending a day on the water with friends. They are a very personalized experience, usually with smaller groups as well.

In addition to offering snorkel sails, **Octopus Cruises** (Borancana 12, departs from Playa Linda beach, 297/593-3739, www.octopusaruba.com, 9am-12:30pm Wed.-Fri., 1:30pm-4pm Mon.-Fri., and 5pm-7pm Tues. and Thurs., $37.50-52.50) offers sunset sails with cocktails and snacks.

The ***Tranquilo*** (Alto Vista 34K, departs from Renaissance Harbor, 297/594-2173, www.tranquiloaruba.com, 10am-3pm Tues., Thurs., and Fri., $85) offers a Romantic Dinner for Two tour ($475), which includes a champagne toast, wine, and a customized menu arranged in advance via email.

Jolly Pirates (J. E. Irausquin Blvd. 230, 297/586-8107, www.jolly-pirates.com, 9am-1pm, 2pm-5pm, and 5:30pm-7:30pm daily, $32-60) offers sunset sails with an open bar in addition to their snorkel sails.

RED SAIL SPORTS DINNER CRUISE

Regularly scheduled dinner cruises depart every Wednesday from **Red Sail Sports pier** (J. E. Irausquin Blvd. 348 A, 297/586-1603, www.aruba-redsail.com, 6pm-9pm, $95 adult, $58 child) next to the Hyatt. Take the island fantasy dinner to a new level without being too hard on the wallet. The *Rumba,* which is 70 feet, has a limit of only 38 passengers. The sunset trip includes a buffet dinner catered by the Hyatt culinary department, known for its quality cuisine, and an open bar.

Sailors can rent small boats to cruise the coastline.

KAYAKING

ARUBA KAYAK ADVENTURES

Aruba Kayak Adventures (Ponton 88, 297/582-5520, www.arubawavedancer.com, 8:30am-2:30pm Mon.-Sat., $83, Sun. on request for groups) runs memorable nature tours. Congenial, entertaining guides Rosendo and Carlos take kayakers, from the novice to the experienced, through the rich biodiversity of the mangrove preserves of Mangel Halto and the south side. Guests are picked up at their resorts and transported to this pristine location. There is a declared limit of 18-20 kayakers per tour, with varying routes for repeat guests. After some snorkeling, lunch is at the quaint Balashi Beer Gardens.

DEEP-SEA FISHING

Deep-sea fishing can be arranged through concierge desks, major water sports companies, or many of the tent operators along Palm Beach; all have some fishing boats on their roster. If you're serious about fishing, it is always advisable to head down to the piers to watch the boats come in and see who is catching. Talk to the crew and the anglers. An amiable captain and crew always add that special something to the enjoyment of the day. Several boats are moored at Hadicurari Pier, between MooMba Beach and the Marriott Surf Club in Palm Beach, or in Oranjestad Harbor. Charter rates vary greatly depending on the size of the boat and length of the trip.

Oranjestad Harbor

DRIFTWOOD FISHING CHARTERS

Enjoy your catch for dinner after fishing with **Driftwood Fishing Charters** (Oranjestad Marina, 297/592-4040, www.driftwoodaruba.com, hours vary, $400-800). Fanatical angler Herby Merryweather will see to it that the catch gets cooked up for no charge that same night at Driftwood, his Oranjestad restaurant. He has two boats; the *Driftwood II* is available only for all-day charters. Merryweather knows where the fish are and loves to catch. In fact, he needs to—to provide fish for his two restaurants, Driftwood and Red Fish.

MAHI MAHI FISHING CHARTERS

You will find equally fanatical guides at **Mahi Mahi Fishing Charters** (Oranjestad Marina, 297/594-1181, www.arubamahimahi.com, hours vary, $400-1,100). They have three boats for charter: the *Kepasa* and the *Mahi Mahi,* both 42-foot Hatteras, and the *Sea-iesta,* a 54-foot Bertram. The congenial crew will clean and prepare 30 percent of the catch for you to take with you. If you do not have kitchen facilities, don't fret: Barney's restaurant in Palm Beach will prepare your catch; you need only pay for any accompaniments.

TEASER FISHING CHARTERS

A consistent winner during annual fishing contests, **Teaser Fishing Charters** (Oranjestad Marina, 297/593-9228, www.teasercharters.com, 8am-noon and 8am-4pm daily, $400-1,000) runs two 35-foot Bertrams: *Teaser* and *Kenny's Toy.* The captain and crew love the sport and share the excitement of the catch. Regular clients cite the friendly crew and their enthusiasm for making a day on the water an enjoyable experience.

Having participated and placed regularly in the annual international billfishing tournament held in Aruba in the fall, Teaser Charters has added a special billfishing run to the regular roster. This is their top-of-the-line all-day excursion.

Hadicurari Pier

CAROLINA CHARTERS

Marcelino and Demian of **Carolina Charters** (Hadicurari Pier, 297/737-4477 or 297/594-3717, www.fishingyachtaruba.com, flexible hours, half day: $350-900) are living their dream by fishing every day. They offer deep-sea and bottom fishing, as well as a special tour for the big game fish. Patrons praise them especially for how well they work with novices and children.

MELINA CHARTERS

For greater convenience to Palm Beach resorts, **Melina Charters** (Hadicurari Pier, 297/593-1550, www.arufishing.com, flexible hours, half day: $300-550) is moored close by. They offer a varied menu of deep-sea, bottom, and inshore fishing, for smaller game. They will gear trips to what is running at the time or a patron's preference. Owner and captain Piet is a personable veteran angler who loves the sport and does his best to find the fish.

KITESURFING, PARASAILING, WINDSURFING, AND SURFING

All along Palm Beach are a dozen or more independent operators with tents that provide spur-of-the-moment, unscheduled activities. These could be banana boat rides, tubing, waverunners, and parasailing, usually sold in blocks of 15-30 minutes. Each resort has at least one vendor; prices and services are the same from one to the next. Fisherman's Huts, north of the Marriott, is Aruba's windsurfing and kitesurfing center, with kiosks and tents where lessons can be arranged or equipment rented to those with experience.

ARUBA ACTIVE VACATIONS

Dedicated to extreme sports, **Aruba Active Vacations** (Fisherman's Huts, L. G. Smith Blvd. across from Bakval, 297/586-0989, www.aruba-active-vacations.com, 9am-7pm daily, windsurfing $50-135, kitesurfing $110-160, mountain biking $25-100, landsailing safari 2.5 hours, $60) is aptly named. Owner Wim Eehlers is the president of the Aruba Windsurfing Association, which conducts the annual Aruba Hi-Winds Pro-Am. He and his crew are fanatical about their activities, offering patient, expert instruction. Aruba is considered to have some of the most ideal conditions for windsurfing in the world: Calm waters and steady winds make it easy to master the sport. Discover a new obsession.

ARUBA SURF SCHOOL

Due to Aruba's calm waters, surfing does not have the thrill of the Pacific or north Atlantic coasts. Thus there is only one operation dedicated to this activity: **Aruba Surf School** (Irausquin Blvd, 297/593-0229, by appt. daily, 2.5-hour lesson and tour $95, rental $35, SUP class $60, $25/hr rental). Still owner and surfing fanatic Dennis Martinez does

Aruba is a prime destination for kitesurfing.

his utmost to provide a fun day of riding the waves. He picks up guests at their resorts and takes them to the best surf for that day—at out-of-the-way coves along the north coast. Expect an outback adventure and surfing safari experience all in one. They also rent stand-up paddleboards (SUP) from their center on the beach directly in front of the Marriott Surf Club.

NATIVE DIVERS WATERSPORTS

You can always count on a friendly chat and conscientious service with Vanessa at **Native Divers Watersports** (Washington 16, 297/586-4763, book at the tent in front of the Marriott Surf Club, 9am-5pm daily, float rental $5/day banana boat; tube rides $20 for 20 minutes; waverunners $65/half-hour; additional $5 per child to share with up to two small children; driver must be at least 16 years old; parasailing $60). She will be happy to arrange all sorts of family activities for playing in the waves, such as tubing, banana boat rides, parasailing, and waverunners, as well as renting out floats, at standard rates. She makes it a practice of directing clients to the most safety-conscious and reputable operators. Her tent is a hospitable place to relax, and she is a fountain of information regarding activities and operators.

FUN FOR EVERYONE

At the north end of the Riu Palace beach you'll find George Tromp and his tent offering **Fun for Everyone** (Borancana 128, 297/640-6603, www.fun4every1.com, 9am-5pm daily, float rental $5/day, banana boat and tube rides $20/half-hour, waverunners $60/half-hour, parasailing $60, beach umbrellas $25/day, beach lounges $5/day). George runs a very friendly operation. He has four fast boats of his own to accommodate all comers. Banana boat rides offer a complete tour of the coastline from Palm Beach to the Westpunt.

He also has beach lounge rental by the day and shade umbrellas for those who are not guests of Palm Beach resorts but wish to spend the day here. This is particularly handy for cruise ship passengers.

VELA SURF CENTER

On the beach between the Marriott and Ritz-Carlton sits **Vela Surf Center** (L. G. Smith Blvd 101, 297/586-3735, www.velaaruba.com, 9am-6pm daily, $60-$125) and a full menu of surfing options. Two-hour beginners' group windsufing and kitesurfing lessons are scheduled four times daily. Advanced private lessons can be set up as well. They also rent kayaks, snorkeling gear, and SUPs. This is one of Aruba's longest established and most respected operators.

Land Tours

Choose from full-size air-conditioned coaches, minibus tours, or safari-type vehicles for large and small groups. The more unique methods, such as trikes and Harley-Davidson motorcycles, take such few numbers that they are practically private tours. Or get off the ground altogether and see Aruba from above, in a skydiving tour.

The advantages of guided tours, whether large or small, are many. Drivers and guides know the island well. Aside from getting you where you want to go with minimal wasted time, guides provide interesting and informative commentary, often seasoned with wit and folklore, making for an enjoyable interlude.

Disadvantages include the need to keep to a schedule instead of exploring or savoring a site for as long as they wish. This is when the smaller, personalized tours with guides who can accommodate patrons' whims deliver. Aruba has a wealth of both large and small tours, allowing everyone to get exactly what they want.

COACHES

DE PALM TOURS

Aruba's most prolific tour operator, **De Palm Tours** (L. G. Smith Blvd. 142, 297/582-4545, www.depalmtours.com, 10am daily, $40 adults, $35 children), has the largest fleet of air-conditioned coaches and a wide variety of tours. Coach tours tend to visit the more easily accessible and prosaic spots, with the obligatory shopping stop at some local souvenir vendor. Those wanting a glance at the island away from the resort centers, while traveling in complete comfort, will find this just about right. Buses take up to 65 passengers.

EL TOURS

A mid-size tour operator and transport provider, **EL Tours** (Ir. Luymestraat 6, Pos Chiquito, 297/585-6730 or toll-free U.S./Canada 866/978-5913, www.eltoursaruba.com, 9am-1:30pm daily, $45 adults, $22.50 child) uses smaller buses and takes fewer passengers. It also visits many of the standard sites, but with an optional stop at Arashi Beach for an hour of snorkeling. Equipment is provided.

MINIBUSES

There are quite a few independent operators who take on small groups of 11-15 visitors at very reasonable prices and flexible schedules. Large families find it easy to arrange a private tour. Most are done at a leisurely pace, allowing personalized exploration of the various sights. Vehicles are well maintained and air-conditioned, offering an attractive alternative that is less commercial than the ordinary bus tour. These independent bus operators are spirited tour guides with a wealth of information about Aruba.

Minibus tours generally operate from in front of the cruise terminal in Oranjestad. They also pick up at hotels when groups hire the entire bus. During the low season they will provide transport for groups, saving money on multiple taxis. Minibus tours tend to stick to the more easily accessed sites and smooth, paved roads.

XCLUSIVE TOURS & TRANSFER SERVICES

Regmy Dubero has been a tour guide since he was 18. He has been in the business over 14 years, the last five on his own. He takes his responsibility as an "ambassador of goodwill" very seriously. Regmy's **Xclusive Tours & Transfer Services** (Rooi Kochi 30 C, 297/593-3551, www.xclusivetoursaruba.com, $25, minimum of 4 passengers for a private tour) makes every effort to entertain guests while proudly showing off his homeland. Tours can be customized to explore particular areas of the island. Favorite spots on the regularly scheduled tours include Casibari Rock Formation, Bushiribana Gold Ruin, Santa Ana Church, and Alto Vista Chapel. A standard tour is two hours, but it can be extended. Passengers can pick the route that interests them most from a menu of tours.

BINNS TOURS

Sonny Binns of **Binns Tours** (Pos Chiquito 81B, 297/568-2028, binns.tours@yahoo.com, $10/hour pp, min two hours) has a larger bus than most independent operators: He handles up to 28 passengers. There are set tours of three and five hours, but time and itinerary are negotiable. Any trip can be customized to the tastes of his guests. Binns is a veteran tour guide who decided to go out on his own, which makes him a very happy fella, indeed. He visits many of the popular spots, offering a selection of sights and timed tours.

HOWARD FOLKES

After more than 24 years as a tour guide, **Howard Folkes** of **HF Tours and Transfers** (Piedra Plat 46H, 297/594-1954, http://folkes-tours.com, $20 pp for two-hour tours, extra time is negotiable) knows every nook and cranny of Aruba. He has two buses: one that handles 29 passengers, the other 15. Trips are customizable. Though his normal point of departure is from in front of the cruise terminal, he will pick up at hotels, even if it's not a private group. Depending on the departure point and time requirements, he will suggest

Drink Water, Cover Up, and Don't Lose Your Wedding Ring!

Aruba's intense sun and temperatures can be extremely taxing, even for the very fit. Continual rehydration is necessary whether you are playing beach volleyball or just lying on the beach. Any strenuous activity should be accompanied by bottles of cool water or frequent stops for refreshments.

When touring in open vehicles, especially mopeds, don't make the mistake of wearing skimpy clothing. Aruba's roads can accumulate blown sand, which can be like driving over ice, particularly on curves. If you skid out, there is the potential for a nasty road rash. You are also likely to run into the foliage, where you can expect cactus with long, sharp thorns. Dress as you would for riding a motorcycle at home: in protective jeans, shirts with sleeves, and, of course, lots of sunblock on exposed areas. Be sure to use the helmet provided.

Tropical temperatures also pose the threat of heatstroke or heat exhaustion when engaging in physical activity, particularly if it is not part of your regular routine. The chronically inactive should think twice about biking long distances at midday or trying any physically demanding activity they are not used to. A completely new sport, or hiking off into some dry, deserted part of the landscape, should not be done alone or without a guide.

Lastly, pay particular attention to that wedding ring. Perhaps due to fingers slicked up by sun lotion, there isn't a week that goes by without a story of some newlywed losing a shiny new ring in the sea. It might happen on a snorkeling excursion or just while swimming offshore. Crews on pleasure boats have gotten pretty good at finding lost rings since they get quite a bit of practice, but why take that chance? Beach boxes will hold wedding rings nicely or lock them away.

a menu of easily accessible sites, such as Santa Ana Church, Alto Vista Chapel, California Lighthouse, and Casibari Rock Formation.

CARAVAN AND SPECIALTY TOURS

Caravan tours offer the best of both worlds: a chance to drive your own 4x4 or heavy-duty safari-type vehicle and a tour guide in a lead car showing the way. Most caravans take 6-10 passengers. These will usually traverse the rougher roads, which are often more direct. Excursions may last a full day with a good number of stops, as standard sights are mixed with those exciting, out-of-the-way locations. Some tour operators also offer shorter jaunts focusing only on off-road sights. Pickup times at resorts are 15-30 minutes prior to tour times quoted, as guests will be transported to a centralized departure point.

EL TOURS

Using Jeep Ramblers seating only four, the **EL Tours** (Ir. Luymestraat 6, Pos Chiquito, 297/585-6730 or toll-free U.S./Canada 866/978-5913, www.eltoursaruba.com, 9am-5pm daily, $93) safari excursions are a bit more intimate, often providing friends or family with their own car. Full-day tours include lunch at the highly recommended B-55 restaurant. Aside from 4x4 tours, EL is also a go-between for interesting alternatives such as guided hiking and mountain biking, horseback rides and Harley-Davidson tours, along with dedicated ecotours. These are customized tours, so prices and hours vary depending on size of group, length of tour, and choosing a guide or exploring on your own.

ABC TOURS

The first safari tours on Aruba were run by **ABC Tours and Attractions** (Schotlandstraat 61, 297/582-5600, www.abc-aruba.com, 9am-5pm daily, $105 adults, $70 children, includes lunch; 8:30am-12:30pm $79 adults, $49 children, no lunch). They set a standard that many still copy. They provide a comfortable ride in canopied Land Rovers and a barbecue lunch at the ABC-owned safari-style restaurant Waka-Waka. Owner

Marvin Kelly is always thinking innovatively and working to make the tours better. Guides compete with each other to make their tours the most interesting and fun. Heavy-duty vehicles mean they can get to the more out-of-the-way spots, including Conchi, Aruba's natural pool on the north coast. Patrons do the driving while following the leader, at least one person in a group needs to know how to use a standard transmission.

ABC provides a variety of half tours, offering sites such as the Ostrich Farm, Ayo Rock Formation, Andicuri Beach, and the Donkey Sanctuary.

★ MADI'S MAGICAL TOURS

Madi's Magical Tours (Shete 19, 297/746-1397, http://madimagicaltours.com, Sunrise Conchi Tour 5:30am-8:30am daily, $75 adults, children half price; 4.5-hour private tours $100) are run by Madi, a fifth generation Aruban who grew up with the countryside as her backyard. She admits to being a *bruha* (a white witch) with an encyclopedic knowledge of island folklore, bush medicine, and out-of-the-way sights. She is more than just a tour guide; her tours always have the feeling of *ban keiro* ("let's go tripping"). They're more like an excursion with family and friends than a commercial operation.

Madi takes very small groups and tries not to tie the guests into a set schedule or routine. Tours usually go well beyond prescribed times because of her charming company. She is quite the character, with memorable, unusual outings. Pick up and return to your hotel will be provided. The safari-type vehicle puts passengers in the car with her, not relegated to the back, so all can enjoy her running commentary.

One outing is a sunrise tour to Conchi, which departs before dawn. Expect some breathtaking photos as the sun rises on this dramatic section of the north coast. Madi is continually adding new, undiscovered areas to her itinerary.

NATURE SENSITIVE TOURS

Nature guide Eddy Croes harbors a passion for the outdoors and Aruban conservation, which he shares during his **Nature Sensitive Tours** (jeep tours begin with pick up at hotel, 297/585-1594 or 297/594-5017, http://nature-sensitivetours.com, hiking tours by appt. $79, full-day jeep tours $85). He was a powerful force behind Arikok National Park becoming a protected preserve and the first to begin identifying and labeling much of the flora found there. His tours are a unique experience, focused not only on the typical sights. He offers a more thorough exploration and understanding of how the many unique outback land formations came to exist.

Eddie has a wealth of stories and folklore to impart and has become something of an Internet personality, so his tours are in demand. He now takes groups of 20 or more for hiking tours using a refitted military truck. The canvas sides of the truck do not allow passengers to view the countryside while moving between locations.

MADAGASCAR ARUBA ADVENTURE

Tourists are raving about Alfredo and his **Madagascar Aruba Adventure** (Caya Seyda 9, 297/746-0572, madagascar-aruba@hotmail.com, 8:30am-1pm and 2pm-6pm daily, $50 adults, $30 children) because of the charm and enthusiasm of the owner-guide. Passengers report tours often go over the allotted time because everyone, including the host, is having so much fun. A little young to be called "Papa Alfred," Alfŕedo is very much all about taking care of his patrons and well informed about the island and the sights. Groups are limited to 12; his shaded safari truck is set up well for taking lots of pictures.

MOTORCYCLES, MOPEDS, AND ATVS

In the past few years, tour operators have realized that getting there can be half the fun when the transportation is funky.

★ BIG TWIN HARLEY-DAVIDSON

On the western outskirts of Oranjestad is the **Big Twin Harley-Davidson dealership** (L. G. Smith Blvd. 106, 866/978-6525 or 297/586-8220, www.harleydavidson-aruba.com, 9am-5:30pm Mon.-Sat., $140-175 half-day rentals, $175-200 full-day rentals), easily spotted by the HOGs lined up in front. If it has always been your dream to be an Easy Rider, you can rent your own or take one of their guided tours for an additional $20 per person fee, gas not included. Riding two on a bike is allowed. Tours lead only three bikes at a time, for a very personal, interesting way to see the island, Availability is limited, so it's best to reserve online before arriving on Aruba. Always attempting to be different, the tour includes a lunch or refreshment stop at Charlie's Bar in San Nicolas.

AROUND ARUBA TOURS

Independent tour companies are meeting the demand for more exciting and engaging methods of exploring Aruba's off-the-beaten-path regions. **Around Aruba Tours** (Alto Vista 116, 297/593-5963, www.aroundaruba.com, 4-hour tours daily, 9am or 2:30pm, $190 per UTV, $100 p/h Jeep Wrangler) is one of the very few to include Philip's Animal Garden in the itinerary. Take a tour in a two-seater UTV or an air-conditioned Jeep Wrangler that seats six. Rent your own if you're feeling adventurous.

GEORGE'S CYCLE RENTAL

For more than 30 years, **George's Cycle Rental** (L. G. Smith Blvd. 124, 297/593-2202, www.georgecycles.com, 9am-5pm daily, mopeds $40-50/day, Yamaha motorcycles $70-100/day, ATVs $120-200/day) has been the number one choice for mopeds and motorcycles. It is on the highway just at the western side of Oranjestad and has a variety of vehicles for rent, from tiny mopeds to ATVs with automatic transmission and hardtop shade canopies. Special discounts are available for longer-term rentals of three or four days. Resort pickup and drop-off plus helmets are part of the service.

MELCHOR CYCLE RENTAL

At the intersection of the Sasaki Highway and Bubali Road is **Melchor Cycle Rental** (Bublai 106-B, 297/587-3448, www.arubamotorcyclerental.com, 9am-5pm daily, mopeds $45/day, UTVs-ATVs $200-240/day, $60-80/h). Although they provide established service for mopeds, they are now more focused on ATV and UTV rentals, with guided tours in the pipeline. They recently acquired a new fleet of ATVs with automatic transmission and reinforced canopy frames for greater safety. They also offer special discounts for longer-term rentals of three or four days and provide resort pickup and drop-off.

★ TRIKES

Show off your sense of style and see the island with **Trikes** (L. G. Smith Blvd. 333, 297/738-7453, www.trikes-aruba.com, office hours 8am-2pm Mon.-Sat., 3.5-hour tours at 8:30am and 1:30pm, $190 for 2, $95 extra for a third person, $50 to drive on the trike with the guide). These motorcycle and car hybrids are very comfortable and easy to drive; a short lesson and practice precedes the actual tour. Some skill with a stick shift helps. Tooling around in these hot-colored three-wheelers is just plain fun; be ready to be noticed.

SEGWAY TOURS

SEGWAY ARUBA

All-terrain personal transporters have finally come to Aruba! **Segway Aruba** (Palm Beach 55, 297/740-7675, www.segwayaruba.com, 2-hour tours daily, flexible schedule, $50-80), not to be confused with Segway Tours Aruba, has a desk next to the Hard Rock Café in Palm Beach. They will conduct a tour with as few as two people. Enjoy the exhilarating sensation of the wind in your face—without having to pedal against it.

The guides are very personable and well informed, and a practice session is provided before takeoff. Refreshments are included in the cost of the tour, and GoPro cameras are available to rent.

SEGWAY TOURS ARUBA

The first to bring personal transporters to the island, **Segway Tours Aruba** (J. E. Irausquin Blvd 230, 297/560-9850, www.segwaytours-aruba.com, 1-5 hours, $45-110) is located within the MooMba Beach complex, between the Holiday Inn and Marriott Surf Club. They offer a brief one-hour tour to the lighthouse, as well as more elaborate packages that include a snorkel trip on a sailboat. If you're coming by cruise ship, you will be met at the terminal in Oranjestad and led through historical Aruba, finishing at Arashi with some beach time and refreshments.

BICYCLES

Portions of J. E. Irausquin Boulevard and L. G. Smith Boulevard north of Palm Beach have designated official bike paths. These areas are painted blue and provide bikers with a legally protected route from Oranjestad to Malmok. The shorefront from Governor's Bay to the Reina Beatrix International Airport has been remodeled to provide safe biking and jogging tracks completely away from traffic. These routes, which offer beautiful views of the shoreline for all seeking to keep fit, are often bustling with both residents and tourists, particularly on weekends, early mornings, and at sunset.

PABLITO'S BIKE RENTAL

Conveniently located for Eagle Beach visitors, **Pablito's Bike Rental** (L. G. Smith Blvd. 234, 297/587-8665, $15/day) provides an easy way to get to town and shops. You will find them on the short road adjacent to Screaming Eagle restaurant, leading to Pearl Residences.

VELOCITY BEACH BIKE RENTAL

Velocity Beach Bike Rental (J. E. Irausquin Blvd z/n, 297/592-1670, 8:30am-4:30pm daily, $15/day) services the Palm Beach area and has brand-new bikes and mountain bikes, including a tandem. They offer a special bargain for

Segway has become a popular mode of touring on Aruba.

weekly rentals: if you rent for seven days, you only pay for five.

JLZ MOUNTAIN BIKE TOURS

Biking fanatic Julien Tromp shares his passion for the sport through **JLZ Mountain Bike Tours** (Bubali 139, 297/660-1731, 1.5- to 5-hour tours beginning at 8:30am or earlier, $40-90). He customizes his tours depending on the skill level of his riders. Beginner tours are around 14 kilometers (9 mi); intermediate, 18 kilometers (11 mi); and the advanced 40 kilometers (25 mi) is 5 hours long with a lunch break. Other tours include cold drinks and fruit. JLZ will pick you up from your hotel and return you to the starting-off point of the trip.

RANCHO NOTORIOUS

Guided mountain bike tours to Alto Vista Chapel and the California Lighthouse are offered by **Rancho Notorious** (Borancana z/n, 297/586-0508, www.ranchonotorious.com, 2.5-hour tours at 8:30am or 3pm daily, $50, 14 years or older), with pickup and return to your resort. Biking is best done in the morning or evening, particularly when pedaling up steep inclines at Alto Vista or California Point in Aruba's intense heat.

HORSEBACK TOURS

★ RANCHO DAIMARI

What's more romantic than riding along the beach by horseback? One of the best ways to see Aruba's north coast is with **Rancho Daimari** (J. E. Irausquin Blvd. 382 A, 297/586-6284, www.arubaranchodaimari.com, 8am and 2pm daily tours, lasting 2 hours, Andicuri Tour $65, Natural Pool $78, resort pickup and return), just north of Arikok National Park. This is one of the best situated and most experienced stables on the island, specializing in treks to the Natural Pool. They also offer more experienced riders the chance to gallop wildly along the beach at Dos Playa. Whichever option you go with, this tour offers an adventure into remote areas rarely visited by anyone on the island.

GOLD MINE RANCH

Alternative north coast destinations via horseback are on the tour route of **Gold Mine Ranch** (Mativadiri 60, 297/585-9870, www.thegoldmineranch.com, depart 9am and 5pm daily, $65-75, private tours available). The tours make seven stops along the way, boasting the only beach trot through the waves. These tours are exclusively for capable and experienced riders. Riders are paired with a horse that matches their riding skill.

EL PASEO RANCH

Closer to Palm Beach resorts and offering horseback tours along the Malmok Coast is **El Paseo Ranch** (Westpunt z/n, 297/593-1440, www.elpaseorancharuba.com, daily tours 9am, 11am, 1pm, and 3pm, $110). This stable is one of the few that includes rides with a snorkel stop in Arashi, a good spot for novice snorkelers. Excursions include drinks and snacks, snorkel equipment, vests, and instruction.

SKYDIVING

★ SKYDIVE ARUBA

If you have an adventurous bucket list, **Skydive Aruba** (Noord z/n, 297/735-0654, http://skydivearuba.com, 8am-4pm daily, every 2 hours, by appt., $250) is a way to check off an item without all the extensive training or first-time anxiety. Jumps are strictly tandem—attached to a veteran instructor—so patrons can relax and enjoy the view. Nowhere on Aruba will you see such a vista as from 10,000 feet up; it is a once-in-a-lifetime experience. Instructors film the entire jump, which will be available for purchase on DVD to be relived over and over again (or to prove to friends that it really happened).

Hiking and Running

RUNNING AND JOGGING PATHS

Naturally pounded dirt paths border the west shore along the **J. E. Irausquin Boulevard** between Manchebo resorts and Palm Beach, providing an exhilarating backdrop for a morning jog. The same paths are found along **L. G. Smith Boulevard** from the Marriott Resort to Arashi Beach. Sunsets are beautiful along these routes.

Jogging and biking paths have also been placed alongside A1 from the Reina Beatrix Airport to Wilhelmina Park in Oranjestad, bordering L. G. Smith Boulevard. These provide a pleasant route along the water, safe from the busy traffic. The length is bisected by the Plaza Turismo, with cafés and bathrooms.

HIKING

Arikok National Park

Aruba's largest natural preserve, **Arikok National Park** (San Fuego 70, 297/585-1234, www.arubanationalpark.org, 8am-4pm daily, $8, with guide $20) occupies 18 percent of the island's landmass. It was designated as a formally protected area in 2000. The park provides over 32 kilometers (20 mi) of hiking trails with various degrees of difficulty. Paved and dirt paths are clearly marked, with flora and fauna identified as well. For a flat fee you can hire on a ranger as guides for the entire hike.

The park is a showcase of native species and Aruba's geological formations. Various trails take visitors to the coastline or the island's greatest heights. There are paved or gravel roads with parking areas paralleling many of the hiking paths, so routes can be reduced according to ability. All quoted distances are calculated with the visitor center at the park entrance as the start and finishing point.

Tour rangers report they will call for a vehicle to pick up hikers who feel too exhausted by the intense heat of the day. It is always advisable in Aruba's tropical heat to hike as early in the day as possible and take plenty of bottled water along to rehydrate frequently.

CUNUCU ARIKOK TRAIL

Cunucu Arikok Trail (3.5 km [2 mi], 1.5-2 hours) leads to an authentically preserved farm with a centuries-old dwelling. It is one of the most popular of all the Arikok hikes and the easiest. Parts of the route pass by Aruba's famous kibrahacha trees, which only blossom a few days out of the year in a burst of intense yellow flowers. Typcial desert flora, including a multitude of cacti with spiny thorns, line the trails.

SEROE JAMANOTA TRAIL

Seroe Jamanota at 184 meters (617 ft.) high offers a remarkable panorama of the entire island from San Nicolas to Westpunt; you can see the curve of the world from its peak. There are two paths to the top. The **Seroe Jamanota Trail** (4.5 km [2.8 mi], 2-2.5 hours) is the easiest and follows a gradual winding road, paved all the way to the summit. Visitors can also park their car at the base and walk this road to the top.

MASIDURI TRAIL

The alternate route to the top of Seroe Jamanota is for the extremely fit and one of the physical trials used to test Dutch Marines. **Masiduri Trail** (7 km [4.4 mi], 5 hours or more) takes a more roundabout path, circling around the south side of the hill. It is required to first climb and descend Seroe Large, which is 114 meters (374 ft.) high, before climbing the steep trail to the top of Jamanota. Park rangers describe it as a true endurance test.

What Exactly are *Cunucu* Houses?

a traditional *cunucu* house

A *cunucu* house is considered the endemic architecture of Aruba. The configuration of what constitutes an authentic *cunucu* house is distinctive for both cultural and practical details. Such houses were built piecemeal as a family grew. The characteristic peaked roof at the center delineates the original home erected for the newlyweds. As occupancy expanded with the births of numerous children, rooms were added to the front, back, and sides.

City homes of wealthier families typically had a second floor for the offspring. These usually were adorned with dormer windows, an architectural feature that traditionally distinguishes the houses in town from their country cousins. More than a dozen children in a family was quite common, and boys and girls would have separate sleeping areas.

The placement of rooms took advantage of Aruba's steady northeast winds. Sleeping rooms were meant to catch the breeze and provide cool comfort, while the west end would be the cooking space with the characteristic *facon,* a fireplace and chimney where meals were prepared. This placement allowed the wind to blow the heat and cinders away from the house. Islanders have such affection for this particular style of architecture that many new homes are still planned this way.

The word *cunucu* is frequently used to describe anything considered rural, while *mondi* is the actual word for deep woods. *Cunucu* is also used to indicate something endemic to the island, such as *cunucu* house or *cunucu* dog, the local mixed breed.

Charles Croes, who has made an intense study of the Papiamento language, claims that *cunucu* does not mean "country." It was the word applied to the perimeter of sand placed around rural homes, which was smoothed out each night before bedtime. Residents examined the sand in the morning for telltale footprints, indicting unwanted visitors such as scorpions or millipedes that may have made their way into the house during the night.

SEROE ARIKOK TRAIL

Aruba's second highest point, Seroe Arikok, is 184 meters (606 ft.). The **Seroe Arikok Trail** (4.4 km [2.7 mi], 3 hours) also offers an easy ascent by paved road to the summit. Close to the height of Jamanota, it offers an equally thrilling view.

ROOI TAMBU TRAIL

Following **Rooi Tambu Trail** (5.5 km [3.4 mi], 2-3 hours) east to the sea takes hikers directly to Dos Playa, a lovely place to sunbathe. Although this spot is popular with bodyboarders, rangers warn about swimming here because of the riptides and undertows. The white sands, surrounding ocher cliffs, and the turquoise Caribbean present a stark contrast and make for beautiful photos.

ROOI PRINS TRAIL

The **Rooi Prins Trail** (5.5 km [3.4 mi], 3-4 hours) takes hikers through a dried-out creek bed and on to Phantage Prins. Hikers can choose to go left to circle back to the park entrance or continue east to the expansive beach area of Boca Prins.

NATURAL POOL TRAIL

Conchi can be reached via **Natural Pool Trail** (Natural Pool; 5.5 km [3.4 mi], 4-5 hours). It heads north to the pool, then circles back following the rugged north coast before turning west to the park entrance. Natural Pool Trail offers the widest variety of scenery of all the trails, passing through cactus and scrub, as well as along the rocky coast.

Golf and Tennis

GOLF

Until 20 years ago, golfers had to make do with the funky San Nicolas Golf Club, where the greens are oiled sand and Astroturf, an interesting challenge that no one took very seriously. Fortunately, since 1990, two world-class courses have been built on Aruba, both surrounded by luxurious communities, with international tournaments conducted regularly.

TIERRA DEL SOL COUNTRY CLUB AND GOLF COURSE

Tierra Del Sol Country Club and Golf Course (Caya di Solo 10, 297/586-0978, www.tierradelsol.com, May 1-Dec. 17, $129 before 1pm/$99 after, Dec. 18-Apr. 30, $159 before 1pm/$129 after) is in Malmok, just at the northwest tip of the island. It is a specially designed 18-hole desert course by the famous Robert Trent Jones Jr., renowned for its breathtaking vistas and very challenging winds. Amenities include a pro shop, day spa, gorgeous pool deck, tennis courts, and gourmet restaurant. Villa rental on-site includes green fees, along with round-trip airport transport and use of all facilities.

DIVI LINKS

In 2004, **Divi Links** (J. E. Irausquin Blvd. 93, 297/581-4653, www.divigolf.com, $90 with a $39 fee for replay winter-spring; $75 with $29 replay) opened a gorgeously landscaped nine-hole course with Prince Albert of Monaco, no less, hitting the first ball. Although part of the Divi complex, Divi Links are open to the public. They have a pro shop, state-of-the-art clinic, and two very appealing restaurants in the clubhouse. Dedicated golfers usually do two rounds to get in their 18 holes.

When carving out the course, the designers did their utmost to preserve the natural wetlands, home to many species of birds. These pools and dramatic formations provide a very unique backdrop when doing the rounds. Thousands of birds have continued to nest here, oblivious to the intruding golfers.

TENNIS

All major resorts have tennis courts for the use of their guests. Courts and lessons should be reserved in advance. Visitors have access to three independent tennis facilities, one for each of the major resort areas. They usually cater to local clientele, but are happy to accommodate guests.

EAGLE INTERNATIONAL TENNIS CLUB

Aruba's first tennis club was the **Eagle International Tennis Club** (Engelandstraat 12, 297/587-5806, 8am-11am and 3pm-11pm Mon.-Sat., $15/hour for a court, $45/hour with a pro, $5 equipment rental). It was part of the exclusive community established for Eagle Refinery executives. The Eagle Tennis Club is a center for the sport on the island and very popular with local players. Co-owner and on-site pro Eddy Ras says they are happy to pair up players that need an opponent or a partner.

The club is one block inland from Oranjestad's westernmost traffic circle. They have a Morning Men's club that starts play at sunup, and vacationers are welcome to see if they can grab a partner. The fee is a donation at the player's discretion. There are six courts and a single practice court for warm up and working on form, as well as a snack bar and refreshments at local prices. Special lights allow for nighttime play.

ARUBA RACQUET CLUB

Close to the Palm Beach and Malmok resorts, **Aruba Racquet Club** (Rooi Santo 21, 297/586-0215, www.arc.aw, 8am-10pm Mon.-Sat., 8am-7pm Sun., $10/hour for a court, $60 lessons with a pro, $5 equipment rental) is an elegantly designed facility with eight beautiful courts and gardens. Amenities include a very cute and inexpensive snack bar and a locally priced spa, perfect for getting a massage after a couple of hours on the courts.

ARUBA TENNIS ACADEMY

Tennis lessons can be arranged at your resort with **Aruba Tennis Academy** (Aloestraat 14, 297/583-7074, www.tennisaruba.com, 8am-11am Mon.-Fri. and by appt., $10-75). The team of pros conducts regularly scheduled free clinics for Hyatt Regency, Marriott, Divi, Tamarijn, and Divi Village Resorts, on alternate days. Check with the concierge to join the morning clinics. Private lessons or a pro as a partner can be arranged by appointment. The Renaissance Resort is included in this service, as well as Boardwalk Small Hotel. Aruba Tennis Academy gives lessons to cruise ship passengers with pickup and return to the Oranjestad terminal included in the package.

BEACH TENNIS ARUBA

Considering the popularity of beach volleyball, could beach tennis be far behind? **Beach Tennis Aruba** (J. E. Irausquin Blvd. 230, 297/592-6421, www.beachtennisaruba.com, 8am-10pm daily, $5/hour pp) has worked hard to make their annual finals an international event. Competitors are welcome to join in the October championships. There are also weekend competitions scheduled throughout the year with new ones cropping up continually as the sport gains an enthusiastic following.

This is a sort of super-charged version of badminton with sand. Players have to get used to the idea of no bounce, which is, of course, different than normal tennis. This is a distinct game, with killer shots the norm, and very physically demanding. If you are a fan, or wish to learn, courts are located at MooMba Beach.

Spas and Yoga

Aruba has an inordinate number of day spas and *estheticas*. Every major resort boasts a spa designed to envelop guests in a soothing and luxurious environment. One extremely popular service is the couple's massage, a special treatment for two with champagne, chocolates, and other accoutrements, including a private whirlpool bath for sharing that sparkling toast.

Local facilities may not be quite as glamorous, but they are usually far more economical. Priced to a local trade of repeat guests, some are also conveniently located near small guesthouses.

SPAS, MASSAGE, AND BEAUTY

CLINICAL MASSAGE ARUBA & SPA

Situated within the Casa Del Mar Resort, **Clinical Massage Aruba & Spa** (J. E. Irausquin Blvd. 51, 297/582-7000, www.clinicalmassagearuba.com, relaxing massage $75, pain management with Flo $135) offers the standard stress relief massage, but specialist Florian Gosset is also certified in pain management. If you have sports injuries, or any back or neck pain, Florian and his staff provide relief through treatments catering to your needs.

This small, intimate spa also offers hot stone, prenatal, and acupressure treatments, as well as body wraps and scrubs.

★ OKEANOS SPA

In Oranjestad, **Okeanos Spa** (L. G. Smith Blvd. 82, 297/583-6000, www.okeanosspaaruba.com, 50-minute Swedish massage $115, 2.5-hour couple's package $440) is a luxurious, full-service spa with a special bonus. The main facility is within the Marina Tower of Renaissance Resort, but another, dubbed The Cove, is out on a secluded peninsula of Renaissance Island. More than one young couple has gotten engaged after sharing a couple's session in this most romantic setting. Cove packages include a 50-minute massage, a bottle of champagne or four frothy, frozen cocktails, and a fruit platter.

Only massages are given in The Cove, no body scrubs or facials. Reflexology or hot stone options are available, as is lunch. Purchasing a treatment on the island also give the visitor access to Renaissance Island for the day, which normally costs $90. Spa guests are not required to be guests of the resort.

The main facility in the resort is very attractive. They have a steam room and community room with snacks and refreshments. An attached outdoor terrace is a place to linger on lounge chairs and enjoy a great view of the harbor.

The Marina outlet carries the full menu of services. Select from exotic body wraps and skin treatments along with salon services. You might want to try the Royal Romance package: a couple's session which includes dinner at the L. G. Smith's Steak & Chop House next door.

SPA DEL SOL

The Manchebo Beach area is home to several facilities, beginning with **Spa Del Sol** (J. E. Irausquin Blvd. 55, 297/582-6145, www.spadelsol.com, 50-minute massage $95, 80-minute $125, couple's massage $180-240) on the beach at the Manchebo Resort. These are the people who brought the first day spa to Aruba. For the full island experience, all massages are administered in a curtained *palapa* on the beach.

Spa Del Sol is particularly known for pampering combination packages, which last several hours. They also include a healthful, holistic lunch. The surroundings are an exotic South Pacific environment of teak and artistic carvings from the owner's collection, acquired from his world travels.

GARRA RUFA WELLNESS FOOTSPA

Annexed to Spa Del Sol is the **Garra Rufa Wellness Footspa** (J. E. Irausquin Blvd. 55, 297/563-7760, 10am-1:30pm daily, $25 for 30 minutes), offering a very unique treatment. A whirlpool footbath is filled with hundreds of the famed "Dr. Fish," which spawn in natural springs in Turkey. Garra rufa have no teeth but love to gently nibble away at dry and flaky skin. It is a surprisingly pleasant and relaxing sensation.

The footbath is sterilized five times an hour with ultraviolet rays. All feet are thoroughly examined before being immersed; only healthy footsies are allowed. The baths are set up so that you can enjoy the view of the beach and sea during treatments.

ZOIA

Perhaps the most beautiful and luxurious of day spas on the island is **ZoiA** (Hyatt Regency Resort, 297/586-1234, http://aruba.hyatt.com, 8:30am-8pm daily, 1-hour massage $145, 1.5-hour $215), just off the lobby of the Hyatt Resort. Completely renovated, renamed, and reopened in 2012, this sumptuous spa features elegant accoutrements. Relax in the community room with all-inclusive snacks, holistic drinks, and continental breakfast. There is a sauna on the premises and terraces that look out on the resort's gorgeous gardens. The menu includes a special line of products by Dinah Veeris, famous in the region for natural skin care potions made from native plants and herbs.

Special all-day packages are conducted in a huge, luxurious room with a private terrace. This is also the room for the couple's massage, sporting a cozy hot tub for two. Each room has a private bathroom to help maintain the mood, allowing patrons to stay within their own special environment. Complete treatments, makeup, and hair packages are offered for wedding parties, for both the bride and groom.

LARIMAR SPA

Aruba's largest spa is **Larimar** (Hilton Aruba Caribbean Resort, 297/526-6052, www.larimarspaaruba.com, 9am-7pm daily, signature Aloe Vera/Rum 80-minute massage with hot stones $185; couple's massage $250), beachside at the Hilton. It is beautifully appointed with a gallery for locally produced art. Spacious, elegant treatment rooms and a stunning community area ensure guests remember they are being pampered in paradise. Larimar is right at the beach, along the Palm Beach boardwalk.

MANDARA SPA

Mandara Spa (297/586-4710, www.mandaraspa.com, 9am-8pm daily, 50-minute massage $120, couple's massage $275) is conveniently located within the Marriott Ocean Club and services three resorts. This is also a very luxurious facility with a relaxation lounge that opens out to enclosed gardens for a serene environment.

MENA'S SKINCARE CENTER

Conveniently located for those staying in guesthouses around Oranjestad and Eagle Beach is **Mena's Skincare Center** (Tanki Leendert, 297/587-6282, 11am-7pm Tues. and Thurs., 9am-5pm Wed. and Fri., 8am-5pm Sat., 1-hour massage $54). It was Aruba's first *esthetica*, specializing in facials, body wraps, and skin treatments. Mena is a living example of the effectiveness of her procedures; she is as youthful as when she first began sharing her skills. This is a local facility, so her prices are geared toward residents with fees that are much cheaper than the usual resort spa fees. There is the standard menu of massages and facials, but the center also specializes in laser depilation and permanent eyeliner procedures ($380 for both upper and lower lids). Mena has a very clean, pleasant space not far from the resorts. It's not quite as glamorous, but neither are the prices. Pickup at hotels can be arranged.

MASSAGE AT HOME

Those staying in smaller guesthouses without spa facilities can enjoy a therapeutic massage, combined with a facial if they wish, right in their rooms. Call **Massage at Home** (Bubali 145, 297/730-6660, www.massagesaruba.com, by appt., 1-hour single massage $100, 1.5-hour $140), run by the skilled, certified therapist Miranda Wever. It's a great time and money saver if a spa is not nearby. Private service in the room is likely to be less costly than some of the more glamorous in-house facilities.

YOGA

SUP YOGA

Condition your body and soothe your spirit with **SUP Yoga** (Vela Windsurfing, 297/593-1793, info@islandsup.com, 3pm Fri. and Sat., $45). Exercise, work on your tan, refresh your chi, and meditate while connecting with nature during yoga on a stand-up paddleboard. Sessions are conducted by Rachel Brathen, on the waters just north of the Marriott Resort.

Beyond the regular classes, Rachel will also put a session together for a minimum of three people. The paddleboard technique is first taught on the beach. Boarders then head out to a secluded area for an hour that engages the entire body. Perfect your balance, both physically and spiritually.

YOGA ON THE BEACH

Beach Yoga has proven so popular that Manchebo has set up **Yoga on the Beach** (Manchebo Beach Hotel, 297/582-3444, info@manchebo.com, 8am Mon.-Sat., 9:30am Sun., 7pm Mon.-Thurs., $15), which offers a variety of classes every day, taught by five instructors of various specialties. Aside from the daily morning Vinyasa Flow, they have Pilates on Tues., Thurs., and Sat. mornings at 9:30am and Sunset Yoga sessions. Tickets can be purchased at the Manchebo front desk and used whenever you please; just show up for class, no prior sign in required.

Yoga on the Beach

Sights

Look for ★ to find recommended sights.

Highlights

★ **National Archaeological Museum Aruba (NAMA):** NAMA is a unique museum with interactive experiences designed to delight all ages. Two floors of exhibits and artwork recreate prehistoric life on the island (page 74).

★ **Fort Zoutman and the Aruba Historical Museum:** Fort Zoutman, the island's oldest structure, houses the Aruba Historical Museum, which features tableaux of antiques from colonial times (page 75).

★ **Butterfly Farm:** Enjoy an inspiring encounter with nature's most beautiful creatures. Bring your camera and escape to a place of utter tranquility (page 78).

★ **Alto Vista Chapel and Peace Labyrinth:** This humble structure is located cliff side on the site of Aruba's first church. The stunning vista and charming chapel encourage peaceful reflection and make for outstanding photo ops (page 78).

★ **Philip's Animal Garden:** This refuge offers an opportunity to interact with exotic animals from over 100 different species (page 79).

★ **California Lighthouse:** Enjoy a 360-degree panorama of Aruba at the site of this lighthouse. The vistas are breathtaking, particularly at sunset (page 81).

★ **Aruba Ostrich Farm:** This private nature reserve offers a memorable encounter with the largest species of bird in the world (page 81).

★ **Ayo Rock Formation:** Quartz diorite formations provide a maze of open caves and passages that lead to summits with stunning panoramic vistas (page 82).

★ **Arikok National Park:** Aruba's largest natural preserve is home to the two highest peaks on the island, some lovely beaches, and lots of interesting flora and fauna (page 84).

★ **Conchi (Natural Pool):** At Conchi, one of Aruba's most stunning natural sites, cooled lava rock has created a dramatic spot for swimming and snorkeling (page 84).

While Aruba is best known for its glamorous hotels and beautiful beaches, there is much more to this island's character. Experience a different Aruba by exploring its museums, historical sites, and natural wonders.

The streets of Oranjestad, Aruba's capital, feature historical structures and colonial homes adjacent to modern buildings. The National Archaeological Museum Aruba, comprised primarily of renovated Dutch colonial buildings, is one of Aruba's most interesting sights.

Nature lovers will appreciate Aruba's biodiversity. The natural flora of this semiarid environment is best observed when venturing into the Aruban outback. Island trees are like giant bonsai due to the constant northeast winds forming them into striking shapes with an artist's hand. The stark limestone cliffs and terraces of the shorelines are a sharp contrast to the lush landscapes of the tourist areas.

A trip to the California Lighthouse and on to the north coast reveals a dramatic lunar landscape. Here you will be transported back to a primordial era where the geological origins of Aruba are evident. At popular sights such as Casibari and Ayo Rock Formations or the Bushiribana Gold Ruin, rock climbing is a popular activity for all ages. Scaling their heights provides a rewarding sense of adventure and some exceptional photo ops. Scattered among the caves and rock formations are pictographs and petroglyphs, coded messages from Aruba's original inhabitants. They date back thousands of years. Archaeologists have catalogued over 300 in various locations. These and other sites provide an authentic impression of the hardships overcome to survive and persist in this harsh environment.

Interspersed among the natural and historic sites, visitors will also find unexpected family-friendly delights. Preserves such as the Butterfly Farm, the Donkey Sanctuary, and Philip's Animal Garden offer enjoyable interludes for interacting with nature.

Aruba offers a diversity of sights that deliver interesting adventures and unique settings for photo enthusiasts. A walking tour of Oranjestad leads to historical insights, while excursions into the island's natural areas reward visitors with dramatic landscapes punctuated by remnants of a prehistoric culture.

Previous: Quadikakiri Cave; California Lighthouse. **Above:** National Archaeological Museum Aruba.

Oranjestad

By strolling the avenues and byways of Oranjestad, you can absorb a lot about Aruba's past. The island's capital is home to the majority of Aruba's cultural and historic sites. Vacationers accustomed to sprawling cities will find the town physically very small. The most interesting historic landmarks and statues can easily be toured by foot in a single day or less as most of the restored landmark structures are clustered near the harbor in an area dubbed "Historical Oranjestad."

The Aruba Monument Bureau was established in 1996 to restore and preserve landmark structures. Since then, a number of Oranjestad's colonial buildings have been returned to their original glory, providing a glimpse of the lifestyle of islanders from centuries past. There are an estimated 100 landmark buildings in Oranjestad alone, and a total of 300 scattered throughout the island. The town has 20 protected historical sights. A number of other landmarks are private homes or businesses. For example, **Kok Optica Opticians** (Wilhelminastraat 11, 297/582-7237) is housed in a landmark building across from Aruba's Town Hall.

Since its inception as a colonial town dating back to the 1600s, the capital city has maintained a warren of narrow, one-way streets. Driving through them can be quite confusing for first-time visitors. There is a large parking lot directly behind the main bus terminal, which is an excellent starting point for exploring Aruba's historic and cultural roots. It is adjacent to one of Aruba's most picturesque landmark buildings, the **Eman House,** now the offices of Aruba Investment Association (ARINA).

MUSEUMS AND HISTORICAL BUILDINGS

★ NATIONAL ARCHAEOLOGICAL MUSEUM ARUBA (NAMA)

The daily life and culture of Aruba's inhabitants prior to the Spanish arrival are the focus of the **National Archaeological Museum Aruba** (Schelpstraat 42, 297/582-8979 or 297/588-9961, www.namaruba.org,

National Archaeological Museum Aruba

10am-5pm Tues.-Fri., 10am-2pm Sat.-Sun., free). NAMA features permanent and temporary displays, with entertaining and informative audio and visual programs. One section of the museum is designated as an extensive research center for archaeology students.

NAMA exhibits are designed to immerse visitors: Sit and examine cooking utensils in an authentically reproduced *maloca,* the habitat of the Caiquetios, the original Amerindians who settled on the island prior to recorded history. Youngsters especially enjoy making their way through a darkened cave to observe glowing pictographs. The attractive displays then transition into colonial times and portray the ethnic diversity of the Aruban people. Fascinating artifacts are displayed in a special environment crucial to the preservation of the ancient urns, tools, and works of art.

NAMA is situated within what were once crumbling Dutch colonial buildings known as the Ecury Complex, now restored to pristine condition. The buildings have a particular historic significance as the birthplace of Segundo Jorge Adalberto "Boy" Ecury, Aruba's great WWII war hero. A history of the famous Ecury family is represented with antique photos and documents in the welcoming foyer.

★ FORT ZOUTMAN AND THE ARUBA HISTORICAL MUSEUM

Aruba's oldest intact landmark, **Fort Zoutman** (Fort Zoutmanstraat z/n, 297/588-65199, museohistoricoarubano@yahoo.com, 9am-noon and 1:30pm-4pm Mon.-Fri., $5), was built in 1796. It is named for Admiral Johan Arnold Zoutman, vice-admiral of Holland and West Friesland. He died in 1785, having never even visited the island. Before the era of luxury hotels began in 1959, **Willem III Tower,** attached to the fort, was the tallest structure on Aruba. The tower was constructed in 1868 as a public clock tower and lighthouse. It was first illuminated on February 19, 1868, the birthday of the Dutch monarch for which it is named.

Fort Zoutman is now the home of the **Aruba Historical Museum.** The fort grounds and museum provide a lively review of island culture, history, and development. The principal exposition rooms in the museum display antiques and artifacts of Aruba's colonial years. Exhibits illustrate the manner in which the people eked out a living as fishers

Willem III Tower makes it easy to find Fort Zoutman.

Memorial Statuary in Oranjestad

Oranjestad displays a good collection of memorial statuary. Most pay homage to local personages who have had a great impact on the island and are set in small plazas.

There are some interesting statuary on both the north and south side of L. G. Smith Boulevard. On the east side of the Parliament building, facing the water, stands a monument to ***Jan Hendrik "Henny" Eman,*** founder of the Arubaanse Volkspartij (AVP). He was the grandfather of Aruba's first and current prime ministers, Henny (named after his grandfather) and his brother Michiel, respectively. Eman initiated the movement for Aruban autonomy and independence, or Status Aparte, from the other islands of the Netherlands Antilles.

A 10-minute walk east from the March 18 Monument is the statue of ***Segundo Jorge Adalberto "Boy" Ecury,*** Aruba's beloved WWII hero. He watches over a triangular traffic island next to a small park. Boy Ecury was attending school in Holland in 1940 during the German invasion and occupation. Boy opted to join the Dutch Resistance during WWII rather than return to safety on his home island. His younger brother Nicky also stayed, but was so young he was not allowed to go out on missions.

Boy's markedly Afro-Caribbean features were an unusual sight in Holland at the time. His having such a distinct countenance made his daring missions even more dangerous. He volunteered to derail train tracks to hinder German troop and weapon movements.

Boy was captured during an attempt to rescue some of his fellow resistance fighters. He died in front of a German firing squad at the age of 22. A feature film of his story made in Holland starred noted Antillean actor and director Felix de Rooy as Boy's father. The film tells of the search for his

or aloe producers, as well as the everyday utensils of home life and conservative dress. One room is dedicated to a broad overview from prehistoric times to the present, titled *Aruba: Milestones and Challenges.* This exhibition was developed in 2001 for a royal visit.

A new exhibit based on island youth getting in touch with their heritage now takes up one of the main rooms. Schoolchildren were asked to investigate the history of heirloom objects passed down through generations in order to reveal and share their cultural and historical impact.

The **Bon Bini Festival** (Fort Zoutman, 297/582-3777, 7pm-9pm Tues., $5), featuring traditional island music and dance, goes on every Tuesday evening in the courtyard of Fort Zoutman.

BESTUURSKANTOOR (GOVERNMENT HOUSE) AND PARLIAMENT BUILDINGS

Observe Aruba's government in action at the adjoined **Bestuurskantoor and Parliament Buildings** (L. G. Smith Blvd. 76, 297/528-4900, 8am-noon and 1:30pm-4pm Mon.-Fri., free) facing directly onto Oranjestad Harbor. These are historic edifices, which include the prime minister's office, where landmark decisions have been made and royalty received. Visitors may find that they are warmly welcomed by an important dignitary, if they care to stop by and inquire on the workings of island government.

There is a spectators' gallery to observe Parliament sessions, which are sometimes heated and dramatic. The entrance is at the side of the building.

MONUMENTS

Aruba commemorates its history and position within the Kingdom of the Netherlands with some very interesting plazas, monuments, and statues scattered along L. G. Smith Boulevard.

MARCH 18 MEMORIAL

One block east of Parliament is a lagoon that divides the town. The northwest corner of the son's remains after the war, with Boy's exploits unfolding as flashbacks. Boy's body was eventually found and received a hero's welcome and burial.

The far eastern end of Oranjestad is marked by the very large Plaza Las Americas rotunda. Fronting the rotunda is Aruba's center for performing arts, the Cas di Cultura. Directly in front of the art center is a small park with a memorial to **Lloyd G. Smith.**

Smith was the first general manager of the Lago Refinery, running the facility from the time it became fully functional through the war years, 1933-1946. His policy of concern and improvement for the island beyond the refinery's gates won him the respect and admiration of his hosts. It exemplifies the very cordial relationship Aruba has maintained with the United States for nearly 100 years.

Wilhelmina Park is also the site of the **Anne Frank Memorial** erected in 2011. The charming, rather wistful statue by Dutch artist Joep Coppens is dedicated to the concept of ethnic tolerance. Its placement was the first official project of the Foundation Respeta bida...semper corda (Respect life...always remember).

The bronze statue depicts Anne Frank with her hands bound, but looking to the sky "in hope of a better world," according to the artist. It stands on a pedestal imprinted with a quote from her diary: "How wonderful it is that nobody need wait a single moment before starting to improve the world." Each side carries the message in one of the languages commonly spoken on Aruba: Papiamento, English, Dutch, and Spanish.

bridge over the lagoon is the site of an attractive plaza called the **March 18 Memorial,** which commemorates the petition for Aruban independence. This is a tranquil place, highlighting an important era in island history. Surrounded by a small park, it offers a pleasant place to stop and relax while enjoying the charming view of the lagoon and sea.

Central to the plaza is a statue of Cornelius Albert "Shon" Eman. Eman headed the delegation that first officially presented the petition for Status Aparte to Queen Juliana on March 18, 1948, during roundtable talks in Holland to determine the future of all Dutch territories in the region. The names of all the 2,147 signatories of that request for Aruban independence are carved in the plates on each side of the memorial's statue.

During the March 18 celebration of 2010 an eternal flame was placed at the memorial. It was lit by Prime Minister Mike Eman, "Shon" Eman's youngest son.

QUEEN WILHELMINA PARK

Directly across from the March 18 Memorial is **Queen Wilhelmina Park.** At the heart of the park is the statue and plaza dedicated to the ruler of the Netherlands from 1898 until 1948. She was the great grandmother of the current Dutch monarch, King Willem-Alexander.

This was Aruba's first commemorative statue, unveiled in October of 1955. The occasion was a royal visit by Wilhelmina's daughter, Queen Juliana. The park is a beautifully landscaped and a pleasant place for a break from walking and touring. The large and decorative plaza is the site for many official ceremonies and important events, most notably Koninginnedag (King's Day) on April 27, an impressive display of loyalty to the monarchy. Visitors to the island on this day are welcome to join the official event, which takes place in the morning.

Palm Beach, Malmok, and Noord

Palm Beach is a relatively modern district with a number of interesting sights. Not far from the busy shopping and entertainment centers are natural areas and attractions. Some, such as the Butterfly Farm, are within easy walking distance.

The area has undeveloped pockets of nature, such as the wetlands known as Bubali Plas Bird Sanctuary across from the Mill Resort. A short drive at dawn provides fabulous sunrise shots from the Alto Vista Chapel. Historic sights like the Santa Ana Church are a reminder of the deep religious faith that is a cultural anchor for many Aruban people.

★ BUTTERFLY FARM

For an exhilarating communion with nature, stop at the **Butterfly Farm** (J. E. Irausquin Blvd. z/n, 297/586-3656, www.thebutterflyfarm.com, 8:30am-4:30pm daily, $15 adults, $8 children) on the land side of the beach road between the Divi Phoenix and Riu Plaza Resorts. The best time to visit the farm is early in the day when butterflies are most active.

Trained guides will explain everything you ever wanted to know about butterflies and moths. Did you know butterflies morph in a chrysalis while moths transform in a cocoon? The most dramatically hued examples of both flitter about freely, feeding on fruit and flowers. There are exotic and gorgeous species from all over the world. It is possible to see one emerge from its chrysalis in one of the breeding boxes.

The Butterfly Farm is a beautiful garden filled with the type of flora on which the various species feed and breed. Relax on one of the benches provided and enjoy the classical music that plays gently in the background.

Consider visiting early in your vacation since the entry fee allows for unlimited returns for the duration of your vacation. Operators Tony and Lori know that one visit will often turn into several. The souvenir shop also features one of the largest collections of butterfly-themed knickknacks to be found anywhere.

SANTA ANA CHURCH

Located at the first major intersection on the Noord-Palm Beach Road beyond the Sasaki Highway (it has a traffic light to distinguish it), **Santa Ana Church** (Noord 16, 297/587-1409, 8am-8:30pm daily) is central to the surrounding community. It was the second church built on the island in 1776, vastly larger than the Alto Vista Chapel, Aruba's first church. The church was rebuilt twice, in 1836 and again in 1886, with major restructuring in 1916.

It is notable for beautiful stained glass windows and an intricate and impressive hand-carved oak altar by artist Hendrik van der Geld, created in 1870. The altar won an award during an exposition of religious art in Rome the year it was built. It was donated to Santa Ana by the Antonius Church of Scheveningen in the Netherlands.

A very interesting aspect of the church is the adjacent cemetery consisting of picturesque family crypts and vaults. Digging into Aruba's foundation of solid rock is a daunting task, so this form of burial is common. Dating back centuries, crypts are brightly painted in the Caribbean way, with epitaphs that offer a peek at local family histories.

★ ALTO VISTA CHAPEL AND PEACE LABYRINTH

Aruba's first Catholic house of worship, the **Alto Vista Chapel** (sunrise-sunset daily, formal services 5:30pm Tues.) was built in 1750 on what was sacred ground to the Caquetio Indians. Spanish padre Domingo Antonio Silvestre led the mission to bring the sparse native population into the fold of Catholicism.

This modest chapel is situated on a cliff with stunning views of Aruba's rugged north coast. The entire area exudes an air of quiet contemplation. The simple, natural setting encourages reflection on the glory of creation, no matter your personal beliefs. There is an annual march at Easter along the winding road leading to its hilltop perch. The parade of worshippers stops at each of the 13 large white crosses along the way to recite a prayer.

As larger churches closer to settlements were erected, the Alto Vista Chapel fell into disuse and crumbled away. A community effort in 1952 spearheaded by Shon Kita Henriquez-Lacle prompted the building of a new chapel on the site. This charming, spiritual place is maintained with devotion by its parishioners.

Around 2005, islander Peter Auwerda constructed a **Peace Labyrinth** in close proximity to the chapel modeled after the Chartres Labyrinth. Visitors are encouraged to walk its 11 circuits. The turns are arranged in four quadrants, with 85 lunations around the perimeter. It is believed to promote meditation and serenity. Annually, on September 21, International Peace Day, a celebration is staged at the labyrinth with the intention of promoting world and inner peace.

To get to the chapel, turn right off the Sasaki Highway and take Noord-Palm Beach Road to the first traffic light. The Santa Ana Church will be across the intersection on the right. Turn left onto the Noord-Westpunt Road for about a half mile. There will be a sign to turn right for Alto Vista. Follow this road to where it ends in a T-intersection. Turn left, and follow this road until it ends at the Alto Vista Chapel.

★ PHILIP'S ANIMAL GARDEN

At his family home Philip Merryweather began at the age of 12 to create the haven for neglected and abused exotic animals that is now **Philip's Animal Garden** (Alto Vista 116, 297/593-5363, www.philipsanimalgarden.com, guided tours 9am-5pm daily every half hour, $10 adults, $5 children under 10). Fortunately, his parents had an exceptionally large property in a rather rural area. His passion for protecting creatures such as ocelots, monkeys, kangaroos, and macaws began

Alto Vista Chapel

Philip Merryweather rescues and rehabilitates abused exotic animals at Philip's Animal Garden.

when he observed how often their owners neglected them after they stopped being cute babies. By the time he rescued them, they were quite a handful, traumatized and aggressive. His patience and determination to learn about their needs and provide a proper environment for each animal contributed to their rehabilitation. Proper care and comfort of such creatures became his mission in life.

For several years, as his shelter grew in size and diversity, he did not permit visitors or conduct tours. Philip now houses more than 600 animals from over 80 species at his reserve. A few years ago, he began hosting special events on national holidays for island youngsters, hoping to teach them about the humane treatment of all animals. His goal was also to make residents aware of the very special care such exotic creatures require and the serious responsibility of possessing what should best be left in the wild. Aruba has since passed stringent laws regulating the importation of exotic animals or trafficking in endangered species.

Philip finally decided to open his doors to the public for regular tours to finance the feeding and care of the animals. Philip's Animal Garden is a nonprofit foundation with all entrance fees and donations going to the maintenance of the facility.

North Coast

The California Lighthouse is the limit for touring in an ordinary car as opposed to venturing into what is truly 4x4 country. The dividing line is the base of the California Lighthouse mount: If traveling beyond, drivers must contend with some grueling gravel roads. A four-wheel drive is best, or an all-terrain vehicle. Sights along the way are for the most part natural formations providing dramatic landscape shots and backgrounds to the rare historic structure. It is a part of the island that is not very well settled to this day.

This is a fun excursion for all who enjoy an off-road trek. North coast sights can also be approached by regular roads passing through Paradera or Santa Cruz, but then it will not be an outback adventure.

Unless otherwise specified, sights do not have regulated hours and can be freely visited without any fees. Most, with the exception of Black Stone Beach and Conchi, are regular stops on all bus tours of the area. The harder-to-reach locations are on the itinerary of most safari tours.

Along the north shore is a stark landscape, dramatically demonstrating Aruba's geological composition. The limestone cliffs carved by the waves and the speckled pillow basalt created by lava bubbling up from eruptions far under the sea make for a stark contrast to resort areas.

The first thing to capture your attention while traversing this north coast road is a proliferation of purposely placed rock piles, some quite artistic, which litter the landscape. How this practice actually began is a mystery. A number of tour guides decided it would add some spice to their tours to tell clients it was an old Amerindian tradition to pile the rocks and make a wish—ideally to return to Aruba. Each guide has their own version of the tale. Since the rock piles first began appearing about 15-20 years ago, it's unlikely that they stem from any ancient tradition. Visitors are welcome to play along with the charade; children love it.

★ CALIFORNIA LIGHTHOUSE

The **California Lighthouse** (Westpunt z/n, 24 hours daily, free) sits on the peak of Westpunt, the northwest point of the island. It is a beacon to a spot that offers some of the most stunning views of the north and west coasts, particularly at sunrise and sunset. These colorful events are dramatically played out daily over California Dunes at dawn and the coastline of Palm Beach and Arashi at dusk. It is an excellent stop for some wonderful photos. The lighthouse itself is closed to the public. There is only one road leading to the north coast, and it rises directly to the peak.

The lighthouse has an interesting history behind its rather atypical name. The Amerindian name for the area is Sasarawechi, but the lighthouse, built in 1916, was named for a wooden U.S. cargo ship that sank nearby during rough seas in 1898. The remains are an established dive site in rather shallow waters.

Contrary to widespread misconception, this is *not* the ship that refused to answer the *Titanic*'s distress call in 1912. That ship was the S.S. *Californian*, a 447-foot steel-hulled ship, which was sunk by a German torpedo in 1915. According to local oral history, the area became popular for salvaging the cargo from the ship, which would wash up on shore. Islanders began referring to the area as California Point.

BUSHIRIBANA GOLD RUIN

Impossible to miss while traversing the north coast road is the almost medieval contours of the **Bushiribana Gold Ruin** (Mativaderi z/n, on the north coast road next to the juncture leading to the Ostrich Farm, 24 hours daily, free). Built in 1874 by the Aruba Island Gold Mining Company of London, the ruins are atmospheric, weather-beaten, and appear far more ancient than they actually are. Youngsters love climbing among the terraces and surrounding rock formations. Combined with the dramatic crashing sea along the coast, the ruins and the view from their ramparts offer interesting photo ops.

This unique stone structure is a remnant of Aruba's gold rush, a repository for the ore turned in by prospectors. It all began when 12-year-old Willem Rasmijn first found traces of gold at Rooi Fluit in 1824 while herding his father's sheep. This discovery heralded a new era of prosperity and increased settlement for Aruba. The ruins are also a landmark for the turnoff to the Ostrich Farm, which is less than a mile inland.

★ ARUBA OSTRICH FARM

A bit of Africa plunked down in the middle of Aruba's outback, the **Aruba Ostrich Farm** (Matividiri 57, 297/585-9630, www.

arubaostrichfarm.com, 9:30am-3:30pm daily, $12 adults, $6 children ages 3-6) is an interesting private nature preserve. Tours are conducted every half hour.

Interacting with these huge, animated, and curious birds will stay with you for some time. It is impossible to visit with them and not be entertained. Be careful with brightly colored cameras and sparkly jewelry. The birds are very attracted to such items, and the adults have *very* long necks. They will attempt to pluck them from your person. You do not want to discover personally that movies depicting the comical consequences of ostriches swallowing valuables are, indeed, based on fact. After your ostrich interlude you will know many more interesting ostrich factoids.

★ AYO ROCK FORMATION

Travel back to pre-ceramic times with a stop at **Ayo Rock Formation** (Ayo z/n, signs indicate turnoff on route 7A, 24 hours daily, free), where huge quartz diorite formations provide a maze of open caves and passages. They eventually lead to summits with stunning panoramic vistas. The area is easily explored. Trails have been carved out by park rangers to provide clear paths leading to the summits.

There is easy rock climbing with beautiful views at the Ayo Rock Formation.

Arawak Indians sought shelter here and their shamans used this place to commune with the spirit world. There are a few particularly spectacular cave paintings in the hollowed out formations. This is Aruba's gold country, and gold dust can be seen glinting in the soil around Ayo's formations. This is an ideal rest stop with picnic tables and public bathrooms.

Santa Cruz, Paradera, and Piedra Plat

These inland areas of Aruba take visitors completely into the realm of everyday island life, far removed from the tourist scene. Residential communities are dense. Scattered throughout are Aruba's impressive rock formations, such as those at Casibari, a busy stop on most tours. Travel through these barrios to reach Arikok National Park.

The Santa Philomena Church in Paradera dominates the skyline, as does the Hooiberg (Haystack Mountain). This is often mistaken as Aruba's highest point. It is a very distinctive element of the island landscape.

HOOIBERG (HAYSTACK MOUNTAIN)

The distinctive profile of the Hooiberg is one of the first things that catches your eye when arriving on Aruba; it is front and center upon exiting the airport. The **Hooiberg peak** (Hooiberg z/n, accessible from roads 4A or 7A to Santa Cruz, a sign indicates the turn leading directly to the base of the stairway,

24 hours daily, free), which means "haystack" in Dutch, offers a remarkable panorama of Aruba. Its location at the middle of the island provides a unique perspective even if it is only the island's third highest point.

No roads or easy paths lead to the top of the Hooiberg. A stairway of 563 steps to the summit can be a challenge. The steps are not comfortably sized or spaced, but there are some places to take a rest along the way. Attempting to climb to the top is only recommended if you are in excellent shape and good health. The reward is fantastic pictures to prove you actually did it: The vistas stretching to all points of Aruba and the mountains of Venezuela make the climb worth the effort.

CASIBARI ROCK FORMATION

The fantastical quartz diorite formations at **Casibari** (Casibari z/n, off of Santa Cruz-Paradera Rd., 24 hours daily, free) are lots of fun for the whole family. The climb can be accomplished easily by almost all ages. Casibari is located just off the principal Santa Cruz-Paradera Road, and the turnoff is clearly marked. The formations are more concentrated and organized than the sprawl of Ayo. Tunnels and byways through the rocks have been tailored and trimmed and are strung with ropes for safety. One passage through is a bit tight, allowing only one person to pass at a time, which might be a bit difficult with very small children. Surrounding the principal attraction are gardens and paths for exploring indigenous flora.

This is a stop on nearly every tour, making it a bustling place with crowds of people at most hours. Across from the entrance is a snack shop to get a cold drink and a bite, and use the lavatories. There is a little snow cone wagon by the entrance that sells authentic coconut water straight from the freshly opened nut, an interesting and invigorating treat.

DONKEY SANCTUARY

Animal and nature lovers will enjoy the **Donkey Sanctuary** (Bringamosa 2C, Donkey Distress Hotline 297/593-2933, www.arubandonkey.org, 9am-4pm daily, free), a refuge and natural park. The donkeys are intelligent, gentle, and friendly, and they eagerly nibble carrot or apple pieces if you bring them.

Casibari Rock Formation

Children especially enjoy getting to know the donkeys. There are always some very young ones on hand.

The sanctuary is a nonprofit foundation, supported by donations from visitors and purchases of some very adorable souvenir items from their shop. It is through volunteer efforts that Aruba's remaining donkey population has managed to survive.

Brought to Aruba by the Spanish 500 years ago, *buricos* (donkeys) were the principal mode of transport on Aruba and an important element of the economy for centuries. They were finally abandoned for internal combustion vehicles with the advent of the Lago Refinery. When the first car was brought to Aruba and assembled in 1915, the island sported a population of around 1,400 donkeys.

Donkey owners released their donkeys into the countryside to survive as best they could. Though they are hardy animals, by 1970 only 20 donkeys could be counted among the wild population. The two main families living in the wild were in a serious state of distress when concerned islanders founded the nonprofit Fundacion Salba Nos Burico (Save our Donkeys) in 1997.

To get to the sanctuary, you must take the Frenchman's Pass turnoff on the Santa Cruz main road, which is clearly marked. It is a steep incline. Turn left at the first paved road, and then take a right at the second turnoff, which is a sand road. After this turn you will see a sign for the Donkey Sanctuary.

★ ARIKOK NATIONAL PARK

Aruba's largest natural preserve, **Arikok National Park** (San Fuego 70, 297/585-1234, www.arubanationalpark.org, 8am-4pm daily, $11) occupies 18 percent of the island's landmass. The park offers more than 32 kilometers (20 mi) of hiking trails with varying degrees of difficulty. There are some lovely beaches along the north shore, particularly popular for bodyboarding. Aruba's two highest peaks, Jamanota and Arikok, are within the park. Trails have been tailored to offer nature enthusiasts journeys through the wild. They can take anywhere from two to eight hours to complete, depending on your degree of fitness. Most major sites can also be accessed by car.

The park was designated a formally protected area in 2000. Becoming a registered foundation made it eligible for funding from the European Union (EU). Island government dedicated monies to the paving of gravel roads though the park without endangering flora and fauna. Funds from the EU allowed the construction of a formal visitor center and ranger headquarters, where you can also gather basic information about the flora and fauna native to the area.

If you are driving a four-wheel-drive vehicle, Arikok National Park can be reached by continuing along the road from the Donkey Sanctuary. It is also accessible over better roads via Santa Cruz, with a pass through Paradera and Piedra Plat on the way from the main resort areas.

★ CONCHI (NATURAL POOL)

The native name for one of the north coast's most breathtaking sights, **Conchi** (access is within Arikok National Park, follow the road to the summit of Seroe Arikok then down its back directly to the entrance, 24 hours daily, free), comes from the bowl shape of lava rock that comprises this dramatic coastal formation. A wall of pillow basalt protects the cove from the huge waves crashing against it, forming a calm pool for swimming and snorkeling. There are various terraces popular for climbing and jumping in the water, effecting a sort of natural water park.

Be prepared on arrival for a long climb down a stairway to the pool and what seems like an even longer climb back up. The beauty of this site is definitely worth the effort, but getting here and back is truly an adventure.

Rugged, winding roads approaching Conchi are impossible to traverse with an ordinary car. It is strongly suggested to leave the driving to an experienced guide with a reliable, tested vehicle, at least for the first

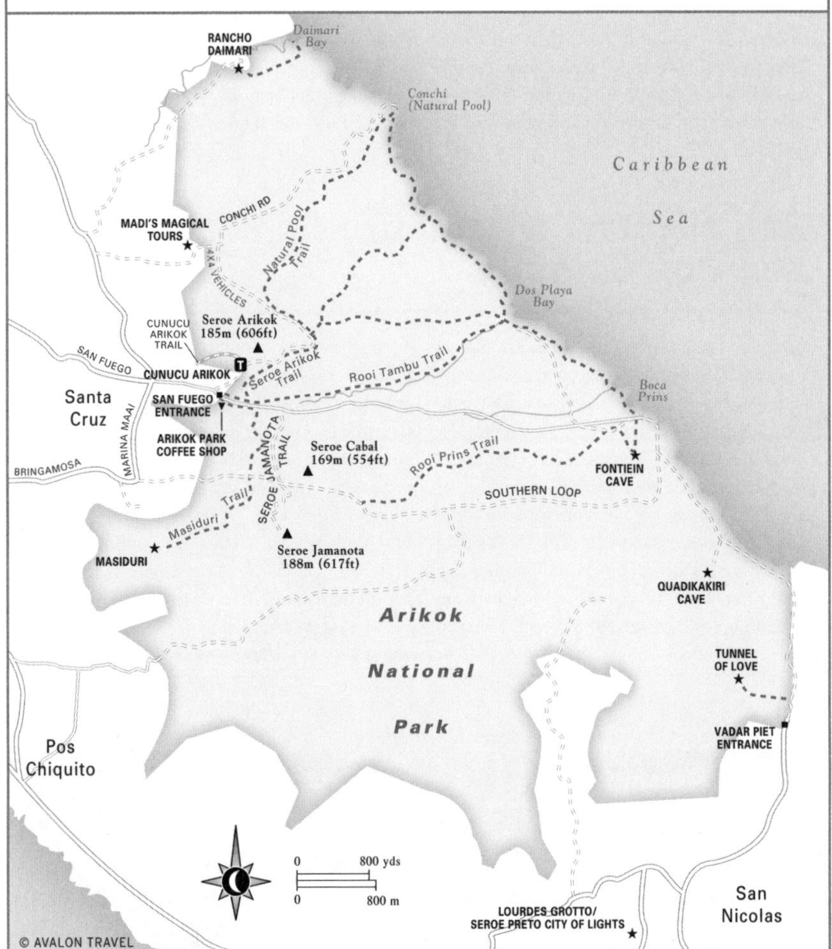

visit. The other option is to arrive by horseback. **Daimari Ranch** (www.arubarancho-daimari.com) at the northern border of the park conducts a trek to the Natural Pool on a daily basis.

QUADIKAKIRI AND FONTEIN CAVES

The **Quadikakiri and Fontein Caves** (Arikok National Park, San Fuego 70, 297/585-1234, www.arubanationalpark.org, 8am-4pm daily, park admission $11) provide easy and safe spelunking opportunities. Both caves have quite a few authentic Amerindian pictographs and dramatic formations. These can be enjoyed without a flashlight as the caves are comprised of large chambers filled with light from natural openings in the ceilings. Park rangers guide visitors through for no fee (though tips are appreciated). They are equipped with flashlights to illuminate some of the more interesting points.

Chambers in Quadikakiri are connected by some easily traversed passages. Some are only four feet high, and most adults will have to bend down to crab walk through them. This will provide a bit of excitement and a real feel of cave exploring without any danger. A closely monitored bat population does no harm.

The caves have dramatic stalagmite and stalactite formations, some still in the process of forming. Safe paths have been laid out for those wishing to do a little exploring on their own. The more hazardous and poorly lit areas have been blocked off. Visitors are asked to respect these limitations for their own safety.

San Nicolas, Savaneta, and Pos Chiquito

Aruba's "Sunrise City," San Nicolas, has an authentic Caribbean feeling to its main street and byways. It is best known as the site of the Lago Refinery and Colony, but has a distinct character of its own. The inhabitants are proud of their multicultural roots. In the late 1920s, many people from all corners of the Caribbean came to San Nicolas to find work at the refinery. They raised families and integrated into the community, enriching Aruba's culture by infusing it with many of their traditions.

Most visitors come to San Nicolas to explore areas such as Baby Beach, but there are also interesting sights, such as Lourdes Grotto. Heading back west toward the hotels, you will pass a number of attractive shore areas in Savaneta and Pos Chiquito.

LOURDES GROTTO

The interesting natural formations that comprise **Lourdes Grotto** (turn left on Pastoor Hendrikstraat at the San Nicolas YMCA where a sign indicates the turnoff, dawn-dusk

Natural limestone caves were converted into the Lourdes Grotto.

Seroe Preto City of Lights

One of Aruba's most attractive sights can only be seen during the holiday season at the end of the year. Those fortunate enough to be on the island in December and early January can enjoy a very special treat: **Seroe Preto City of Lights** (Seroe Preto z/n, 24 hours daily, free). Volunteers join together in this community effort to build a fantastical town out of colored lights with a different theme each year. It is extensive, taking up the entire hillside. Walkways allow visitors to climb the hill and immerse themselves in the experience. Usually the festival includes at least one notable Aruban landmark. For impressive pictures, bring a tripod or improvise; you will need some way to keep a camera steady.

The City of Lights is only on display from the first weekend in December to Three Kings Day (January 6). It is a labor of love by the **Stichting Hunbentud Uni Seroe Preto** (United Youth Foundation of Seroe Preto). The average annual cost is $12,000 to construct the scene, not including the utility bills. The project is funded by donations and fundraising events throughout the year. The first efforts began back in 1957. These were very simple compared to the elaborate work of art the project is today.

Most nights during the week, Seroe Preto is relatively quiet and ideal if you wish to take pictures without too many people around. During the holiday break and on weekends it gets very busy. Friday and Saturday nights mean musical performances by seasonal singing groups called *gaita* until late. There are often wagons selling snacks and refreshments as well. It is all very festive.

On the final night volunteers host a blowout farewell bash before turning off the lights. Everyone brings food and drink and the music performances go on until dawn. The tone seesaws from "Silent Night" to "Don't Stop the Party" as Carnival bands take over to mark the beginning of the incoming season. This is a joyous, authentically Aruban holiday experience.

daily, free) are dominated by a 700-kilo (1,543-lb.) statue of the Virgin Mary. The area has an ethereal quality that inspires spiritual reflection. It is a shrine to St. Bernadette, the Lady of Lourdes, and many believe it offers healing properties, like its namesake. The grotto is a natural formation in the rock cliffs on the road to Seroe Preto, or Black Point, clearly indicated with road signs.

Local oral history reports some islanders having a vision of the Blessed Mother at this spot. A community effort realized and maintains this tribute with candles and fresh flowers. Each year **St. Theresita Church** (St. Theresitaplein 8, 297/584-5118) in San Nicolas organizes a pilgrimage to the site on February 11, the Feast Day of Our Lady of Lourdes, which culminates with a mass. The site was first unveiled in 1958, 150 years after St. Bernadette had her original vision.

Food

Aruba's repeat visitors often claim that the food is one of the reasons they keep coming back to the island. The superb quality and selection of restaurants have generated a loyal clientele. The diversity of Aruba's population is reflected in the wealth of authentic ethnic restaurants scattered around principal tourist areas. Not only can you choose a different place for dinner every night, but you can also indulge in a different cuisine.

This explosion of eateries took place primarily over the last 15 years. Previously, fine dining was the ken of the hotels. There wasn't much competition from independent restaurants, and, generally, the hotels were relatively pricey.

Now many excellent spots for breakfast, lunch, and dinner are within easy walking distance of resorts. As a result, hotels have reevaluated their menus in order to compete. Patrons will find hotel dining usually priced the same as independent restaurants, with culinary teams striving to be trendy and innovative.

An influx of classically trained chefs from Europe and the United States has resulted in fusion cuisine holding sway over island kitchens. This melding of regional flavors and fresh, local ingredients with Cordon Bleu cooking is producing some tantalizing original dishes with Caribbean flair. Adventurous eaters who sample local dishes, such as *sate* with *pinda* (peanut) sauce, *cabrito stoba* (stewed goat), *keshi yena* (filled cheese), and other recipes of the region, are generous with their praise.

For Americans looking for familiar food, a good steak, hamburger, or pizza is never far away from major resorts. International food franchises are abundant, but so are many independent restaurants with interesting and unique menus. Quality, moderately priced meals are readily available. Aruba also boast authentic Thai, Bavarian, Belgian, Indian, Filipino, Chinese, and Middle Eastern eateries run by members of the local immigrant communities.

Aruba is also home to a well-respected culinary institute, where graduates receive

Previous: beachfront dining at sunset; fresh ceviche. **Above:** refreshments served on the beach.

Look for ★ to find recommended dining.

Highlights

★ **Smit & Dorlas Coffee House:** Aruba's first coffee shop is still its most charming. Relax with a good cup of coffee and one of the shop's complimentary cookies (page 96).

★ **Twister Café:** The owner of this cozy Dutch pub is one of the island's top gourmet chefs. Aside from the usual delicious and inexpensive offerings, Twister hosts three special nights of culinary magic the last weekend of each month (page 97).

★ **Casa Vieja:** For budget-friendly, authentic regional cuisine, Casa Vieja is your best bet. Their specialties are fish and meat platters that easily feed three and Colombian "stew soups" (page 98).

★ **Yami Yami:** With good Chinese food at local prices, this is Aruba's favorite fast food (page 102).

★ **Passions:** This beachfront restaurant is unquestionably one of the most romantic dining spots on the island, with excellent food and a tranquil ambience (page 103).

★ **Carte Blanche:** Enjoy fine gourmet dining in a cozy, friendly place. The hosts and chef make it an utterly memorable evening (page 107).

★ **Terrazza Italiana:** Indulge in a hearty plate of pasta or snack on some Italian tapas at this reasonably priced restaurant. They also serve up stunning views of the shoreline from their beachfront terrace (page 109).

★ **The Old Cunucu House:** Find authentic Aruban cuisine inside this 150-year-old farm-house. They have excellent fresh fish and international specialties at extremely reasonable prices (page 110).

★ **Amuse Bistro:** Enjoy gourmet French food with a touch of the Caribbean at this pleasant open-air eatery in the Playa Linda Resort (page 116).

★ **Marina Pirata:** Savor a dockside dinner with fish fresh off the boat at this island institution. Congenial hosts and a reasonably priced menu add to the appeal (page 122).

★ **Zeerover:** This is where to go for the very freshest of fish. It is a beautiful spot on the water with an authentic Caribbean ambience (page 122).

certification from the American Culinary Federation. The institute attracts students from all the Americas, producing a new generation of young chefs who are passionate about cooking and local cuisine.

One of the most enjoyable pastimes on the island is beachside dining. The vibrant blue seas, cooling trade winds, rustling palms, and breathtaking sunsets enhance the flavor of a meal as much as any seasoning. Romantic dinners under the stars are available in countless venues with memorable settings, even on a beautiful sailboat. Each night, dinner can be a gourmet adventure in some dazzling locale or a simple meal in cozy surroundings.

Many of the smaller restaurateurs don't have the budget for a full-fledged dedicated website. They do however take advantage of the free pages of major social media sites like Facebook and Twitter. These pages will most likely provide detailed menu descriptions, special offers, or changes in hours or location.

Oranjestad

Unlike what you will find in Manchebo Beach and Palm Beach, most restaurants in town are filled with islanders on their way to work in the morning or on a lunch break. In atmosphere and clientele, dining in Oranjestad is a very different experience from the beachside eateries in the resorts. Here, you are in native territory with a definitive regional ambience, and food is more reasonably priced to accommodate the locals.

ARUBAN

CAFÉ MARYLI

A bastion of authentic *cuminda criollo* (local cuisine), **Café Maryli** (Caya Ernesto Petronia 72, 297/588-9781, 11am-6pm Mon.-Sat., $10-13.50) is a very clean, tiny place at the very northern border of town. It occupies the front corner of the small Heimee shopping mall.

The specialty of the house is Aruban stews and soups made from whatever is fresh and available. The menu is posted on a small chalkboard and changes daily. Platters usually come with pan-fried pork chops, roast chicken or ribs, and a choice of fresh fish, grilled, fried, or Creole style. This is where to find authentic local dishes such as *pan bati* or *funchi,* usually served with fish or soup.

Most islanders order takeout as the teeny-tiny dining room offers few tables. Eating in has a certain island charm, however, and tables open up after the lunchtime rush.

ASIAN

Sushi has become very stylish on Aruba and not only among visitors. Pacific Rim cuisine, featuring flavors from all corners of Asia and surrounding island nations, is very much in vogue on Aruba.

Chinese food has been the number one choice among natives for fast food since the first immigrant opened a restaurant decades ago. The "Chinese/Dutch," restaurants, which are the most common type on Aruba, always have some Indonesian dishes on their menu. Generally, you can get tasty, filling meals at most Asian venues with prices that please the budget-conscious traveler.

ASIAN DELIGHT

Particularly busy with a takeout trade, **Asian Delight** (Wilminastraat 68, 297/583-7751, 11:30am-9pm Tues.-Sat., $6.25-16) is the top choice among islanders for their yummy, yummy value-priced Yami-Yami special. In addition to takeout, there is a very small dining area for eating in.

The à la carte menu also features inexpensive Chinese and Indonesian dishes with generous, family-size portions, but most customers pick up their Yami-Yami. This is a combo meal of appetizer and main course served on a bed of either *bami* or *nasi.* Choose from mini spring rolls or three different soups (wonton, egg drop, hot and

Aruban Cuisine

Aruban food has been influenced by island history and by the diversity of cultures hosted here. It has some very surprising elements. The Dutch left their mark by integrating into island cuisine traditional dishes from another former colony, Indonesia. The seasonings and mainstays of this Pacific country are very much in evidence at nearly all local restaurants and a part of most islanders' everyday diet.

Basic dishes of the Indonesian kitchen are **bami** and **nasi goreng,** which traditionally consist of leftovers and whatever is handy. Meat, chicken, and vegetables are stir-fried and mixed with lo mein noodles (*bami*) or fried rice (*nasi*). All chefs have their own recipe.

Most Asian restaurants serve a *bami* or *nasi* special, which is a sampling of Indonesian dishes with a local touch. The rice or noodles are surrounded with small servings of *sate* (pork, chicken, or beef mini-kebabs) with *pinda* (peanut) sauce, coconut shrimp, chicken, fish, fried sweet banana, sometimes breaded, and other traditional items.

Another holdover of colonial days is a favorite snack called **loempia,** large egg rolls second in popularity only to **pastechi,** tender, half-moon-shaped, fried pastries filled with perhaps cheese, or chop suey, curried chicken, fish, or beef. They are not empanadas, which are made with cornmeal and also a popular item. *Pastechi* is the Aruban way to start the day, usually paired with a *malta,* a strong root beer.

A dish unique to the ABC islands is **keshi yena,** or "full cheese." Traditionally, edam cheese came in a large ball and was eaten by cutting or scooping out the soft cheese and leaving the hardened rind. This rind would then be filled with a stew of chicken, beef, or seafood and the halves wrapped together in foil to be baked in a slow oven. It was served whole and opened at the table by cracking it with a ritual hammer. Today, any restaurant claiming to serve local food will have this on the menu, but the hours-long traditional method of preparation has been replaced by surrounding the basic stew with melted gouda, which is milder than edam.

Aruban food could be described as peasant food, since it is based on what could be found regionally and cheap. **Stoba** (stew) is a mainstay. It can be made of chicken (*galena*), meat (*carne*), goat (*cabrito,* tastes like lamb, usually a touch gamier), or *konkomber,* a sort of local squash. "Pigtail" is exactly what it indicates; nothing is wasted here!

Favorite side dishes include **pampona** (pumpkin), plantain (fried banana), or **funchi** (the local version of polenta, very firm cornmeal that can be sliced or cubed). *Funchi* is often fried and served with melted cheese (you can feel your arteries hardening even as you eat it), which is a beloved treat. Another standby is **pan bati,** meaning beaten bread; it's a cornmeal pancake that is nothing like a tortilla, sort of a firm breakfast pancake.

Aruban food really shines in the assortment of fresh Caribbean fish available on most menus and fundamental to the island diet. If you have never had fish from this part of the world before, you will find it a revelation. The sweet, moist, clean taste of the local catch can convert the most ardent fish hater.

Ciguatera, a type of seafood poisoning that can be a concern when dining on species high on the food chain, such as snapper or barracuda, is not an issue here. Fish from local waters are completely safe to consume.

sour) as an appetizer, then select from 10 different main courses. Most are surprisingly good, in particular the chicken and fish dishes. Try the Tjap Choy, a fresh blend rich with crispy vegetables and tender chicken in mild sauce.

The regular menu is extremely diverse. Several Indonesian and Thai dishes are featured. Specialty dishes range from Japanese teriyaki chicken or "old-fashioned" fried rice with absolutely everything.

Asian Delight is not far from L. G. Smith Boulevard. It is best reached by walking up the street on the west side of the lagoon that divides the town (aptly named Lagoonweg), which takes you directly to their door.

FUSION DELI

For something really different, try cuisine from Suriname at **Fusion Deli** (Caya Betico Croes 49A, 297/588-3588, 8:30am-7pm Mon.-Sat., $3.15-5.50). This country located along the northern coast of South America also experienced the influences of Dutch colonialism. Indonesian dishes are a staple. Most of the plantations in Suriname, however, had many East Indian laborers, and the country has a substantial Hindu population, which has impacted the national cuisine.

Curried foods are typical, wrapped in large, round flat Indian breads and called roti. Fusion Deli is a center for this hearty dish, which attracts many of the office workers in town during lunch. Diners select from tasty, filling, and inexpensive meals of roti and Surinamese *broodjes,* Dutch for "small breads." Interesting typical drinks of coconut, ginger, or almond milk complete this exotic experience.

TATAMI SUSHI HOUSE

A bit off the beaten track, **Tatami Sushi House** (L. G. Smith Blvd. 124, 297/582-9945, 11am-2:30pm and 5:30pm-10:30pm Tues.-Fri., 4pm-11pm Sat., 5:30pm-10:30pm Sun., $8.40-14.30) is a cozy place hidden at the back of a very modern building at the west edge of town. (The building is called the Portofino Mall, but you will have absolutely no way of discerning that.) CMB Loan Division is out front as a landmark.

Tatami Sushi House offers a very nice, personalized selection of sushi made fresh to order, with some very interesting creations from the chef. There are conventional items such as California rolls as well as exotic combinations and some reasonably priced assortment platters. They have some cute Papiamento names like "Bon Bini" (Welcome), which comes with 12 pieces of sushi, or a big "Mi Dushi" (My Sweetheart) special for two. The dining room is tiny, so reservations are recommended.

BEACHSIDE DINING

At the very eastern border of L. G. Smith Boulevard is Surfside. This is the principal spot for beachside dining in Oranjestad, apart from the new boardwalk at Governor's Bay. Four eateries at Surfside provide a special environment and good food. Here you will find some of the most romantic restaurants in town.

Tatami Sushi House

BAREFOOT

Uniquely designed, **Barefoot** (L. G. Smith Blvd. 1, 297/588-9824, www.barefootaruba.com, 5pm-10pm daily, $24.50-39.50) takes its name from the central dining room of a sandbox with tables, where patrons are encouraged to take off their shoes and wiggle their toes in the sand. There are also no-sand options if the sandbox is not for you.

The circular dining area is an open-air terrace looking out on one of the most appealing locales for sunset watching. The elegant gourmet cuisine from European chef-owner Gerco is earning rave reviews. Dishes emphasize seafood, such as fresh crab cakes or seafood ragout. A reasonably priced three-course meal varies daily. Preparation and presentation are beautiful, but expect somewhat smaller portions in the European fashion.

REFLEXIONS BEACH RESTAURANT AND LOUNGE

Adjacent to Barefoot, **Reflexions Beach Restaurant and Lounge** (L. G. Smith Blvd. 1A, 297/582-0153, www.beach-aruba.com, 10am-11pm daily for meals, bar open until 4am daily, $19.50-43) features a revamped and elegant menu. The shoreside eatery and bar is an all-day spot with a shaded club area and a pool on the dining terrace. The beach and restaurant are lined with stylish couches and lounges. They offer snack service on the terrace or beach for soaking up the island ambience. Most local patrons on the weekends linger through the day and well into the night.

The dinner menu strongly features gourmet appetizers and seafood. During the day, enjoy platters of assorted local and Dutch snacks. When they have it, they will offer a fresh snapper platter prepared in classic Aruban fashion for only $20.

On weekends they often host some high-decibel music events during a two-for-one happy hour 4pm-6pm, and the party continues until the wee hours, changing this quiet beachside eatery into a trendy club.

PINCHOS GRILL AND BAR

A distinctive menu and memorable location mark **Pinchos Grill and Bar** (L. G. Smith Blvd. 7, 297/583-2666, www.pinchosaruba.com, 5pm-midnight Sun.-Thurs., 5pm-1am Fri.-Sat., $19-44) as one of the most romantic places to dine on Aruba. The ultracool ambience and live, mellow music on weekends makes it a popular place for chic, elite businesspeople to stop by for a relaxing cocktail.

Veteran restaurateurs Robby and Anabella Peterson realized a dream when they opened Pinchos. It is named for the skewers on which many of the main courses are cooked over an open, wood-fired grill. The restaurant is known for distinctive dipping sauces and unique marinades. The chicken kebabs and Black Angus rum-infused blue cheese tenderloin are delicious and different, as are the jumbo shrimp and chunky fish kebabs. They also have a selection of main courses off the skewer, but *pinchos* are their claim to fame.

Set on a dock out over the water, it is, without a doubt, one of Aruba's most romantic spots to watch the sunset, and the decor is keyed to encourage this coziness. There are hammocks for two, and huge throw pillows and low couches for lounging while dining at low tables (great for drinks and cuddling, but not so much fun if you have to balance your plate on your knees). They do have normal seating as well.

THE WEST DECK

The upgrading of the Oranjestad shorefront has resulted in a charming eatery at the center of the town called **The West Deck** (L. G. Smith Blvd. z/n at Governor's Bay, 297/587-2667, www.thewestdeck.com, 10:30am-11pm daily, $9.95-45.95). Diners can sit on the expansive deck overlooking the water or at picnic tables on the sand. The eclectic menu has been influenced by a range of Caribbean cuisines.

Choose from Bahamas-style conch fritters, jerk chicken wings, West Indian samosas, enormous burgers, or fresh, whole baby red snapper, Aruban-style. All the finger-food appetizers can be ordered by the dozen for large parties that want to enjoy the sunset while nibbling and sipping on stylish cocktails served in jelly jars. A single menu offers options for lunch, dinner, or snacking. Depending on what you order, a meal can range from quite inexpensive to pricey, especially if you're ordering a lot of side dishes priced à la carte. But all of the food is prepared and presented with flair.

The West Deck attracts a lot of tourists, but is also popular with a very chic local crowd. Islanders will usually come with large groups for extended, very social evenings by the water. Reservations are a must; the location and congenial staff have made it quite a hot spot, particularly around sunset. It is not nearly as crowded for brunch or lunch.

BREAKFAST, LUNCH, AND COFFEE SHOPS

For lighter fare look beyond the international franchises such as Starbucks and Dunkin' Donuts. Oranjestad has no end of attractive coffee shops and breakfast and lunch spots.

COFFEE BREAK

Local caffeine addicts usually choose **Coffee Break** (Caya Betico Croes 101A, 297/588-5569, 7am-6pm Mon.-Sat., lattes $2.80) as the place to get their morning fix and meet with friends. This is a very cute, clean, cozy spot done in old-fashioned soda shop decor with rounded, padded stools along the counter. Comfy sofas for reading the morning paper fill one corner of the café and they have free Wi-Fi.

The coffee beans are freshly ground; imagine all those fancy coffees you know and love, priced to the local trade, in florins instead of dollars. This means prices are about 45 percent less than what the resorts and high-profile outlets charge.

Local snacks and pastries are the food fare, as well as waffles, the pie of the day à la mode, and a changing selection of fresh gelato. They also offer elaborate, iced-coffee treats and ice cream floats. Find seasonal specials listed on their Facebook page.

COFFEE 4 U

Extremely popular with island intelligentsia is **Coffee 4 U** (L. G. Smith Blvd. 108, 297/582-2906, 7am-7pm Mon.-Fri., 8am-6pm Sat., 8am-2pm Sun., $4.50-10), just past the gas station on the western end of town. The specialties here are Italian cappuccinos and lattes, enjoyed at a very stylish, contemporary collection of banquettes and couches. Free Wi-Fi makes this a favorite meeting spot for convivial business conferences.

The restaurant has expanded its menu beyond pastries and paninis to full breakfasts with fruity waffles and very rich, savory crepes. Quiches come in alluring combinations, such as spinach and feta or bacon and brie. A lunch special changes daily.

DE SUIKERTUIN

Fashionable islanders love lunch at **De Suikertuin** (Wilhelminastraat 64, 297/582-6322, www.desuikertuin.com, 7am-4pm Mon.-Sat., $4.85-14). "The Sugar Garden" is aptly named. Housed in a landmark *cunucu* house, it features a beautifully landscaped patio in the backyard for outdoor dining. Or choose the quaint, air-conditioned, and authentically maintained indoor rooms.

De Suikertuin offers a rather typical Dutch-European menu with Aruban touches. Try the very nice pumpkin soup, a local delicacy. Luncheon baguettes hold anything from peanut butter with sprinkles (a Dutch thing) to smoked salmon with dill dressing. Other options are quiches and a changing menu of hot dishes.

DJESPIE'S PLACE

Attached to Coffee Break and sporting the same decor, but separated by a door, is the cute little snack stop **Djespie's Place** (Caya Betico Croes 101, 297/588-5569, 7am-6pm Mon.-Sat., $1-4 snack or sandwich), a popular hangout with islanders. The focus is on an authentic Aruban snack menu. Quick lunch options include *pastechis* and croquettes, or well-stuffed sandwiches and hamburgers.

★ SMIT & DORLAS COFFEE HOUSE

Aruba's first coffee shop, **Smit & Dorlas Coffee House** (De La Sallestraat 30-A, 297/588-4888, http://coffeehousearuba.com, 9am-6pm Mon.-Fri., 9am-2pm Sat., lattes $2.50) offers 14 freshly ground coffees from around the world and 40 loose teas, both black and herbal, in the most delightful surroundings imaginable. Styled after vintage Viennese pastry shops, it not only serves excellent coffee, but delicious paninis, a quiche of the day, and baguette sandwiches. It is also famous for fresh-made cakes, all reasonably priced. Coffee House is the embodiment of why enjoying a cup of coffee or tea with a friend is such a treasured institution; it's the sort of place where you will want to linger.

Hot beverages are served with delicious complimentary cookies, which will entice you back for more. There is no other place on Aruba to purchase these cookies. The shop also sells unique, hard-to-find, designer coffee and teapots made for two that can be lovely gifts.

Coffee House is not far from the main post office, which is a 10-minute walk inland from the Renaissance Resort. Take a right turn at the traffic light just past the post office, at De La Sallestraat, and find it five minutes farther along on the south side.

STARBUCKS

If you can't live without your **Starbucks** (Renaissance Mall and Renaissance Marketplace, 297/523-6750, 7am-10pm daily) then never fear, they are here. There is a Starbucks at the very center of the Renaissance Mall, next to the pier for the boat to Renaissance Island. The mall has a chic, award-winning Caribbean design and air-conditioned surroundings and the Starbucks lounge area has deep couches for relaxing and checking your email with free Wi-Fi.

The Renaissance Marketplace Starbucks is across the main street, right on Oranjestad Harbor, a setting with a lovely view. Here you can relax on the outdoor terrace and enjoy the breeze. This is a nice place to watch the fishing boats make way early in the morning or government officials grabbing their caffeine fix before sessions of Parliament.

Both cafés sell a collection of dedicated Starbucks Aruba logo gear, for those who take their coffee souvenirs seriously or are seeking a gift for the fanatic back home.

CARIBBEAN FUSION

Unadulterated, full-blown French cookery is hard to find on Aruba these days. Instead, it is considered quite fashionable to incorporate regional seasoning and indigenous fruits and vegetables to liven up the menu. Chefs are also more health-conscious in their cooking style, with less emphasis on rich, heavy sauces. Passion fruit sauces and mango salsas produce exotic flavors that chefs find enchanting, and the customers seem to agree.

IGUANA JOE'S

A trendy Caribbean menu is the signature of **Iguana Joe's** (L. G. Smith Blvd., 297/583-9373, www.iguanajoesaruba.com, 11am-midnight Mon.-Sat., 5pm-11pm Sun., $15-25). Located on the second level of the Royal Plaza Mall, it was first in a very successful local franchise, followed by Smokey Joe's and Iguana Cantina in Palm Beach. Famous for their island potions, they also serve traditional local favorites, including *keshi yena* and Aruban-style fresh fish. Regional specialties such as jerk chicken and jambalaya spice things up. The ribs are also very popular. The food is always good, and they have a funky, fun decor with a great view of the harbor and boulevard, ideal for observing island life.

THE PADDOCK

Very popular with young Dutch students interning abroad, **The Paddock** (L. G. Smith Blvd. 13, 297/583-2334, www.paddock-aruba.com, 9am-10:45pm, bar open until the last patron leaves, $7-22.25) occupies a prime spot right on the water.

Talk about funky decor! You can't miss the velociraptor hanging out on the roof, right next to the Volkswagen. As a venue that attracts poor students, it has a reasonably priced menu and an ambience that appeals to all ages. It becomes a hangout for younger folks after the dinner hour. Every night features drink specials and some sort of happy hour; three nights a week local bands play until 2am.

Dutch baguette sandwiches are a standard here, from the local favorite of cheese and pickles to paper-thin carpaccio. *Tosties* (the local version of grilled cheese), hamburgers, and sharwarma (their spelling!) are considered specialties. There is a very diverse dinner menu with an emphasis on fish and seafood. Every Wednesday evening is an all-you-can-eat rib special (9am to closing, $13). Visit the website for an amusing hint of what to expect from this distinctly Dutch eatery.

QUE PASA

A longtime Oranjestad favorite with an eclectic menu, **Que Pasa** (Wilminastraat 18, 297/583-4888, www.quepasaaruba.com, 5pm-11pm daily, $17-27) features regional cuisine with European flair. Lively Caribbean decor in a landmark building showcases a great deal of original art. A second level with a terrace offers alfresco dining overlooking the street.

Loyal patrons rave about the tomato soup, very good ribs, and fresh catch of the day. The offerings also include carpaccio, tuna tataki, or duck breast salad. Que Pasa is best known for its fresh specials of the day, which could be fish, steak, or something else altogether. The exceptionally friendly staff is happy to recite the specials and offer an honest opinion of what they recommend.

7 WEST

On the north side of the harbor, **7 West** (Weststraat 7, 297/588-9983, www.7-westaruba.com, 9am-4:30pm and 5pm-10:30pm daily, $7.25, $10 daily specials, $15 all-you-can-eat ribs Fri.) is often overlooked because of its second-story location. However, the appealing open-air eatery is in a prime spot. Terraces provide a great view, and it is priced for a local crowd. The recently redecorated interior is quite attractive, with rounded booths providing a cozy environment.

Lunch platters of ribs (which are excellent, tender, and tasty), fried chicken, or jerk chicken are uniformly priced. They also feature a daily lunch special: Usually (but not always) it is fresh fish, depending on Chef John Boomkamp's whim. The signature burger is done the Dutch way, with a fried egg, bacon, gouda, and sautéed onions. There is also a children's menu. No additional service charge is added to the bill.

★ TWISTER CAFÉ

Deep in the heart of Oranjestad find the surprising **Twister Café** (Dominicanessenstraat 10, 297/583-9077, twistercafearuba10@yahoo.com, 5pm-2am Mon.-Sat., $10-18.50, culinary weekend $42.50) to enjoy an unexpected gourmet treat.

Twister has a cozy, intimate neighborhood pub ambience, with a dedicated Dutch clientele. Owners Linda and Annie are congenial hosts. For over 10 years, Linda was executive sous-chef and then executive chef of what was always considered Aruba's premier gourmet restaurant, Chez Mathilde. After it closed, she completely focused on Twister. She brings her deft touch to the kitchen, at extremely reasonable prices.

The menu ranges from authentic Dutch *stampot*, a unique mix of vegetables, mashed potatoes, and meat, to tournedos of beef. The plat du jour could be duck breast or whatever is fresh; Twister is also known for hearty soups.

Every last weekend of the month, Annie and Linda host a special "Culinary Weekend." They devise a unique menu and seat up to 30. The five-course meal consists of soup, two appetizers, a main course, and dessert, for one very reasonable price, drinks not included. The same meal is served over three nights: Friday, Saturday, and Sunday, beginning at around 8pm. Doors open 45 minutes prior for a meet and greet. Sunday evening is strictly no smoking. If you have particular dietary concerns, they will prepare an alternate dish. It is a leisurely, congenial evening of wine and food appreciation.

Main courses for this culinary adventure could be beef Wellington; pan-seared lamb and duck breast; a combination of Chilean sea bass, salmon, and a fresh local offering; lamb three ways; or a poultry medley with ostrich and duck leg. The focus alternates between meat and seafood from one month to the next. You can expect something special and memorable since Linda has a fine reputation as an innovative and intuitive chef.

COLOMBIAN

Aruba's rapidly expanding expatriate Colombian population has resulted in a number of informal cafés serving authentic cuisine. Colombians like their big meal at lunchtime, and typical dishes are *sopas,* huge bowls filled with meat or fish, tons of veggies, and some broth; it's almost a stew. The other favorite dish is a mixed meat platter typical to Latin America; each country has its own version. These include several different cuts of beef, pork, sausage, and organ meats. If you have a taste for tongue, liver, kidney, heart, and tripe, you will be very happy with this, or you could ask them to substitute an extra piece of chicken or sausage.

★ CASA VIEJA

Among Aruba's population of Colombian spots, **Casa Vieja** (Cumana 8, 297/588-1627, 7:30am-11pm daily, $3.50-20) is one of the most authentic. It is on the eastern end of town along the Caya Betico Croes. In this tiny place, food is served on a small covered patio with a thatched roof and a few garden chairs and tables. This is a good spot for inexpensive breakfasts, which are served all day. The food is simply prepared, there is a lot to eat, and it is dead cheap.

One of the delicious soups can either be enjoyed as a first course or a whole meal. Sunday is the day for the house specialty, Sopa de Mariscos (seafood soup), and the enormous mixed meat platters that easily feed two or three heaped with beef, chicken, pork, thick bacon, chorizo, and whatever else is on hand, plus steak fries and authentic tostones, or flattened plantain chips, which are more like crispy flat potatoes. Many from Aruba's Colombian community come here to enjoy their Sunday meal.

LA ESQUINA

There is a cluster of budget-priced eateries in the middle of the Caya Betico Croes, the main shopping street. **La Esquina** (Caya Betico Croes 49A, 297/588-0108, 9am-11pm daily, $5.50-20) is another cute little hole-in-the-wall with just a few tables doing a brisk local business.

This tiny café on a corner is rustic and popular for the *sopa di dia.* The Sunday seafood soup usually runs out by the afternoon since it is such a beloved item. Mixed meat platters range from the smaller-sized "Peasant" to the "Big Mixed Platter," enough for three or four people. Fish stews or shrimp and fish platters, grilled or fried, are also nice for non-meat eaters.

The menu has a translation of the Spanish names of dishes, but not too thorough an explanation of what you get, which may be challenging on the mixed platters. The crew tends to be a bit weak in English, but you can point at what you want.

CUBAN

CUBA'S COOKIN'

Inspired by a bygone era, **Cuba's Cookin'** (L.G. Smith Blvd., in the Renaissance Marketplace, 297/588-0627, www.cubascookin.com, 10:30am-11pm daily, $26.50-43) strives to create that carefree, vivacious ambiance that was pre-revolutionary Havana of the 1950's. Aside from a lively menu, the restaurant features a live band nightly, plus a salsa show and lessons every Monday. The open air eatery has a very congenial staff and an atmosphere that encourages you to linger well past your dinner.

The menu is diverse, with a strong emphasis on Caribbean style seafood and classic Cuban Ropa Vieja and ribs. It is the only restaurant on Aruba to have Matzoth Ball Soup on their menu, if you have a hankering. The chef is also attentive to the needs of certain dietary requirements and has devised some very tasty vegan and gluten-free dishes; the "Mean Women's Pasta" is a good example.

ITALIAN

CASA TUA

Casa Tua (Renaissance Marketplace, 297/583-1990, www.casatuaaruba.com, 11am-11pm daily, $12-36) was Aruba's first gourmet pizzeria. The Oranjestad outlet (there is also one in Palm Beach) has an elegant vibe and a terrific location by the water end of the mall. There is indoor and outdoor dining, situated so patrons can enjoy the free nightly shows at the bandstand.

Patrons rave about the pizza and reasonably priced pasta. Order a medium for two to share rather than the personal pizza special, as the latter are often premade and reheated. Other dishes tend more toward seafood, with only a few meat dishes, but no veal.

MIDDLE EASTERN

SULTAN

The original Middle Eastern restaurant, and still considered the best by many, is **Sultan** (Caya Betico Croes 229, 297/588-2598, www.sultanaruba.com, 11am-3pm and 5:30pm-11pm Mon.-Sat., 5:30pm-11pm Sun., $8.85-18). It is found just a bit beyond the eastern edge of Oranjestad, on the Cumena traffic circle.

This cozy, simple place tries to recreate a Middle Eastern decor and atmosphere. Arabic pop videos play on a plasma screen. There is a party room in the back for groups to lounge on colorful cushions and dine while reclining. The menu declares that they are determined to make you "weak in the knees" with their authentic cuisine.

Main courses feature a mix of Middle Eastern favorites, kebabs of chicken, lamb, or tenderloin or a platter of large falafel, which is perfect for vegetarians. Shawarma is their specialty. All main courses are accompanied by ample portions of excellent hummus, tabouli salad, and saffron rice or baba ganoush and pita bread. If you have a large party, try the expansive sample platter of every kind of kebab and regional delicacy ($55 flat rate). Every dish comes with homemade sauces; the creamy garlic sauce is tasty, mild, and definitely worth trying. Approach the tomato-based salsa with caution: It is *super* spicy.

PERUVIAN

DELIMAR

Authentic regional cuisine from Lima, Peru, distinguishes **Delimar** (Wilhelminastraat 4, 297/582-6139, 11:30am-9pm Mon., Tues., Thurs.-Sat., 11:30pm-4pm Sun., $18) from other fish and seafood restaurants. Since Lima is a port town and central to the coastal region, it relies heavily on seafood, cilantro, and particular regional dried peppers for its distinctive cuisine. Delimar owners, chef Marco and his wife Lorena, have imported these directly from their homeland for an authentic flavor.

The couple is passionate about what they deliver to the table. Dishes are made to order, allowing patrons to specify the degree of spiciness they prefer, or dishes can be pretty hot. If you're looking for a really different style of preparing fish, this is the place. Allow for the preparation to take time, and don't be in a hurry. Generous portions of seafood are served as *arrisotado,* the Peruvian version of risotto; *tacu-tacu,* with rice and beans; or *cau-cau,* seafood only. For a refreshing and unique dessert after some very spicy seafood, try the fresh passion fruit mousse. In keeping with the cuisine, the bar is stocked with Peruvian beers and some liquor from the region.

Here is where Peruvian expatriates and families go for their Sunday lunch. It is conveniently located just behind the Renaissance Resort. Look for Delimar on Facebook.

LA GRANJA

This Floridian franchise began in Aruba. **La Granja** (Hospitaalstraat 2, 297/583-5602, www.lagranjarestaurants.com, 11:30am-10pm daily, $9-17) originally specialized in barbecue chicken but has vastly expanded the menu to include ribs, chops, steak, shrimp, and the Peruvian specialty of fresh ceviche. An average meal is half a bird cooked over a wood-fired grill in classic Peruvian rotisserie style. Other main courses are a full pound of steak or grilled pork. Try some of the Peruvian condiments, more like relishes, which lend a new and exciting taste to familiar poultry.

The restaurant features quick, cafeteria-style service and a rustic setting with picnic-type tables. Find it by going inland from the far eastern end of Caya Betico Croes, where the tram rails end. The building takes up an entire corner just a block beyond Coffee Break.

PORTUGUESE

GOSTOSO

For a very long time **Gostoso** (Caya Ing Roland H. Lacle 12, 297/588-0053, www.gostosoaruba.com, noon-3pm and 6pm-10pm Tues.-Fri., noon-4pm and 6:30pm-10pm Sat.-Sun., $21-33), which means "delicious" in Portuguese, was rated Aruba's number one restaurant on the most popular review sites on the Internet. As would be expected from the seafaring Portuguese, fish and shellfish are big on the menu. The owner-operated eatery also features some Aruban dishes.

The food is excellent, and they make great white sangria. Steaks are prime Black Angus beef. Particularly recommended is the Espetada Marinara, a very unique presentation of surf and turf, or order Catch of the Day in Mango Sauce, made with grouper or Chilean sea bass; portions are very generous.

This charming little place tucked away on an Oranjestad side street does have one or two drawbacks. Rather poor acoustics means it gets quite noisy when filled (and it usually is). Its popularity can possibly result in a long wait for a table after 7pm. Don't have a heart attack when first perusing the menu; prices are in Aruban florins, not dollars.

SEAFOOD

Aruba is a fish and seafood lover's paradise. Clean waters guarantee a catch of the freshest and most delicate flavor. An authentic catch of the day is always a treat, but make sure the restaurant actually uses fresh, not frozen, fish.

AQUARIUS

A favorite lunch spot for island movers and shakers is **Aquarius** (L. G. Smith Blvd. 82, 297/523-6195, 7-11am, noon-3:30pm, and 5:30pm-11:30pm Mon.-Sat., 7-11am and 5:30pm-11:30pm Sun., breakfast buffet $18, Sunday brunch $30, lunch buffet $15-20, dinner seafood buffet $39) next to the reception desk of the Renaissance Marina Tower. The restaurant has a pleasant, chic decor and an extremely friendly and accommodating staff.

It is entirely possible to find bank presidents or an important minister or parliamentarian dining at the next table or lining up for the fabulous lunch buffet. There are two choices: cold, which consists of just the salad bar, soup of the day, dessert table, and unlimited ice tea, or full buffet, with a selection of local dishes.

The cold is a delicious and diverse array of all-you-can-eat fresh sushi, some gourmet cold fish dish of the day, a variety of ceviche and seasoned salads, and all the greens and accompaniments you could possibly imagine, with fresh-made dressings. The soups are always good, as is the dessert assortment, which changes daily.

Dinner adds to the buffet a fresh fish station where patrons choose from at least a few different kinds of fish and shellfish, sautéed before their eyes and to their specifications. Try the yummy mango salsa to accompany your fish.

THE OLD FISHERMAN

Ask an islander where to go for fresh fish in Oranjestad and anyone will tell you **The Old Fisherman** (Havenstraat 36, 297/588-3648, http://oldfishermanaruba.com, 8am-11pm daily, $22-44). It started out as a tiny hole-in-the-wall right on the water at the harbor, where local anglers would drop off their catch. Food was sold only to take away. It was so popular with islanders wanting fresh fish that it had to move into the present cozy surroundings with a distinctively local decor. Find The Old Fisherman on the side street next to the bus station.

Platters of fresh fish and seafood are named for friends and family, and prepared as you like it: sautéed, breaded and fried, with creamy garlic sauce, or meunière. The signature dish here is the "Claudio Wolfe"—a whole red snapper fried, grilled, or stewed. The dining room is filled with natives, and there is always a feeling of being with a family and their friends, rather than at a commercial establishment.

STEAK HOUSES

Most steak restaurants go beyond their advertised specialty, offering fish and poultry to accommodate patrons who might be in the mood for something else. Usually, it is a mediocre offering. The same is usually true for fish houses offering beef. It's best to stick to the fine fish restaurants for seafood and to the steak houses for steak.

EL GAUCHO

No conversation about Oranjestad steak houses is complete without mentioning **El Gaucho** (Wilminastraat 80, 297/582-3677, www.elgaucho-aruba.com, 11am-11pm daily, $37), Aruba's first and, still considered by many, foremost Argentine steak house, though much pricier than it used to be. There are mixed reviews on some items on the menu, such as the short ribs, but the *churrasco,* the Gaucho Steak, is an 18-ounce hunk of boneless sirloin that is consistently excellent. It's usually enough for more than one person.

There is a kids' menu with favorites such as macaroni and cheese and hamburgers, plus a video game room to keep the little ones busy. Mariachi singers perform every night, which is very interesting if you are new to experiencing them live.

L.G. SMITH'S STEAK & CHOP HOUSE

Aruba has some very fine eateries where the staff is fanatical about every dish being superlative. One such restaurant is **L.G. Smith's Steak & Chop House** (L. G. Smith Blvd. 82, 297/523-6115, www.lgsmiths.com, 5:30pm-11pm daily, early bird special 5:30pm-7pm

an elegant dessert at L.G. Smith's Steak & Chop House

daily, $26-44, $79-90 for three-course special with wine pairing).

Gourmet food and fine wine pairing are the restaurant's passion. At least once a year a celebrity chef is brought in from Europe or the United States to devise a special limited-time menu of unique and impressive dishes. Average pricing for the special menus is $44-60 per person for a three-course dinner including several options. Wine pairing with each course costs an extra $30-37 total.

The regular à la carte menu specializes in certified Angus prime beef steaks, ranging from a petit filet mignon to a massive 20-ounce Porterhouse. There are also some gourmet vegetarian dishes, such as vegetable Wellington, and elegant desserts.

On the Renaissance Mall mezzanine level, a wall of picture windows provides a gorgeous view of the harbor. The restaurant's decor is elegant "island chic." Attached to the Crystal Casino, the restaurant also has a lounge bordering the gaming area, where light fare is served after midnight. They also work with Okeanos Spa, next door, to offer a "treatment and dinner" package.

YAMANJA WOODFIRE GRILL

Regulars rave about **Yamanja Woodfire Grill** (Wilminastraat 2, 297/588-4711, www.yemanja-aruba.com, 5:30pm-10:30pm Mon.-Sat., $25 and up, prix fixe menu $42.50-55) directly behind the Renaissance Resort Marina Tower. This charming restaurant occupies a landmark building and offers indoor and outdoor dining.

Grilled meats are the specialty with mesquite wood imparting a singular flavor. U.S.-certified Angus beef is served, which does make the à la carte menu somewhat pricey. Though ostensibly a steak house, Yamanja offers several fish and seafood dishes from the grill, as well as a number of unique vegetarian dishes. For families and the budget-minded, there are a less expensive kids' menu and a three-course early bird special.

Eagle Beach and Manchebo Beach

Aside from resort restaurants, this area has traditionally had few eateries compared to Oranjestad and Palm Beach. Now that it is quickly becoming Aruba's center for beachfront condominium complexes, there are a lot more options for dining out, from local cuisine to gourmet.

Most restaurants are lined up along the beach, within the resorts, or across Irausquin Boulevard. The proliferation of malls on the Sasaki Highway has resulted in one or two eateries worth the short walk from the hotels. Farther inland along Bubali Road there are a few interesting venues, such as the elegant Madame Janette and Quinta Del Carmen, and the bargain-priced Yami Yami. Most restaurants in the resorts feature a mix of typical lunch fare such as hamburgers, wraps, and Caesar salads during the day, but offer more innovation and romance once the sun goes down.

EAGLE BEACH AND VICINITY

Aruba's southwest point, Punto Brabo, ends at Costa Linda Resort, the dividing line between Manchebo Beach and Eagle Beach. Aside from Passions, all resorts and restaurants along J. E. Irausquin Boulevard are found on the land side of the street, across from the beach. Eagle Beach ends at Aruba's famous fofoti trees, a distinctive landmark: This is the base of the Bubali Road, which leads across the Sasaki Highway to some interesting places to dine.

Asian

★ YAMI YAMI

The Bubali Commercial Center (BCC) is a small strip mall on the Bubali Road. It is where you will find the suburban outlet of Asian Delight, called, appropriately, **Yami Yami** (Bubali 69C, 297/587-0062, 11:30am-9pm

Dining Alfresco

One of the great attractions of the tropics is a romantic sunset dinner on a beach or in some delightful gardens. A lovely meal under swaying palms with the cooling trade winds rustling is a fantasy come true; though, not so much when the wind nearly blows the food off your plate. Aruba is known for some particularly strong winds, and many restaurants have been designed with that in mind. Several places set up windbreaks or have designed the building to provide a tranquil environment.

Unfortunately, this can lead to open-air dining areas getting uncomfortably warm, especially if the heat from the kitchen is blowing your way. Dress lightly, but bring a sweater just in case.

Dressing lightly exacerbates the other issue with dining outdoors: mosquitoes or sand fleas becoming pests, particularly around sunset, when they are most active. Everyone enjoys the casual atmosphere of the island and the option to dine in Bermuda shorts and light clothing. But bare legs under a table are an immediate attraction for some annoying insects, especially if there was rainfall in the previous weeks.

This is a problem all over the Caribbean, even more so on other islands where it rains a bit nearly every day. A windy desert island such as Aruba has an advantage, but that is no guarantee of being entirely bug-free. It is not usually such an issue at restaurants situated where there is a steady breeze or not much greenery.

Long pants with shoes and socks are suggested. If you wish to completely enjoy that fantasy meal with large areas of skin exposed, invest in some bug repellent, particularly in the mid to late fall.

Tues.-Sun., $6.50-16) after the bargain-priced meal that is a staple for many islanders. For those on a budget, the Yami Yami combo is filling and tasty, with over a dozen choices for the main course. The regular menu is also very reasonably priced, offering generous portions of high quality and high end dishes that won't wallop your wallet.

This outlet also has a pleasant and slightly more spacious dining room than its predecessor, and a sushi bar. Made-to-order sushi combos start at $15 for a 21-piece platter. "Party Platters" are only made to go, which is useful for entertaining in your suite or for devouring outside while watching the sunset.

Beachside Dining

★ PASSIONS

Actually on Eagle Beach, **Passions** (J. E. Irausquin Blvd. 252, 297/587-0110, www.passions-restaurant-aruba.com, beach bar 10am-11pm daily, restaurant noon-4:30pm and 6pm-9:30pm daily, $22.50-51.50) is the only shoreside restaurant between Manchebo Beach and Palm Beach. It rates as one of the most romantic spots on Aruba's entire west coast, truly set apart from all the others. The location on the beachfront of the Amsterdam Manor Beach Resort lends a particular air of tranquil seclusion.

The menu is the epitome of Caribbean fusion, with an emphasis on fresh fish and seafood. Dishes range from chicken breast and a variety of fish and shellfish to a surf and turf of filet mignon and lobster tail. Innovative sauces and presentations have earned this restaurant a high rating, but the real attraction is the setting and singular ambience. For a special anniversary dinner or a marriage proposal, it is ideal. Mellow singers with a romantic repertoire are regularly featured.

Caribbean Fusion

CARAMBOLA

Martijn Haselhoef, well known to many island visitors for his years as maître d' at the famous Ventanas Del Mar, has realized his dream restaurant with **Carambola** (J. E. Irausquin Blvd. 64, 297/587-6695, www.carambola-aruba.com, 8:30am-10:30pm Tues.-Sun., $25-45). He and his wife, Sarmie, share a reputation for their exacting attention to detail and exceedingly friendly reception.

This restaurant is a particularly lovely spot in the Paradise Beach Villas. The decor is elegant, with a winding staircase to a cozy mezzanine level, perfect for large groups and special occasions.

A diverse menu of classic dishes is punctuated with the local touch. Try the peanut soup, which will surprise you, and the fresh fish. Diners have the option to customize their surf and turf: Filet mignon can be matched with a choice of shrimp, scallops, or lobster, and is priced accordingly. Martijn personally produces all of their fresh pastas daily. Another must-try is the CCC chowder (clams, crab, and conch) served in a bread bowl—delicious, and a meal by itself.

This venue is particularly known for gourmet holiday buffet brunches offered on Thanksgiving, Christmas, and Mother's Day, but also added on to the schedule at other times according to demand.

MADAME JANETTE

Beautiful gardens and excellent food have made **Madame Janette** (Cunucu Abao 37, 297/587-0184, www.madamejanette.com, 5:30pm-10pm daily, $28-45) a consistent favorite with longtime visitors. Regulars have their pet menu items, but the interesting seasonal menus and daily specials always attract interest.

Host and part-owner Ramon is an island expert on obtaining the freshest of exotic and fine-quality comestibles, while Karsten is the certified master chef. Together they founded the restaurant and garnered a loyal following almost immediately for their gourmet preparation and value. Even after more than a decade, reservations are still required days in advance to get a table.

Seafood specialties include bang bang shrimp, fresh catch of the day, Asian honey soy sea bass, and whole deboned yellowtail snapper, adding a fresh twist to standard dishes. Asparagus season, showcasing those large, white stalks highly valued by Dutch chefs, is from mid-April to late June and results in a continually changing menu of asparagus-based recipes.

Dress is casual and comfortable, and it is advisable to wear light clothing. It can get warm because of the windbreaks. Madame Janette also features appropriate nightly entertainment.

QUINTA DEL CARMEN

A short distance inland from the Super Food Plaza on the Bubali Road is the exceedingly charming **Quinta Del Carmen** (Bubali 119, 297/587-7200, www.quintadelcarmen.com, 5pm-10pm daily, $27-45), housed in lovingly maintained landmark building that was Aruba's first hospital. Originally built by one of the "founding families" as a weekend country cottage, it is named for their beloved daughter, Carmen. Dr. Horacio E. Oduber conducted the first organized medical clinic on the premises, and it was also deployed by the Arends Oil Company as the hospital for their employees.

Now it is home to a gourmet restaurant, from the same people who run Barefoot in Oranjestad. Dining is mostly al fresco in the rear courtyard. There are tables set up in the very elegant interior rooms, but they use no air-conditioning. The windows and doors are left open to allow the breezes to cool the rooms naturally. This works for the most part, but some may find it rather warm, particularly in the early fall, when winds die down.

Their interesting appetizer menu is reminiscent of traditional Aruban cuisine, including pumpkin and local seafood soups and cheese croquettes. There are a number of dishes categorized as "Grandma's Favorites," such as Sucade Lappen, a very Dutch beef stew, typical Dutch cookies and ice cream, and a chicken soup Aruban style (which means it has a little bit of everything).

SCREAMING EAGLE

Many veteran visitors will point to **Screaming Eagle** (J. E. Irausquin Blvd. 228, 297/587-8021, www.screaming-eagle.

net, 6pm-11pm daily, $27.50-59) when asked what is considered one of the great bastions of gourmet cuisine on Aruba. Chef-owner Erwin Husker has a reputation for his flair in the kitchen and for producing very interesting, inventive recipes with a distinctive touch. Prices are high, but food fanatics and dedicated patrons insist that the experience is worth it. The menu includes tender tournedos with a pepper sauce prepared fresh at your table, and crêpes suzette flambéed with cognac.

A fine wine cellar and a quirky but chic decor, along with the exquisite recipes, have proven a very successful formula. Here you can dine lounging on bed-like couches; but there is also normal table seating for the less adventurous.

Along with seasonal offerings, the fluid menu offers a chef's signature special of the day. Always extremely inventive and delicious, the special costs what one might pay for an entire meal. The Screaming Eagle is a spot for discerning diners with expansive budgets.

TULIP

Tulip (J. E. Irausquin Blvd. 240, 297/587-0110, www.tulip-restaurant-aruba.com, 7:30am-10am, noon-4pm, and 5pm-10:30pm Wed.-Mon., $12.50-44.95) is an appealing place to dine alfresco for breakfast, lunch, and dinner. In addition to its Caribbean cuisine, it is also a good place to find distinctly Dutch dishes.

Tables are scattered around the terrace and the very lovely gardens. The offerings include a giant pork schnitzel, *sate, bami* and *nasi goreng,* and Tulip signature *keshi yena,* the standard of stewed chicken smothered in gouda cheese.

The majority of the dinner menu focuses on international cuisine: fresh fish and shrimp, chateaubriand for two, and an assortment of steaks and chops with some Dutch and local side dishes.

Tulip is a bit north of La Quinta Resort and screened by shrubbery; the nondescript entrance is on J. E. Irausquin Boulevard and can be easy to miss.

MANCHEBO BEACH AREA

Within this cluster of resorts just on the edge of town are some excellent restaurants, and the clubhouse at the Divi Links contains two fine places—one somewhat pricey, the other comparatively moderate—with spectacular views of the golf course and surrounding area. Divi Resort management has had a definitive hand in advancing the quality of dining choices now available to those staying at the low-rise resorts.

Barbecue

HOLLYWOOD SMOKEHOUSE

The loyal clientele of **Hollywood Smokehouse** (J. E. Irausquin Blvd. 47, 297/280-9989, 5pm-10pm Mon.-Thurs., 12pm-10pm Fri.-Sat., $7-21) headed in droves to the eastern end of Aruba for the "low and slow" smoked brisket, ribs, chicken, and pulled pork. Now the restaurant has conveniently relocated within the Alhambra Shopping Bazaar, only a short stroll from all the Manchebo Beach resorts. A stint as a gourmet snack truck won them the number one spot in Aruba's annual Food Truck Championships for two years running.

Hollywood Smokehouse is known for huge portions; platters can be solo or combined and often come with enough food for two. Platters are served with three kinds of barbecue sauce, all very spicy. Pulled pork and brisket sandwiches are available. This is perhaps the only restaurant on Aruba serving beef brisket; if you miss your family's pot roast, try this excellent, tender, smoked version.

Located directly across from Fusion Wine Bar, Hollywood will often partner with them for rousing events in the mall's open-air gallery. Live bands and specialty drinks combined with delicious offerings from the grill have considerably livened up the evenings around this quiet area. See the Hollywood Smokehouse Facebook page for more updates.

Beachside Dining

ELEMENTS

A chic, contemporary eatery situated in the Bucuti & Tara Beach Resort, **Elements** (J. E. Irausquin Blvd. 55B, 297/583-1100, ext. 109, www.bucuti.com, bar 10am-12pm daily, lunch 12pm-5pm, dinner 5pm-10:30pm, lunch $8.50-20, dinner $18-35) maintains a strict adults-only policy. That can make it an elegant oasis among the mostly family-friendly timeshares that surround it, which are usually heavily populated with groups and children, particularly around holidays.

Elements offers an expansive deck right on the beach with lounges surrounded by curtains. The air-conditioned section features wall-to-ceiling windows for an unobstructed view of the sea and the most expansive beach on Aruba.

The menu reflects the tastes of a more discerning, health-conscious patronage, with a diverse selection of vegan, vegetarian, and gluten-free dishes. Lunch items are a bit higher-priced compared to nearby beachside eateries, but there is the advantage of dining without fractious children anywhere in the vicinity.

Even the most standard offerings of wraps and sandwiches have a gourmet touch. Smoked salmon for the salmon tempura salad is not lox, but the fresh and delicate variety. The Mediterranean bread bowl, a grilled chicken breast salad with kalamata olives and chickpeas, is served in a crusty edible bread bowl, as is the creamy seafood chowder.

The dinner menu is not quite as inventive with steaks, seafood, and pasta, plus some vegetarian dishes. There is also a special area set aside for a romantic dinner on the beach: only three tables for two, with two sittings per night at 6pm and 8:50pm. The romantic dinner includes complimentary wine or champagne and three courses with appealing choices; the service charge is included in the package.

MATTHEW'S BEACHSIDE RESTAURANT

Casa Del Mar Resort had seen a number of places come and go in this charming spot by the sea. With **Matthew's Beachside Restaurant** (J. E. Irausquin Blvd. 51, 297/588-7300, www.matthews-aruba.com, 7:30am-10pm daily, $24.95-45, all you can eat ribs $23, early bird $27.95, private beach dinner for two $150) it is a win-win situation. Owner Stefan Legger and his wife Milca built their reputation with the very popular Rumba, in town, but decided to move to the beach. Loyal patrons rave about the food, staff, and that very appealing sea view.

The restaurant features a nice, but fairly standard, à la carte menu. Emphasis is on grilled shellfish, snapper, grouper, and various sizes and cuts of steak. The specialty nights are the real attraction. The all-you-can-eat spareribs special on Tuesday is a big draw, with reservations recommended. Friday is the Italian menu with lots of pasta dishes but also osso buco for those who want something less basic. Matthew's also offers special private dinners for two on the beach, which include a complimentary bottle of champagne. These should be arranged well in advance.

RICARDO'S

Timeshare owners at Aruba Beach Club are thrilled by **Ricardo's** (Pool Deck of the Aruba Beach Club, 297/582-3000, breakfast 7:30am-11:30pm daily, lunch 1pm-5pm, and dinner 5pm-10pm, 2-for-1 happy hour 4pm-6pm daily, $15-23), which upgrades the standard lunch menu through exotic items, an attractive wine closet, and generous portions. The main restaurant is on a deck overlooking the beach, but there are also shaded tables around the Aruba Beach Club (ABC) pool deck. The hotel provides mellow, live entertainment during the evening happy hour. The "drink of the day" is two for one throughout the day.

When ABC owners want a casual dinner and don't feel like traveling outside the resort, they readily choose Ricardo's. Host Ricardo Chirino was the extremely popular maître d' of Matthew's Beachside Restaurant, as well as the emcee for its karaoke nights. He brings the same charm and energy to his own eatery.

His famous Karaoke Dance Parties are held on Thursday nights.

Monday and Wednesday evenings are all-you-can-eat rib and grouper nights, respectively, both priced at $23.95. The fish is fresh-caught, and the ribs are tender and tasty. Both are served with fries and salad.

International

★ CARTE BLANCHE

Within eight months of opening their doors in 2010, Chef Dennis and partner Glenn Bonset, the driving force behind **Carte Blanche** (within Bucuti & Tara Beach Resort, L. G. Smith Blvd. 55B, 297/586-3339, http://carteblanchearuba.com, 7pm-11pm Tues.-Sat., $95, wine pairing $79) saw this innovative restaurant shoot to number one on Internet review sites. It attained the rarified designation of a perfect score from over 100 reviewers. All describe the meal as one of the best they've ever had, anywhere, and find that the quality has stayed consistent. Expect a stunning dining experience, with dishes beautifully presented and superbly prepared.

Patrons are seated at a curved counter, allowing them to chat with Dennis and Glenn as they prepare the meal and beverages. Dennis is the sort of cook who keeps pots of herb plants by the stove to pluck and crush fresh into bubbling saucepans. Recipes can be adapted to fit any dietary needs (low fat, food allergies, no sugar), and substitutes are possible, if necessary. Be sure to call ahead to check the menu and inform them if you have any food issues.

The five-course Chef's Surprise is a prix fixe menu, without wine pairing or cocktails. Carte Blanche also offers an à la carte menu. Both are fluid, changing with the season and by the day.

Reservations should be made 3-4 months in advance at the very minimum via the form on the website. Guests are required to confirm when they arrive in Aruba, or the restaurant will take someone on standby. During high season (Dec.-Apr.), they are booked up to five months in advance.

THE FRENCH STEAKHOUSE

One of Aruba's most famous, upscale restaurants, **The French Steakhouse** (J. E. Irausquin Blvd. 55, 297/582-3444, www.manchebo.com, 5:30pm-10:30pm daily, $28-33,

one of the beautiful dishes at Carte Blanche

prix fixe early bird $35) was opened by legendary hotelier and restaurateur Ike Cohen. After almost five decades, it still maintains a loyal clientele who enjoy the company of a congenial waitstaff, many who have worked there almost as long as the place has been open. This doesn't mean that they are old, but that they were trained to provide the ultimate in courtesy and service, a holdover from times gone by.

Ike is gone, and chefs come and go, but the restaurant has maintained its standards, a charming garden atmosphere, and moderate pricing. Chef George Hoek, a regional culinary icon, now rules the kitchen. Classic dishes such as rack of lamb, giant T-bone steak, fresh fish, and shrimp scampi are the fare. The French Steakhouse also offers what it calls a five-course menu, which is still very nice despite coffee or tea being considered a course. It does include an appetizer, soup or salad, main course, and dessert with choices such as surf and turf with a lobster tail, which is excellent. Mellow nightly entertainment on the piano provides just the right touch.

MULLIGAN'S

The lower level of The Links's clubhouse is home to **Mulligan's** (J. E. Irausquin Blvd. 93, 297/523-5017, www.mulligansaruba.com, 6:30am-1am daily, $6.50-28), an open-air eatery with a spectacular panorama of the golf course and surroundings. This is a more casual golfer's lounge, with very early breakfast served before the first tee time of the day. The lunch and dinner menu is reasonable; sandwiches, burgers, and pizza all have a gourmet touch. Baguettes are priced equally to most local Dutch sandwich houses. The stone-oven pizza menu has some very interesting and original recipes. Try the Asian pizza with duck and cilantro-ginger sauce or a shawarma pizza with ground lamb, for something really different.

WINDOWS ON ARUBA

Elegantly prepared food and an equally elegant Louis XIV decor are the trademarks of **Windows on Aruba** (J. E. Irausquin Blvd. 93, top floor of the Divi Links Clubhouse, 297/523-5017, www.windowsonaruba.com, noon-2:30pm and 6pm-10:30pm Mon.-Sat., 10:30am-2pm Sun., $28-56, Sun. brunch $42.50), along with an absolutely breathtaking view. A great local jazz trio or guitarist Ivan Jansen entertains three nights a week.

One of their most popular offerings is the gourmet Sunday brunch with unlimited mimosas or champagne. Each dish is plated and made fresh. There is an endless choice of items, such as crêpes suzette, escargot, scallops, duck breast, and smoked salmon omelets.

The regular menu focuses on fine dining. Standard items like fresh grouper, prime steaks, and lobster tail are prepared with flair. This is one of the few venues to offer classic chateaubriand for two, a dish that is not readily available at most restaurants. To truly appreciate the restaurant's atmosphere and assets, go for an early dinner to catch the sunset.

Italian

ELLIOTI'S

The area has two connected Italian restaurants, outside of the all-inclusive resorts, with dual personalities but the same owners. **Ellioti's** (J. E. Irausquin Blvd. 59, 297/593-6919, 6pm-10pm Mon.-Sat., $18-37) is more elegant with a spacious, air-conditioned dining room, though most patrons prefer the outdoor deck. It is conveniently located at the juncture of the Costa Linda and Bucuti Resorts, an easy stroll from all the hotels.

For years, executive chef Jeffrey Elliot was the sous-chef of one of Aruba's most famous but now defunct Italian restaurants, Valentino's. He gets high marks from reviewers for his shrimp fra diablo and pasta sauces. Owner Adrianna is a lover of fine food, particularly Italian, and a most congenial host. Dedicated patrons are enthusiastic about the preparation, personable staff, and the pleasant atmosphere of the terrace.

PIZZA BOB'S PUB

The Bucuti side of the Ellioti's restaurant complex houses **Pizza Bob's Pub** (J. E. Irausquin

Blvd. 59, 297/588-9046, 11am-10pm daily, $17-25), which is more of a comfortable hangout than just a restaurant. Pizza Bob's has a tiny dining room (nice for lunch in the heat of the day), but the action is at the outdoor patio and bar, with a giant screen for sports events. Local singers provide mellow music nightly.

Popular for its thin-crust pizza, Pizza Bob's offers some restaurant specials as well as build-your-own options. A wee bit pricier than most island pizza joints, it does offer an early bird special 5pm-7pm, when a 14-inch pizza goes for the price of a 12-incher. The greatest asset of both Ellioti's and Pizza Bob's is their convenience to the low-rise resorts, and in a relatively quiet area, they provide nighttime entertainment.

PIZZA & MORE

The best prices anywhere on Aruba for great pizza and pasta are found at **Pizza & More** (Orange Mall; see Facebook page for more information) on the main shopping street in the center of town. It is a very small, simple place right next to Maggy's Emporium. This is where locals go when they want good pizza or pasta at a fraction of what is charged by spots close to the resort areas.

There are changing specials every day. The chef makes lasagna with meat, chicken, and seafood, but is also delightfully inventive with vegetarian versions as well, using mushrooms, eggplant, spinach, or whatever is fresh. The menu includes homemade hearty soups of the day served in a good-size bowl with crusty focaccia. There are no veal dishes or beef beyond meat sauce and meatballs. The main courses of chicken with mushrooms or curry shrimp or scampi, served with salad and pasta, are also tasty. The restaurant caters and delivers to your resort for no extra service charge.

Pizza & More is moving from Oranjestad to the Orange Mall in Eagle Beach. Check their Facebook page for more details.

★ TERRAZZA ITALIANA

The charming folks from Pizza & More in Eagle Beach took over the oceanfront terrace at Paradise Beach Villas to establish the delightful **Terrazza Italiana** (J. E. Irausquin Blvd 64, 297/561-1699, 5:30pm-9:30pm Mon.-Sat., $7-17). Maintaining very reasonable prices, they serve up fresh hearty soups, a variety of delicious pastas, and innovative lasagnas and risottos.

This formerly neglected terrace on the third floor of the resort offers incredible views of the shoreline. The breeze naturally cools the eatery, though sometimes too much—bring anything lightweight. The spot is as popular with islanders as it is with tourists for its excellent food and fantastic location. This is a great place to kick back with some sangria, snack on Italian tapas, and watch the sunset without walloping your wallet.

Seafood

RED FISH

An authentic Aruban fish shack can now be found within easy walking distance of the Manchebo and Eagle Beach resorts. **Red Fish** (Orange Mall, 297/280-6666, www.redfisharuba.com, 7pm-10pm Wed., $10.95-45) is named for the red snapper regularly featured on the menu. Owner Herby Merryweather is a veteran charter fishing captain, who founded the popular Driftwood restaurant and charter fishing boats in Oranjestad.

Red Fish features a diverse seafood menu, plus poultry and steaks for landlubbers. It is a place to go for fresh fish, usually grouper or snapper, prepared as moochi, which is the favorite Aruban style—cut into fish steaks and flash fried. The catch of the day platter comes in two sizes—half or full pound—with side dishes of sweet fried bananas, fries, and *funchi*. The expansive menu also has mixed shrimp and fish platters, whole snapper, and a lobster and filet mignon surf and turf.

This eatery has a rustic charm, even though its location on the highway does not particularly convey island ambience. Still, it is the best place within the area for fresh fish at the sort of prices locals pay to eat out.

Palm Beach, Malmok, and Noord

The question in Palm Beach is not "where will we find a nice place to eat?" but more, "how can we choose from so many options?" According to various review sites there are 86 listed restaurants within these limited borders. New eateries are opening regularly, and consequently a number are closing; it is almost like the turnover in New York City.

The main strip, J. E. Irausquin Boulevard, is packed with restaurants and shopping malls, which also contain several places to dine. It is a bustling center of neon and bright lights. Fusion and Italian cuisine tend to dominate. Not far inland, away from the heavily populated thoroughfare, are some very interesting places with more tranquil and genuine island atmosphere.

ARUBAN

★ THE OLD CUNUCU HOUSE

Housed in a landmark colonial farmhouse dating back over 150 years, **The Old Cunucu House** (Palm Beach 150, 297/586-1666, www.theoldcunucuhouse.com, 12pm-11pm daily, $16-35) is a charming bit of authentic Aruba. The menu features traditional island dishes along with elegant and very reasonably priced international favorites. The indoor dining room maintains the simple decor of an old-time Aruban home, while the outside terrace is surrounded by charming gardens.

It is located in a cul-de-sac at the end of a side road off the Noord-Palm Beach Road; a sign clearly marks the turnoff. The tranquility of the spot and the picturesque surroundings will make you feel you have been transported back in time, away from the hustle and bustle of the tourist scene. There is little to be heard but the rustling of the trees as you dine alfresco on the terrace.

Typical fare such as conch and *keshi yena* and Aruban side dishes of *pan bati*, banana *hasa* (plaintains), and *funchi* are the house specialty. The fresh catch of the day, served

Service Charge

First-time travelers beyond U.S. borders will likely be puzzled by the extra 10-15 percent service charge tacked on to their check, particularly if the waiter tells them emphatically that it is not a tip. In most cases, this is at least partially true; the servers usually do not receive the full amount. Most restaurants keep 7-10 percent of the service charge to cover breakage and laundering. They rarely keep it all, but they could (although they wouldn't keep employees for long, if that were the case).

The remainder is divided among all the restaurant staff including the kitchen help and maître 'd. This usually works by a point system, with the "higher-ups" getting the lion's share. The bus person who worked so hard to clear your plates and keep the water glasses filled doesn't see much of it.

For restaurant patrons unaccustomed to an added service charge, be aware that this is a common practice in Europe, Latin America, and other parts of the world. Some island eateries have eliminated it as a draw for customers. If it bothers you, check websites and menus, which will usually state clearly if a service charge is included, or ask before making reservations or being seated.

A good rule of thumb: If you have had highly satisfactory, friendly service, leave anywhere from half the service charge or more to reward their diligence. This too will go into a pot (or is supposed to) to be divided by the staff at the end of the night. Your individual servers still don't get it all, but they are most likely being paid minimum wage and depend highly on gratuities, so it will be appreciated.

This should also be kept in mind for tour guides, boat crews, and other employees of vacation activities and services.

a variety of ways including "Aruban-style" with Creole sauce, is outstanding, as is the succulent rosemary rack of lamb. One appetizer plate meant to be shared offers ample samplings of several favorite Aruban snacks: *pastechi*, calamari, fish cake, and meatballs.

CHEO'S CORNER

A small kiosk next to the carousel in Paseo Herencia Mall houses **Cheo's Corner** (J. E. Irausquin Blvd. 382-A, 297/562-9520, 8:30am-1pm Mon.-Sat., 5pm-midnight daily, $3-30). It sports a small collection of tables for open-air dining, and the enthusiasm of the charming owner/operator, Cheo, provides great ambience. He serves his native Venezuelan staple, arepas. There are few things more filling than an *arepa con queso* or *con* carne mechada (with stewed, shredded beef). *Arepas* are thick, fried cornmeal buns that are cut open and filled with cheese, meats, or chicken.

Also on the menu are equally filling *empanadas* (a sealed cornmeal pastry that is fried whole) and *chachapas* (a stuffed cornmeal flatbread, much like tortillas). They offer a reasonably priced list of coffees and exotic fruit *batidos* to accompany your early morning *arepas*. Those seeking a hearty dinner will find that the huge, family-sized mixed meat platters (beef, chicken, and sausage) with avocado and choice of fries or *arepas* will easily satisfy three to four people. Cheo's Corner is an inexpensive oasis of authentic regional food in Palm Beach.

ASIAN

AZIA

Confessions nightclub was converted into a chic, bistro/club combination and reopened in 2015 as **Azia** (J. E. Irausquin Blvd. 348, 297/586-0088, www.giannisgroup.com, 5pm-1am Sun.-Thurs., 5pm-3am Fri.-Sat., $12.50-19.50). The menu is Pan-Asian, featuring dishes from India, China, Japan, Korea, Mongolia, and Indonesia. The concept is smaller servings, tapas style, so you can snack lightly or order several different dishes from the extensive menu and fill up nicely. They have some interesting soups; a selection of sushi and dim sum, and distinctive seafood and meat presentations, all served in smaller portions.

Seating is indoor/outdoor. The al fresco section offers more couches and lounges and

Cheo's Corner is next to the carousel in Paseo Herencia Shopping Mall.

an open area for dancing. This is a good spot for late night snacking, exotic drinks, and socializing until the wee hours.

J.H. YEE'S ASIAN BISTRO

Located on the mezzanine of the South Beach Center, **J.H. Yee's Asian Bistro** (Palm Beach 55, 297/586-3888, 12pm-3pm and 6pm-11pm daily, $14.95-39) offers a diverse menu of Asian dishes from China, Thailand, Mongolia, and Japan, along with some very tempting lunch and early bird dinner specials. There are also two teppanyaki tables, which should be booked well in advance.

The restaurant is huge and the decor is elegant. Window seats offer a spectacular view of the Palm Beach strip and nightlife. J.H. Yee's serves up some of the best Asian cuisine in the Palm Beach area and is just a short stroll from all the major hotels. The amiable staff and service has earned it a dedicated repeat patronage.

BARBECUE

NEW WEI TAI

When passing **New Wei Tai** (Palm Beach 4, 297/586-8864, 11:30am-10pm Sun., $8) on the Palm Beach-Noord Road any Sunday, you will see islanders lined up for the weekly barbecue special. Huge portions of either ribs or chicken or a combo of the two are piled on an enormous heap of fried rice in takeaway containers, to be consumed on the beach. If you're not given enough barbecue sauce, ask them to put on a bit more.

Most customers usually get their food to go, but you can also have it plated to eat in the air-conditioned dining room for a nominal extra charge.

CHÉ BAR

For authentic Argentine BBQ and a friendly, family ambiance, nothing beats **Ché Bar** (J.E. Irausquin Blvd. 382-A, 297/586-1696, 6pm-11pm Tues.-Sun., $9.50-42.50), located on the northern sidewalk of Paseo Herencia Shopping Mall. Expect ample and tasty portions of pork ribs or Argentine beef steak prepared on a wood fire grill.

The house specialty is their home country's famous mixed meat platter. It can be ordered as a small sample platter with "bits and bites"of chorizo and blood sausage, rib eye steak, and chicken, or as a bountiful dinner for two with the addition of short ribs.

This cozy outdoor eatery has proven very popular. It has the ambiance of a European sidewalk café. The prices and the portions are appealing.

BEACHSIDE DINING

Well aware that a fantasy of most couples is to dine along the shore at sunset, every resort in Palm Beach has some sort of eatery fashioned to fully exploit the romantic setting. All have open-air casual restaurants along the stretch of boardwalk running the length of the strip, so guests need only put on a little beach cover (or not) during the day. Menus are typical lunch and snack bar fare: hamburgers, hot dogs, Caesar salads, chicken strips, with the occasional fillip of gourmet crab cakes or quesadillas, depending on the star rating of the resort. Most usually have a kids' menu and several will take orders and deliver lunch to your beach lounge chair.

For dinnertime they switch to more elaborate and diverse menus. A few also set up tables right along the water's edge for a "toes in the sand" experience. These are very popular, so reservations for the high-demand sunset hours should be made well in advance. Seating is usually quite limited and at a set hour (but not always) coordinated to sunset. Some offer a prix fixe three- or four-course meal.

A few resorts have the option of arranging a private dinner for two. Enjoy a dedicated waitstaff in a more secluded area of the beach for the most romantic experience imaginable. It is perfect for a marriage proposal or a special occasion (like being in Aruba). The arrangement should be made with your concierge immediately upon arrival or in advance by email.

Private Beachside Dining

For true romantics, a private dinner for two on a remote corner of the beach can be arranged at a few of the larger resorts. These usually include a choice of preset menus with a range of prices. Additional amenities, such as private photographers, flower arrangements, and personal musicians are available. This is the dream setting for a marriage proposal or just a special evening for eternal honeymooners. Main course choices usually include a surf and turf with lobster tail, rack of lamb, or fresh fish dish. Menus are fairly standard from one resort to the next.

The Hilton Caribbean calls its private affair **La Playa Torchlight Dinner** (J. E. Irausquin Blvd. 77, 297/586-6555, hiltonconcierge@depalmtours.com, $65 pp). This includes a three-course meal that must be ordered at least 24 hours in advance. Choices include surf and turf, fresh fish, and chicken. While there is no additional setup fee, there is a 15 percent service charge and 3 percent sales and health tax added.

Hyatt Regency wants to see you **Pampered in Paradise** (J. E. Irausquin Blvd. 85, 297/586-1234, www.aruba.hyatt.com, $96 pp) under a private *palapa*. It comes with a four-course meal, including appetizer, soup or salad, a choice from six gourmet main courses, and dessert. There is a 17 percent service charge for the personal waitstaff and an additional $50 sétup and breakdown fee for the private arrangement.

Marriott Resort (L. G. Smith Blvd. 101, 297/586-9000, www.marriott.com, $95-135 pp without drinks) offers three different menus. The $95 meal has four courses, and the others, for $115 or $135, serve five, although you could debate whether champagne sorbet is a course. There is a $25 setup fee and an additional service charge of 18 percent. These dinners require a dedicated service staff, so resorts usually set a limit of one or two tables nightly. It is strongly advised to arrange such a special evening via email before arriving on Aruba, or check with the hotel concierge for availability when you arrive. Seating times are at your convenience.

BUGALOE

At the end of the De Palm Pier you'll find **Bugaloe** (J. E. Irausquin Blvd. 79, 297/586-2233, www.bugaloe.com, 8:30am-midnight daily, $8.50-27), an extremely popular nightspot for tourists and locals. Whether you are seeking coffee and light breakfast, lunch, dinner, or late-night snacking, you will get it along with a view and ambience that are unmatched. The lively, friendly service makes returning patrons feel like friends.

Wraps dominate the menu and are available all day and night. There is also a diverse selection of finger foods that will pair perfectly with an exotic frozen drink or ice-cold beer. Main courses on the dinner menu are mostly fish and seafood, plus one steak platter. The star item is whole red snapper; on "Crazy Mondays" the chef comes back from the docks with a fresh catch and there is a $5 discount.

FOOTPRINTS

The Hyatt Regency Resort converts its patch of beach into a restaurant called **Footprints** (J. E. Irausquin Blvd. 77, 297/586-1234, www.aruba.hyatt.com, 6:30pm-10pm Fri.-Wed., $35-52 pp) Friday through Wednesday. The restaurant offers a small selection of dishes among three courses and requires guests to order an entrée and at least a starter or dessert. The Hyatt chefs are particularly inventive and attentive in designing their menus. The resort's culinary department has partnered with island growers to feature freshly harvested local ingredients in their dishes and established an herb garden on the hotel's grounds. There is a real effort to elevate the quality of the menus while injecting an authentic touch of Aruban cuisine beyond the standard hotel fare.

Emphasis is again on fresh, local fish, whether blackened, Cajun style, or seared with stir-fried fresh vegetables. The menu also has a seafood pepper pot with shrimp, scallops, mussels, clams, and Aruban *funchi* (the standard island accompaniment to seafood). Dessert choices are very tempting: passion fruit crème brûlée, Aruban coconut cream cake, or tres leches cake.

Only five tables are available, and reservations are recommended well in advance.

PELICAN NEST

At the north end of the beach, between the Playa Linda and Holiday Inn, **Pelican Nest** (Pelican Pier, 297/586-2259, www.pelican-aruba.com, 11am-11pm Tues.-Sun., $19.50-38) features an open seafood grill for healthy dining. The ceviche is rated by some as the best on the island. The restaurant generally gets low marks on service, but the location is so pretty, you might just want to order another glass of wine and enjoy it.

PURE OCEAN

Formerly the Sunset Beach Bistro, **Pure Ocean** (J. E. Irausquin Blvd. 75, 297/586-6066, www.sunsetbeachbistro.com, 7am-11am and 5pm-11pm daily, $20-43) at the Divi Phoenix Resort is famous as the first restaurant in Palm Beach to offer dining right at the water's edge. There are a limited number of tables just at the shoreline, but ample seating elsewhere on the beach and in the open-air covered terrace looking out on the sea. Reserve well in advance for a shoreside table.

A longtime standby with veteran visitors for more than 15 years, the restaurant reopened in early 2013 with a refreshed menu of fusion cuisine. Fresh local fish is the focus. The fish is grilled with Aruban Creole sauce and served on a bed of couscous, or it comes with coconut curry sauce. For landlubbers, there are plain steaks and a sprinkling of Italian dishes, such as osso buco, chicken saltimbocca, and rigatoni and meatballs.

SIMPLY FISH

At the far northern end of Palm Beach at the Marriott Resort, **Simply Fish** (L. G. Smith Blvd. 101, 297/520-6600, www.marriott.com, 6:30pm-10:30pm daily, $38-60) is a venue that offers an à la carte menu as opposed to prix fixe.

This is one of the most expensive of the beachfront eateries, with a menu leaning largely to standard offerings from northern waters, such as tuna, sea bass, and halibut, instead of fresh local Caribbean fish. Lobster tail, on its own or paired with filet mignon, is typical of the menu. The surroundings are lovely, and the staff is very friendly, accommodating.

INTERNATIONAL

BARNEY'S

Those who like discovering a comfortable neighborhood hangout for a mature crowd, while at the same time a fun place for families, will really enjoy **Barney's** (Palm Beach 21A, 297/586-5420, www.barneysaruba.com, 5pm-10pm Tues.-Sat., $9.50-29.50). Owners Ron and Elina have a very congenial division of labor: He loves being bartender while she sees to it that everyone is well satisfied with their meal. Patrons praise their spicy firecracker shrimp and mushrooms stuffed with escargot. They offer a diverse menu, and chef Hans has a deft touch in the kitchen. Try the smoked trout filet for a real gourmet treat.

Four nights a week, the place is busy with themed specials: Tuesday is Schnitzel Night, with a choice of chicken or pork schnitzel prepared any of five ways; Thursday features unlimited ribs; and Saturday is limitless (until they run out) rib eye steak. On Friday evenings they host a fun karaoke party.

TASTE OF BELGIUM

Popular with fashionable islanders, **Taste of Belgium** (Palm Beach Plaza, L. G. Smith Blvd. 95, www.tasteofbelgium.aw, 297/586-6388, 8am-midnight daily, $7.50-42.50) sports contemporary decor while exuding old-world charm. The restaurant centers around the fireplace lounge, where friends gather for conversation, wine, and snacks or Italian lattes and pastries.

Taste of Belgium offers a choice of Belgian

continental, full English, or full American breakfasts, including fresh-squeezed orange juice. European baguettes and wraps are typical lunch fare, while the extensive dinner menu has a distinctly Belgian touch. Choices range from vegetarian herbed pasta to *slibtong* in *citroenboter* (sole meunière). Main courses are always accompanied by the famous *frites,* the best fries you will ever have, made a special, secret way. Some come just to order the fries, with a choice of all sorts of sauces; they're perfect with some Belgian beer.

On Sundays, Taste of Belgium features a brunch menu for a fixed price that allows you to order a limitless number of gourmet treats from 11am until 2:30pm. Advance reservations are required, as it is very popular with islanders.

TWO FOOLS AND A BULL

Described as a "gourmet studio," **Two Fools and a Bull** (Palm Beach 17, 297/586-7177, www.2foolsandabull.com, 7pm-11pm Mon.-Fri., $100), with its partners Fred Wanders and Paul Faas (aka Pablo Diablo) features an intimate chef's table concept, allowing patrons to enjoy their meal preparation as entertainment.

The beautifully renovated classic landmark house is only a short distance up the Palm Beach-Noord Road from the Sasaki highway. It provides an intimate environment for the curving counter surrounding the chef and host. With only 16 patrons at a seating, everyone is made to feel like a guest, rather than a customer. Start the night with a welcome drink and a "meet and greet." If you didn't come for dinner with some friends, by the end of the evening you will have a roomful.

Like Carte Blanche, there is a flat rate for the five-course meal. The menu changes daily with their whims and what is fresh. A typical meal could include as appetizers terrine of fois gras, veal with apples and pickles, rouleaux of Cornish hen stuffed with sweetbreads, seafood symphony with lobster sauce, to name only a few. Chef Fred made the name of some of Aruba's top gourmet kitchens and has a wide repertoire. The main course is always three meat cuts grilled on the fire wall. A gourmet dessert concludes this delightfully decadent meal.

Suggested wine pairings are posted for each course. After less than a year, Two Fools became the number two rated restaurant on Aruba. It continues to receive rave reviews.

LA VISTA

If you're a super hearty-eater with a taste for buffets, **La Vista** (Marriott Resort, L. G. Smith Blvd. 101, 297/520-6601, 5:30pm-10:30pm daily, Sunday Brunch 10:30am-2:30pm, $40-65) offers an excellent value for the quality and diversity of dishes offered. While it may seem that $40 is high for a buffet, by comparing the quality and prices of many restaurants on Aruba, this is a good value. Wednesdays cost more because they include unlimited king crab and shrimp, and Saturdays cost more because they include unlimited baked, whole Caribbean lobsters. Tuesday (italian) and Sunday (International) are the least expensive nights. Mondays feature a live folkloric show and Thursdays feature a live carnival show, with regional Aruban cuisine to match the entertainment. Friday evening is all about the grill, including prime rib, prawns, and crab claws. There is always Häagen-Dazs ice cream at the sundae station of the dessert bar, an example of the attention to quality in everything offered.

Expect casual dining and very clean surroundings. La Vista also has a terrace adjacent to the beach, and walls of windows for watching the sunset. The restaurant is known for its special holiday buffet brunches, and offers an à la carte menu. One drawback: drinks are rather overpriced, even nonalcoholic ones. They do have a 50% discounted Happy Hour daily from 5pm-7pm.

PAPIAMENTO

Considered one of the most romantic restaurants on Aruba, **Papiamento** (Washington 61, 297/594-5504, 6pm-9:30pm Mon.-Sat., www.papiamentoaruba.com, $19.50-58) is housed in a beautifully restored landmark country manor built in 1886. Most of the dining is outdoors among the lush gardens surrounding a swimming pool, though there are a few tables within the elegant interior. If you are perhaps planning a marriage proposal, Papiamento offers the perfect romantic atmosphere.

The Ellis family is famous on Aruba for their gourmet savvy. This is one of the foremost eateries to offer a very unique and delicious version of Keshi Yena. Generally, the emphasis is on very fine quality steaks and seafood. Their seafood fishes are especially innovative in their flavoring and preparation. Try the Cazuela, a fusion of shrimp and rock lobster in an Aruban coconut milk chowder, or the Aruban Bouillabaisse.

They also offer several surf and turf dishes served sizzling on a lava stone, lightly seasoned and served with tasty dipping sauces. The quality of the beef is superb and this technique is especially suited to produce moist, tender shrimp, fish, and lobster.

As this restaurant is very popular with veteran visitors, reservations are strongly recommended.

FRENCH

★ AMUSE BISTRO

For elegant gourmet dining in Palm Beach, few restaurants can match **Amuse Bistro** (J. E. Irausquin Blvd. 87, 297/586-9949, www.amusearuba.com, 5:30pm-10:30pm daily, $22.50-28.50) for creative cooking and value. Patrick is a classically trained chef with an impressive résumé. His attention to detail and stringent standards of preparation are evident in the quality of the food; he even churns his own, very rich, ice cream. Dishes are made to order, so be prepared for a leisurely meal. Despite this, devoted fans report dining here several times during their one-week stay.

The restaurant is attractively laid out in the arcade of shops and eateries that front Playa Linda Resort. Dining is alfresco, and there are some cozy couches for romantic dinners. One unique and practical amenity is the option to order main courses full size or a half plate as an appetizer, and vice versa. It allows diners to have more of what they consider a good thing, or try a bit of this and that. A "half plate" is $10 less than a regular main course price.

Grilled scallops with ginger sauce and the goat cheese salad are highly recommended. Be sure to save room for dessert, as the pineapple carpaccio with cinnamon ice cream is to die for. The basic menu is rotated three times a year to offer variety in addition to the daily specials.

THE CRÊPE BAR

If you're planning to visit the Butterfly Farm, allow an extra hour to enjoy a delicious breakfast or brunch with Anton, owner of **The Crêpe Bar** (J. E. Irausquin Blvd z/n, 297/586-6926, www.thecrepebararuba.com, 7:30am-7pm daily, $6-9), which is attached to the farm. If you are out jogging or walking along the Palm/Eagle Beach road, it provides an excellent place to relax and enjoy a reasonably priced meal. Anton, originally from Montreal, is passionate about his made-to-order crepes. Choose sweet or savory, and it will be cooked up fresh. He has put together a number of crepe specials that are very appealing, but he is always willing to customize your dish. Alternatively, you can order bagels with cream cheese and lox.

This is open-air dining in the charming gardens of the farm and an easy stroll from the Palm Beach resorts. It offers a delightful alternative to hotel breakfasts.

PAPILLON

A bastion of classic French cuisine on Aruba, **Papillon** (J. E. Irausquin Blvd 548A, 297/586-5400, www.papillon.com, 5pm-10:30pm daily, $26-43) is a cozy outdoor eatery tucked away at the rear of The Village Mall across from the Hilton Caribbean Resort. The decor recreates a rustic countryside inn. There are very few indoor tables, but since the interior is not air-conditioned, dining under the awning is preferable.

An interesting selection of hot and cold starters includes lobster bisque and a creamy roast pepper soup along with a goat cheese and nut salad. Enjoy entrées such as classic duck à l'orange, various cuts of steak with béarnaise sauce, and local and Atlantic fish. Service can be slow; be prepared for an evening of leisurely dining.

INDIAN

TANDOOR INDIAN GRILL HOUSE

A contribution from another expatriate group on Aruba is **Tandoor Indian Grill House** (South Beach Center, 297/586-0944, www.tandooraruba.com, 6pm-10:30pm Mon.-Fri., noon-3pm and 6pm-10:30pm Sat.-Sun., $16-24, weekend lunch buffet $22), the place for authentic East Indian cuisine. Dishes are prepared in a tandoor, a cylindrical clay oven, for characteristic taste and tenderness. Overall, the food is very reasonably priced.

The lunch buffet on Saturday and Sunday provides an excellent opportunity to sample a variety of flavors and textures. The assortment includes curried shrimp, chicken, chickpeas, tandoori chicken, saffron vermicelli, and a batch of vegetarian dishes along with a very simple salad bar. It is worth trying every dish to understand the range and appeal of Indian cooking.

The regular menu is extensive, a dozen different ways of preparing lamb, chicken, or fish, offered in degrees of spiciness from extremely mild to murderously hot. The buffet is generally on the mild side. It can be spiced up with some green chili sauce and other garnishes on the salad bar, which will make you sweat. Sample the purple *ras golla* (cottage cheese balls cooked in sugar syrup) for dessert. They are very sweet, an interesting surprise that puts out the fire.

ITALIAN

Palm Beach hosts a staggering number of Italian restaurants for such a small area. Local restaurateurs are quite convinced that vacationers from the United States can't survive a week without at least one Italian dinner and are consistently proven correct, so they offer plenty of options.

Several Italian restaurants are within the malls on J. E. Irausquin Boulevard or adjacent, with more in the resorts. Most are uniformly overpriced for pasta and carry the standard Italian dishes on their menus. Some feature a unique, regional pasta specialty prepared for two or more: A sauce incorporating vodka, tomatoes, and seasoning is tossed and flamed with pasta inside a giant parmesan cheese wheel imported from Italy. This is done at your table and quite a show.

ANNA MARIA'S

Authentic southern Italian cuisine prepared with enthusiasm is the fare at **Anna Maria's** (Kamay 25-M, 297/586-2833, www.annamariasaruba.com, 6pm-10pm Mon.-Sat., $17-46), a labor of love by the chef/owners, Anna Maria and her husband Christian. He is native-born Aruban with Sicilian grandparents and describes his wife as "pure Napolitano."

Sharing their enthusiasm for "Italiano Autentico" cuisine became an enterprise after first feeding friends. It started with just a few tables on the charming back patio of their impressive home. In a few years it has grown to include accommodating waitstaff and a continually expanding menu.

Hot and cold appetizers include a tasty *chupe de camarones,* a Peruvian shrimp chowder, reflecting Christian's direct parentage. Main courses are based mostly on pasta dishes, starting with fettuccine Alfredo to linguini al frutti di mare. Everything is made to order, so patrons relax and enjoy the surroundings while waiting for their food. You can also watch the hosts puttering around in their kitchen.

Anna Maria's is located in a residential area off the Avenida Frans Figaroa, heading north past the commercial area around the Santa Ana Church. Turn left just before Ng's market and they are a short distance down the road.

SOLE MARE

One of the longest established Italian restaurants on Aruba is **Sole Mare** (Palm Beach 23, 297/586-0077, 5:30pm-11pm daily, $15-45). It has a loyal clientele and a menu that sports a wide assortment of traditional dishes, including the famous "pasta in parmesan" dish prepared tableside.

Portions are extremely generous. They do an excellent and reasonably priced Ossobuco, one of their house specialties. The Branzino Al Sale is also a favorite. The entire fish is baked en croute with a salt breading, and then filleted at your table. They offer a large selection of pastas with various sauces, but are very accommodating about adjusting their menu standards to suit patrons' personal preferences.

SEAFOOD

WHACKY WAHOO'S

Great fresh fish and a feeling of visiting with friends has made **Whacky Wahoo's** (Palm Beach 33B, 297/586-7333, http://wackywahoo.com, 5:30pm-10pm Mon.-Sat., $22-28.50) a top-rated restaurant on Aruba. Chef and owner Harald is a good friend to all the fisherfolk and an enthusiastic fisherman. This guarantees fresh fish on the table every day for his customers. A best bet in Palm Beach for fish lovers, the main course is usually caught that morning and on your plate the same day.

Harald was a master chef-in-training with Cunard Lines when he met lovely Arubiana Roxy while he was exploring Aruba during shore leave. Both the charms of the lady and Aruba brought him back. He established the reputations of a number of island restaurants before finally opening his own place, the Hadicurari fish center. It became a very popular hangout on the beach for tourists and local anglers. Circumstances have brought him to the present location, about a 15-minute walk inland on the Noord-Palm Beach Road.

The catch of the day might be two or three different kinds of fish listed on a chalkboard, served a choice of five different ways. Whacky Wahoo's is about fish and seafood, and Harald has devised some very interesting and diverse recipes for preparing shrimp and conch. Good-quality steak and duck with very tasty sauces are options for landlubbers. There are also some really tempting desserts; try the fresh baked brownies. The dining room has limited space, and reservations are strongly recommended.

STEAK HOUSES

TEXAS DE BRAZIL

Aruba's bastion of Brazilian cuisine is the *rodízio steakhouse* **Texas de Brazil** (J. E. Irausquin Blvd. 382, 297/586-4686, www.texasdebrazil.com, 6pm-10:30pm Mon.-Sat., 5pm-10:30pm Sun., $45, $30 for salad bar only). Patrons control the service, with a gadget that displays a "red light" or "green light." Once you have indicated you are finished with the salad bar and are ready for the main course, congenial waiters visit your table in a continual stream offering various cuts of beef, chicken, pork, and lamb, cooked over an open wood fire and served on giant swords. Diners give the nod or say "no" to each dish; this will continue endlessly until you say "uncle."

The continually changing salad bar features distinctive hot dishes such as seafood thermador and saffron rice, which are good alternatives to the parade of meats. Everything is quite tasty and satisfying, with some original and unique marinated salad items and a delicious seafood chowder. Dessert is not included, but who has room? The cost is nearly what most Aruban steakhouses charge for only a main course, so if you are really hungry, this is a great deal.

Located on the second level of La Hacienda Mall, it also has an elegant cocktail lounge on one side with a lovely view. The dining room is across the way, divided by an open-air courtyard.

North Coast

ITALIAN

LA TRATTORIA EL FARO BLANCO

Next to the lighthouse at the top of California point is **La Trattoria El Faro Blanco** (California Lighthouse z/n, 297/586-0786, www.aruba-latrattoria.com, 9am-11pm daily, mini menu 3pm-6pm daily, $16-48), a misnomer for those who understand the true meaning of trattoria, as it is anything but. An utterly delightful arrangement of open-air terraces looks out on the remarkable vista of the entire northwestern shore of Aruba. One can see to nearly Oranjestad and far inland. The staff is extremely congenial. There are mixed reviews on the food, from excellent to mediocre and overpriced, but the location and atmosphere are unmatched.

Santa Cruz, Paradera, and Piedra Plat

While you are touring in Aruba's outback, a number of small, local snack shops can be found or a surprising quantity of international fast-food franchises for a quick lunch. They usually feature an abundance of fried foods, stews, and barbecue with fries and rice, and some lettuce and tomato passing for a salad, but they are quite inexpensive and offer great value for the money. More important sights, such as Arikok National Park, Natural Bridge, and Casibari Rock Formation, have places that will sell you a cold drink and a *pastechi* or sandwich.

ARUBAN

DON PINCHO

Rowigini Center in Santa Cruz is home to **Don Pincho** (Papillon 53, 297/585-8459, 10:30am-10pm daily, $8-15), a favorite among the residents for island food and entertainment. Just south of the Santa Cruz business district, it offers generous, bargain-priced specials on BBQ and traditional island dishes. This is how Arubans like to eat and relax.

URATAKA CENTER

On the road to Arikok National Park, **Urataka Center** (Urataka 12, 597/585-5212, 11am-4pm daily, $2-14) is a popular, local hangout, replete with pool table and domino tables for tournaments. They tout that they serve "the best pizza," but that is because pizzerias are rare for that area.

The real gems on their menu are local favorites. This is a good place to try island standards off the grill, such as a chicken wing "basket," a heaping helping of crispy, flash-fried wings without breading, or barbecue ribs. More substantial platters are pork chops or grilled chicken "a la plancha," served on a wooden plank, which is less expensive than pizza.

It gets busy on the weekends. It is a good place to stop for a cold beer and an authentic slice of island life.

CAFÉS

ARIKOK PARK COFFEE SHOP

After hiking around the park for a couple of hours, you will find that the simple fare on the terrace of the **Arikok Park Coffee Shop** (visitor center, main entrance Arikok National Park, 297/585-5200, 8am-4pm daily, $1.50-2.50) tastes just about right. It is a tiny little place offering local snacks, *pastechis*, croquettes, hot dogs, and tuna sandwiches. The seating on the deck, where you can relax with a light meal, provides an absolutely gorgeous view of the park.

HUCHADA

One of Aruba's favorite stops for fresh breads, cakes, and snacks is **Huchada** (Santa Cruz 328, 297/585-8302, 6am-8pm Mon.-Sat., $3-4). The specialty is stuffed sandwiches on a choice of fresh-baked rolls, often still warm from the oven. The basics include ham and cheese and tuna salad, with some interesting combinations. Try one or two items from their great assortment of cakes, pastries, and cookies, boxed up to take back to the room. Essentially a bakery, Huchada has a few tables to sit and take a break.

San Nicolas, Savaneta, and Pos Chiquito

Aruba's eastern and southern shores have yet to be greatly developed for tourism, though there is much potential and it will come. Most places to dine are aimed and priced to islanders (with some notable exceptions) and will be very busy with a local crowd around lunchtime or on weekends.

INTERNATIONAL

B-55

The terraced restaurant on a hill called **B-55** (Balashi 55, 297/585-2111, b55-aruba@yahoo.com, 10:30am-10pm daily, $16.80-22.50) boasts a spectacular vista of Aruba's south side and midlands. B-55 gets rave reviews from those who have stumbled upon it in their travels, giving it a "5 out of 5" rating. It's ideally located to be breezy and comfortable; you won't feel bothered by insects or tropical heat, even at the lunch hour.

Popular with islanders, it is known for good food and a very diverse menu, with excellent daily specials. Recommended choices are the "famous seafood soup" and the barbecue combo; portions are very generous. Dinners come loaded with side dishes, and fresh fish is served in a choice of seven intriguing styles. They now have a stone pizza oven, and their pizzas for two are reasonably priced and accompanied by curry coleslaw. The wine list, sold by the bottle, is exceptionally reasonable.

CHARLIE'S BAR

No trip to San Nicolas is complete without a stop at the legendary **Charlie's Bar** (B v/d Veen Zeppenfeldstraat 56, 297/584-5806, http://charliesbararuba.com, 11:30am-9:30pm Sun.-Thurs., 11:30am-10pm Fri.-Sat., $16-30), if only for a glimpse of the highly idiosyncratic decor. It features possibly the largest collection of miscellaneous memorabilia squeezed into one spot, even the bathroom walls are filled with curiosities and original art.

Charlie's has always been famous for their fresh shrimp, steamed or scampi, and steak sandwiches. Dishes are served with "Honeymoon Sauce" by chef Rosalba, which they also sell by the jar.

The bar is named for its founder, the late Charlie Brouns II, an island character if there ever was one. He left an indelible mark on San Nicolas and its people, and his son keeps his memory alive in this famous local hangout, where tourists are always warmly welcomed.

Becoming a tourist attraction has spiked the prices considerably. Located in the heart of Aruba's red light district, Charlie's Bar is more appealing to visit in the daytime for a snack and drink, especially if you're traveling with a family.

CARIBBEAN FUSION

COSTA RIBA

Kamini Kurvink is an expatriate from Trinidad who has realized her dream by taking over **Costa Riba** (Christoffelbergweg 9, San Nicolas, 297/564-2303, noon-9pm Sun.-Thurs., noon-11pm Fri.-Sat., $10.25-20), an interesting place that can't be missed on the way to The Colony and Baby Beach. The menu is diverse and regional with East Indian elements that reflect her background. The menu's artwork also reflects Kamini's good nature and philosophy; pages are filled with humorous homilies about the pleasures of fine food and drink.

A varied menu leans heavily toward seafood dishes, many of them curried. Kamini prepares excellent whole fresh snapper. For a touch of the exotic, check out the *cabrito* (goat) stew wrapped in Indian flatbread or other roti, which comes with pumpkin, *chana* (an Indian chickpea garnish), and curried potato.

Kamini has been the chef-proprietor since 2011, and her enthusiasm lends a decidedly personal touch. She has garnered a dedicated following who particularly appreciate her warm, welcoming presence in addition to what have been described as "the best chicken wings EVAH!"

FLYING FISHBONE

If you are searching for the most romantic dining experience possible, **Flying Fishbone** (Savaneta 344, 297/584-2906, www.flyingfishbone.com, 5pm-11pm daily, $30-50) is a top choice for many visitors to Aruba. The restaurant was the first to establish the toes-in-the-sand concept, and it has the perfect secluded cove to make it work.

The menu has a nice diversity, from refreshing gazpacho and shrimp tempura to gourmet seafood and prime steaks. It offers a delectable lobster thermidor. Everything is beautifully presented and delicious, though portions tend to be small.

Sunset is considered the optimal time to fully experience the locale; reservations are recommended well ahead for that time slot. One drawback, cab fare from major hotel areas is almost equal the price of a dinner, and actually the same as a compact car rental for the day. If you are planning to rent a car, take advantage of having the transport and reserve that night for an out-of-the-way place like Flying Fishbone. It isn't hard to find, just keep following the IA, which parallels the sea; signs will indicate where to turn right.

GENERAL STORE CAFÉ

The pleasant eatery at **General Store Café** (Savaneta 225E, 297/584-1189, 10:30am-2:30pm Mon.-Sat., $7.80-8.50) behind the hardware and home center of the same name will surprise first-time visitors. General Store Café was originally an independent eatery set up with a stylish, homey interior. The hardware store took it over to provide a congenial lunch place for its employees, but welcomes the public. Many come from around the neighborhood to enjoy the ambience and take advantage of the bargain menu.

Food service is cafeteria style, with everything served in large takeaway foam containers. The menu is posted at the beginning of the week with menu items changing daily: Each day there is a choice of four new main courses and a soup. Options can be anything from fresh wahoo with white wine, beef or vegetable lasagna, or breaded shrimp. There is always some sort of *stoba,* a dish that is authentically Aruban. All main courses are served with mashed potatoes, vegetables, and plantains. If it's too heavy on the carbohydrates, they will gladly substitute more steamed vegetables.

Cold options include attractive, creative salads, wraps, and hero sandwiches. The staff is extremely friendly and accommodating. It is a very nice place to relax and get out of the heat after a long morning of touring.

The hardware store is on the highway, bordered by a dirt road. Turn inland at that road and find the restaurant directly behind.

RUM REEF BAR

Located next to JADS Dive Shop, **Rum Reef Bar** (Seroe Colorado, 297/584-2569, 11:30am-6pm daily, $4-16) offers a lovely view overlooking the expanse of Aruba's southeastern point. The open-air terraced eatery is the only one next to Baby Beach. The menu is simple: sandwiches, hamburgers, hot dogs, platters of chicken wings, and *sate* or grouper Aruban-style with Creole sauce.

JP, the owner of both JADS and Rum Reef, fancies himself something of a mixologist. If you are in the mood to relax and linger over an exotic frozen concoction, put yourself into his capable and creative hands. The ambiance is extremely congenial; you'll arrive a patron and depart as a friend.

SEAFOOD

★ MARINA PIRATA

One of Aruba's original "local" fish restaurants, **Marina Pirata** (Spaanslagoenweg 4, Pos Chiquito, 297/585-7150, 6pm-10pm daily, $20-40) offers that dining-on-a-fishing-dock charm, with a bit more elegance. Twinkling lights and hurricane lamps have prompted patrons to describe the atmosphere as "magical." A longtime favorite of veteran visitors, it is famed for its fresh fish and prompt, amiable service. This is where they brought Gloria Estefan for dinner when she wanted to eat somewhere "authentic." Kids love feeding the fish that come right up to the dock in large schools, attracted to underwater lights.

Marina Pirata offers a half dozen ways to sample the fresh catch of the day. It is a great place for whole red snapper and fresh Caribbean lobster. The signature dish is the Spaans Lagoen special, a seafood mix. It is prepared à la *coquille St. Jacques* in a creamy sauce ringed with cheese-crusted mashed potatoes.

Driving to Marina Pirata can be confusing because the road seems to end at nothing. The restaurant is right on the water, out of sight, down some steps leading to the shore. It is clearly marked with an archway and sign, but you can't see the proper entrance from street level.

★ ZEEROVER

Fish fanatics and shrimp lovers cannot miss a meal at **Zeerover** (Savaneta 270, 297/592-9080, 11:30am-8pm daily, kitchen closed Mon. but bar is open, $8-15). This is hands-down the best place on the island for fish. Since it's right on a dock where a number of fishing boats are moored, don't be surprised to see your meal carried in fresh while you wait to order. Patrons stand on line at one window to order food and a second window to order drinks.

The menu is simple: whatever fish is on hand and fresh shrimp. The attendant taking your order will show you what they have, and you pick out the fish filet, steak, or whole fish of your choice: It could be grouper, wahoo, marlin, snapper, etc.. Shrimp can be medium or huge, or a bit of both. The selection is then weighed and the check is tallied.

Pick out a table, either in the shade of the terrace or out on the dock. Enjoy a cold beer while you wait, which won't be too long. Your entire order is combined in a single basket, family-style, with some plastic plates and forks (some regulars bring their own sturdier silverware). Most end up eating with their fingers, so sinks with soap and towels are distributed around the restaurant. There is always one conveniently close by.

Fish and shrimp are flash-fried; there is no other option for preparation. It is consistently excellent and fresh. Try the papaya pica relish for some zing. It is a locally produced relish that is very spicy; just a little goes a long way, but really enhances the fish.

Zeerover is popular mostly as a lunch place. Dinner is a hit-and-miss proposition: Food is served only as long as fresh fish is available. It is not unheard of for them to close the kitchen by 5pm because they have run out of fish. Even with dinner reservations, it is advised to call and confirm.

On an island of elegant restaurants, Zeerover is an authentic Caribbean fish shack, though quite a bit more comfortable and elaborate. Popular with the seafaring crowd and church-goers, it's mobbed on Sundays and the wait to order can be an hour or more. Service is fine once the order is in, but choose a weekday if you don't care to stand in line for so long.

Entertainment and Events

Look for ★ to find recommended entertainment and events.

Highlights

★ **Bugaloe:** Bugaloe's authentic island atmosphere is a favorite with all ages. Located out on the water, Bugaloe features great bands and a popular dance floor (page 128).

★ **Señor Frog's:** This Mexican restaurant becomes a fun singles' club late at night. It remains one of the best places in Aruba for young people to connect (page 130).

★ **Carnival:** The Carnival celebration dominates the island from the first Saturday after New Year's Day until Ash Wednesday, with a seemingly endless lineup of parades, musical events, beauty pageants, and themed street parties (page 135).

★ **Himno y Bandera Day and International Half Marathon:** Aruba's National Day, March 18, encompasses elegant protocol events, a joyous celebration of national identity and pride, and a half marathon (page 135).

★ **May Day:** On the first day of May, the Royal Dutch Marines turn their camp into a theme park for a day. There's music and food, as well as aerial and sea-based demonstrations of mock battle (page 136).

★ **Soul Beach Music Festival:** Top R&B singers and big-name comedians converge in Aruba for Memorial Day weekend, with five days of concerts, media events, and parties (page 136).

★ **Aruba Hi-Winds Pro-Am:** For over 25 years Aruba has been hosting the most renowned Pro-Am windsurfing and kitesurfing competitions in the world (page 137).

★ **Caribbean Sea Jazz Festival:** The last weekend in September is a time for interpretive music under the stars. Local and international jazz, innovative art, and gourmet food are all served up at bargain prices (page 138).

★ ***The Nutcracker:*** The immortal ballet has become a holiday tradition in Aruba thanks to famed former Bolshoi and New York City Ballet star Leonid Kozlov (page 139).

★ **New Year's Eve:** Island-wide pyrotechnics start the new year with the biggest bang heard anywhere (page 140).

Whether you're into music, art, culture, or comedy, Aruba will have something exceptional for you.

Top Latin, jazz, soul, and classic rock groups, including superstars such as Marc Anthony, Chaka Khan, Alicia Keys, and Crosby, Stills, and Nash, can all be found in concert at Aruba's many fine venues, and at ticket prices much lower than in the United States. Free shows are featured at most busy entertainment centers nightly, and scores of special events associated with national holidays and weekly festivals amuse and enlighten while sharing traditional island culture with visitors.

Almost all the large hotels have in-house casinos and cozy lounges or sport bars for relaxing and socializing after dinner. All-inclusive resorts feature organized, live entertainment nightly. Though visitors need not venture out from their major resort to find entertainment, if they don't they will miss out on one of Aruba's most appealing attributes: what some dub an "all-inclusive island." Unlike at many resort destinations, on Aruba tourists easily mix and mingle with local residents who equally enjoy the many amenities of the more populated tourist areas.

It is safe for visitors to roam around principal tourist areas at night in search of amusement. Oranjestad and Palm Beach are the hubs for lounges, discos, and free entertainment. Well-lit and bustling shopping malls contain elegant or casual family eateries, late-night lounges, and stages for nightly free shows. Most are set up to provide entertainment to diners. Several shops and souvenir kiosks are open during the evening hours as well.

Oranjestad is the epicenter of most special events on Aruba. The biggest Carnival parades, national holiday celebrations, conventions, conferences, sporting events, and most concerts are here. The early months of the year are filled with an unending parade of Carnival events, but Aruba really begins to "heat up" starting in late spring with exciting events like the Soul Beach Music Festival, Caribbean Sea Jazz Festival, and sporting events such as the Aruba International Regatta and Aruba International Pro-Am Golf Tournament. The island's physical attributes and weather attract world-class athletes from around the globe to such events as the Aruba Hi-Winds Pro-Am windsurfing and kitesurfing competition in July and the International Beach Tennis Tournament in November. These are exciting days for both participants and spectators.

Previous: a Carnival dancer; pageantry during Carnival. **Above:** salsa at Bugaloe.

Nightlife

In Palm Beach every sort of nighttime activity is just a short stroll from any resort. Visitors can check out clubs, restaurants, shows, and even late-night shopping. Visitors staying in Oranjestad and Manchebo Beach will find convenient casinos and clubs, with most nightlife focused around the major resorts and the casinos in their area.

ORANJESTAD

Oranjestad generally tends to quiet down at night, except for the few blocks along L.G. Boulevard surrounding the harbor. The Renaissance Marketplace, right on the water, is always lively with musical performers nightly at the waterside bandstand. Many of the clubs within the mall arrange their own entertainment. Outside the mall, several venues that are cozy eateries during the day turn into hot nightspots until all hours once dinner is over. With clubs lining the water, there are always lovely views and a distinct island feel.

CAFÉ CHAOS

One of Oranjestad's most popular nightspots, **Café Chaos** (L. G. Smith Blvd. 60, 297/588-7547, 5pm-1am Mon.-Thurs., 5pm-3am Fri.-Sat., happy hour 10pm-11pm Sat., no cover charge) has a cozy, European pub ambience: all dark wood paneling, humorous signs, and good cold beer on draft. It is right across from Wilhelmina Park.

Café Chaos morphs from a quiet place early in the evening to a busy, raucous hangout as the night wears on. Weekends feature some of the island's top bands on its small stage. The crowd often overflows out onto to the sidewalk after midnight.

CAFÉ THE PLAZA

A favorite spot to enjoy free nightly musical performances is **Café The Plaza** (Seaport Marketplace, 297/583-8826, www.cafetheplaza.com, 8am-1am daily, no cover charge), a very popular hangout with most of Aruba's Dutch community. The restaurant is open for breakfast, lunch, and dinner until midnight; tables are usually pretty well filled inside and out from the lunch hour on. Patrons particularly enjoy the outdoor terrace for drinks and platters of typical Dutch snacks such as *bitterballen* or *frikendel*. This congenial spot is perfect for lingering while listening to great bands on the Renaissance Marketplace stage.

CILO CITY LOUNGE

Find a chic and relaxed spot for a quiet drink by the harbor at **Cilo City Lounge** (Seaport Marketplace, 297/588-7996, www.cilo-aruba.com, 7am-1am daily) on the L. G. Smith side of the Renaissance Marketplace. It is a popular after-work "meet and greet" spot for island movers and shakers who can walk directly across the street from Parliament. There are live performers nightly 7pm-10pm.

GRAND CAFÉ TROPICAL

Grand Café Tropical (Seaport Marketplace, 297/582-8577, www.grandcafetropical.com, 4pm-1am Mon.-Thurs., 4pm-2am Fri.-Sat., happy hour 4pm-7pm daily, no cover charge) is a cute and cozy club where patrons are welcomed by friendly owner Evert. The bar's comfy neighborhood ambience encourages participation in Karaoke Wednesdays and dancing to live music on weekends on the tiny dance floor. Seating is principally on the outside terrace, with a nice view of the harbor. The daily happy hour features fancy martinis for $3.

JIMMY'S PLACE

Though they just consider their establishment "a typical Dutch bar," **Jimmy's Place** (Windstraat 17, 297/582-2550, www.jimmysaruba.com, 5pm-2am Mon.-Thurs., 5pm-4am Fri.-Sat., 8pm-2am Sun., no cover charge) has long been the island's unofficial gay and

Party Buses

When looking for a happening nighttime hot spot, you want the scene to be fun and busy. However, Aruba's club crowd works during the week and usually saves their partying for Friday and Saturday nights. Locals commonly hit the clubs following some other event or after a night shift, so places don't begin to fill up until late.

For vacationers, every night could be a party night, and one of the best ways to guarantee a hopping atmosphere is to sign up for one of the *paranda* tours, or party buses. Wherever you go on a party bus, you bring the party with you. Why try to locate an obscure, out-of-the-way local club on your own or risk driving under the influence? Wildly painted buses pick up guests at their hotel and safely drop them back afterward.

Party buses boast friendly hosts and drivers who are there to lend to the hilarity. The hosts are well practiced at getting the party started. One tour option is to leave earlier in the evening to enjoy a champagne toast on a secluded beach at sunset; dinner at a local restaurant follows. The rest of the evening is spent at picturesque local bars, with a drink included at each stop. More drinks can be purchased at special prices—usually only a dollar or two. Another option is to dine on your own with a pickup time later in the evening; this option is popularly known as a "pub crawl" and only includes the barhopping portion of the tour.

Two of the longest-running and most respected *paranda* tours are the **Kokoo Kunuku** (Noord 28 P, 297/586-2010, www.kukookunuku.com, 6pm-midnight Mon.-Sat., $65, with dinner, Pub Krawl 9pm-12:30am Mon.-Sat., $40) and the **Banana Bus** (SchubertStraat 10, 297/593-0757, www.bananabusaruba.com, Tues.-Thurs., Pub Crawl $45 pp). "Going local" has never been easier.

lesbian hangout. The crowd is usually a 50-50 mix of straight and LGBT. The polished wood tables and lovely rear gardens are very pleasant and homey here. This spot is the most fun on the weekends when there is a live DJ. As with most of Aruba's clubs, things pick up late at night after locals get off of their shift at the resorts and restaurants.

BEAM

Oranjestad has an interesting new meeting place called **BEAM** (Steenweg 17, 297/735-4242, lamperaquel@gmail.com, 10am-6pm Mon.-Sat., 9pm-midnight last Sat. of the month, no entry fee). Its primarily an art gallery, where island artists rent stalls to create and sell their work. If you are an art buff who likes to chat with artists and understand their motivation, you will find the atmosphere very stimulating.

Beam is operated by island artists and musicians and attracts an elite, cultural crowd with their night events, which take place on the last Saturday of the month and are expanding to more evenings. You can e-mail Raquel Lampe (see email above) to find out their current schedule. The events usually include original live music, poetry readings, a holistic drinks menu, and a bar featuring beer at local prices (5 florins instead of dollars). If you happen to be visiting at the right time and enjoy art, this is a unique environment and experience that you shouldn't miss.

EAGLE BEACH AND MANCHEBO BEACH

The preponderance of timeshare and condominium resorts with family clientele has kept this area relatively quiet at night. The Alhambra Casino complex, which reopened in 2012 after a complete makeover, is the center for most of the nighttime excitement. It is within easy walking distance of almost all the Manchebo Beach resorts. A free tram service to and from the center to the more distant Tamarijn or Dutch Village runs until all hours of the night. For the cluster of resorts farther north on Eagle Beach, the casinos at the Tropicana and La Cabana Resorts provide most of the entertainment.

CAGE

Described as a club for everyone of all orientations, **Cage** (King Plaza, Caya Harmonia 9, 297/593-3550, 9pm-3am Wed.-Sun., $6) is also Aruba's current LGBT hot spot, particularly popular with the yuppie crowd. The clientele is generally mixed with straight and LGBT patrons. Despite the modest entry fee, the space is quite big, and the decor chic. Mezzanine seating provides a place to cool off after a hot time on the dance floor. Cage is on the north side of the Sasaki Highway, in the large mall between the Bubali Road and the large roundabout. A nonsmoking policy means Cage is a breath of fresh air compared to the typical smoke-filled venue.

DJs play some house and rock, but mostly Caribbean and Latin dance music—a favorite with islanders. Ladies Night is on Wednesday, with free drinks for the femmes 9pm-10:30pm. On Saturday the club features live bands, which mostly play Latin and regional dance music, and the cover charge climbs to $14 but includes two drinks.

FUSION WINE AND PIANO BAR

A sophisticated upscale local clientele has made **Fusion Wine and Piano Bar** (Alhambra Shopping Bazaar, 297/280-9994, 6pm-1am Mon.-Thurs. and Sun., 6pm-2am Fri.-Sat., no cover charge) their favorite place to while away the late-night hours. They offer an extensive wine cellar and gourmet tapas menu, with live music on weekends. There are front and back open areas for enjoying the balmy Aruban evenings, along with excellent and attentive service, comfy lounges, and a tasteful ambience.

STAR KARAOKE

Indulge your inner rock star at **Star Karaoke** (King Plaza, Caya Harmonia 9, 297/594-3988, 8pm-3am Tues.-Sun., no cover charge), a cozy hangout with two rooms for singing the night away. Karaoke is very popular on Aruba, particularly with the expat Filipino community. There is a special VIP Room for classic KTV, which can be rented for $20 an hour if you want to host a private party. You are welcome to bring your own food to the VIP room, but drinks must be purchased from the house bar.

PALM BEACH, MALMOK, AND NOORD

Palm Beach is unquestionably Aruba's center for nighttime excitement. It offers a wealth of evening activities, mostly within the many large malls that line J. E. Irausquin Boulevard. There are several eateries that segue into appealing cafés and popular gathering places as the night wears on. Many feature live musical performances for free. Shopping is also a prime after-dinner activity, with scores of stores and kiosks around the area offering their wares until 10pm or later.

SAND AT BRICKELL BAY

Aruba's chicest open-air nightclub is the **Sand at Brickell Bay** (J. E. Irausquin Blvd. 370, 297/280-9967, www.arubasandbar.com, 11am-1am Sun.-Thurs., 11am-3am Fri.-Sat., no cover charge, over 21 only), right on the main Noord-Palm Beach Road bisecting J. E. Irausquin Boulevard. For those who love the shore, the beach bar feeling has been transplanted to this convenient location.

The club features a VIP section with dedicated waitstaff and a stage surrounded by a dance floor for live music. On select Sundays they host a pool party from noon to late night, with live entertainment during the happy hour (4pm-7pm) and special prices on all drinks, including premium brands. Wednesdays are "Ladies Night Out" with $5 champagne cocktails and 2-for-1 mojitos (8pm-9pm). Generally nice prices on exotic, frozen cocktails are part of the regular menu.

For more entertainment options, there are a plethora of plasma screens for catching PPV sporting events, and a hookah lounge called I ♥ Hookah, which offers an enormous selection of inhalants, from flavored tobaccos to chunks of fresh fruits. Hookahs can include up to six mouthpieces for large parties.

★ BUGALOE

The charming eatery known as **Bugaloe** (water end of the De Palm Pier, 297/586-2233, www.bugaloe.com, 9am-midnight daily, no cover charge) recommended for breakfast, lunch, or dinner, turns into one of Aruba's favorite nightspots when the sun sets. A diverse, all-ages crowd enjoys the casual atmosphere and authentic island feel of the pier. This spot never gets steamy, smoky, or hot as you are always bathed by the trade winds. There are great live bands on Tuesdays, Wednesdays, and weekends, plus free salsa lessons on Wednesday nights. The music and mood are friendly and welcoming, with the dance floor filled with jolly people most of the night.

DREAM BOWL

For some after-dinner family fun, **Dream Bowl** (L. G. Smith Blvd. 95, 297/586-0809, www.dreambowlaruba.com, 4pm-11pm Sun.-Thurs., 4pm-midnight Fri.-Sat., lanes $35/hr, up to 6 shoe rentals included) in the Palm Beach Plaza Mall offers bowling jazzed up with a stylish, modern decor. The hall is all black lights and neon-glow colors, right down to the bowling balls, for a new twist on a favorite family pastime. On Tuesday, Wednesday, and Thursday happy hour features bargain buckets of beer. Thursdays are particularly special for being "Red Pin Night"—hit a strike when the red head pin appears and win a free drink!

Aside from the six lanes, there are pool and foosball tables, air hockey stations, and a complete arcade to keep young hands and minds engaged. It also sports a pizza bar, if you are in the mood for a nice, casual evening and an informal meal.

GARI & WASABI

Though actually a sushi restaurant, **Gari & Wasabi** (Palm Beach 6-D, 297/586-0078, www.gariandwasabi.com, 5pm-2am daily, no cover charge) is most appreciated as a "meet and eat" by its clientele. Very stylish art deco surroundings are perfect for healthy snacks along with exotic martinis. Most patrons stay on well after a late dinner or gather here after some fashionable evening event. Regular events such as ladies' night and happy hour with $1 sushi rolls and $4 mojitos and sangria attract island fashionistas. Continually changing specials are posted on their Facebook page.

GUSTO

Islanders in their mid-twenties flock to **Gusto** (The Village Mall, 6pm-1am Mon.-Thurs. and Sun., 6pm-3am Fri.-Sat., happy hour 9pm-11pm daily, no cover charge) directly across from Señor Frog's in The Village Mall. It is a cozy bar with a chic, casual atmosphere; dress up or down as you please.

There is a nightly happy hour with all drinks half price. Check the Facebook page for themed events on weekends with local or international celebrity DJs. The music varies between all genres of popular music, from trance, house, and hip-hop to salsa and meringue. There is no entrance fee, except for special events.

LOCAL STORE

Oranjestad's former hot spot for the younger crowd is now in Palm Beach. The **Local Store** (Palm Beach 13A, 297/586-1414, www.localstorearuba.com, 5pm-11pm Tues.-Sun., no cover charge) took over a popular little rum shop and added some local flavor. On Friday afternoons, island yuppies flock to the little cocktail tables scattered about the front yard for happy hour.

The club presents live music on weekends, with local bands specializing in the Caribbean sound. Expect lots of reggae, trance, house, and reggaeton. They offer a diverse, international menu that includes ice-cold craft beers and buckets of spicy chicken wings.

MOOMBA BEACH BAR & RESTAURANT

The distinctive and funky beachfront **MooMba Beach Bar & Restaurant** (J. E. Irausquin Blvd. 230, 297/586-5365, http://moombabeach.com, 8am-1am daily, happy hour 6pm-7pm daily), wedged between the Holiday Inn and Marriott Surf Club, attracts all ages, but holds a singular position for nightlife in Palm Beach as one of the most popular places for young people to connect.

Casinos

Aruba boasts 13 casinos. Palm Beach resorts alone host eight busy gaming rooms within easy walking distance of each other. **Manchebo Beach resorts** have the **Alhambra Casino** only minutes from their doors; Eagle Beach is home to the homey **Tropicana Casino** and **Glitz Casino** in **La Cabana Resort.** Oranjestad is serviced by **Crystal and Seaport Casinos,** part of the **Renaissance resort.**

All of these casinos tout a player's club with a VIP card that costs nothing to obtain and brings an immediate reward of a $10 play coupon. Using the card when playing slots and table games puts credits on the member's account. Points can be redeemed for logo items, or many resorts will give credit toward dinners in their restaurants. Other services, such as spas and extra nights in the resorts, are also awarded for points. Membership allows winnings to stay credited to an account, so vacationers keep their winning safe until they are ready to leave the island.

The **Hilton, Occidental,** and **Holiday Inn Resorts** have dedicated poker rooms, where tournaments of Texas Hold 'Em are conducted nightly. Other Palm Beach resorts with casinos are the **Marriott Hotel** proper, **Hyatt Regency, Riu Palace, Riu Caribbean,** and **Ritz-Carlton.** All have standard table games: craps, roulette, and blackjack, as well as hundreds of slot machines accepting various levels of bets, from a penny to hundreds of dollars. The Crystal Casino has a special bank of slots that award a brand-new car for hitting the big jackpot. The casino gives away around six cars a year. Casinos also host special slots and blackjack tournaments sporadically through the week. It is best to check with the casino in your resort, as schedules change regularly. There are often special international tournaments, particularly around holidays.

Crystal and Seaport Casinos (www.arubacrystalcasinos.com) are right by Oranjestad Harbor. Crystal is the only casino on Aruba open 24 hours a day, to date. The Seaport Casino offers an elaborate sports book gallery, with real-time broadcasting of races and sporting events. Most casinos also host some afternoon **bingo,** which is very big with the locals; a small investment can reap a modicum of rewards. Bingo may not be for high rollers, but it provides a congenial break from the afternoon heat, with door prizes, drinks, and snacks.

Aruba is also known for **Caribbean Stud Poker,** where you play against the house with

On the weekends it is filled with families enjoying the beach and restaurant, as well as guests from smaller resorts who have an arrangement with MooMba to use their beach.

Its bar and outdoor lounge area embody the fantasy of island life and leisure and stay busy at all hours for events, beach tennis, and great bands on the weekends. The main bar is always hopping at happy hour and well into the night. It is surrounded by shops that are open until 10pm.

★ SEÑOR FROG'S

The Aruban outlet of the famous **Señor Frog's** (J. E. Irausquin Blvd. 348 A, 297/586-8900, www.senorfrogs.com, noon-1am Mon.-Thurs., noon-3am Fri.-Sat., 5pm-1am Sun., no cover charge) dominates The Village Mall. It is still one of the best places to go wild along with dinner or late-night Mexican snacks. Everyone wants to go home with a signature souvenir YARD, the super tall glasses that you get to keep when you order the 28-ounce drink and then pay less for refills.

This is most definitely a young person's place for late-night fun, though it's popular with families for lunch and dinner, when the atmosphere is decidedly different. After 10pm it changes gears to become a nightspot of calculated craziness and most definitely not a family place. For example, there's a Spring Break Bikini Contest for the late crowd starting at midnight, with all girls dressed only in bikinis getting free shots. As you might assume, much drunken naughtiness ensues.

SOPRANOS PIANO BAR

At the south end of Arawak Gardens, **Sopranos Piano Bar** (J. E. Irausquin Blvd.

Alhambra Casino

progressive jackpots based on the returns from all the tables. This unique game has resulted in surprisingly frequent big winners, sometimes well over $50,000 or $100,000. Aruba levies no taxes on winnings, but a person can transport a max of $10,000 cash when traveling. Island casinos will provide the service of keeping the money in an account for regularly returning visitors. Such wins are sometimes credited with an increase in timeshare and jewelry sales because as the saying goes, "you can't take it with you!" Well, you can, with some clever planning and cooperation from many friends, depending on the size of the win.

370, 297/586-9944, www.sopranospianobar.com, 5pm-2am Mon.-Thurs., 5pm-4am Fri.-Sun., two-drink minimum) features excellent local entertainers with the occasional imported pianist performing for a month or so. There is a request and tips jar; the latter is required to attain the former. This is an after-dinner drinks and cigars place with cozy booths on the terrace and a very atmospheric interior. Named and styled after the famous TV show, it draws a mixed crowd. The patrons set the pace, as requests and music create the mood, from mellow tunes to classic rock. You will not hear house, trance, or hip-hop here.

SOUTH BEACH LOUNGE

Aruba's pretty people like **South Beach Lounge** (Palm Beach 55, 297/586-6766, 6pm-1am daily). The stylish and contemporary open-air deck is set up with various seating arrangements to suit the mood. Take a high stool around the bar to watch a sporting event, sprawl on a lounge chair or couch, or hit the dance floor to listen to live bands on a Saturday night. South Beach is most active from 11pm until 1am on the weekends and usually quiet during the week. The crowd is eclectic, from young people on vacation to a more mature crowd of resident fashionistas.

DE OLDE MOLEN (THE MILL)

Undoubtedly Aruba's largest nightspot, **De Olde Molen,** or **The Mill** (J. E. Irausquin Blvd 330, 297/586-6766, 10pm-3am Sun.-Fri., 1am-6am Sat. $10 for inside disco), is housed in the landmark mill itself and takes up the entire lower level and most of the parking lot for inside/outside mingling. While the cover provides access to the air-conditioned interior, two bars, a DJ, and space for unlimited dancing keep most of the crowd outside. The Mill is open very late (or rather early), attracting many of the casino employees who like to relax after getting off from late shifts. Not much happens before midnight, and things don't really get going until 2am or later, which has earned The Mill the nickname "The After Party."

The entire facility is broken up into areas that seem to cater to certain demographics. The music inside the main club right under the windmill is hard-core techno and attracts a much younger crowd. The enclosure on the eastern end, where the DJ plays mostly salsa, *bachata,* and more classic rock, has become the favorite with tourists. Expect a very mixed crowd.

Shows and Concert Venues

Aruba's primary concert venues are the Aruba Entertainment Center and Cas di Cultura, both on the western outskirts of Oranjestad. Scattered around the island are several sports arenas and community centers, which will often host large concerts with imported and local talent.

The wider beaches are commonly employed for concerts—most frequently, Surfside Beach, which annually hosts the Soul Beach Music Festival. Concerts on Aruba are not about staying planted in your seat; they're about socializing, dancing, and grooving to the music. Ample refreshment booths encourage a party atmosphere.

ARAWAK GARDENS

Enjoy dinner theater at no extra cost when dining at one of the five restaurants at **Arawak Gardens** (J. E. Irausquin Blvd. 370, no phone, 7pm-10pm daily for the show, no cover charge), just across from the Occidental Resort. Singers and musicians entertain, and all restaurants have outdoor terraces surrounding the gazebo where they perform. The music is usually mellow: classic rock, golden oldies, and show tunes. Visitors can dine at Salt & Pepper (Dutch-continental cuisine and tapas), Fishes N' More (seafood), Casa Tue (pizza and Italian), Tango Argentine Grill (steak

Ray Ellin (right) with Chuck Nice, a regular guest at Aruba Ray's Comedy Club

house), or even a Burger King with island ambience.

ARUBA RAY'S COMEDY CLUB

Once upon a vacation, New York comedian Ray Ellin fell in love with Aruba, coming to spend five to six months of the year at his island retreat. His unflagging enthusiasm for this tropical paradise prompted his comedy cohorts to dub him "Aruba Ray," and thus was born **Aruba Ray's Comedy Club** (Amsterdam Room in the Marriott Resort, 297/749-4363, www.arubacomedy.com, nightly 8:30pm-1pm, $36). Ray lures some of the best and brightest talents from New York and Los Angeles for four to six weeks of shows, around four times a year. These times are not set in stone, but usually strike around major holidays (Thanksgiving, New Year's, Valentine's Day); check scheduling and performers on his website.

This is entertainment for mature audiences. Ray is an extremely congenial host with a droll, lighting-fast wit. His style of humor involves and engages his audience, but in the nicest, most inoffensive manner. Many will recognize his rotating roster of guest comics from late-night TV talk shows and cable comedy hours. The price of a ticket includes a promotional perk from the Stellaris Casino in the Marriott and a discount coupon for La Vista restaurant. Tickets may be purchased online or at the door. For an additional $22, enjoy four hours of access to a premium open bar during the show and afterward at the casino tables.

CAS DI CULTURA

Aruba's **Cas di Cultura** (Vondellaan 2, Oranjestad, 297/582-1010, www.casdicultura.aw) is the performing arts center where classical music concerts, dance recitals, plays, and myriad other events are staged. It has a 400-room auditorium that hosts local and imported talent.

The theater is flanked by the Rufo Wever School of Music and the Da Vinci Piano School, both of which frequently conduct concerts in the auditorium. The Cas di Cultura hosts the annual holiday production of *The Nutcracker,* which is performed by **Kozlov Dance International** (www.koslovdance.com) and stars Leonid Kozlov. The Cas di Cultura also has an exposition room where smaller events are conducted, and art or educational exhibits are displayed.

At Aruba's "House of Culture" performances are usually dedicated to classical, jazz,

a free evening show at Paseo Herencia Shopping Mall

and island music and dance. The center has no house orchestra, so programs are entirely dependent on whichever group is renting the auditorium. There are usually shows every Friday and Saturday night, and often during the week. Upcoming performances are posted on the website.

PASEO HERENCIA SHOPPING MALL

Great for all ages, *Waltzing Waters* is a sound, water, and light show in the **Paseo Herencia Shopping Mall** (J. E. Irausquin Blvd. 382-A, 297/586-6533, http://paseoherencia.com, 7:30pm, 8:30pm, 9:30pm, and 10:30pm daily). The mall also features numerous special events during the year on national and international holidays. Monday through Saturday they stage free shows beginning at 8pm encompassing a wide variety of entertainment, including concert violinists, folkloric dancers, steelpan drummers, and talented local singers. There is even a salsa night and *Cirque Aruba* fantasy program of tumblers and clowns.

The mall runs a horse-drawn carriage, which will take people back to their hotel at the end of the evening; a ride along the boulevard is $30 for 25 minutes. Shetland pony rides for kids around the mall are $5 for about 5 minutes.

Festivals and Events

Within one week of the New Year, Aruba begins a long calendar of special events, punctuated by ebullient parties. Weeks of Carnival happenings heat up the winter months beyond the tropical temperatures. The "low season-slow season" months are enlivened by numerous festivals, international sports competitions, and concerts to attract visitors with diverse interests. Something exceptional is taking place nearly every month of the year—additional motivation to choose Aruba as a destination.

WEEKLY FESTIVALS

BON BINI FESTIVAL

The long-running **Bon Bini Festival** (Fort Zoutman, 297/582-3777, 7pm-9pm Tues., $5) features authentic insight into traditional island culture, music, and dance. Regional instruments such as the "caha di orgal" (an organ grinder), the *wiri,* and steelpan accompany enthusiastic young dancers in native costume. There are booths for inexpensive local art, handicrafts, and snacks.

Performers change from one week to the next, so there is no predicting the program. Count on either folkloric or carnival dancers. This is a pleasant way to spend two hours, and a nice segue into having dinner at one of Oranjestad's excellent restaurants.

CARUBBIAN FESTIVAL

Established in 2011, the **Carubbian Festival** (Bernardstraat, San Nicolas, 297/582-3777, 6pm-10pm Thurs., $64 adults, $32 children, purchase voucher at De Palm desks) is a celebration of the multicultural heritage particular to San Nicolas. Every Thursday night the main street is converted into an elaborate street fair. Three stages offer music, but the big action is on the main stage. Acts change weekly, but the grand finale is always a rousing Carnival show with audience participation. Vouchers provide prime seating and table service for drinks. A pan-Caribbean menu reflects the many nationalities that made San Nicolas their home when the refinery first opened. Three generations later, their cultural traditions and diversity carry on.

A standard package includes a choice of meal, transportation by bus to and from San Nicolas, and a drink. More drink tickets can be purchased at the festival. There are some very interesting regional beverages, most nonalcoholic, with purported natural, healthful properties. They are worth trying for the unique experience. Many booths are on hand selling local arts and crafts, as well as logo souvenirs.

JANUARY AND FEBRUARY

★ CARNIVAL

The festive events of **Carnival** (multiple venues, parades free, musical contest and election $5.50) start the Saturday after New Year's Day (unless New Year's Day falls on Thurs., Fri. or Sat., then they will wait another week) and can last 4-10 weeks depending on the advent of Ash Wednesday. A full calendar with times, description of events, locations, and parade routes can be found in English on www.visitaruba.com.

For islanders, Carnival is the most anticipated event of the year, beginning with a nighttime parade through Oranjestad called the *Fakkeloptocht,* Dutch for Torch Parade. Carnival events will be going on most weekends until the arrival of Ash Wednesday, except for the final week when they are nearly every night. There are music contests, queen elections, and parades, parades, parades, day and night. This is a chance to sample local, original music composed each year just for Carnival. Live bands are vital to the parades, moving along in specially designed trailers, while thousands of participants garbed in sumptuous costumes dance alongside. Each group is judged for their artistic floats and exotic road pieces.

The major parades after the Torch Parade are the Balloon Parade (San Nicolas), Children's Parade (San Nicolas and Oranjestad), Youth Parade and Tivoli Lighting Parade (Oranjestad), Jouvert Morning (San Nicolas), Grand Final Parades (San Nicolas and Oranjestad), and finally, the Burning of Momo (Aruba Entertainment Center, Oranjestad).

At the Aruba Entertainment Center, Carnival queens are selected during extravagant pageants in four age categories, from child to a mature Mrs. Carnival. Two of the biggest events are musical contests, the selection of the Tumba King or Queen and the Roadmarch and Calypso King or Queen (San Nicolas).

The party ends at the stroke of midnight marking the beginning of Ash Wednesday with the burning of an effigy of Rey (King) Momo, a pagan figure who rules over revelers and the dark of night.

The ritual commencement of the new Carnival is announced annually on November 11, at 11 minutes after 11am. The same evening an inaugural event will be held, usually at a venue close to most resorts, to initiate island visitors into the traditions and excitement of Carnival, Aruban-style. It varies from one year to the next.

Aside from the official activities, many resorts will schedule "jump-ups" for their guests. These open-air festivities usually feature one of the more popular Carnival bands, beer stands, and lively entertainment.

A shorter Carnival season means more frequent events; none are sacrificed due to lack of time. Aruba's Carnival is rated as second only to Brazil. If your vacation preference leans toward unbridled indulgence, this is the time to visit Aruba. Many come every year just to enjoy the spectacle.

BETICO DAY

The first official national holiday of the year is on January 25. **Betico Day** (Plaza Betico Croes, behind the Cas di Cultura, 5pm-10pm) honors the memory of "El Liberatador," Gilberto Francois "Betico" Croes. A solemn ceremony of remembrance is followed by a cultural night of speeches, musical performances, and folkloric dance.

MARCH

★ HIMNO Y BANDERA DAY AND INTERNATIONAL HALF MARATHON

Aruba's National Day, March 18, or **Himno y Bandera Day,** begins before dawn with an **International Half Marathon** starting in San Nicolas and ending in Oranjestad. This has traditionally attracted runners from Latin

America, the United States, and Europe, with cash awards and trophies. The day of celebration continues with festive events and an elaborate street fair and national show at night in the Plaza Betico Croes; entrance is free. This is the best place and time to buy Aruba souvenirs, as the fair features authentic, locally made handicrafts. It is remarkable how many ways Aruba's attractive flag can be incorporated into alluring garments and jewelry; you name it, you'll find it here.

WENTE/PAPIAMENTO GOLF TOURNAMENT

The famous California Wente Vineyards partners with local restaurant Papiamento to put on the **Wente/Papiamento Golf Tournament,** a weekend of golf and gourmet food for a good cause. Proceeds go to a different Aruba foundation each year. Events are punctuated by a welcome reception in Papiamento Restaurant's elegant gardens. Unlimited Wente vintages flow throughout the weekend (wine tastings along the greens are actually a part of the competition).

Arion Wine Company (Ponton 38 Q, 297/583-3325, www.arionwinecompany.com) sponsors the event and handles registration. Eric Wente, head of the famous winemaking family, plays host for the weekend. The first prize is a trip to the Wente Vineyards in the Livermore Valley, with a weekend of golf on their famous course. The tournament is by invitation only, but visitors can leave their name at Tierra Del Sol Pro Shop in Malmok to participate on a stand by basis. Contact the shop for more information.

APRIL

KING'S DAY

The month ends with the most important Dutch holiday of the year, **King's Day,** on April 27. It is a time for revelry and activities of all kinds. Visitors are welcome to observe the protocol ceremony honoring the monarch at Wilhelmina Park beginning at 10am in the morning. All through the day there are flea markets, classic car club and Harley-Davidson motorcades, kite competitions, and open houses at all island museums.

MAY

★ MAY DAY

The best way possible to start a month is with a holiday. On May 1, **International May Day,** the Royal Dutch Marines open their camp in Savaneta (turn off for the camp from Hwy. 1A is clearly marked, 9am-6pm) and turn it into a giant theme park. The day is filled with the island's best flea market, inexpensive food stands, musical performances, boat rides, and aerial and sea-based demonstrations of mock battle. It's a great way to mix and mingle and observe island life; all proceeds from the day are donated to a local charity.

★ SOUL BEACH MUSIC FESTIVAL

The **Soul Beach Music Festival** (multiple venues, musical concerts at Surfside Beach, comedy at Aruba Entertainment Center, www.soulbeach.net, combo package for all parties and VIP concert seating $365), founded by comedian and actor Sinbad, has a home on Aruba. It is a Memorial Day weekend tradition for thousands. Five days of media events along with beach and after parties culminate in three concerts by chart-topping R&B, hip-hop, and soul performers. One night is dedicated to the hottest comedians of the moment. Alumni include Jamie Foxx, Jennifer Hudson, Toni Braxton, Alicia Keys, R. Kelly, L. L. Cool J, and comedians Kevin Hart and Mike Epps; expect to see top talents for a fraction of the price it would cost in the United States. Packages and charter flights can be arranged through the website.

JUNE

ARUBA INTERNATIONAL TRIATHLON

June ends with the **Aruba International Triathlon** (contact IBISA at idefre@setarnet.aw, 297/585-4987), which consists of a 1.5 kilometer (1 mi) swim, a 40 kilometer (25 mi) bike race, and 10 kilometer (6 mi) run, with cash prizes and trophies for the winners.

The main event begins at Eagle Beach across from the MVC-Club, next to the Tulip restaurant. It starts with a two-loop 1.5k swim, then a 40k bike segment (eight loops along Irausquin Blvd. from Costa Linda Resort to Divi Phoenix Resort), and ends with a five-loop run along the same bike course. Around 400 athletes from Aruba, the United States, Europe, and Latin America compete.

JULY

★ ARUBA HI-WINDS PRO-AM

One of the most respected amateur windsurfing and kitesurfing competitions in the world is the annual **Aruba Hi-Winds Pro-Am** (Fisherman's Huts, L. G. Smith Blvd., Malmok, www.hiwindsaruba.com, no fee for spectators). Expect to meet some of the greatest names in windsurfing in the region, including the PWA Women's World Champion in Freestyle Windsurfing since 2008, Sarah-Quita Offringa, a native Aruban. She often lends her presence to this event in which she first competed and which holds a special place in her heart.

The entire week is punctuated with beach parties, fashion shows, and breathtaking demonstrations of athletic prowess, including the celebrated nighttime aerial kitesurfing display. Spectators are welcome to join the fun, where cheap, icy-cold beer never stops flowing.

AUGUST AND SEPTEMBER

ARUBA INTERNATIONAL REGATTA

Aruba's premier all-class sailing event is the **Aruba International Regatta** (Surfside Beach, http://aruba-regatta.com), which is growing in scope and attendance annually, but still maintains the atmosphere of a grand beach party. It is a great weekend for sailing enthusiasts, with everyone from windsurfers through cruising class 36-footers competing. Even if you don't sail, it is a friendly event with wonderful opportunities for some very striking photos. It takes place on the third weekend of August.

ARUBA INTERNATIONAL PRO-AM GOLF TOURNAMENT

At the end of August or beginning of September, golf fanatics can join or watch the **Aruba International Pro-Am Golf Tournament** (Tierra Del Sol Country Club and Golf Course, Malmokweg z/n, 297/586-0978, www.tierradelsol.com), attracting golf pros and players from around the world. The

Aruba International Regatta

36-hole tournament guarantees one highly respected pro mentoring each four-person team. The event encompasses three days of competing on the Tierra Del Sol course for great prizes and beautiful trophies. The weekend includes elegant evening events and organized activities for nongolfers.

OCTOBER

★ CARIBBEAN SEA JAZZ FESTIVAL

The **Caribbean Sea Jazz Festival** (Renaissance Marketplace and Convention Center, 297/588-0211, www.caribbeanseajazz.com, $50 pre-sale, $70 at the door) has become a destination for many on the last weekend of September. This is two nights of great music, gourmet food for pennies, and original art created just for the event on exhibition and for sale. International stars join renowned regional performers under the stars. CSJF has welcomed David Sanborn, Chaka Khan, Oscar D'Leon, Angie Stone, and Candy Dulfer, to name only a few. The party starts well in advance with the featured artists performing free warm-up events at local venues.

NOVEMBER

ARUBA INTERNATIONAL BEACH TENNIS OPEN

Whether you are a fanatical player or a spectator, find the world's top-seeded players and all levels of competition at the **Aruba International Beach Tennis Open** (J. E. Irausquin Blvd. 230, 297/592-6427, www.beachtennisaruba.com, mid-Nov.). International sports journalists credit Sjoerd de Vries, founder of Beach Tennis Aruba, as the premier promoter of the sport in the Americas.

Professional players from around the globe converge on Eagle Beach for a week of thrilling matches and nightly parties. There are 30 courts and constant action throughout the day.

Athletic tournaments on Aruba always provide a congenial, party atmosphere for competitors and the audience, in addition to the exciting sporting action, and this event particularly embodies all these aspects.

DECEMBER

During Christmas and New Year's, Aruba is packed not only for the escape from winter's

the Caribbean Sea Jazz Festival

Ending the Year with a Bang!

As New Year's Eve approaches on Aruba, fireworks mean bidding farewell to the old and greeting the new. Fireworks go on sale just after Christmas, and the nightly displays don't stop until everyone runs out of rockets.

This is particularly noticeable on the last business days of the year. Tradition demands that businesses set off a *pagara,* a roll of various-sized firecrackers that can number anywhere from 5,000 to 5,000,000. The most famous is the one set off in Oranjestad by MetaCorp, usually stretching the entire length of the Renaissance properties and beyond. It holds up traffic for nearly an hour and takes about 20 minutes to run its course. *Pagaras* are said to chase away any ill will or *fuku* (FOO-KOO, this is really the name for the bad vibes). Once a business establishment or home has set off its *pagara,* it is now cleansed for the coming year.

At the stroke of midnight on New Year's Eve, homes and restaurants alike set their *pagaras* alight. The New Year starts with Aruba enveloped in a fog of firework smoke. Resounding through the night is the noise of hundreds of millions of firecrackers exploding simultaneously. Bring your earplugs!

worst but also for the great excitement of the season; Aruba has its own lively traditions, music, and events associated with the holidays.

Check www.aruba.com for the calendar of special events, as the ever-changing roster features new festivals, sporting meets, and concerts; onetime happenings are regularly added to the calendar.

SINTERKLAAS FEAST DAY

Aruba's loving observance of Dutch traditions is never more evident than on the **Festival of Sinterklaas** (island-wide, Dec. 5). This beloved figure was the precursor for Santa Claus, and based on a very real person. He arrives on Aruba 2-3 weeks prior to his feast day, greeted at the port by thousands of children and their parents.

On December 5, the eve of his actual feast day, the stately gentleman will be seen everywhere, including many resorts, distributing toys and sweets to both island and vacationing children. In accordance with Dutch tradition, Sinterklass is accompanied by Zwarte Piet, a black Moor dressed in Renaissance attire. Some celebrants will also dress up as Zwarte Piet, donning blackface and Moorish costume. This has become a controversial part of the tradition in recent years, but is still a part of the celebration in Aruba. Be sure to keep this in mind if you plan on visiting during the holiday.

HOLIDAY SHOPPING IN ORANJESTAD

The capital's merchant association members turn Oranjestad's "Caya Grande" into a festive holiday celebration on the weekends (MAMBO, Caya G. F. "Betico" Croes, 10am-6pm every Sat. until Christmas). All through the day there is entertainment from seasonal local singing groups called *gaita,* performing a lively regional music of the same name.

At the beginning of the month, there is a visit from Sinterklaas prior to his feast day, after which Santa Claus holds court with young children at various venues.

★ *THE NUTCRACKER*

Russian ballet star Leonid Kozlov, formally the principal dancer of the Bolshoi and New York City Ballets, and his wife Adriana, a prima ballerina herself, settled permanently on Aruba in 2013. They opened the first academy dedicated to classic ballet on the island and have trained some of its most talented dancers. Leonid and Adriana dance the principal roles as well as bring in notable guest performers for their annual recital of Tchaikovsky's ***The Nutcracker*** (Cas di Cultura, 297/593-2036, www.kozlovdance.

com, mid-December weekend, 7pm, $20). The stunning sets, gorgeous costumes, and beautiful choreography have created a delightful new holiday tradition, which Aruban audiences have enthusiastically embraced. If you have yet to introduce the family to this seasonal treat, you can do it on Aruba for a fraction of what it would cost in the states.

Shows are frequently sold out, so be sure to purchase tickets online in advance. The exact weekend and number of shows vary from year to year; check their website for details. Vacationers staying at the Occidental Resort can enjoy an abridged version of the show during the weeks of Christmas and New Year's.

ARUBA DANDE FESTIVAL

Another beloved holiday tradition is the local version of caroling, which is focused on the New Year. The annual **Dande Festival** (changing venues, various community centers, www.visitaruba.com, begins at 8pm on a weekend between Christmas and New Year's, free) is a competition, lasting almost until dawn, to select the next Dande King or Queen. Many resorts host Dande exhibitions for their guests around this time.

Traditionally, the New Year's "serenade" of Dande is performed by roaming minstrels who travel from home to home. Employing "inside information" from an informant within the household, they usually personalize the song's lyrics to the lives and foibles of the residents, always in a most humorous manner. An important part of the ritual is the passing of the hat and a small monetary reward from each family member for their entertainment.

During the Dande Festival, lyrics are far more topical and occasionally contain scathing political and social commentary. Most often, however, they deliver a message of enjoying life and of good wishes for the coming year.

★ NEW YEAR'S EVE

Those who think watching a ball drop while freezing is the epitome of New Year's Eve excitement have yet to experience the change of

The Nutcracker

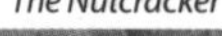

year on Aruba. As the year's end approaches, a frenzy of fireworks can be seen and heard everywhere. At the stroke of midnight, the sky fills with pyrotechnics from every neighborhood, after which the professional displays begin!

The streets of Oranjestad are usually filled with spectators for a magnificent fireworks show over the harbor, sponsored by the Renaissance Resort.

Vacationers find that nearly every resort on Aruba hosts a special dinner for their guests to celebrate the year's end. Many restaurants also host special evenings lasting until midnight, with champagne included.

Most hotels will stage fireworks displays, especially on the beach, for their guests. Most notable are those put on by the Divi and Tamarijn Beach Resorts by the Manchebo Beach and Eagle Beach area; Hyatt Regency Resort in Palm Beach; and Renaissance Resort in Oranjestad.

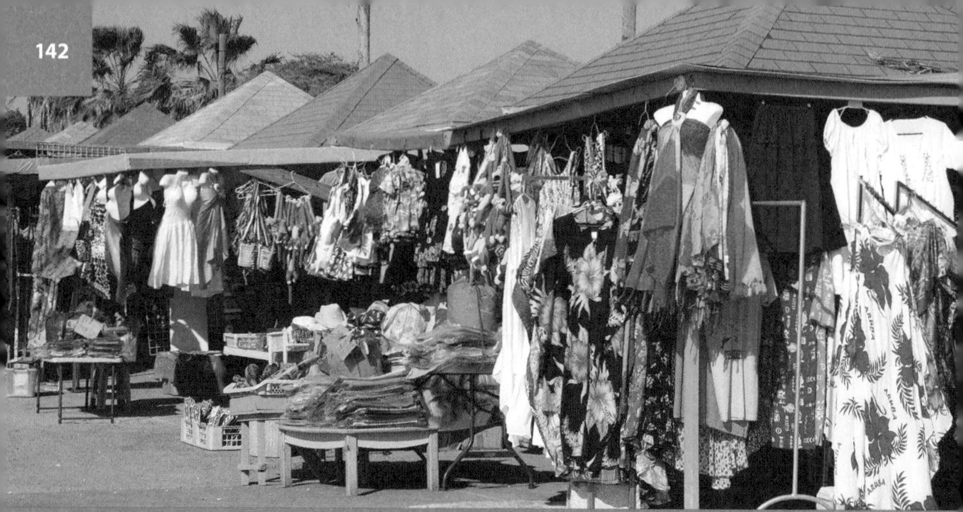

Shops

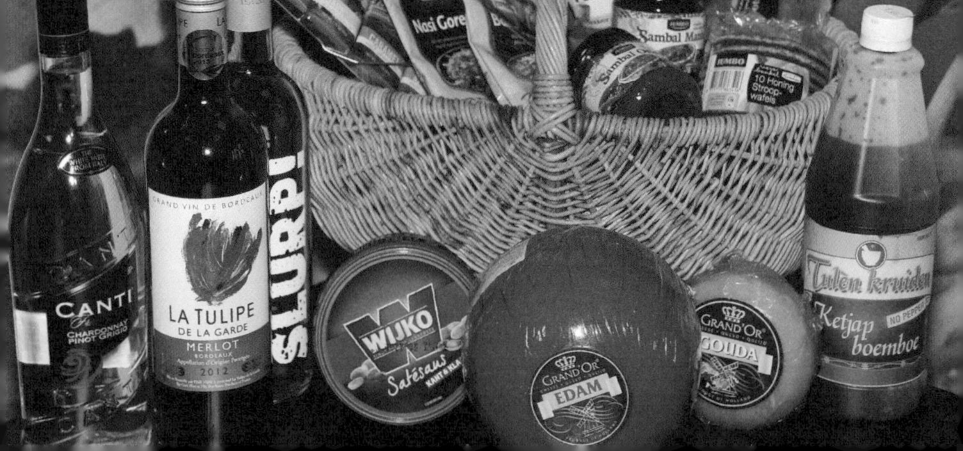

If you want a unique memento or great bargain, you're looking in the right place. Aruba offers a variety of shopping options, including signature designer stores, countless jewelry shops, souvenir and handicrafts shops, and flea markets.

Some of the best buys are at the open-air markets. A small group of native artisans produces interesting handicrafts and original paintings and watercolors. These can be found for sale at various festivals conducted by the resorts. Crafts such as macramé and appliqué are more the ken of Latin American cultures. Many attractive items from these countries from handwoven hammocks and embroidered garments are a common item at various markets.

The smaller jewelry stores are known to perform their "calculator dance" when a shopper inquires about a particular piece. Being knowledgeable about gemstones and having a taste for bargaining certainly help in haggling for some remarkable discounts, but it requires patience and determination. This practice is not particularly Aruban, but it has been a fairly common practice since the new millennium.

European perfumes and high-end cosmetics and skin care products are comparatively good buys, as are wines from Europe and Latin America. Canadians report that famous U.S. brands are as much as 25 percent cheaper than what they pay at home.

Hard liquor is discounted at the duty-free shops at the airport, but not beyond, except for the locally bottled Ron Superior and Palmera rums. It is best to buy your favorite liquor on your way in or your way off of the island. Smokers also declare cigarettes on Aruba cost much less than in the United States. Dutch cheeses are an excellent buy, and as long as they are uncut and sealed in the original rind, they can be carried into the United States. The best places to pick these up are at the supermarkets.

Cigar lovers will be thrilled to know that Cuban cigars of every brand are widely sold here. Aruba has it own brand, Aruhiba, made of locally grown tobaccos, which can be taken back to the United States without fear

Previous: Oranjestad flea market; a selection of edible souvenirs from an island market.
Above: downtown Oranjestad.

Look for ★ to find recommended shops.

Highlights

★ **Cosecha:** Chat with island artists regarding their work at this government-endorsed center for authentic, local handicrafts (page 146).

★ **Mopa-Mopa:** The Quillasinga people of Colombia still produce the beautiful handicrafts sold here in the same way that their ancestors did in centuries past (page 146).

★ **Gandelman Jewelers:** A respected regional family operation, Gandelman is the exclusive agent for watch brands like Rolex and Patek Philippe on Aruba (page 148).

★ **Renaissance Mall:** If designer labels are your obsession, then this is the place to indulge. The greatest concentration of top American, European, and Latin designer shops will be found in these elegant corridors (page 149).

★ **Super Food:** Food shopping can be gift shopping for lovers of Dutch cheeses and exotic spices. Aruba's most popular market is distinctly Dutch, and the quality of the products is exacting (page 154).

★ **Terrafuse:** Don't go on a hunt for that unique souvenir, make it yourself at Terrafuse's glass art classes (page 155)!

★ **Aruhiba:** This store has the largest and most diverse selections of Cuban, Honduran, and Dominican cigars on Aruba. Aficionados, however, should try Aruba's own homegrown and rolled brand, which costs far less (page 156).

★ **Caribbean Queen:** This sparkling boutique showcases handcrafted jewelry and accessories by local artisans, each of them a queen of their craft (page 156).

★ **Paseo Herencia Shopping Mall:** This lively shopping center offers a variety of restaurants and shops and provides free entertainment nightly (page 160).

of confiscation. More locally manufactured items come from Aruba Aloe, which offers products for hair and skin care.

Well-known names such as Louis Vuitton, Gucci, Mario Hernandez, Montblanc, Salvatore Ferragamo, Ralph Lauren, and Tommy Hilfiger all have dedicated outlets either in Oranjestad or Palm Beach. Aruba, however, is not a true duty-free port. European designer goods are marginally discounted over what they would cost in the United States. Other items, especially electronics like cameras, mobile devices, and video games, are uniformly more expensive.

Oranjestad is best known for daytime shopping. Until 2006, it could claim Aruba's only shopping center. Since then, "mall fever" has struck Palm Beach. One multipurpose mall after another has cropped up, with a plethora of goods, restaurants, and activities. Shops at the Palm Beach malls usually open in the late afternoon hours. Mindful that most visitors prefer to spend their days on the beach, they offer the convenience of nighttime shopping often accompanied by entertainment.

Oranjestad

Downtown Oranjestad is Aruba's daytime shopping destination. Stores in town open their doors anywhere between 8:30am and 10am and close between 6:30pm and 8pm. There was a time not so long ago when almost all stores closed for an extended two-hour siesta. Modern times and more competition have eliminated such island practices completely—a boon for fanatical shoppers. There are only a few die-hard "local" shops that don't remain open all day. Nearly all stores are closed on Sunday, except for a very few on L. G. Smith Boulevard that will open when a cruise ship is in port.

The area around the cruise terminal could rightfully be dubbed the local "diamond district." One store after another boasts well-known names of fine-quality jewelry and gemstones. Several are internationally affiliated, with service outlets in the United States. A few have their own on-site artisans creating original pieces.

Downtown Oranjestad offers great shopping.

Most stores and malls are clustered around the harbor. Within their halls are name brand designer shops, complemented by attractive cafés and stylish surroundings. Caya G. F. Betico Croes has always been considered the town's main shopping street. One half has high-end stores displaying well-known brands, but the eastern end is mostly dedicated to local shops with lower-end goods. A free tram service to and from the cruise terminal will take you directly to the vendors in downtown Oranjestad.

ART, HANDICRAFTS, AND SOUVENIRS

Aruba's traditional native crafts practiced by the Amerindian population are long lost. But many of the people who have come to live here kept the connection with their homeland and brought with them several of the native handicrafts still practiced in Venezuela, Colombia, and other Latin countries. Most offerings can be found at flea markets and souvenir shops.

Aruba does have an active and talented community of artists and painters whose works can be found for sale at a number of surprising venues.

ARTISTIC BOUTIQUE

A very eclectic collection of giftware is showcased at **Artistic Boutique** (L. G. Smith Blvd. 90-92, 297/582-3142, 10am-6pm Mon.-Sat.), a long-standing favorite among islanders. They carry fine and semiprecious jewelry, NAO by Lladró, and a very unique selection of authentic East Indian garments, rugs, sculptures and home decor items.

Artistic Boutique is Aruba's last bastion of fine table linens—always among one of the island's real bargains, especially compared to linen prices in the United States. If you are the kind of person who still sets an elegant holiday table or are looking for a special bridal shower gift, be sure to check out their selection of hand-embroidered and appliquéd linens.

Though close to the cruise terminal, the store is easy to miss. The entrance is in the large parking lot adjacent to the Breitling watch store.

★ COSECHA

Authentic local arts and handicrafts can be found at **Cosecha** (Zoutmanstraat 1, 297/587-8709, www.arubacosecha.com, 9am-6pm Mon.-Sat., $7-200), directly behind the Renaissance Marina Tower in Oranjestad. You can find anything here, from inexpensive handmade costume jewelry to handcrafted skateboards made of driftwood. Each day, one of the artists on display will be present to discuss their work or take special commissions.

HENDRIK SCHOUTEN STUDIO

Transplanted Dutch artist Hendrik Schouten performs his craft before visitors' eyes in his Renaissance Marketplace studio. He has an imaginative way with portraiture and an arresting artistic style. He is quite prolific, and there is enormous demand for his work. If you are interested in original art, it's worthwhile to stop by the **Hendrik Schouten Studio** (L. G. Smith Blvd. 82, 297/585-3374, www.hendrikaruba.exto.org, 2:30pm-6pm Mon., 2:30pm-7pm Fri., 10:30am-5pm Sat.).

★ MOPA-MOPA

Aficionados of genuine, artfully crafted handiwork should not leave Aruba without visiting **Mopa-Mopa** (Renaissance Marketplace, L. G. Smith Blvd. 82, 297/588-7297, www.mopamopa.com, 10am-6pm Mon.-Sat.). Though not produced on Aruba, the arresting and beautiful pieces on sale here are unique.

These works are the result of a complex process handed down through the generations of the Quillasinga tribe of Colombia and still done as it was before the Spanish came to the New World. The buds of the mopa-mopa tree, a bush that grows in Putumayo province in the Amazon basin, are boiled to produce a resin. Natural plant dyes give the resin distinctive colors. The artisans then chew the resin to soften it, so it can be stretched and cut into intricate designs. Most works communicate the Quillasinga culture through natural

Authentically Aruban

If you're looking for a unique gift that truly represents Aruba, be sure to check out some of these places.

Since the mid-20th century, nearly 99 percent of the island's foodstuffs have been imported, as the harsh desert climate is inhospitable to agriculture. Recently, new technologies and a "green" sensibility have resulted in widespread cultivation of hardier fruits and vegetables, as well as the production of some very interesting liquors and condiments, such as Madame Janette relish and Papaya Pica. You can find these goods at **Super Food** and the **Alhambra Shopping Bazaar** in the Eagle Beach area.

Ha'Bon (Coconuts and Van Dorp stores, various hotel sundry shops, Island Breeze at Airport, 297/594-5777, www.habonaruba.com,) is a line of all natural soaps handmade in Aruba. They are very gentle and designed for all skin types. This small company hires mentally and physically challenged individuals as staff and also recycles their unused soap to donate to care facilities for the elderly. The various soaps are delightfully scented with fresh flowers and herbs and very attractively packaged for gift giving.

Collectors seeking authentic local arts and handicrafts should visit **Cosecha** (Zoutmanstraat 1, 297/587-8709, www.arubacosecha.com, 9am-6pm Mon.-Sat., $7-200), directly behind the Renaissance Marina Tower in Oranjestad. Housed in a beautifully restored landmark building over 100 years old, Cosecha is government sponsored and aims to encourage local artisans to pursue their passions.

The collection is quite diverse, and the artists produce much of it by recycling what most consider useless debris. You will find jewelry made of djucu nuts that have floated over the sea from Venezuela, skateboards made of driftwood, and remarkable accessories fashioned from old inner tubes. Every item is officially certified as being "Made in Aruba." Different artists visit daily to discuss their work.

subjects, such as flora and fauna, ceremonial masks, or stories of their everyday life. The results are items anyone would be proud to own and display. This traditional Colombian craft cannot be readily found outside its home country.

POST ARUBA

A visit to Aruba's post office or central bank would not usually be at the top of most souvenir shopping lists. These are two places, however, where ideal gifts and mementos can be found for stamp or coin collectors. **Post Aruba** (Irausquinplein 9, 297/528-7678, www.postaruba.com, 7:30am-noon and 1pm-4:30pm Mon.-Fri.) headquarters in Oranjestad has a philately desk where collectors can find beautiful first-day-of-issue ensembles of commemorative stamps. The post office issues 10-12 commemorative collections annually. Each is created from original artwork by local artists who also design the special envelope and cancellation stamp standard to a first-day ensemble.

UNOCA GALLERY

The government-funded foundation that supports cultural projects, **UNOCA** (Stadionweg 21, 297/583-5681, www.unocaruba.org, 8:30am-noon and 1:30pm-5pm Mon.-Fri.) maintains a permanent collection, but also hosts temporary shows with works for sale. Aruba's most respected native artists thus have an excellent venue for showing their work. Art collectors interested in exploring Aruba's artistic past and present will be enlightened—and perhaps find a worthwhile piece.

CLOTHING AND FASHION

LA LINDA DEPARTMENT STORE

The invasion of designer brand shops has transformed many islanders into walking fashion plates. They are thoroughly informed in the trendiest names in garments and accessories. Still, the island has shops that Arubans always turn to first for everyday needs, which have a special place in the community. **La Linda Department Store** (Caya G. F. Betico Croes 3, 297/585-2120, 9am-6:30pm Mon.-Sat.) is such an island institution.

It started out as a tiny notions store back before WWII, carrying "a bit of this and a bit of that." This family business, for decades one of the largest stores on the island, still has the same philosophy. Consumer demand has expanded enormously, and so has the inventory. If misdirected luggage has left one or more family members without a change of clothes, a quick fix can be found here for any size and gender. It is one of the few stores on Aruba to stock tall and big men's clothing, as well as stylish plus sizes for women.

La Linda is an anything and everything store. Find beachwear to formal clothing, beach toys to bicycles, brand name athletic shoes, or blow-dryers and reading glasses, all moderately priced.

PALAIS ORIENTAL

Popular with island women for trendy and timeless tropical wear, **Palais Oriental** (Caya G. F. Betico Croes 72, 297/585-1422, 8:30am-6:30pm Mon.-Sat.) offers a vast selection of casual and career clothing for sizes 6 to 26, at very comfortable prices. While their collection is not exclusive to curvier fashionistas, it features the most diverse and stylish options on Aruba for plus size women.

The shop is also famous for the exceptionally friendly and helpful staff, who make shopping for bargain-priced resort wear all the more enjoyable. A number of annual vacationers make it a rule to travel with a lighter suitcase, knowing they will be paying Palais Oriental a visit.

JEWELRY STORES

A concentration of fine-quality jewelry stores radiate out from the cruise ship terminal. It is possible to spend an entire morning, or longer, examining the inventory of several shops to find that special piece. Be prepared to perhaps spend another hour bargaining for it. Shoppers who know their gems and understand current trends in the market can do well. Haggling over prices is not a practice of the finer stores.

★ GANDELMAN JEWELERS

One of the best known names for fine designer goods and watches is **Gandelman Jewelers** (Renaissance Mall, L. G. Smith Blvd. 82, 297/529-9900, http://gandelman.net, 10am-8pm Mon.-Sat.; branch stores in Hyatt Regency and Marriott Resort 9am-midnight Mon.-Sat.). For generations, this has been where residents of Curacao and Aruba shop for high-quality jewelry. It is a successful family business with a superlative reputation.

Gandelman is the exclusive agent for Rolex, Cartier, Patek Philippe, Carrera y Carrera, Bulgari, Breguet, and David Yurman. They also have the largest collection of Baccarat jewelry and giftware. Famous names in luxury accessories are discounted by 5-20 percent over U.S. retail prices.

NOBLE JEWELERS

Nash, the owner of **Noble Jewelers** (Westraat 4, 297/583-8780, nash@setarnet.aw, 9am-6pm Mon.-Sat.), is an icon of the jewelry trade on Aruba. He has clients who return annually and swear by the quality, price, and service of his store. Noble is the exclusive dealership for Hearts on Fire diamonds in Oranjestad. The brilliant stones are particularly known for the exceptional quality and fire, due to their unique, multifaceted cut. Noble is also very community-minded, annually providing the volunteer foundation Friends of the Handicapped with its most important fundraising raffle prizes.

PERFUME AND COSMETICS

Still one of the traditionally great buys of the Caribbean, European perfumes can be found at shops in all the main tourist areas. Prices are exactly the same on the island as at the airport. There is no need to wait until your departure to purchase that favorite fragrance—or to discover a new one. Exclusive brands of skin care products, such as La Prairie, are also discounted compared to U.S. rates.

DUFRY

One of the best known names internationally for duty-free scents and cosmetics is **Dufry** (Caya G. F. Betico Croes 29, 297/582-2790, www.dufry.com, 9am-6pm Mon.-Sat.). There are three stores in Oranjestad and two at the airport. An enthusiastic crew of cosmetic artists is always ready to provide patrons with a new look and to advise on skin care.

MAGGY'S EMPORIUM

Since 1955, **Maggy's Emporium** (Caya G. F. Betico Croes 59, 297/582-2113, www.maggysaruba.aw, 9am-6pm Mon.-Sat.) has been Aruba's place to shop for the finest in cosmetics and fragrances. A fully trained staff of enthusiastic makeup experts awaits patrons, ready to provide the latest tips on makeup trends and new scents.

During the first week in June every year, the shop conducts a weeklong beauty festival. This entails workshops with visiting specialists from top cosmetic companies. Sessions are usually free with the purchase of a package that includes a choice of items. Glamorous bachelorette parties end the day here with wine, hors d'oeuvres, and exotic cocktails.

PENHA

A well-established name in the Dutch Caribbean, **Penha** (Caya G. F. Betico Croes 11, 297/582-4160, www.jlpenha.com, 9am-6pm Mon.-Sat.) has a full selection of the most sought-after fragrances and famous brand name cosmetics. It is also the exclusive agents for Karen Kane resort wear and MAC cosmetics on Aruba. The dedicated MAC boutique maintains a staff of expert cosmeticians ready to do hair and makeup for weddings and special occasions.

SHOPPING MALLS

★ RENAISSANCE MALL

Aruba's greatest concentration of signature designer stores is in **Renaissance Mall** (L. G. Smith Blvd. 82, 297/582-4622, www.shoprenaissancearuba.com, 10am-8pm Mon.-Sat.), an enclosed mall within the Renaissance Resort. The shops here feature designer brands, such as Louis Vuitton, Adolfo Dominguez, Carolina Herrara, Custo Barcelona, Gucci, Furla, Ermenegildo Zegna, Vilebrequin, Faìonnable, Dolce & Gabbana, EPK, Diesel, with Apriori, Samoon, Erfo, Joseph Ribkoff, Hammer, Hammerle, and Gottex sold in the Entre Nous/Eva Boutique.

The mall has Aruba Aloe and Dufry outlets. Scattered among the clothing shops are the fine-quality jewelers Chopard Boutique, Colombian Emeralds, Gandelman, and Jewelry Warehouse. Cigar Emporium sells Cuban cigars and the most diverse and unique collection of decorative lighters to be found on Aruba.

The mall is the ground floor of the Renaissance Marina Tower. Hotel restaurants offer excellent choices for dining. The focal point of the mall is a Starbucks that won awards as the most beautifully designed outlet in the Caribbean.

RENAISSANCE MARKETPLACE

Though it is home to a number of shops, the open-air mall called **Renaissance Marketplace** (L. G. Smith Blvd. 82, 297/582-4622, www.shoprenaissancearuba.com, stores 10am-8pm Mon.-Sat., restaurants and clubs 10am-1am daily) is best known for its restaurants and nightlife. The shops here carry more standard souvenir stock. Adjacent to the water, a row of dining spots, including Cilo, Hung Paradise, Sushi-Ya, Sea Salt, and The Dutch Pancake House, offer harbor views for breakfast, lunch, and dinner. Plaza Café, Casa Tua, Grand Café Tropical, and Cuba's Cooking provide dinner and entertainment until the wee hours of the night.

Interspersed among the restaurants and clubs are some interesting shops, including a **Mopa-Mopa** store (297/588-7297, www.mopamopa.com, 10am-6pm Mon.-Sat.), which specializes in unique handicrafts from Colombia. Rage is famous for its sterling silver jewelry. The collection includes a huge selection of stylish studs for a piercing anywhere on the body. Champagne has an attractive collection of costume jewelry and moderately priced accessories. City Fashion outfits men and women with tropical resort wear. Souvenirs and sundries can be found at Captain Cook's, open until late at night.

Hendrik Schouten (297/585-3374, www.hendrikaruba.exto.org, 2:30pm-6pm Mon., 2:30pm-7pm Fri., 10:30am-5pm Sat.) maintains an art store and studio, where he gives painting lessons. Aruba's original movie theater, The Cinemas, is in this mall, showing first-run films.

ROYAL PLAZA MALL

Aruba's first giant, multiservice mall was **Royal Plaza Mall** (L. G. Smith Blvd. 94, 297/588-0351, 10am-6:30pm Mon.-Sat.). Architecturally, it is a frothy confection dominating the boulevard and harbor. The first thing to catch the attention of arriving cruise ship passengers is its ornate facade and the sun glinting off its golden dome. Three stories house dozens of shops, plus restaurants and nightclubs that overlook the harbor.

The tiers surround a large courtyard populated with kiosks selling bargain-priced knickknacks. Among the 50 shops and eateries are respected jewelers such as Shiva's, Pearl Gems, Little Switzerland, Royal Jewels & Diamonds, and My Time and Spare Time watch stores.

Dufry (297/582-2790, www.dufry.com, 9am-6pm Mon.-Sat.) is famous for fine cosmetics and perfumes. Bula Surf Shop is Aruba's center for the most popular names in surfing gear, sandals, sunglasses, and board shorts. Among the souvenir and resort wear stores are Fantasea, Little Holland, Yellow Submarine, Souvenir Outlet and More, Bob the Fish, Del Sol, Shipwreck, Beach n' Wear, and Alcy's Boutique. The mall is also home to a cigar store, Casa Del Hubano.

SUPERMARKETS

Most of Aruba does their supermarket shopping on the western end of Oranjestad. Circumstances have resulted in Aruba's major markets setting up business in close proximity to each other. The convenience of their grouping allows shoppers to go from one place to the next to check off all the items on their list, as it is rare for one market to have everything you seek. This is simply an aspect of island life.

Supermarket shopping on Aruba is quite an interesting experience. Expect a diversity of goods from around the world, most likely several that are never seen in most U.S. markets. Some may lament the paucity or expense of the American brands. This is to be expected, as all items are imported, with freight and taxes added on to the cost. Compensating for the additional prices is the opportunity to sample how the rest of the world eats, and their equivalents to standard U.S. goods. You will find that many basic items, such as Dutch butter, coffee, chocolate, and tea, are far superior and less expensive than their U.S. counterparts. European produced foodstuffs are forbidden from using dyes; try these breakfast cereals for a more natural product.

The mélange that is the Aruban community is evident in the diversity of comestibles carried by most markets. Products direct from China, India, Indonesia, and the Philippines are standard stock to service the expatriate communities. Goods that one would normally have to seek out in specialty shops in the United States are normally found on most island supermarket shelves. The markets can be surprising and inexpensive sources of souvenir gifts for any cooking enthusiast. Attractively priced and packaged exotic spice packets, local relishes, and other unique items are easy to travel with, and will be appreciated by foodies who want to expand their culinary repertoire.

Aruba Aloe

aloe vera plants

Since the late 1800s, Aruba has been considered one of the world's top producers of aloe vera products. The extract from this cactus has proven to have remarkable healing properties; it was always favored as a pure, natural product for treating burns and irritated skin. The world lost interest in aloe in the 1950s, but a resurgence in holistic healing and skin care has again prompted a thriving industry.

The **Aruba Aloe Museum and Factory** (Pitastraat 115, 297/588-3222, www.arubaaloe.com, 9am-5pm Mon.-Fri.) in Hato welcomes tour groups and individuals, providing a fascinating history of aloe harvesting on the island. In 2000 it acquired a new owner and a complete renovation of the field and factory. The R&D department developed a prescription-strength product that has been tested and praised by burn wards across Europe.

Aruba Aloe produces several lines with varying scents and concentrations. There are sunblocks, after-sun soothing gels and creams, body and face lotions, and hair care products. Fourteen outlets are scattered about the island, including one at the airport next to the departure lounges. Store hours depend on location. Oranjestad stores are open during the day. Palm Beach and Eagle Beach outlets stay open until 10pm. These products can also be found in most hotel mini-markets.

Aruba Aloe outlets are at the following locations:

- Alhambra Shopping Bazaar
- Arawak Gardens
- Reina Beatrix International Airport
- cruise ship terminal
- Divi Village Resort lobby
- La Cabana Hotel lobby
- Palm Beach Plaza
- Paseo Herencia Shopping Mall
- Renaissance Mall
- The Village Mall
- Caya Betico Croes 78
- Marriott Ocean Club
- Occidental Resort
- Riu Resort

Aruban chocolate bars

One drawback of island life is the highly anticipated weekly shipment of fruits and vegetables, dairy products, and other fresh items. Shopping the day before they arrive can be very disappointing, as it is sometimes difficult to find fresh milk, lettuce, and other standard items. This is becoming less of a problem, but is still an issue during busy holiday weeks. If you are arriving on a weekend and staying in a place where you plan to cook, it's best to stock up immediately.

LING & SONS

Aruba has two exceptionally well-stocked markets, one of which is **Ling & Sons** (Italiestraat 26, 297/588-7718, www.lingandsons.com, 8am-9pm Mon.-Sat., 9am-6pm Sun.). Their slogan, "groceries just like home," refers to a diverse selection of popular U.S. brands, including the generic IGA line. They are also, however, the island source for Albert Heijn products, the trademark brand of one of the largest market chains in Europe known for quality goods. These products are far less expensive than familiar American brands and definitely worth trying.

Ling & Sons has always been considered one of the finest food outlets for its fresh specialty salads department, bakery, meats and produce, and enormous diversity of inventory. It is very popular and enjoys a brisk trade, ensuring a fast turnover of fresh products. This is also the single largest source of kosher food items on Aruba year-round.

Eagle Beach and Manchebo Beach

Because of the easy access by foot to all of Oranjestad shopping, this area was traditionally more resort- and beach-oriented. The proliferation of condominium complexes is resulting in a rash of malls along the Sasaki Highway. They have not yet, however, been populated by very interesting enterprises aside from a couple of restaurants. The sleek Alhambra Shopping Bazaar houses some interesting shops and a gourmet mini-market. A few local stores can be found on Bubali Road once you cross Sasaki Highway, but carry little of interest in the way of souvenirs and gifts. Most resorts have newsstands with small sundry and souvenir shops attached. A very few facilities—such as the Divi, Tamarijn, and Casa Del Mar—have arcades with resort wear, jewelry, and perfume outlets.

ART, HANDICRAFTS, AND SOUVENIRS

THE CENTRAL BANK OF ARUBA

Aruba's financial agency, **The Central Bank of Aruba** (J. E. Irausquin Blvd. 8, 297/525-2141, www.cbaruba.org. 8am-noon and 1pm-4pm Mon.-Fri.) not only regulates the island's commerce, but is also the agent for stunning commemorative coin collections. The proofs are high-quality silver or gold limited issues. Special collections celebrate a diversity of events, beginning with Status Aparte and Aruba having its own money. Among the coin issues that are not sold out is one dedicated to the Royal Visit in 2011. Aruba's 25th anniversary of Status Aparte is available in both silver and gold proofs, as are memorial issues of inauguration of King Willem-Alexander in 2013. They are minted in Holland and beautifully boxed for display or gift giving.

MANA AT LA CABANA RESORT

La Cabana Beach Resort in Eagle Beach decided to show its support for the local art community by turning the main lobby and mezzanine into a giant art gallery. **Movimiento di Arte Nobo Aruba** (MANA; J. E. Irausquin Blvd. 250, 297/594-2233, 24 hours daily) is the curator for the exhibits that change every three months. Aruba's top artists are challenged to create fresh works around particular themes. The works can be viewed at any time of the day or night, but to arrange a purchase, call the contact number between 1pm and 6pm daily.

SHOPPING MALLS

ALHAMBRA SHOPPING BAZAAR

The sleek and stylish center for shopping and dining in the low-rise areas is **Alhambra Shopping Bazaar** (J. E. Irausquin Blvd. 47, 297/583-5000, shops 10am-10pm daily, dining and entertainment 7am-2am daily). Peruse The Lazy Lizard for tasteful knickknacks and resort wear. An Aruba Aloe outlet meets all your needs for locally produced sun protection and hair and skin care products. There is an official Aruba logo shop, with a distinctive graphic emblazoned on an assortment of garments for all ages. Bijoux Terner has big floppy beach hats and other great accessories at a standard price of $10 per item. Diamonds International offers top names in designer jewelry and watches, while R. Glass has a wide assortment of handcrafted costume jewelry and accessories. You will also find Shalom Body & Soul Spa here.

The Market, a very well outfitted mini-market, has an excellent wine selection and prepared foods for an easy meal. An expansive, charming dining patio is surrounded by a budget-priced food court with Little Caesar's Pizzeria, Dunkin' Donuts, Subway, and a Baskin Robbins. There is also a Juan Valdez coffee shop, and Twist of Flavors has an assortment of Dutch pancakes and a daily Early Bird Dinner special.

Flea Markets

Though weekend flea markets are a Dutch tradition, it is the influx of immigrants from the Caribbean and Latin America that are largely responsible for their spreading on Aruba. Since 2000 flea markets have come to dominate some shopping areas and are always popular for bargain souvenirs. These amalgams of street stalls offer inexpensive resort wear and accessories, T-shirts, and decorative gewgaws, at the cheapest prices. Among them you will find some original Latin American handicrafts, but for the most part, they sell mass-produced cheap imports, much of which you have likely seen at other destinations, silkscreened with a different name.

Upon exiting the cruise terminal, visitors are presented with a cluster of stalls: **The Terminal Flea Market** (directly across the street from the terminal, 10am-6:30pm Mon.-Sat.). Another flea market lines the **waterfront along L. G. Smith Boulevard** (8am-6:30pm Mon.-Sat.), which was traditionally the fruit and fish market in decades past.

Tourist Go Flea Market (L. G. Smith Blvd. 144, 297/592-2424, 8am-8pm Sat.-Sun.) is so well established, it even has a Facebook page. Dozens of stalls with authentic regional crafts and inexpensive Aruba logo gear set up on the weekends. The parking lot of what was the local paint factory takes on a whole new personality. An easy walk from the Manchebo Beach resorts, and right next to the major supermarkets, it is one of the best spots for browsing for all sorts of unexpected goodies.

Nighttime bargain hunters enjoy trawling the numerous kiosks that open at sunset along **J. E. Irausquin Boulevard in Palm Beach.** They operate seven days a week and offer inexpensive but stylish sunglasses, handicrafts, T-shirts, handmade costume jewelry, and attractive accessories of every stripe. **The Village Mall** hosts a flea market in its courtyard (7pm-10pm daily) with a very festive atmosphere.

SUPERMARKETS

SAVE-A-LOT

Affiliated with the well known U.S. SavMor franchise, **Save-A-Lot Supermarket** (J. E. Boegoroi 4, 297/587-1090, 8am-8pm daily) carries many of the "exclusive brands" budget-conscious U.S. shoppers know well. For canned and packaged goods, dairy products, and a wide assortment of comestibles, this is Aruba's bargain-priced grocery store. Geared to the Aruban market, those familiar with the chain will also find an expanded inventory including many Dutch brands.

Though the deli and meat department may not be as varied and elegant as neighbor Super Food, there is a very nice bakery. As a rule, fresh produce and dairy, along with frozen food items, are generally much more reasonably priced than the other markets, as are the generic brand soft drinks and juices.

★ SUPER FOOD

Aruba's first building designed to be totally energy self-sufficient through renewable sources houses **Super Food** (Sasaki Hwy. z/n, 297/588-6040, http://superfoodaruba.com, 8am-8pm Mon.-Sat., 9am-6pm Sun.). It is impossible to miss at the Sasaki Highway and Bubali Road intersection, directly across from the Tropicana Resort. More of a mall than a market, it has always been regarded as Aruba's Dutch grocery, known for its inventory from Holland. It is considered to have the best deli and cheese departments, as well as diverse, quality produce and meat markets and an exceptional bakery. This is Aruba's most complete source of gourmet and exotic items from around the world.

The island's largest market is clean, and fresh food products are beautifully presented. The arcade of shops surrounding it contains opticians, a fresh fish store, a pharmacy, MIO mobile providers, and a very attractive and reasonably priced eatery called Jack's Cafe, named for the market's owner. Next to the front entrance is an Aruba Bank ATM.

Palm Beach, Malmok, and Noord

Palm Beach after dark has been enlivened by a phenomenon that only materialized since 2006: nighttime shopping. This was previously unheard of on Aruba. Savvy entrepreneurs figured out that most vacationers would rather spend their days indulging in other activities or laying on the beach, rather than shopping, and the ploy has proven to be very successful. In the evenings, most malls host special events, and dining venues offer free entertainment to make nighttime shopping even more attractive.

ART, HANDICRAFTS, AND SOUVENIRS

POST ARUBA

Post Aruba (Palm Beach Plaza, 297/528-7678, www.postaruba.com, 8am-6pm Mon.-Sat.) is conveniently situated near the major resorts. This branch also sells commemorative stamps, plus another very special item only available here: personalized Aruba stamps. Bring your camera's memory card with some exciting pictures of the family and have them digitally inserted into one of seven design choices of artful, usable stamps. Beautiful illustrations feature Aruba's most famous landmarks. Imagine a rendering of Alto Vista Chapel with a photo of your family actually at the chapel, integrated into the design of the stamp. Sold in sheets of six, they can be used to send postcards out to friends and family anywhere in the world.

★ TERRAFUSE

Make your own Aruba mementos at **Terrafuse** (Turibana 14, 297/592-2978, www.arubaglassceramics.com, 3pm-6pm Tues., 9am-noon Thurs., $85 pp). The studios offer a singular experience for the crafty: classes in the art of glass bead-making. Participants learn a new skill along with personally creating a very unique and individual souvenir. Returning students receive a discount on the class fee.

Ciro and Marian Abath are internationally recognized artists. Ciro's work greets island visitors at the airport in the *Water* exhibit. Both he and his wife have traveled the world and studied with masters of glass art. Their studio is on the grounds of their quaint and lovingly maintained landmark *cunucu* house. Not far from the hotels, it is on the way to the Alto Vista Chapel.

Workshops in glass bead-making are held twice a week. Special arrangements can be made for groups of 4-6. You will also be treated to a demonstration of glassblowing. They use imported Moretti glass from Italy. This saves you the trouble and time of traveling to Venice to see this craft in action!

Ciro and Marian have a boutique on the premises with an exquisite collection of their original glass pieces. One-of-a-kind mementos from Aruba can be found here. A taxi ride to the studio is $7; they will provide transportation back to your resort.

THE MASK

The Mopa-Mopa outlet for Palm Beach, **The Mask** (Paseo Herencia Shopping Mall, 297/586-2900, www.mopamopa.com, 10am-10pm Mon.-Sat., 5pm-10pm Sun.) offers night shoppers the opportunity to obtain these unique and impressive pieces.

I ♥ HOOKAH

One of the shops in the arcade surrounding Sand at Brickell Bay Lounge is **I ♥ Hookah** (L. G. Smith Blvd. 370, 297/600-7116, Ilovehookaharuba@gmail.com, 3pm-1am Sun.-Thurs., 3pm-3am Fri.-Sat.), a fun and funky mini-market that sells and rents hookahs and also carries anything else you can imagine that has to do with smoking, including Cuban cigars. If you are also in need of aspirin or have an upset tummy, the shop carries an assortment of over-the-counter remedies and is about the only spot staying open until the wee hours.

The inventive owners have a startling selection of fruits, spices, and other surprising non-nicotine inhalants for their hookahs, so you do not have to carry the guilt of puffing away. It is all part of the service they offer to the Sand Lounge customers, but this is an independent store, with very diverse inventory of all sorts of unique items you might find you need in the middle of the night, including condoms.

CIGARS

★ ARUHIBA

Cigar aficionados recommend Aruba's own **Aruhiba** (L. G. Smith Blvd. 330, 297/585-7833, www.aruhibacigars.com, 9am-6:30pm Mon.-Sat., 9:30am-4pm Sun.) for a good buy and a pleasant surprise. The cigars are cultivated and rolled on the island, with no chemicals used to hurry the fermentation process. Aruhiba produces 16 different cigars of varying length, strength, thickness, and price. Cigar lovers report they are a very enjoyable smoke. Lack of import and shipping costs make them a bargain compared to imported stogies from Cuba, Honduras, and the Dominican Republic. A diverse selection of cigars from the entire Caribbean is also offered in the shop, which has one of the largest inventories of such stores on Aruba. Find it among the cluster of kiosks next to the Olde Molen. Interested parties are invited to tour the cigar factory in Moko by appointment.

CLOTHING AND FASHION

Palm Beach fashion shops tend to focus on resort clothes and swimwear. There are several shops with beautiful items that customers can put on to wear immediately on the beach. Among them are some haute couture stores with exotic European fashion for those who like to make a statement with their beachwear.

BACI DA ROMA

The owner of **Baci da Roma** (Paseo Herencia Shopping Mall, J. E. Irausquin Blvd. 382-A, 297/586-7986, bacidaroma.aruba@yahoo.com, 10am-10pm Mon.-Sat., 5pm-10pm Sun.), or "Roman Kisses," could be a model for her elegant collection. In fact, she once was, so she knows her stuff when ordering inventory. Fine-quality English couture from Traffic People and Paradise is suitable for Aruba's tropical surroundings or an elegant cocktail party back home. The timeless styling with trendy touches at reasonable prices will undoubtedly make you fall in love with something in this store.

★ CARIBBEAN QUEEN

Bring on the bling is the motto of **Caribbean Queen** (Palm Beach Plaza, L. G. Smith Blvd. 95, 297/586-8737, 10am-10pm Mon.-Sat., 5pm-10pm Sun.). It's a most unusual accessory store for the woman who wants to rule any room she enters. Every item in this shop makes a distinctive statement, from crystal barrettes and earrings, adorable flowery leather sandals, to lizard-skin luggage ensembles.

Each month the shop features one-of-a-kind work by a local female artisan, the "Caribbean Queen of the Month." It could be a collection of costume jewelry made with Elizabeth van Brede's handcrafted porcelain beads and pendants. Look over the unusual clutches and belts made from recycled inner tubes by Carina Molina. (They are far more impressive than you might think!) You may even find hand-painted silk scarves created using a specialized resist and dye technique by the author of this book. These distinctive original works are the central theme of the store, but there are lots of other unique items to catch a shopper's eye.

KAPRICHO

This is a great place for both genders to perk up a vacation wardrobe. **Kapricho** (Paseo Herencia Shopping Mall, J. E. Irausquin Blvd. 382-A, 297/586-6510, kapricho@setarnet.aw, 10am-10pm Mon.-Sat., 5pm-10pm Sun.) has a beautiful selection of resort wear and accessories for women as well as an exceptionally attractive collection for men. The store features soft, comfortable shirts from Tommy Bahama and Tori Richards, which have the tropical look without being too flowery or garish.

JEWELERS

Palm Beach does not quite have the concentration of jewelers as Oranjestad. Still, there are more than enough scattered among the various shopping centers and hotels to provide excellent variety and range of quality. They are frequently situated close to casinos. They know big winners need an outlet for those big cash payoffs that are hard to transport back home. Colombian Emeralds, Gandelman Jewelers, and Little Switzerland, all well-known regional franchises, can be found in the major hotels.

GEMSTONES INTERNATIONAL

The congenial lady giving you expert advice during a visit to **Gemstones International** (J. E. Irausquin Blvd. 370, 297/583-0663, gemstonesaruba.com, 4pm-10pm daily) is the owner Sarita, who knows her stones and has exquisite taste. If you cannot find something that is quite what you are looking for, her artisans will create an original new piece. She carries a diverse collection of loose precious and semiprecious stones to choose from, and guarantees all work.

JEPACALAOS

Unique handcrafted jewelry and art objects can be found at **Jepacalaos** (Palm Beach Plaza 218, 297/741-8442, www.jepacalaos.com, 10pm-10pm daily). A large part of the interesting collection of jewelry features the Larimar stone, a form of pectolite containing strains of cobalt that impart a unique blue coloring. The shop's artisans will also produced custom pieces to order, given sufficient time.

Those who appreciate fine handicrafts will be drawn to the collection of tamo, which is rather similar to mopa-mopa, but using natural wood colors, rather than black backgrounds. The colored pieces are then inlaid so the final product looks nothing like mopa-mopa work, but has its own distinctive finish. The various vases, jewelry boxes, tables, and other decorative items are very eye-catching.

JEWELS IN PARADISE

An intimate shop in Palm Beach Plaza called **Jewels in Paradise** (L. G. Smith Blvd. 95, 297/586-7433, jewelsinparadisearuba@setarnet.aw) takes great pride in carrying

Sales Tax

Aruba has a 1.5 percent sales tax, which is actually a turnover tax called "Belasting op Bedrijfsomzetten" or BBO. It was introduced in January of 2007 and lowered from 3 percent to 1.5 percent in 2010. In 2015, a 2 percent "health tax" (BAZV) was implemented, bringing the sales tax total to 3.5 percent.

Certain enterprises and goods are exempt, such as the medical profession and prescription drugs. Commercial enterprises, particularly supermarkets, apply the sales tax. Other venues, such as jewelers, which cater specifically to tourists, usually absorb the tax expense or build it into the cost of goods, rather than adding it on to a purchase.

Diamond Shopping

THE FOUR C'S

It is vital while looking for the best deal in diamonds to know the "Four C's" of gemstones: clarity, color, cut, and carat. In these politically correct times, a new C of country may also be a consideration. Most consumers usually have another "C" in mind—cost.

Carat refers to weight or size, and cut refers to the fashion in which the stonecutter has tried to best enhance the natural virtues of the gem. Multiple facets and the depth of the cut affect the brilliance and scintillation. When a round or pear-shaped diamond is well cut, light enters through the flat part of the stone then travels to the angled underside. Here, it is reflected repeatedly before bouncing back out to the observer's eye. This light is the scintillation—the flashing, fiery effect that makes diamonds so mesmerizing. A stone of a high carat may be poorly proportioned and heavily "discounted." This gives a false impression of a great deal. The brilliant fire that dazzles is the measure of a quality stone.

Color and clarity are the other two most important variables. Diamonds are graded against a white background. Grade is calculated by the hue of the stone compared to a set of master stones graded by the Gemological Institute of America (GIA). There is a wide range of color designations, starting with the purest white and the alphabetic letter D and working their way down the alphabet, all the way to the Z, which is the deepest yellow of colors, referred to as canary yellow diamonds. Jewelry fashions change to also deploy champagne, chocolate, and black diamonds, their value dictated by current trends. The diamonds most used in multi-stone pieces are the "near colorless" categories G and H.

A very important factor that will make a simple, one-carat stone cost thousands more than a gem three times the size is clarity. Vendors are impressed by patrons who understand what grades of clarity signify. It is a description of the stone while still in the rough, uncut stage.

FLAWS

- **FL**—Flawless, the rarest and most valuable of diamonds.
- **IF**—Internally flawless, with only external flaws while in the rough stage.
- **I1-I3**—You can see flaws with the naked eye.
- **SI1-SI2**—Slight Inclusion: You can easily see flaws with a 10X microscope.
- **VS1-VS2**—Very Slight Inclusion: You need not be an expert to see flaws with a 10X microscope, but it takes a long time (more than about 10 seconds).
- **VVS1-VVS2**—Very, Very Slight Inclusion: Only an expert can detect flaws with a 10X microscope.

There are wide varieties of flaws; many do not affect the integrity of the gem. A diamond doesn't need to be flawless to be gorgeous. Flaws can be crystal growth, which sometimes looks like a diamond within the diamond. The extent of the flaw and how it detracts from the beauty of the diamond affects its investment value. Buyers beware of I1-I3 level diamonds.

ETHICAL PRACTICES

The term "blood diamond" refers to gems that are mined under repressive regimes with forced labor. African countries in political upheaval are known for this. Famous personalities have endorsed certain brands of diamonds with ethical practices of avoiding blood diamonds. These stones may be more expensive, but the people that work the mines have humane conditions, with all labor law benefits. These diamond companies have invested in and bettered the communities near the mines, providing schools and scholarships. These gems are engraved with a microscopic logo to prove their pedigree.

one-of-a-kind items. The owner Dinesh also has a varied collection of jewels, priced to any budget. Find silver and semiprecious stone pieces or a seven-carat emerald pendant; the selection is that diverse. Whether your taste runs to simple and delicate Italian design or something from their "Maharani" Collection, inspired by traditional East Indian fashion, you can find something interesting here.

KRISTIE'S JEWELS

A cozy family operation dedicated to quality, **Kristie's Jewels** (J. E. Irausquin Blvd. 382A, 297/586-0598, kristiesjewels@gmail.com, 4pm-10pm daily) is the Palm Beach agent for Hearts on Fire diamonds. The collection consists of unique items designed and manufactured in Italy. The elegant store offers a tasteful, attractive selection. As agents for Silverado charms, they have an "I Love Aruba" charm with a divi tree crafted exclusively for this shop.

SHOPPING MALLS

The Palm Beach area holds Aruba's greatest concentration of malls, and a concentrated dose it is. Shopping, dining, and entertainment are all contained in bustling beehives spread over a half mile of J. E. Irausquin Boulevard. The promenade attracts islanders and tourists equally. Shopping hours uniformly end at 10pm, but clubs and cafés stay open until at least 1am, and 2am or later on Friday and Saturday nights.

ARAWAK GARDENS

Though principally a dining and entertainment center, **Arawak Gardens** (J. E. Irausquin Blvd. 370, shopping 5pm-11pm daily, dining and nightlife 11am-2am daily) hosts a plethora of cozy shops and kiosks with a diverse selection of souvenir items. Piles of T-shirts, beach covers in bright colors, and Aruba logo gear of every stripe, can be found in the various venues.

DE OLDE MOLEN

Visitors can't help noticing an arresting sight when they first enter the modern area of Palm Beach: An authentic Dutch windmill over 200 years old. **De Olde Molen foundation** (L. G. Smith Blvd 330, 8am-2am daily) is the site of a strip of nightspots, and the grounds offer a number of kiosks. These include **Prima Casa Real Estate,** and the official **Aruhiba outlet** for Aruban-made cigars.

The windmill was originally built in 1804. It was used in Friesland for dredging water out of the sub-sea level lands. After being damaged by a storm in 1878, it was disassembled and rebuilt in Holland. There it was used as a grain mill, but fell into disuse after new storm damage in 1929. A Dutchman with dreams of living in the tropics purchased what remained in 1960. It was finally rebuilt on Aruba over a two-story foundation.

PALM BEACH PLAZA

The physically largest shopping center in the area is **Palm Beach Plaza** (L. G. Smith Blvd. 85, 297/586-0045, www.palmbeachplaza.com, shops 10am-10pm, dining and nightlife 7pm-2am). The three floors shelter 32 stores, the island's largest movie theater, bowling alley, video game center, restaurants, cozy bars, and family entertainment.

Unique to Palm Beach Plaza are Salvatore Farragamo, Montblanc, and Lalique outlets. Jewelry stores include Shiva's, Monarch Jewels, Rage Silver, Jewels in Paradise, Jepacalaos and My Time, for budget-priced timepieces. Fashionistas will love Benetton and Totto clothing and accessories, Panache, Giordano, and Caribbean Queen.

San Marino and Basinger are the shops for elegant shoes, as well as a Birkenstock store, while Goofy Gecko and Art Fusion provide those unusual souvenirs you seek. The mall also has outlets of Post Aruba and Western Union.

Customs Allowances and Restrictions

Travelers returning to the United States are required to declare the following on a CBP form in U.S. currency:

- Items purchased.
- Items received as gifts.
- Items bought in duty-free shops, on the ship, or on the plane.
- Repairs or alterations to any items taken abroad and then brought back, even if the alterations were performed free of charge.
- Items brought home for someone else.
- Items intended to sell or use in a business, including merchandise taken out of the United States.

To avoid being charged a duty upon return, it is advised that costly electronic items that are less than six months old be registered upon departure from the United States.

EXEMPTIONS

Travelers returning from Aruba have an $800 standard duty-free exemption. It will be applied in the following instances:

- Items for personal or household use or intended to be given as gifts.
- Items declared to CBP. If not declaring an item that should have been, there is the possibility of forfeiture or penalties.
- Items classified as accompanying baggage, returning with the traveler. Mailed items do not qualify.
- Purchases of fine art, such as original paintings or sculpture, are duty-free.

Exemptions are applicable on a cumulative basis. Frequent travelers must take into account items declared 30 days or less prior to their present return. Items declared on previous journeys less than 30 days past will be deducted from the $800 exemption.

Two liters of alcoholic beverages, as long as one was produced in a U.S. Insular Possession (e.g.,

★ PASEO HERENCIA SHOPPING MALL

The first major mall in Palm Beach, **Paseo Herencia Shopping Mall** (J. E. Irausquin Blvd. 382-A, 297/586-6533, http://paseoherencia.com, shops 10am-10pm daily, dining and nightlife noon-2am daily) offers several unique shops. Most notable about this mall is its community spirit, with walls and corridors filled with island information. Displays showcase important moments in Aruba's history and internationally famous Arubans, and impart a sense of island culture.

For European couture, DGL specializes in Diesel, Gaastra, and Villebrequin. There is a large Tommy Hilfiger outlet, and Kapricho carries elegant tropical clothing. Here you'll find the only Hunkemoller on Aruba—the European version of Victoria's Secret. La Langosta and Agua Bendita sell exclusive lines of Latin designer swimwear. Mario Fernandez of Colombia is one of the most respected names in designer leather goods. Maxi-Pet offers a stunning selection of chic fashion for your favorite canine or feline companion, from full outfits to sparkling collars.

Puerto Rico), are allowed when combined with liquors distilled and bottled in the Caribbean basin or Andean countries. Otherwise, the limit is one liter. Travelers carrying alcohol must be over 21 and returning to a state that has no restrictions on its import. Normally, no more than 200 cigarettes and 100 cigars are exempt, if they are within the $800 allotment ceiling. The same double allowance for liquor can be applied to cigarettes and cigars, when half that allowance is purchased in a U.S. Insular Possession.

Travelers might avoid duties for a total of over $800 in goods depending on circumstances and the items. If a piece of fine jewelry costing $700 is received as a gift, while other miscellaneous goods were purchased, the official may waive the duty, even if the total exceeds $800.

Cruise ship passengers who have stopped in multiple Caribbean basin or Andean countries may receive an allowance of $1,600 for duty-free purchases. This is applicable if one of the ports of purchase was a U.S. Insular Possession such as Puerto Rico or the U.S. Virgin Islands. Duty-free purchases from the Caribbean basin or Andean countries are limited to $800. An additional $800 in duty-free purchases will be allowed from the Insular Possession for a total of $1,600. A number of cruises stopping in Aruba embark from Puerto Rico. This regulation allows travelers additional purchases from the embarkation point. It is essential to retain receipts on all purchases.

PROHIBITED ITEMS

- Cuban cigars
- Live birds of any kind—exotic, domestic, or wild (they may carry a strain of avian flu)
- Live fish, marine animals, and mollusks
- Meats, fruits, vegetables, plants, seeds, animals, and plant and animal products (including soup or soup products)
- Prescription drugs

Some items, such as cooked foods, may be exempt. A full declaration of nature and origin should be made to a customs officer. Travelers departing Aruba will be passing through customs prior to their return flight. If you purchased fruit (unsealed), local snacks, or sandwiches to eat on the plane, be sure to inform the customs officers.

Jewelers include Kristie's, Little Switzerland, Pandora Boutique, Pearl Gems, Times Square, and Sparkles. They offer a range from handcrafted costume jewelry to top-of-the-line precious gemstones. A two-story Maggy's Emporium has a complete menu of spa treatments and salon services, along with all popular brands of scents and cosmetics. There is a dedicated Crocs store and the YOLO (You Only Live Once) brand has both a high-end clothing store and discount shoe store. The Palm Beach outlet for mopa-mopa crafts is also here at The Mask. Paseo Herencia is home to The Cinemas, which shows first-run films for far less than in the United States.

SOUTH BEACH CENTER

South Beach Center (J. E. Irausquin Blvd. 55, shops 10am-10pm daily, dining and nightlife noon-2am daily) occupies a very large complex at the corner of J. E. Irausquin Boulevard and the Noord-Palm Beach Road. Just look for the giant Hard Rock Café neon guitar and you are there. This is an amalgam of local and international eateries, with a few shops and a spa interspersed between them. Most shopping is done at the kiosks lining the sidewalk. They offer all sorts of bargain-priced souvenirs.

Formal shops include a Lazy Lizard, for some stylish resort wear and amusing gifts.

Island Treasures stocks inexpensive beach bags, sandals, wraps, and other typical tropical gear in flowery prints. Restaurants include Rembrandt, with a distinctly Dutch pub vibe, and the local Hooter's and Benihana outlets.

THE VILLAGE

A standout from the standard Miami Beach architecture of the area is **The Village** (J. E. Irausquin Blvd. 348, shops 5pm-10pm daily, dining and nightlife 7am-2am daily), modeled to look like a community of classic Aruban *cunucu* houses. This is a happening place for all ages. Aside from the massive flea market occupying the main courtyard at night, The Village is lined with a number of souvenir and resort wear shops.

Señor Frog's and Gusto are places the club crowd favors, with a highly distinctive atmospheres. Papillon gourmet restaurant occupies the main building.

North Coast

Aruba's traditional wilderness offers little shopping outside of a few of the tourist sites where small shops offer standard, factory-produced souvenir fare. Most carry typical items, like flowery beach covers and logo T-shirts. The shops of the Donkey Sanctuary and Ostrich Farm offer some very unique mementos and giftware.

GIFTS AND SOUVENIRS

AFRICAN ART BOUTIQUE AT OSTRICH FARM

After taking a tour of the Aruba Ostrich Farm, make sure to visit the farm's unique **African Art Boutique** (Matividiri 57, 297/585-9630, www.arubaostrichfarm.com, 9:30am-5pm daily) for a peek at the surprising collection. Home fashion, furniture, original carvings, kitchen linens, and the like are distinctive and extremely attractive. It isn't necessary to travel halfway around the world to obtain some authentic African art. Another unique item is the artwork made from hollowed out ostrich eggs. Collectors of the unusual will find these hand-painted creations most intriguing.

DONKEY SANCTUARY

In addition to an entertaining encounter with some charming residents, the **Donkey Sanctuary** (Bringamosa 2C, Donkey Distress Hotline 297/593-2933, www.arubandonkey.org, 9am-4pm Mon.-Fri., 10am-3pm Sat.-Sun.) has a shop of unique crafts and gifts to support the work. The collection of donkey paraphernalia is quite large, many items custom-made crafts and original paintings donated by top island artists. A charming wall calendar with great donkey photos is issued annually. All proceeds assist in the care and feeding of the denizens of the sanctuary.

Santa Cruz, Paradera, and Piedra Plat

The best of Aruba's shopping is focused in the commercial areas of Oranjestad and Palm Beach that serve both tourists and residents. The dedicated residential areas of Santa Cruz, Paradera, and Piedra Plat have some souvenir shops offering logo shirts and tropical pattern resort wear attached to such sights as the Casibari Rock Formation. Their inventory is the same as similar shops found within the popular tourist areas.

The most unique shop here is the Rococo Plaza, which is a must-visit for collectors and those that enjoy antiques hunting.

the distinctive towers of Rococo Plaza

ANTIQUES

ROCOCO PLAZA

Aruba's only antiques center is **Rococo Plaza** (Tanki Leendert 158-G, 297/741-5640, http://antiquesaruba.com, 9am-1pm and 3:30pm-5:30pm Mon.-Fri., 9am-1pm Sat.), which can be spotted from afar by its unique dual-tower entrance. While touring some of the standard sights, you are bound to pass by Rococo Plaza. It is on the way to Arikok National Park and worth a stop for antiques enthusiasts. The store is enormous. Allow some time to peruse the 20 rooms of curios from diverse eras. Most of the inventory is imported from Europe, and there are some truly fascinating items. Collectors will have a field day.

Expect to find vintage cameras and photos, standup pianos, art deco sconces, and authentic Louis Quinze furniture. Naturally, some chaff surrounds the gems. Though there is quite a lot to work through, many unique treasures await those with a penchant for collecting.

Where to Stay

Some of Aruba's greatest attractions are the glamorous, elegant resorts that line the shore along Palm Beach, Eagle Beach, and Manchebo Beach. The original pioneers of Aruba's tourism industry had a personal vision of the atmosphere that would best suit each area when the first resorts were built along the shore. Their vision set the tone for later projects, with each resort designed to meet the particular desires and expectations of their guests. There are large, bustling, full-service resorts with casinos and clubs for nighttime excitement, or small, tranquil getaways for those seeking to escape from their workday world and fully relax.

Most of these options are usually members of the Aruba Hotel and Tourism Association (AHATA). AHATA member resorts offer excellent service, quality accommodations, and are sincerely concerned about the satisfaction of their guests. They maintain a standard that the Aruba Tourism Authority (ATA) endorses. Many travel agents have inspected these facilities as well and are very comfortable recommending them. Smaller, independent, non-AHATA facilities often deliver the same standards, but they do not have marketing resources equal to the big resorts, so they rely on the endorsements of their patrons. Thanks to the Internet, these places are becoming easier to discover.

Whether choosing a large, full-service resort or one of the smaller guesthouses, the famed hospitality of the island is a consistent element. When veteran visitors explain the reasons they return to Aruba annually, they mention the reliable weather and beautiful beaches, but the sincere welcome they receive from resort staff and island residents is paramount.

In the 1960s, when Aruba was first trying to build a tourist market, families actually welcomed vacationers into their homes for no charge when the few existing resorts were filled. This demonstration of authentic hospitality inspired the mission and values behind the chain of Divi Resorts, one of the largest and most popular local franchises on Aruba.

Smaller lodgings like guesthouses and apartment complexes are great for visitors

Previous: Palm Beach; waterfront pool in Savaneta. **Above:** Aruba Reef Apartments.

Look for ★ to find recommended lodging.

Highlights

★ **Wonders Boutique Hotel:** This attractive, elegant guesthouse is convenient to the best shopping, dining, and entertainment in Oranjestad (page 170).

★ **Renaissance Resort:** Oranjestad's only full-service resort, the Renaissance Resort has excellent restaurants, a beautiful spa, and all the amenities of a Palm Beach resort for far less money (page 170).

★ **Divi Dutch Village:** Surrounding the lush Divi Links golf course and one of the most gorgeous pool decks in Aruba, these apartments offer everything for golfers and their families (page 174).

★ **Beach House Aruba:** Hosts Ewald and Doris provide their guests with incredible hospitality. Their cozy inn on the Malmok Coast is what island life is all about (page 177).

★ **Villa Sunflower:** Rock-bottom rates, unique ambience, and proximity to Palm Beach are Villa Sunflower's trademarks. Free mosaic lessons are just the cherry on top (page 179).

★ **Villa Bougainvillea:** Staying at one of the spacious apartments attached to this private home will make you feel like a guest, not a customer. Each apartment has its own terrace (page 180).

★ **Boardwalk Small Hotel Aruba:** This tranquil oasis has 13 spacious casitas surrounded by lush gardens. It is a beautiful, clean facility with homey touches and personality (page 180).

★ **Aruba Reef Apartments:** Realize your fantasy of a tropical paradise at this converted seaside home. Stay in an eclectic apartment with a private beach for the most romantic getaway imaginable (page 185).

who want to be truly immersed in the local environment, away from the tourist scene. A number of guesthouses and vacation apartment complexes scattered around the island also boast hospitable staff and quality rooms (though usually not a large number of rooms). There is often a very cozy ambience at these establishments, which allows guests to get to know the owners and feel like they are staying in someone's home. Guesthouses, in most cases, require walking some distance to a beach. A rare few actually abut the sea. Renting a car is almost always necessary if you stay in this type of accommodation. However, some guesthouse owners assist with arranging a car rental by making reservations and taking guests to the rental office or having the car delivered. They can also procure discounts on weekly rates.

For such a small island, Aruba has a great number of accommodations to suit all tastes. Whether you are choosing escape or excitement for your Caribbean vacation, you will find a resort or area that fits your mood. The main tourist areas of Palm Beach, Manchebo Beach, Eagle Beach, and Oranjestad are in such close proximity to each other that their particular amenities are easily accessible to vacationers wishing a change of scene for the day or evening. Resort staff readily welcomes visitors who are not guests to sample shops, restaurants, and casinos.

CHOOSING AN ACCOMMODATION

Aruba's capital **Oranjestad** is mostly populated with guesthouses and smaller apartments. It has two AHATA members, Renaissance and Talk of the Town. The less expensive accommodations are within a similar price range, but some rent only by the week. A few are converted homes that are exceptionally charming.

Generally, accommodations in Oranjestad are far less expensive than the principal shorefront areas of Palm Beach, Manchebo Beach, and Eagle Beach.

Staying in the island's capital imparts an authentic feeling for island life, with restaurants geared and priced for locals just minutes from your door. Most of Aruba's historical sights are within easy walking distance. For fans of Carnival events, these are the ideal accommodations for easily taking in the parades and many of the nighttime festivities.

What the accommodations in Oranjestad generally lack is the immediate access to the beach and sea that some consider an essential aspect of a Caribbean vacation. However, there are a few public beaches within easy walking distance of most guesthouses. Renaissance Resort has compensated by creating a beach for its guests and providing access to a private island with beautiful, tranquil beaches via regularly scheduled boat transport.

The first resorts built on **Manchebo Beach** were very small enterprises, only 20 rooms each, with casual, "barefoot elegance." For decades, Manchebo has been the center of timesharing on Aruba. **Eagle Beach** has become a focus for condominium development. Many of the facilities offer unoccupied units for rent. Families seeking spacious accommodations that allow them to cook find this appealing, as do those vacationers who want to be away from the hustle and bustle of the very large Palm Beach resorts. These resorts do not have long lines waiting for beach towels, lounge chairs, or a *palapa* for shade, which the large Palm Beach resorts often require guests to reserve. On weekdays, the nearby undeveloped beach areas are empty, though they can get busy with islanders on the weekends.

Timeshare rooms are usually a touch more luxurious and larger than the standard hotel room, as they were built to be sold, not rented. All come with either a full kitchen or a very well equipped kitchenette, nice for families that prefer to eat in and save money for a couple of meals out. Most rooms have at least one separate bedroom and a sofa bed in the living room to accommodate a family of four comfortably.

Palm Beach is a mile-long strip of glamorous, high-rise resorts, bustling with activity both day and night. Palm Beach is where the mega-resorts cluster, each offering every sort of amenity and service imaginable and consisting of 300 rooms or more. These glitzy, elaborate facilities are designed to meet guests' needs and desires without them ever having to leave the premises. They offer myriad dining choices and cocktail lounges, spas, shopping arcades, casinos, shows, game rooms for the kids, access to beautiful beaches and stunning pool decks, and exceptional catering and event departments for weddings and conventions.

The major Palm Beach resorts may vary slightly from one to the next—perhaps some are a bit more exclusive (or exclusively priced) in amenities and accoutrements—but all conform to a certain standard. Most operate under some large, international, corporate hospitality brand which usually carries with it an adherence to the star system rating, and, to some extent, the corporate guarantee of satisfaction.

If your taste runs to quiet little guesthouses far from the madding crowd, with a more personal touch and usually a relationship with the owner, then look beyond Palm Beach proper to the adjacent **Malmok.**

Aruba's hinterlands of **Santa Cruz** and **Savaneta** offer a scattering of guesthouses, with some on the southern shore boasting a bit of private beach. They generally offer very personal service, vastly reduced rates over the western shore resorts, and some surprising amenities, such as an on-site spa, breakfast included, or exceptionally attractive pool decks. They are almost all set up as apartments, uniformly outfitted with kitchens and extra beds or sofa beds to easily accommodate four or more.

Oranjestad

A stay in the island's capital immerses vacationers in island life, history, and activities. Scores of restaurants and shops are close by, but beaches require a bit of travel. Smaller guesthouses tend to be mostly inhabited by a business trade, rather than tourists.

$50-100

ARUBA HARMONY

Situated in Ponton, an area bordering north Oranjestad, **Aruba Harmony Apartments** (Palmitastraat 9, 297/593-7661, www.arubaharmony.com, $89 studios, $179 two-bedroom suites) is secreted away in an upscale neighborhood, surrounded by attractive homes. Ten rooms circle a courtyard with a small pool. There is an abundance of picnic tables and comfortable deck chairs for dining outdoors, and all rooms are equipped with full kitchens. The clientele is largely European.

One unique aspect: The place gets its name from owner-operator Barbara Arends's enthusiasm for the practice of feng shui. The rooms and their placement take this into account, designed to be beneficial to your chi. Barbara also offers special packages attuned to an individual's Chinese zodiac sign and horoscope that include treatments in the onsite spa. They are intended to create harmony and balance. Less expensive European spa treatments are also an option.

Activities packages in conjunction with scuba and deep-sea fishing operators can also be arranged, along with ecotours. When making reservations, send flight and arrival time and you will be greeted at the airport.

$100-200

ARUBA SURFSIDE MARINA

A very clean, modern facility, **Aruba Surfside Marina** (L. G. Smith Blvd. 7, 297/583-0300, www.arubasurfsidemarina.com, $145, minimum of four nights) has only a few rooms. The upper level holds three

Alternative Accommodations

Families on a budget or groups of friends looking to save may wish to explore the option of renting a house while on Aruba. There are quite a few gated communities offering condominiums, town houses, and villas while owners are off island. Aside from these communities, there are also several freestanding homes available for at least a week at a time. If you prefer privacy and are looking for an island hideaway, the cost and logistics of renting a home are ideal. Many are only minutes from the beach. Nearly all have swimming pools.

Prices vary from as little as $650 per week for a comfortable one- or two-bedroom home to as high as $10,000 for some of the luxurious mansions within the Tierra Del Sol Country Club and Golf Course. Minimum one-week rentals are required, and long-term rentals of a month or more obviously have better rates. Rental homes are usually equipped with all appliances, including TVs, and other conveniences, such as linens and tableware.

Here are four reliable brokers for villa rentals:

- **Aruba Happy Rentals** (Boegoeroei #13-D, 297/586-2662, U.S. 866/978-6986, http://arubahappyrentals.com)
- **Aruba Palms Realtors** (J. E. Irausquin Blvd. 370, 297/566-0339 or 877/586-8962, www.arubapalmsrealtors.com)
- **Aruba Villa Rentals** (Salina Cerca 35E, 297/586-4290, www.arubavillarentals.com)
- **Prima Casa Real Estate** (J. E. Irausquin Blvd. 330, 297/583-3350, http://aruba-realty.com)

studios plus two suites with all oceanfront terraces. Each unit comes with fridge, microwave, coffeemaker, and utensils. The first floor is entirely for meeting and conference rooms, so it does get some traffic for events and business presentations on a daily basis, and is popular with business travelers. Room rates include a continental breakfast for two served on the room's balcony.

The expansive courtyard makes this a popular place for local weddings and other catered events. There are a gazebo, gardens, and a beautiful view of the sea and shore, but no pool. Instead, you have immediate access to a very quiet, semi-secluded beach area. This is a good spot if you planning a destination wedding and wishing to be away from the tourist crowds. The management is well versed in arranging wedding events, as this is their specialty.

CADUSHI APARTMENTS

A pleasant but plain collection of 15 apartments close to the airport, **Cadushi Apartments** (Stadionweg 4B, 297/593-1770, www.cadushiapartments.com, $170) is just a short walk from Surfside Beach, where they have beach lounges for their guests, and the main part of town. The exterior decor is clean and contemporary, and there is a small pool.

The apartments are spacious and include a living room, separate bedroom, fully equipped kitchen, and free Wi-Fi. Free snorkel equipment and a cooler to take to the beach are also included. They offer services such as doing laundry (no ironing) and stocking the cupboard pre-arrival.

CAMACURI APARTMENTS

The description of **Camacuri Apartments** (Avenida Milio J. Croes 46B, 297/582-6805, www.camacuriapartmentsaruba.com, studios $139-194) as "a hideaway" is right on the money. Thirty-nine apartments are tucked away behind houses bordering a field and a major stadium. Camacuri can only be found by turning down a dirt road across from the Aruba Entertainment Center. There is no indication of where to go, but once you know, it is easy to find. It does offer a surprisingly tranquil oasis, just on the eastern outskirts of town, with sprawling gardens and a nice pool.

Spread out over an extensive patch of land are a main area of rooms around a courtyard and scattered, two-story casitas with suites. The largest, top-of-the-line suite has a master bedroom in a loft with its own separate bathroom. All come equipped with kitchens, even the studios. The main part of town is perhaps a 15-minute walk away; for grocery shopping, a small market is nestled in an extensive commercial area nearby.

★ WONDERS BOUTIQUE HOTEL

Wonders Boutique Hotel (Emmastraat 63, 297/593-4032, www.wondersaruba.com, $119-149) is an exceedingly charming alternative to formal resorts and perfect for those seeking something out of the ordinary. It only has eight, large, air-conditioned studio rooms with very spacious bathrooms on a well-maintained property. Each room comes with a well-stocked and reasonably priced minibar and a coffeemaker. A warm welcome with an exotic cocktail sets the mood for your stay.

Formerly a very large, two-story home, the hotel is extensively decorated with original art. Though the pool is small—just big enough for a cooling dip—the entire back courtyard is delightful, with lush gardens. There is a grill and a well-equipped shared kitchen available for guests. The management also offers breakfast on the premises, although not included with the price of the room and a little pricey compared to nearby cafés geared to locals.

The clientele is mixed, though usually with a European flavor. The hotel is only a short walk to a number of fine Oranjestad eateries, shopping, and principal attractions. The owner will provide round-trip transport to and from the airport for a fee, as well as shuttle service to Eagle Beach or Palm Beach departing daily at 10:30am.

If you really want to feel a part of island life, this is a very good place to be; it is rated superb by reviewers on a number of websites. Host Gaston is trying to do something special here, and he is succeeding!

OVER $200

★ RENAISSANCE RESORT

Oranjestad has one full-service resort, the **Renaissance Resort** (L. G. Smith Blvd. 82, 297/583-6000 or toll-free in U.S. 800/421-8188, www.marriott.com, Marina Tower $600, Beach Tower $764), which dominates the harbor and L. G. Smith Boulevard. Though operating under the Renaissance name, this is the only major resort wholly owned by a local family business. Incorporated into the resort properties are two elegant shopping malls, two casinos, a convention center, Oranjestad Harbor, and—offshore—Renaissance Island. The two sections of the resort are well separated by L. G. Smith Boulevard and the Renaissance Marketplace, but both have appealing views. A free tram runs between them. Discounts of up to 40 percent on room rates are continually offered, but can be time-sensitive and dependent on availability. Count on paying less than the full rate, except for holiday weeks.

The Marina Tower is adults-only and looks out on the harbor. The lobby, which doubles as a mall, is filled with designer name signature stores. Central to the mall is the dock for the ferries to Renaissance Island. The general ambience defines "island chic." The clientele is diverse; though on weekends it is decidedly wealthy South Americans enjoying a couple of days of shopping and play. The pool deck is on the mezzanine level and overlooks the harbor and L. G. Smith Boulevard.

Beach Tower is family-friendly, and has one- and two-bedroom suites with full kitchens, as the complex was originally planned and sold as timeshares. It has its very own attractive lagoon, huge free-form pool deck, and artificial beach. Each section of the resort has a dedicated concierge, activities desk, and car rental service.

Renaissance Island is a beautiful facility with a restaurant and spa, water sports operator, plus three separate beaches (including a secluded adults-only section for topless sunbathing), included in the package for all guests. It is quite popular for elegant, catered affairs—particularly weddings. The island is accessed by speedboats departing from two locations every 15 minutes, and it takes about 15-20 minutes to reach the island. Day passes are sold to non-hotel guests at the concierge desks for $90, which include lunch, a drink, and a choice of water activity equipment.

This is a resort with high standards, a smoke-free policy, and the added benefit of being in town. Its accessibility to Oranjestad offers the opportunity to get a better feel of the island and its culture.

Eagle Beach and Manchebo Beach

The resorts run by Divi Properties dominate much of the Manchebo Beach area. This concern also runs The Links golf course, with surrounding condos and timeshares, and the Alhambra Shopping Bazaar. However, each resort has a distinctive personality.

Divi Properties all started when a lawyer from upstate New York, Wally Wiggins, brought his family on vacation to Aruba in 1965, beginning a decades-long love affair with Aruba. Wally built the first Divi resort because he wanted to have a place to stay on the beach and zoning laws would not allow a private home. They started with 20 rooms, as a permit would allow no less. It opened the same day Neil Armstrong walked on the moon. One small step for Mr. Wiggins, family, and friends, became a giant step for Aruba's tourism.

$100-200

QUALITY APARTMENTS

Many timeshare owners elect to extend their stay at **Quality Apartments** (Schotlandstraat 70, 297/582-0697, www.arubaqualityapartments.com, from $143). This family-run facility offers a nice pool, plus large, comfortable, and very clean rooms. There are studios with loft bedrooms and one-bedroom suites. The entire facility has 73 units. It is on a fairly busy commercial thoroughfare and not far from major supermarkets and shopping, but most rooms are set back from the street and quiet.

Amenities include a multi-machine laundry, fitness room, free Wi-Fi in all rooms, plus a computer station for guests who don't like to travel with their toys. Over the years, guests have left behind their books, resulting in an extensive lending library of ideal beach reading, in several languages.

$200-300

ARUBA BREEZE CONDOMINIUMS

Luxurious but very reasonably priced accommodations are found at **Aruba Breeze Condominiums** (J. E. Irausquin Blvd. 232A, 297/732-2788, www.arubabreeze.com, from $225, $10 for each additional person, children under 3 free), a condominium complex that regularly rents out at a nightly rate.

Located in a cul-de-sac at the juncture of Manchebo and Eagle Beaches, the facility has 25 identical two-bedroom duplex town houses outfitted with everything a family needs. There are two spacious bedrooms upstairs, each with their own bathroom, and a half-bath on the first level. The town houses have beautifully appointed kitchens, spacious living rooms, and a terrace on each level, with high-quality furniture and fixtures. Balconies overlook two rather utilitarian pool decks, which are rarely crowded.

Conference and fitness rooms are situated off the lobby. They keep two grills by the large shade *palapa* at the main pool and an ice machine with bags of ice, to fill coolers for the beach. The concierges in the lobby assist with tours, car rentals, and more; they are very amenable and eager to please. Daily maid service is included, which is rare for a condo complex. This is a very quiet place with Eagle Beach only five minutes away on foot.

Extended Stays

Travelers planning to stay more than the automatically allotted 30 days may need to file a form with **DIMAS** (Paardenbaaistraat 11, 297/522-1500, www.dimasaruba.aw, 7:30am-11:30am and 2:30pm-4pm Mon.-Thurs.), the Department of Immigration. Officers at the airport issue a visitor's visa for one month; anyone planning to be on Aruba longer should inform the officer while passing through immigration. Traveling as a tourist allows visitors to stay on Aruba a total of 180 days out of a year without a work or residence permit.

At the airport extending a stay for more than 30 days but not exceeding 180 days can be carried out immediately by nationals of the Kingdom of the Netherlands or its territories and independent entities, the United States, Canada, the United Kingdom, Ireland, and the Schengen Territory. Those with property on Aruba, such as a house, condominium, apartment, or timeshare, can also immediately request to extend their stay if prepared to show proof of ownership. Individuals who are only renting, particularly at smaller, cheaper guesthouses, may find officials a bit less cooperative in automatically extending their stay.

The immigration officer can grant up to 90 days if satisfied that the visitor has sufficient funds to cover an extended stay. All tourists applying for an extension beyond 30 days are required to have valid travel insurance (medical and liability) for the duration of the extended stay.

Those wishing to extend a stay beyond what has been indicated by an immigration officer can file an application at the DIMAS offices. There is no filing fee for a tourist extension application. Required forms can be downloaded from the website. Applicants should have copies made of all filled out forms before applying.

The following documents must be presented:

- Original application form for extension of tourist stay.
- Copy of the profile page and all the written and stamped pages of the petitioner's passport, valid for at least another three months from when the extension is applied for.
- Copy of Embarkation-Disembarkation form (ED-Card).
- Copy of a valid return ticket.
- Copy of valid travel insurance (medical and liability) for the duration of the extended stay.

If the petitioner is not staying at their own private residence or a hotel, they need to present a declaration of guarantee from a resident of Aruba who will accept liability for expenses incurred during the petitioner's stay. Anyone planning to stay longer than 180 days in Aruba will need a residence permit and will not be considered a tourist.

PARADISE BEACH VILLAS

Another attractive, intimate timeshare renting by the night is **Paradise Beach Villas** (J. E. Irausquin Blvd. 64, 297/587-4000, www.paradisebeachvillas-aruba.com, studios $175, one-bedroom suites $265). Situated on the south side of La Cabana Resort, this small complex has something of a history. The developers went bankrupt and were going to abandon the facility, but the owners rallied together to purchase it and salvage their investment. Because of this there is a strong sense of community here. Rooms are rented out, but the general clientele is long-term repeat visitors who have a tangible stake in the facility. This is a family-oriented resort, and there is a palpable relationship between staff and guests. The rooms are spacious and nicely appointed. There is also an excellent on-site restaurant, Carambola, which offers discounted rates for those staying at the resort. Guests must cross J. E. Irausquin Boulevard to access the beach.

TROPICANA RESORT & CASINO

Tropicana Resort & Casino (J. E. Irausquin Blvd. 248, 297/587-9000, www.troparuba.com,

$239 for one-bedroom suite) was originally built as an annex to the La Cabana Resort. This very large facility (over 360 rooms) changed hands a few times, but was acquired in 2011 by the Tropicana hospitality chain of Atlantic City. Since then, there has been a long process to renovate the rooms, and they are about halfway done. Until completion, bargain rates are in effect.

The complex wraps around a very attractive pool deck with two large free-form pools. One pool has a waterfall and the other attracts most of the kids with its waterslide, but also has a swim-up bar. Whirlpools and kids' pools are separate. It is a long walk to the beach.

There are no real grounds beyond the pool deck, but you can't beat the bargain rate. The rooms were originally timeshares, so they have full kitchens and are spacious, though showing their age. The new management has attractively renovated the community areas. The affiliated casino, tennis courts, and restaurant are located in the vast parking lot. And for all of your snacking needs, there is a small snack bar around the pool, a Dunkin' Donuts and Baskin Robbins on the premises, and a mini-market.

$300-400

AMSTERDAM MANOR BEACH RESORT

The noticeably unique architecture of the **Amsterdam Manor Beach Resort** (J. E. Irausquin Blvd. 252, 297/527-1100 or 800/969-2310, www.amsterdammanor.com, standard studios $335) exterior captures one's attention. It is a bit of Bavaria in Aruba, looking something like a medieval turreted castle, yet cozy at the same time. The rooms were originally done in a very heavy, European old-country design, but have been redecorated for a much more sleek, modern look. The results are very attractive. This resort is EarthCheck certified and award-winning for its ecofriendly practices, including being nonsmoking throughout.

There is a tiny pool deck, but the beach is easily accessed by crossing the road. With few rooms but a long stretch of beach, the resort is never crowded. It has an excellent, romantic restaurant on the beach, called Passions.

ARUBA BEACH CLUB AND CASA DEL MAR

Though physically connected and appearing as one large resort with contrasting architecture, **Aruba Beach Club and Casa Del Mar** (J. E. Irausquin Blvd. 53, Aruba Beach Club 297/582-3000, Casa Del Mar 297/582-7000, www.arubabeachclub.info, www.casadelmar-aruba.com, studios $200, one-bedroom suites $325 and up) are two separate corporate entities, each with their own general manager, reception, and expansive pool decks. (This all has to do with tax structures.) They also have separate activities directors, guest lounges, and waterfront restaurants, but share tennis courts and other facilities. Each has pleasant and reasonably priced beachfront restaurants, which are independently owned. Lounge chairs and pool decks can be used interchangeably by all guests. A separate section away from the beach is called the Ambassador Suites. This area has a small pool and lower rates.

Aruba Beach Club (ABC) was the island's first timeshare facility, opening its doors in 1979. It has a very devoted clientele, many of them staying for months during the winter, a real "home away from home." Most bought in during the groundbreaking, and now are vacationing with their grandchildren. Both ABC and Casa Del Mar (CDM) have creative, energetic activity directors who specialize in keeping kids entertained. They often moonlight as babysitters. There is daily bingo and other such pastimes. Families will find they soon feel connected to an extended "Aruba family."

CDM has a more contemporary pool deck, but both have plain, rectangular pools, not the free-form works of art that are standard now. If you need to be near the action and nightlife, or around other singles, you might prefer staying somewhere else.

★ DIVI DUTCH VILLAGE

The huge, rambling facility of **Divi Dutch Village** (J. E. Irausquin Blvd. 93, 297/583-5000 or 800/367-3484, www.dividutchvillage.com, Dutch Village $338, Divi Village $343, Divi Golf Village $381) is ideal for golfers and their families who want other activities. The closer to the course, the more expensive the rooms, but also the more luxurious and newer the buildings are.

Dutch Village is adjacent to the Tamarijn on the water side of J. E. Irausquin Boulevard, which also allows direct access to the beach. The buildings are spread out and arranged around three separate swimming pools with lush gardens. These are the oldest units in the complex, but newly refurbished and redecorated. The top two floors are duplexes with master bedrooms and private baths on the upper level. All the rooms have individual hot tubs on the terraces. As timeshares, the facility has a generally mature crowd, with lots of grandchildren around during peak holiday weeks.

Divi Village is newer and across the road from the beach. The pool deck looks out on the main thoroughfare. It is the tennis center for the resort complex and closer to the golf course, offering golfing villas for better access.

The final section of Divi Village, Divi Golf Village, is adjacent to Divi Links golf course. These apartments are set far back from the main road and beach. To compensate, there is the Infiniti pool with one of the most sumptuous and expansive pool decks on Aruba directly overlooking the fairway. These buildings are also closer to the clubhouse, an attractive facility with two fine restaurants, Mulligan's and Windows on Aruba.

$400-500

BUCUTI & TARA BEACH RESORT

For a truly tranquil getaway, the owner-operated boutique resort **Bucuti & Tara Beach Resort** (L. G. Smith Blvd. 55B, 297/583-1100, www.bucuti.com, $448-513) is adults only. The 104 rooms are divided between two sections: the original Bucuti rooms with balconies and the 40 suites of the Tara, which are more luxurious and spacious. All Tara rooms have a direct ocean view. Room prices are on a modified European Plan, which includes a gourmet, full American buffet breakfast; all room taxes and service charges; plus no extra fee for local calls, which usually cost around $5+ everywhere else. Each room is provided with its own Lenovo netbook upon check-in. Skype is installed to use for emailing or chatting with the folks at home at no additional cost. There is free Wi-Fi throughout the resort. A unique perk to the Tara suites is a huge bathroom, with a cable television screen set up in a section of the equally huge mirror. If you can't stand to miss a minute of a show or a big game for a pit stop, you don't have to.

Guests are greeted with a complimentary champagne toast. A gift souvenir water bottle, in keeping with the strict environmental care policy, is part of the welcome. Bottles can be refilled at various water stations on the beach. The resort and its owner, Ewald Biemans, have been cited internationally several times for their pioneering sustainability policies.

Bucuti & Tara Beach Resort also has two gourmet, adult-only restaurants. The staff is vigilant about service and making sure the sense of quiet seclusion is maintained. Guests are given a red flag to hold up if they wish to order food or drinks while on the beach. Servers will not interrupt reading or dozing to take an order. The resort also houses a mini branch of Intermezzo Spa, offering a full menu of massages and skin treatments, and an air-conditioned fitness room. The pool is very small, but the resort is on the widest beach on Aruba.

COSTA LINDA

Costa Linda (J. E. Irausquin Blvd. 59, 297/583-8000 or 888/858-0845, www.costalinda-aruba.com, two-bedroom suites $378-589) was the last timeshare resort built by Sun Development, the founders of timesharing in Aruba, and one of the most luxurious of the four facilities it left in its wake. All units are very spacious and beautifully appointed two- or three-bedroom suites. The ocean-end rooms have enormous patios for outdoor entertaining, with their own gas grills and whirlpool tubs.

This very large facility has one of the widest beachfronts on Aruba. The attractive free-form pool deck has an adjacent restaurant. It is family-oriented and quiet at night, but Alhambra Shopping Bazaar is just outside the door and past the parking lot.

MANCHEBO BEACH RESORT

Manchebo Beach Resort (J. E. Irausquin Blvd. 55, 297/582-3444, toll-free 888/673-8036, www.manchebo.com, $420) is a cozy, full-service resort with a superior beachfront. It opened within months of the Divi Resort in 1969 and reflects that time, with an informal, open-air lobby. There are only two stories, and all rooms have an ocean view. The rooms and grounds were renovated and refreshed in 2011.

Sitting right on the island's southwest point, it has the widest beach on Aruba. This is where Spa Del Sol has an attractive facility. Massages are done in curtained kiosks on the beach. Yoga sessions are also conducted daily in the shade of the spa.

The resort is an institution for much of its clientele. It is a mix of mature American and European crowds who have been staying here for years. The lobby leads directly to an equally informal open-air restaurant, which at night becomes Ike's Place. The poolside bar has a stunning view and is where most end up around sunset for happy hour. The deck is small and an extension of the restaurant, with an appealing setup for dining. When Ike Cohen opened the resort, he installed one of the island's most famous gourmet restaurants, The French Steakhouse, which is still a great value. Chamber music recitals are hosted here once a month on Sunday mornings.

OVER $500

Two sister resorts, Divi and Tamarijn, were built on the same concept: two-story casitas with terraces or patios facing directly out to the sea. They are separated by a small stretch of sand, and guests can use the restaurants and bars interchangeably, along with fitness rooms, tennis courts, and more. Frequent tram service takes guests between the two, at all hours of the day and night.

DIVI MEGA ALL-INCLUSIVE

Divi Mega All-Inclusive (J. E. Irausquin Blvd. 45, 297/525-5200 or 800/554-2008, www.diviaruba.com, $660 garden view, $675 ocean view), which opened back in 1969, is a long, rambling resort with rooms directly on the beach or in a new section set back within lush gardens. Along with its sister resort, the newer Tamarijn, they are generally considered "honeymoon hotels."

The rooms are not large; all first-floor rooms have direct access to the beach. The resort turned all-inclusive in the late 1990s. Since many of their loyal patrons spent their honeymoons at the Divi 25 or 40 years ago, they are now no longer a clientele comprised of only newlyweds, but of all ages and quite diverse. They have formed very congenial groups who usually gather during happy hour (which at an all-inclusive, is all day) at the famous Bunker Bar at the Tamarijn, which hangs out over the water. The success of the first Divi Resort resulted in expansion and in the Tamarijn, which shares grounds with the Dutch Village timeshares.

Divi has recently undergone complete renovations. The community areas are elegant. A chic, stunning, contemporary pool deck abuts the beach, and the lobby has an Internet center and shops. There is nightly entertainment, and family-oriented amenities and organized activities are offered daily.

Aside from the family-type buffet center near the beach, the resort is home to the famous Red Parrot Restaurant, featuring fresh fish and international cuisine. The themed restaurants require advance reservations. For an all-inclusive facility, the quality of cuisine and variety are way above par.

TAMARIJN BEACH RESORT

The Divi's sister resort, **Tamarijn Beach Resort** (J. E. Irausquin Blvd. 41, 297/525-5200 or 800/554-2008, www.tamarijnaruba.com, $620 ocean view), is located just south of the Divi and a little closer to Oranjestad. It has also undergone extensive renovations, and has been given a more contemporary look best described as island chic.

Adjacent to the Divi Dutch Village timeshares, the grounds boast some very lush, beautiful landscaping on the land side of the beach. The resort's Overlook Bar and Bunker Bar offer some of the most beautiful views of the Caribbean at sunset. Guests from both resorts like to gather at either spot at day's end.

The rooms of "the Tam" are small, but provide the feeling of the beach being a part of the accommodations, as terraces and patios open to the very beautiful, tranquil shorefront.

There are no elevators, so individuals with physical restrictions should specify that they require a ground-floor room when making reservations.

Most of the themed restaurants shared by the two resorts are within the Tamarijn. They include Paparazzi, for Italian cuisine; Fusion, for Pacific Rim; Palm Grill, for fresh stir-fried dishes; as well as an all-day stone-oven pizza bar for snacking and meals from early in the day until late at night. Themed restaurants only serve dinner, and reservations are required well in advance. The Cunucu Terrace, adjacent to the pool deck, serves breakfast, lunch, and dinner buffets, and is the spot for nightly entertainment.

Palm Beach, Malmok, and Noord

Since Palm Beach boasts the greatest concentration of accommodations and activities, it may likely be a vacationer's default choice, particularly if selecting a package through a travel agency or wholesaler, which tend to work mostly with the AHATA member resorts. During holiday time many will only accept reservations for a minimum of 10 days that include both Christmas and New Year's. Bookings often are required more than a year in advance.

Beginning from the Eagle Beach approach, these giant hotels line up along a boardwalk that has been laid out from the southernmost end of Palm Beach to the Marriott Complex and is a popular spot for a morning run or

Hot Water

Visitors staying in guesthouses and alternative accommodations might be taken aback when they first see only one faucet in most sinks and showers. Since forever, the island has relied on the tropical sun to heat the water, and it does a fine job. A shower anytime from around noon till sunset has surprisingly warm water and very comfortable; at times, it's perhaps even too hot. It all depends on the weather, which is usually reliable. First thing in the morning is the time to grab a cold shower, for those who need it.

Major resorts understand that their guests expect hot water at any hour of the day and night, and they have hot-water heaters to provide it. Unfortunately, what comes out of the cold-water tap is the same sun-heated water the rest of the island is using, so there is no cold water to temper the hot. Running the cold-water tap will not result in the water getting colder; it will likely get warmer. Keep this in mind when stepping into the shower or filling a bathtub. Be sure to check first to avoid scalding temperatures. If you are fanatical about cold drinking water, make sure to locate the ice machine down the hall when you arrive.

walk. It also allows easy access to the various restaurants, casinos, and shops within the resorts.

$100-200

ARUBA BEACH VILLAS

Looking out on the water when you first get into Malmok, **Aruba Beach Villas** (L. G. Smith Blvd. 482, 297/586-1072 or toll-free in U.S. 800/320-9998, www.arubabeachvillas.com, studio suites $178-238) is a favorite destination for dedicated windsurfers as an ideal location for the sport. Aruba Sailboard Vacations and Fiberworx board shop are attached, convenient for equipment and spare parts, waxes, and more. Aruba Sailboard works with the Villas and, during high season, room rates include unlimited equipment rental. (During the off-season, rooms are half price, but no equipment is included.) Initial lessons are not free. Those really interested in spending a vacation learning the sport should be prepared to dedicate several hours toward mastering it.

Owner Phil is an expatriate American who never wanted to leave Aruba and very happy to be a host. Rooms are rustic, but quite spacious, with big closets and bathrooms, even in the studios, and all have fully-equipped kitchens. The oceanfront rooms have wooden decks for enjoying the view, and the beach is just across the road. There is a small pool in the back. Less expensive rooms are simple and bare-bones, suited for people who will be out on the water most of the time. A charming, open-air community area faces the sea and is a popular place to kick back and talk windsurfing with other fanatics.

BANANAS APARTMENTS

A popular spot with Europeans and families, **Bananas Apartments** (Malmokweg 19, 297/586-2858, www.bananas-resort.com, studio apartments $770/week, extra person $15/night, children under 6 free) is just a short distance down the Malmokweg, which runs perpendicular to the beach road. All rooms have fully equipped kitchens. Cleaning service and fresh towels daily are included, with oversize beach towels distributed by the pool.

Converted from two adjacent houses, each section has a small pool and one whirlpool spa. The older section has a sprawling backyard and lovely gardens with shade trees. The newer section has an open, paved pool deck and is still in the process of becoming as homey as the original. Don't balk at taking an "older" room: They have more charm and nice big wooden picnic tables on the patios for family meals.

★ BEACH HOUSE ARUBA

Among the Palm Beach guesthouses, **Beach House Aruba** (450 L. G. Smith Blvd, 297/593-3991, www.beachhousearuba.com, $100-140) is one of the few with its own patch of shorefront. Hosts Ewald and Doris are known for their hospitality, and they enjoy a very dedicated and loyal clientele. Located on the Malmok strip just north of Fisherman's Huts, this converted home boasts a quiet bit of beach just across the boulevard, where they have placed a *palapa* for shade and some lounges.

The 10 units vary in size, but all come with an air-conditioned bedroom separate from the kitchenette/lounging area. Ewald based the room design on the Hawaiian concept of lanai, taking full advantage of Aruba's climate and breezes for his guests to experience outdoor living at its best. Most units are centered around a community area in the back of the house, where he has built a power pyramid to fully recharge your chi during organized yoga sessions. There are a few front units with beautiful ocean views, which also look out over the pool area. The decor is eclectic and quaint, and each unit unique.

Coolers to take to the beach, storage for windsurfing equipment, and complimentary lounges at MooMba Beach are all included. To boot, Ewald is known to offer a masterful cappuccino while socializing with his guests. As a former windsurfing instructor, he is ready and willing to share his insights into the sport. All in all, Beach House Aruba

Resort Hopping

The major resorts, with the exception of the all-inclusive hotels, welcome nonguests to their premises to use their restaurants, spas, casinos, and shops. This particularly applies to Palm Beach, where resorts are in close proximity to each other. Vacationers can easily walk from one to the next, either on the beach boardwalk or the boulevard promenade. Walking the strip is a favorite nighttime activity. A preference for the ambience of a certain casino or poker room can easily be indulged, as can seeing a show at another resort, usually only minutes away on foot. Pool decks, however, are for the use of guests of the resort only.

Since Riu and Occidental are all-inclusive, they screen those trying to enter from their pool decks for identifying bracelets. Nonguests are turned away. Visitors are welcome through their main entrances if they wish to use their casinos. Inquire at their concierge desks about day passes to fully sample the facility.

offers an absolutely delightful and very personal island experience.

BRISAS STUDIO APARTMENTS

If you want to be far from the madding crowd, but not too far, **Brisas Studio Apartments** (Keito 8B, 297/592-8631, www.brisasaruba.com, studio apartments $105) is a secluded, serene hideaway; brisas means "quiet" in Papiamento. Located on the eastern outskirts of Palm Beach, it is owned by the same people who manage Wonders Boutique Hotel and consists of only two charming apartments. There are mini-markets and some nice restaurants close by, but you will most likely need a rental car.

Amenities include coolers, snorkeling gear, beach towels, and fold-up lounges to take to the beach. There is a grill on the premises. Each apartment has a nicely equipped kitchenette. Rooms come with a queen-size bed, but an extra fold-up bed will be provided on request. The rooms are quite spacious and can accommodate extra occupants.

CARIÑAS VACATION HOME & APARTMENTS

Spanking new **Cariñas Vacation Home & Apartments** (Palm Beach 360, 297/592-8631, www.arubacarinas.com, studio apartments $125, bungalow $170) offers two interesting options: a two-bedroom bungalow that has its own private entrance or one of five spacious studio apartments with kitchenettes. The complex is located in the residential area of Palm Beach but in sight of the main hotel area, and only a 10-minute walk from the beach.

Each apartment has a spacious terrace for enjoying meals outdoors. The bungalow has a very large living room and its own private outdoor patio away from those of the apartments; it sleeps six comfortably. The complex has laundry machines for all to use. The neighborhood is very quiet, but conveniently close to all the action of this busy area, including several restaurants, stores, and casinos. It does not have a pool, but does offer charming community areas for relaxing, socializing, and taking in some sun. The clientele is a mixed crowd, mostly Europeans who have a penchant for community living, in addition to North and South Americans.

COSTA ESMERALDA VILLAGE

Convenient to all the Palm Beach action, **Costa Esmeralda Village** (Washington 61B, 297/567-5611, www.costaesmeraldaaruba.com, $120-175) still features a tranquil environment in a quiet neighborhood only minutes from bustling nightlife, casinos, activity centers, dining, and great beaches. The rooms are attractive and contemporary, and sizes range from typical hotel studio to one-bedroom suite to duplex town house with two bedrooms and baths.

The rooms are light and spacious and the

bathrooms are huge. Suites have complete kitchens, and the studios have kitchenettes. The facility sports two moderate-size pools, one of which is designed specifically for swimming laps, and a whirlpool spa. The community area also has a gas barbecue for guest to use. The management is extremely personable and will assist in car rentals and arranging tours. Costa Esmeralda Village is right next door to Papiamento Restaurant, which offers superb gourmet dining.

★ VILLA SUNFLOWER

Villa Sunflower (Salinja Cerca 25E, 297/593-0409, www.arubasunflower.com, studio apartments $110), also nestled in a very quiet residential area adjacent to Palm Beach, provides a true "guest in a home" experience. Your hostess, Rienk, lives on-site and is a delight, as are her six apartments, each unique and artistically decorated.

Rienk is an enthusiastic mosaic artist, and the entire complex is connected by a labyrinth of her stunning mosaic walks. The walls and doors of the rooms, as well as nearly every tabletop in sight, are mosaic masterpieces, with sunflowers and underwater seascapes frequently popping up. There is a good-size pool surrounded by art, and a community barbecue/dining area completely adorned with mosaic and tiled surfaces. Lush greenery provides ample privacy for each unit. Rienk will even give free mosaic instruction to anyone interested in learning the craft.

The rooms are airy and spacious, each with a kitchenette and a full-size fridge, air-conditioning, cable TV, and free Wi-Fi. There is an all-day communal courtesy coffee/tea stand, and inexpensive laundry machines are available. Fisherman's Huts are very close, and the beaches north of the Marriott are about a 20-minute walk. Villa Sunflower is on a rather narrow street, and there is no dedicated parking. Depending on how busy they are, this might be inconvenient if you have rented a car for the week. The place is guarded by two dogs that warm up to guests very quickly. They are pet-friendly for smaller dogs.

DEL RAY APARTMENTS

North of the Santa Ana Church in Noord is a side street where **Del Ray Apartments** (Caya Calco 13D, 297/586-3309, www.delreyaruba.com, $145) is tucked just a bit off the beaten

community area at Villa Sunflower

track, but only minutes from the beach by car. It's also close to shopping and only five doors away from Anna Maria's Italian restaurant. Twenty-six comfortable, clean apartments surround the large pool deck and playground. This option is a good value for spacious rooms in a quiet corner that is still close to Palm Beach. This nice mom-and-pop operation, with a largely European and Latin clientele, has an arrangement with MooMba Beach for lounge chairs for guests.

LA BOHEME

Just inland along the Bakval Road, across from the Marriott, is **La Boheme** (Bakval 2E, 297/593-6512, www.labohemearuba.com, $165-185), a delightful new addition to Aruba's growing list of guesthouses. It is comprised of four one-bedroom apartments surrounding a charming pool deck. Each comes with a kitchenette, a giant plasma TV, and a spacious terrace. Grills are on hand for a cookout, and coolers for trips to the beach. La Boheme also has an arrangement at MooMba Beach Bar to provide lounges for its guests.

La Boheme is located in a very quiet residential area within very easy walking distance of all the major Palm Beach action. All units are pretty standard, with one just a bit larger than the others, and very slightly higher priced. Since it is so intimate, friendly relations with the other guests seem to develop naturally. The clientele is a mixed crowd; North Americans, Europeans, and Latin Americans seem equally attracted to this cozy place.

★ VILLA BOUGAINVILLEA

Staying at **Villa Bougainvillea** (Malmokweg 4, 297/526-1055, www.villabougainvilleaaruba.com, $119-149 for up to four) is a unique experience indelibly stamped with the character of hostess Rona. It is located nearly at the main sea road and is a short walk from the nice beach at Boca Catalina.

Three utterly charming apartments with mini-kitchens are attached to the proprietor's home and give patrons the feeling of being a visitor rather than just a tenant. Each has its own entrance and a key to the gate for security. The rooms are very spacious and decorated with fine and eclectic taste, creating a unique ambience. Bathrooms have tubs as well as showers, which is unusual at most budget places.

Each room has a little terrace and looks out on a charming backyard with a pool and grill. "When the spirit moves her," Rona will cook up a storm of gourmet snacks and mix a pitcher of sangria to treat her guests to a little "get acquainted happy hour."

Three good-size *cunucu* dogs (the local mixed breed, which were rescued) have the run of the house and property. They warm up to renters quickly, but if you choose to stay here, you should be completely comfortable with dogs.

$200-300

★ BOARDWALK SMALL HOTEL ARUBA

The first in line of the Malmok off-the-beach resorts is **Boardwalk Small Hotel Aruba** (Bakval 20, 297/586-6654, www.boardwalkaruba.com, one-bedroom suites from $295, $15 pp for more than four guests, children under 12 free), where one really has a sense of being in a tropical paradise.

Formally known as Boardwalk Retreat—a very appropriate name—this is a lovely, tranquil place with 13 casitas surrounded by lush gardens. It is removed from but still in close proximity to all the Palm Beach action—the Marriott Casino is just across the road.

Rooms are spacious, sleeping four comfortably, with high ceilings, large closets, dressing rooms, and fully equipped kitchens. Each has its own patio or terrace with an individual grill that housekeepers keep clean. Generally, the rooms are spotless.

There is a small pool and whirlpool, and arrangements for guests to use the lounge chairs at MooMba Beach Bar between the Holiday Inn and Marriott Surf Club. Shuttle service to the beach is provided along with individual coolers for ice and refreshments.

The owners, twin sisters Kimberly and Stephanie Rooijakkers, took over in 2011, and their enthusiasm for Aruba and this charming facility is infectious. They are also pet-friendly; expect their adorable longhaired dachshund to greet you in the lobby.

BRICKELL BAY BEACH CLUB & SPA

Being close to, but not on the beach, makes adults-only **Brickell Bay Beach Club & Spa** (J. E. Irausquin Blvd. 370, 297/586-0900 or toll-free in U.S. and Canada 866/332-3590, www.brickellbayaruba.com, $248) a good value. It is in the heart of Palm Beach and well situated for enjoying the nighttime action. Room rates include a continental breakfast.

An unimpressive exterior and lobby mask pleasant and freshly renovated rooms. A spacious and attractive pool deck with bar is where the Orchid Day Spa is located. Patrons can enjoy a pool view while getting a massage, facial, manicure, or pedicure at comparatively reasonable rates. Only 98 rooms guarantee that the pool never gets crowded, and they have just added on an expansive and glamorous bar and nightspot called Sand Bar & Lounge, with nighttime beach tennis courts. Lounge chairs on the Occidental beach are made available for guests.

Tomato Charlie's Pizzeria and Italian restaurant is attached, with a terrace dining room looking over the thoroughfare à la European café style. It serves breakfast, lunch, and dinner; the food is affordable and pretty decent, with room service provided as well.

CARIBBEAN PALM VILLAGE

Caribbean Palm Village (Palm Beach Rd. 43-E, 297/526-2700, www.cpvr.com, $258 one-bedroom), about a mile inland along the Noord-Palm Beach Road, was originally built as a timeshare complex. Aside from the studio rooms, they have very spacious one- and two-bedroom suites, and two attractive pool decks. There is a community lounge and fitness center, and an independent restaurant on-site serving breakfast, lunch, and dinner. Community barbecue and picnic areas and a day spa are part of the complex as well.

The resort is across the street from Santa Ana Church and smack-dab in the middle of a commercial area, with a supermarket, department store, and drugstore next door. In addition to having every convenience at hand, there is a busy, bustling center just beyond the resort's walls.

HILTON ARUBA CARIBBEAN RESORT & CASINO

Aruba's first major resort, and still one of the most elegant and attractive hotels on the island, is now a Hilton: **Hilton Aruba Caribbean Resort & Casino** (J. E. Irausquin Blvd. 81, 297/586-6555, www3.hilton.com, $244-319 plus taxes). Aruba's "grande dame" still exudes charm and elegance, harking back to a bygone era. It has had a number of incarnations since first opening as the Aruba Caribbean, and its newest one as a Hilton took place in June of 2015. It is living history for Arubans. It was going to be purchased by the RIU chain before being bought by the Hilton, but a consortium of local businesspeople stepped in to ensure it would retain its non-all-inclusive status, as well as its particular character. One change to keep in mind: it has become a 100 percent nonsmoking facility.

Rooms in the main section may be older, but they are well maintained with rather unconventional room dimensions. If you are offered a room in the "old section," take it—they are very spacious, with high ceilings and huge dressing rooms and closets. They are a throwback to the day when people came to the island and wore gowns and tuxedos at night. (Former James Bond actor Roger Moore used to stay here regularly.)

Two additional sections of more pedestrian design were added over the years. Since 2010, the hotel has undergone millions of dollars of renovations and refurbishments. One of the most notable additions of the changeover was the complete sculpturing of the pool deck to create the feeling of sitting on the beach, with lushly landscaped paths. It is one of the most gorgeous pool areas on Aruba. This area is also home to one of Aruba's most interesting unofficial attractions: Victor, the Birdman, who cares for the exotic birds around the gardens.

There is a special "Plaza Club" on the upper floors with more elaborate rooms and suites, a personal concierge, and complimentary continental breakfast, afternoon tea, and happy hour, with snacks and drinks included. There is an in-house casino, and the detached Larimar Day Spa is the largest and one of the most luxurious on Aruba. Under the Hilton flag, the amenities and restaurants for which the resort is known have remained in place, with the added advantage of being able to earn and deploy Hilton points under the franchise's reward system.

OCEAN 105

Ocean 105 (L. G. Smith Blvd. 105, toll-free in U.S. 866/978-6986, www.ocean105.com, one-bedroom units $216-$325) is one of two Malmok guesthouses actually on the water, with direct access to the beach. It is adjacent to Boca Catalina, which is popular with islanders on the weekend. Guests have a small patch of beach to call their own. Ocean 105 is also bordered by two nice snorkel spots for beginners, with easy shore access. A number of sailboats stop in the bay daily with charter trips.

The two-story guesthouse has only four apartments: a single one-bedroom and three two-bedroom units, which are very spacious and elegantly decorated. (The owner also has a chic, contemporary furniture shop.) There are sofa beds in the living rooms, fully equipped kitchens, and terraces or patios that hang out over the sea, but there is no pool. Maid service is provided twice a week.

THE MILL RESORT

Across the street from the beachfront resorts, **The Mill Resort** (J. E. Irausquin Blvd. 330, 297/526-7700 or toll-free in U.S. and Canada 800/992-2015, www.millresort.com, $280) is right next to the area's signature landmark, for which it was named. Rather unique, it is a sprawling facility in the low-rise mode and was a concept ahead of its time. It was intended to be a condominium complex, with exceptionally large three-bedroom units that could be divided into separate apartments by closing the doors. Now living spaces have been divided into studios, junior suites, and royal accommodations, each with either full or mini-kitchens. Royal suites have a private whirlpool bath in the middle of the room. Families can combine junior or royal suites with a studio for the kids, with its own bathroom. Up to two children ages 12 and under stay free in the same room with parents.

Two hundred rooms surround a very spacious and attractive pool deck with three free-form pools, a restaurant, and a bar. The bar is very popular with locals on Friday evenings for the lively happy hour and local band. Shuttle service is provided to the beach. They have staked out a section of beach just south of the Riu where they distribute lounge chairs. There is a mini-market on the premises as well as the Intermezzo Day Spa, which has a luxurious couples' room.

$300-400

BLUE RESIDENCES

Just on the border of Eagle and Palm Beach is the fairly new **Blue Residences** (J. E. Irausquin Blvd. 266, toll-free in U.S. 866/728-4910, www.bluearuba.com, $300, one-, two-, and three-bedroom units $400+). These very attractive condominiums are rented out as hotel rooms. They have been set up so those selecting the $300 option get the standard amenities, a king-size bed and bath, and no kitchen. However, larger groups and families opting for one bedroom or more can expect a full and beautifully appointed apartment. These are exceptionally spacious and have ocean views.

Since the facility is all condos, the decor of each unit reflects the individual taste of its owner. The ground-floor apartments each have whirlpool spas on the terrace, but no privacy—so no skinny-dipping. There is a very attractive pool deck, designed for swimming laps. Other services include an on-site day spa, mini-market, restaurant, and fitness room. Aside from holiday weeks, the facility is usually not very busy. Blue Residences is situated directly across J. E. Irausquin Boulevard from the Baranca Plat beach. The resort has not placed *palapas* or lounges on the beach, so it still remains a rather quiet, secluded spot.

DIVI PHOENIX BEACH RESORT

The checkered past of **Divi Phoenix Beach Resort** (J. E. Irausquin Blvd. 75, 297/586-6066, www.diviresorts.com, $310) and a number of incarnations have resulted in two sections of disparate configurations and price. Divi Properties acquired a failed project, restoring and enhancing the original plan. Hence, the name Phoenix, as it was rescued by a respected hospitality franchise to rise from the ashes.

They parlayed this coup into a very popular resort, where the rooms are all suites with fully equipped kitchens, a step up from your average hotel room, especially in the new section. The original resort has a cozy, simple pool deck, and one of the first restaurants to actually provide the toes-in-the-sand waterfront dining experience at Pure Ocean.

The sumptuous new section opened in 2008. It now houses the main lobby and a luxurious free-form pool; all rooms have spacious balconies facing out over the pool or with ocean views. The poolside restaurant and bar is also beachfront, with a swim-up bar. Naturally, the newer, more luxurious area has the higher-priced rooms.

Divi Phoenix totals 214 suites; those available for rental are mostly studios (the bedroom can be closed off with accordion doors and living rooms have sofa beds) or one-bedroom units, nice for families.

The resort has a mini-market, additional casual sandwich spot, business center, concierge and car rental desks, on-site day spa, and a very friendly, accommodating staff. It is slightly set apart from the strip of resorts, so there is a more tranquil atmosphere around the beach.

OVER $400

PLAYA LINDA BEACH RESORT

Playa Linda Beach Resort (J. E. Irausquin Blvd. 87, 297/586-6100, www.playalinda.com,

the swim-up bar at Divi Phoenix Beach Resort

Timeshare and Condominium Rentals

Timeshare rooms are a hybrid of hotels and condominiums, usually with the amenities of housekeeping and easy beachfront access. They provide concierge desks, activities coordinators, plus homey touches such as laundry rooms and mini-markets.

Families with young children often find these facilities ideal. They allow privacy for parents as well as meals in the room. With young, sometimes fussy eaters, not having to spend on costly restaurants is a worthwhile savings.

It isn't easy trading a timeshare at another location for one on Aruba, particularly during busy holiday weeks. Each timeshare has a rental office with quite a few listings, though many owners prefer to rent direct and keep the commission. Direct listings can be found on the numerous Aruba bulletin boards online or via classified ads in Aruba's English-language newspapers.

Popular online forums with listings can be found on www.aruba.com, www.visitaruba.com, http://aruba-travelguide.com, http://arubabound.com, and http://aruba-bb.com. There are also individual bulletin boards from the various timeshare resorts. If someone has not already listed a timeshare unit for sale or available for rent in the time frame you seek, join the bulletin board and post what you are looking for, include the particular weeks and locations you desire. There are also a number of independent travel brokers specializing in renting out timeshares.

The spate of new condo resorts on Aruba promises even more luxurious digs for fantastic rates. Condo owners wish to earn back or make money on their investment by renting it out. Often their owners use them for only a few weeks a year, much less than a hotel room is used.

A website dedicated entirely to connecting directly with owners of timeshares and condominiums is **Vacations Rentals by Owners** (www.vrbo.com). Listings are by owners eager to rent their property and willing to pay to list their properties, so bargains can often be found on this site. There are hundreds of listings offering a wealth of options.

studios or one-bedroom units $455) is more than just hotel rooms; it is the first, the coziest, and one of the most luxurious timeshare resorts on Aruba. It is located in a prime spot and won awards for design when it first opened.

The resort hosts a mini-market, as well as a number of shops and restaurants both on the street side and on the beach boardwalk. It offers a very nice day spa, fitness room, tennis courts, and a beautiful pool deck that was completely renovated in 2015. The overall feel is most definitely family-oriented. Most guests have owned timeshares here for years. They are veteran visitors with a lot of good advice about the island that they are eager to share.

An independent Playa Linda online bulletin board on the website has entire sections dedicated to those looking for tradeoffs or rentals, and another for those offering them, where great discounts can be found. Since the average maintenance fee for the top-of-the-line rooms is around $900 per week, you can save substantial money by finding a place being rented out directly from owners, who are looking to just earn back their fees.

A dispatch office for an ambulance service and an EMT center are headquartered in the parking lot. Because of this, the resort's clientele is generally mature. It would also be a good idea for someone with a chronic condition to take this into account when choosing accommodations.

Santa Cruz, Paradera, and Piedra Plat

Beyond the principal tourist areas, accommodations are few and far between. Aruba's government encourages tourism projects in these currently undeveloped areas, but investors are still focused on Aruba's west coast and beachfront.

$100-200

CUNUCU VILLAS

Lia Lopez is the sweet, friendly host at **Cunucu Villas** (Santa Cruz 23, 297/585-1616, www.cunucuvillasaruba.com, one-bedroom suites $117, for two adults and two children, $20/night for each extra person). She has 12 identical units on two levels. The upper rooms have a very nice view of the surrounding countryside. Set back on a dirt road at the end of a residential street, Cunucu Villas has an attractive pool deck with a community grill and large picnic tables under a shaded terrace. Rooms have simple decor and full kitchens.

Despite its rather out-of-the-way location, it is only a 10-minute walk to Huchada Bakery, and Santa Cruz's principal commercial area is only a bit farther on. It is also quite close to Arikok National Park.

PARADERA PARK APARTMENTS

Providing quicker access to Arikok National Park for dedicated hikers and nature buffs, **Paradera Park Apartments** (Paradera 203, 297/582-3289, www.paraderapark-aruba.com, $174 studio, $20/night for each extra person) is a very friendly, family-run operation with a dedicated following. They get a surprising number of long-term guests who have been vacationing on Aruba for years, as the accommodations are clean, attractive, and the owners are quite personable.

Paradera Park Apartments is comprised of a small complex of studios and one- and two-bedroom suites, tucked away down a side street in what is a purely residential area. The turnoffs to get here are clearly marked. There is also one duplex suite with the bedroom and master bath on the second level. All rooms include full kitchens. The focus of the complex is a small pool with an attractive deck and garden and a community center.

San Nicolas, Savaneta, and Pos Chiquito

It is rare to find accommodations in Aruba's more rural areas, which are either deserted stretches of scrub or a national park, enjoyable for a day of exploring. However, more small guesthouses are situated on or near the scattered coves of Savaneta and Pos Chiquito, where there is close access to some lovely beaches that see very little traffic.

These primarily residential areas have some attractive and relatively inexpensive facilities. Some are particularly aimed for those who really want to get away from it all. Most provide an apartment setting, targeting budget travelers and including full kitchens, as restaurants and cafés are few and far between. If seeking a sense of being isolated on a tropical island, these places certainly deliver, but renting a car is definitely required.

$100-200

★ ARUBA REEF APARTMENTS

Aruba Reef Apartments (Savaneta 342 C, 297/735-2053, www.arubareef.com, $187) is about as close as you will come to your fantasy of a tropical island getaway. Parts of this expansive waterfront home have been converted into the most delightful apartments, where you can literally roll out of bed (or your personal hammock) onto a lovely private beach.

Each of the five units has a kitchenette with a full-size fridge, a terrace, and a very spacious, newly refurbished bathroom. Fred has a house in Bali, so the ambience is a mix of Caribbean/South Pacific, and the surroundings are covered with his remarkable art collection from around the world. He is an erudite aficionado, and his love of art infuses every aspect of the place.

The beach has a volleyball court and plenty of lounges. There are a few communal areas, a grill, and even a "meditation zone" on a deck next to the water. Free kayaks and snorkel gear are on hand so you can explore the stunning waters along Aruba's south coast.

The complex is adjacent to Flying Fishbone restaurant, and is only five doors down from Zeerover. The current host, Raffy, took over from his father Fred, the original owner of the property, when he passed in 2016. Raffy lives on the premises and is a congenial host, full of information about the island. Fred had the word "Paradise" engraved in the home's quaint entrance—and it truly feels like it.

SEABREEZE APARTMENTS

Perfectly situated to enjoy the great beaches of Pos Chiquito, **Seabreeze Apartments** (Malohistraat 5, 297/585-7140, www.seabreezeapartments.com, $105) is a delightful new complex comprised of 10 studio and one-bedroom units, each with a kitchenette, cable TV and free Wi-Fi. It is a five-minute walk from Mangel Halto Beach and some sensational snorkeling and diving. Free coolers are provided for anyone planning to spend some time there.

The owner, Joey, is thrilled to be hosting his own facility and thoroughly enjoys the company of his guests. The charming complex has a very appealing community area with both a pool and whirlpool spa. It has been designed to encourage congenial repartee. Right next door is a small supermarket and Chinese restaurant, and Marina Pirata restaurant is within walking distance.

the pool at Seabreeze Apartments

THE HIDEAWAY

If you're looking for a bargain accommodation that will leave you feeling like you have your own luxurious villa in paradise, aptly named **The Hideaway** (Pos Chiquito 273F, 297/596-0197, capeskris@aol.com, $213) fits the bill. This two-story home is comprised of three apartments, each of which can sleep six or more comfortably, that have beautifully outfitted kitchens. The top unit has a "nanny's room" and all of the terraces have stunning views. This is a great place if you have a large group or a few families vacationing together. The room rates are a flat rate, so the bigger the group the cheaper it gets per individual—no additional fees for extra bodies.

The property is made for entertaining, with a spacious patio, pool and spa, large gas grill, and spectacular sound system. Maid service is available at a very reasonable extra cost. The house is fairly new, nicely decorated, and designed for renters. Each apartment closes off completely from the others. A rental vehicle will be necessary, as it is in a somewhat secluded location, but the beautiful beaches of Savaneta and Pos Chiquito are only five minutes away by car.

OVER $200

CLUB ARIAS BED AND BREAKFAST

The rather surreal, idiosyncratic facade of **Club Arias Bed and Breakfast** (Savaneta 123-K, 297/593-3408 or in U.S. 917/508-7210, www.clubarias.com, $250 and up, includes breakfast) disguises a charming courtyard with surprisingly large pools and attractive gardens. The courtyard is the focal point, surrounded by 10 very spacious rooms, each uniquely decorated with original art and knickknacks.

Each room has its own kitchenette, and one unit has a full kitchen. But the community area sports a cozy open-air restaurant where Cordon Bleu-graduate chef Gabriel prepares gourmet omelets for the breakfast part of the bed-and-breakfast. Breakfast is served 7:30am-10:30am, and Gabriel is available for private dinners on request. You do not need to stay at the resort to order breakfast, but it is only free for guests. Residence at Club Arias, named for its owner from New York, Arias Schwarz, also includes high tea with fresh pastries at 4pm.

It is located directly on the main highway that runs the length from Oranjestad to San

Rooms surround the pool area at Club Arias Bed and Breakfast.

Nicolas, a very busy thoroughfare. But it's set back a sufficient distance for quiet, particularly the back rooms.

VISTALMAR

One of Aruba's first out-of-the-way apartment and resort facilities, **Vistalmar Apartments** (Bucutiweg 28, 297/582-8579, www.arubavistalmar.com, $945/week) has garnered a dedicated clientele. There is no beach to speak of, but there is a private dock along one of the prettiest sections of the south shore. It is very close to two yacht clubs, which is nice for dedicated deep-sea fishing fanatics.

The rooms have fully equipped kitchens and terraces looking right out on the sea and the sunsets. Breakfast is provided on arrival day, with the understanding that the cupboard is likely empty, and fresh bread is delivered daily. The owners offer airport shuttle service on arrival and departure days. Other amenities include snorkel gear, coolers, and bicycles. A car rental can be arranged as part of the package for a special discounted rate.

Background

The Landscape

A phrase from the chorus of Aruba's national anthem, "Aruba Dushi Tera" ("Sweet Land Aruba"), describes this island nation as *Nos baranca tan stima* (Our beloved rock). This simple phrase conveys the distinct self-awareness and great affection Arubans have for their unique desert island.

Aruba is a relatively flat island with three major peaks: Seroe Jamanota, 188 meters (617 ft.); Seroe Arikok, 184 meters (606 ft.); and Hooiberg, 165 meters (541 ft.). Constant winds continuously buffet the island from the northeast, traveling thousands of miles across open sea. Combine this with the geological makeup, and Aruba's north coast is a lunar landscape of limestone outcroppings. These are interspersed with quartz rock and pillow basalt. All were formed when undersea volcanoes initially created the submerged landmasses that would become the ABC islands of Aruba, Bonaire, and Curacao. Along the north coast, heavy waves dramatically crash and spume, occasionally broken by small coves and beaches.

The land resembles an elongated triangle. The south shore is dotted with small beaches, mangrove formations, and limestone cliffs. The western or leeward side is home to the miles-long stretch of beaches that so attract visitors and real estate developers. These areas from Palm Beach south have been exclusively zoned for tourism.

Located north of the equator at 12°32'28"N and 69°57'30"W, Aruba is 31 kilometers (19 mi. long and 9.65 kilometers (6 mi.) wide at its widest point. Approximately 116 square kilometers (72 mi.), the island is divided into seven zoning districts, each containing multiple barrios. The closest major landmass is the Paraguaná Peninsula of Venezuela, 19 kilometers (12 mi.) south; Caracas is 68 kilometers (42 mi.) from Aruba. Sister islands of Curacao and Bonaire are 88 kilometers (55 mi.) and 103 kilometers (64 mi.) east, along the 12° latitude line. Aruba is the physically smallest of the ABC islands, but it has a population of 107,000 compared to only 15,000 living on Bonaire, which is 179 square kilometers (111 mi.) in size. Curacao, at 275 square kilometers (171 mi.), is the largest of the three and has a population of 141,766. It takes only 20 minutes to travel from Aruba to Curacao by prop plane, but the sea voyage is a challenging 15 hours through very rough waters.

GEOLOGY

Studies propose the initial undersea landmasses were formed around 95 million years ago, finally making their way to the surface through tectonic activity around 30 million years later. Aruba was formed from three kinds of rock: igneous, which is a cooling and solidification of magma; metamorphic, a rock formed from a previously produced rock; and sedimentary, resulting from the continual deposit and hardening of other rocks.

The fantastical pillow lava formations found primarily around the north coast confirm the underwater accretion of the land. After the original volcanic eruptions, a continuation of the magma flow over the rock, a process called plutonism, created layers. The majority of the island's landscape, named the Aruba Lava Formation, is a part of a huge geologic formation called a batholith. Of this, only a minor portion has been exposed after weathering, erosion, and being pushed up by the earth's movement.

The carved limestone cliffs populating coves along the shoreline are the most recently

Previous: Aruba's rugged north coast; cacti.

Hooiberg, Aruba's third highest peak, in the distance

accumulated rock. Close examination of the terraces reveal a wealth of interesting marine fossils and coral impressions.

WEATHER

One of Aruba's great assets is the reliable weather: a sunny 28-33°C (82-92°F) year-round. Its proximity to the equator defines it as a tropical island, but constant breezes and sea currents keep the temperature comfortable. The sea is surprisingly cooler than expected. Temperatures are ideal for coral growth and a proliferation of colorful fish life.

Aruba is considered to be south of the Hurricane Belt and therefore is rarely subject to the devastating storms for which the Caribbean is known. Usually, Aruba's weather, if it is an issue at all, is most unstable from around mid or late August until the end of November. This is a time when named storms are more likely to form in the Gulf of Mexico. Each year, weather pundits predict an increased number of greater strength for the Atlantic, Caribbean, and Gulf regions. The records show it is very rare for them to approach Aruba. For the most part, they turn north from the gulf as they make their way across the Atlantic from Africa.

Occasional weather fronts behave utterly contrary to what is expected, of course. Hurricanes Dean, Lenny, Ivan, and Francis are examples of some systems that were so huge and powerful, even Aruba experienced heavy seas and hard rains, just from the ripple effects. Sometimes storms far away will produce small occlusions that can result in rough waters or occasional squalls. Still, it is unheard of for travel plans to the island to be canceled because of weather on Aruba.

The most common effect of the big storms is for Aruba's ever-present wind to die down, causing it to become oppressively humid. There is no predicting this well in advance. In 2015, Aruba was declared to be in a "medium drought" situation, and rains have been scarce. Conditions have been consistently breezy and dry since 2012.

Environmental Issues

OVERDEVELOPMENT AND POPULATION

Aruba faces the conundrum of many Caribbean islands: progressing economically and technologically into the 21st century, while attempting to maintain its cultural identity. Unbridled construction and development may create jobs and business opportunities, but at what cost to the physical aspects that define the island's character and support its economy through tourism?

This has now become a concern for not only the government and dedicated groups, but also the average citizen. Islanders are dismayed to see developers callously bulldozing acres of land, which are habitats for countless endemic species of flora and fauna. Coastal areas and the essential mangrove formations with their delicate ecosystems are particularly endangered. Aside from some cases of completely unwarranted waste, other projects beg the question: Does the island really need another shopping mall or upscale housing complex? There is already an overabundance of both. This is another dilemma, as property owners wish to generate profit from undeveloped land, which may have been in the family for generations. Legislation requiring environmental studies and prohibiting threats to endemic endangered species is not in place to curb these actions. Aruba's enormous success with tourism has exacerbated its sustainability issues, and it doesn't help that tourism has been the island's primary financial pillar since the last half of the 20th century.

For decades Aruba has been a golden land of opportunity within the Caribbean, attracting immigrants from other islands as well as South and Central America. The rapidly burgeoning population on a physically small piece of rock naturally created stresses on various systems and the infrastructure, despite the native population readily accepting and integrating these various groups socially.

Aruba's advanced system of water distribution, and an attractive social and educational system under the Dutch, has provided benefits and support that many immigrants from the immediate region could not find in their homelands. Much of this came with the Lago Refinery, along with especially skilled labor that more than tripled the island population when it first opened.

For the quarter of a century since Status Aparte, immigrants could always count on jobs in tourism, construction, and menial positions. When Aruba achieved Status Aparte in 1986, the population was estimated at 72,000. The 2010 census counts over 107,000 legal residents. The demands on the infrastructure, the loss of natural lands cleared for all the needed housing, as well as the boom in development of tourism venues has caused great concern among environmental groups. Add to that the further strain created by a visiting population of more than 1.5 million per year, and the waste this produces on a land of very limited area to store it.

TRASH AND RECYCLING

Unfortunately, the region is still generally well behind the times compared to the United States, Canada, and Europe in regard to recycling or a general attitude toward maintaining the environment through the proper disposal of litter and mass waste. Many people are very sensitive to this situation; hence hard legislation was enacted in 2012 to address the issue. Severe strictures to inhibit illegal dumping have been enacted. It is encouraging that travel executives who regularly visit Caribbean nations for business report that they find Aruba far cleaner than most other destinations in the region.

Aruba maintains an official landfill on the south shore at Parkietenbos, where the trash is burned. There is regular weekly collection conducted in almost all communities, as well as private operators for businesses and hotels that require more frequent service. However, large items and appliances or large quantities of debris from yards are not carted away by the public service.

Collaborating with private waste haulage services, various foundations and companies have organized a number of island-wide cleanups. There are at least three beach cleaning efforts annually sponsored by various concerns when hundreds, sometimes thousands, of volunteers participate; tourists are welcome to join in.

Until the summer of 2012, some individuals owning unused parcels of land had turned them into dumps for profit; this is now banned without exception—a policy that has been fully enforced. The landfill also eliminated any charge for dropping off large amounts of refuse. Unfortunately, a public recycling plant constructed by a U.S. concern to produce "Fluff" broke down after only a few months and was subsequently shut down. Since then, Ecotech, a private waste management company, and WEB, the island's water and power plant, have been trying to create a more viable solution.

Ecotech opened a sorting service, and all materials collected are now shipped off to be recycled. In the fall of 2014, a biogas production plant was opened to process all organic refuse. WEB refitted one of its power plants to deploy the recycled fuel, which is expected to provide 8 percent of Aruba's energy needs by 2020. Presently, the system only processes the waste collected by Ecotech's private service. They are in negotiations with the governmental garbage collection agency, SERLIMAR, to also process the public collections.

Incentive programs have been established to encourage the public to sort and turn in their waste in order to win prizes. Concerned interests tour the schools giving lectures along with hosting contests for students to collect recyclable waste, conditioning the next generation for what is necessary for a sustainable Aruba.

AIR POLLUTION

A glance at a chart compiled by the U.S. Department of Energy's Carbon Dioxide Information Analysis Center (CDIAC) in 2008, based on information gathered by the United Nations Statistics Division, reveals Aruba is number nine in the world regarding carbon dioxide emissions in metric tons of carbon dioxide *per capita*. This is among 214 nations. Without question, the refinery in San Nicolas was directly related to this standing. Figures show the now defunct Netherlands Antilles, which was dissolved in 2010, was rated the number four country with the most emissions *per capita* in the world, likely due to the huge Shell refinery in Curacao. The Valero refinery has been idle since April of 2012, which has proven beneficial to Aruba's emission rating.

All refining operations ceased completely in 2014, and the area is being utilized as a transshipment station, loading oil from small lake tankers to the larger oceangoing vessels. Recurring rumors of recommencing production have yet to result in definitive action. Informed parties hold little hope of the antiquated facility being viable again, as the cost of repair and modernization does not really make it an attractive investment.

The CDIAC chart tracked emissions from 1990 to 2008, and there are sharp declines in the years when Aruba's refinery was inactive. A similar study conducted at the end of 2013 by The Shift Project (http://www.tsp-data-portal.org/) did not list Aruba in the top 20 nations for carbon dioxide emissions.

Despite the refinery's emissions, and those of WEB's power plant at Balashi, along with the burning of trash at the landfill on the south side, visitors have always found Aruba's air delightfully fresh, for the most part only carrying the scent of clean salt seas.

It is possible that when planning these facilities, the engineers kept in mind the prevailing northeasterly wind, which pushed all the fumes away from the island immediately. Even when frolicking at Baby Beach or Roger's Beach, in the very shadow of the refinery, people could see the emissions, but not smell them.

RENEWABLE ENERGY

WEB, Aruba's other great source of carbon dioxide emissions, is also working diligently in conjunction with the government to reduce and possibly eliminate entirely the island's dependence on oil for power and water to reduce its carbon footprint. The primary concern is not necessarily the environment but the practicalities of a very turbulent and speculative oil commodity market, driving prices up to a point where average islanders cannot afford to pay their electric bills. Purification of the air will of course be a very positive outcome of reducing Aruba's oil use.

Other renewable energy technologies are being pursued. In 2009, the Vader Piet Wind Farm, consisting of 10 giant wind turbines, began operating on the far northeast coast of Aruba. The government and the company running the wind farm had hoped to establish a second at Urirama, near the Alto Vista Chapel, but this was met with strong resistance from nearby residents; the situation created a stalemate. The government has made clear its intention to see this wind park realized, but the project is still not underway.

A large solar field was completed at Aruba's airport. It also acts as shade for the parking lot. This now provides all the power for the airport, and produces 3 percent of Aruba's energy needs. Import taxes on materials and equipment to harness clean energy sources have been drastically reduced, encouraging residents to find alternatives to power their homes by feeding energy back into the grid. WEB has switched over to reverse osmosis water purification, which requires far less energy. In 2011, a program was implemented called "Save Together with Us" encouraging consumers to be frugal in their energy consumption. Items that reduced water and electricity consumption were distributed as gift bags to all low-income neighborhoods.

The declared goal of island administrators is to make Aruba completely oil independent by 2020. They have been vigilant in reaching out to every possible international organization toward that goal. In 2012, the Carbon War Room, founded by Sir Richard Branson, officially endorsed and affirmed its support to make Aruba the first completely oil independent nation in the world. This is a process that will require not only installing new means for harnessing energy from low emission-producing sources, but also an effort to change wasteful energy habits on the part of residents.

The Dutch energy think tank TNO established its first Caribbean branch in Aruba in 2011. It connects scientists, technology, and stakeholders to devise plans that will assist various communities in fulfilling their energy needs. In October of 2012 they broke ground on a Smart Community, in the centrally located barrio of Kibaima. This experimental community will consist of 15 homes that will operate solely on renewable energy sources and five control homes that do not, in order to provide comparative statistics. TNO describes Aruba as "the perfect springboard for markets in the United States and South America." Its involvement in this project and Aruba's own goals will hopefully stimulate interest from European private companies in investing in the Caribbean and Latin energy markets. TNO's stance, and that of the Aruban government, is that investment and business in renewable technologies can provide opportunities for jobs, profit, and an improved quality of life for the entire region.

Islanders are being encouraged to make the switch to electric or hybrid cars. Some entities, such as Divi Properties Aruba, are actually awarding small electric cars to those who purchased condominiums. Aruba's power distributor, ELMAR, is conducting programs to promote the import and purchase of electric cars and the construction of solar energy structures to house and charge them. Duties on electric automobiles have been reduced from the usual 40 percent for gas-burning vehicles to only 2 percent to further encourage consumers to make the change.

LITTER ON BEACHES

Efforts continue to make individuals and large concerns like resorts aware of the multiple consequences of plastic cups, plates, and straws, as well as foam containers to Aruba's environment. Some are proposing that only reusable glasses, dishes, and silverware be used anywhere near the beach.

It is very common for resorts to provide meal and drink service to guests on the beach in disposable foam containers, with plastic cutlery, and drinks in plastic cups. If these are not disposed of immediately and properly, the trade winds will likely blow them about. Not only is it unsightly litter, but far worse, it can end up in the sea, where it can become deadly.

Various types of marinelife, particularly turtles, feed on jellyfish; plastic and foam cups and the plastic rings that hold together a six pack of cans, can easily be mistaken for their favorite food. This can result in a turtle choking to death—a far more common occurrence than most would imagine and a serious threat to a number of species. The cups and foam debris accumulate under the water and litter the marine environment. The same holds true for sailing cruises when drinks are served; care must be taken so that the cups do not blow overboard. Paper goods are at least biodegradable, but these should also be disposed of quickly and properly, especially newspapers, which do tend to get blown about.

Conscientious guests at resorts should not hesitate to speak up if a facility does not provide a sufficient number of conveniently located waste disposal units. If trash bins are filled beyond capacity before the end of the day and there is spillover, bring it to the management's attention; they will respond.

Saving Aruba's Turtles

a baby leatherback turtle

Every year during between March and November sections of beach may be cordoned off, particularly around Eagle Beach. This is to protect the eggs and hatchlings of Aruba's local and migrating sea turtle population, which mate and nest here during these months.

Four species in particular are the concern of **TurtugAruba** (hotline 297/592-9393, http://turtugaruba.org), the local foundation that works to protect the island's turtle population. The green sea turtle and the hawksbill are native to Aruban waters and can be spotted year-round while snorkeling and diving, though the hawksbill is considered a critically endangered species.

Leatherbacks and loggerheads normally feed and live in far distant oceans, usually in the North Atlantic, but will travel thousands of miles to return to the same waters where they first entered the sea to mate. The females lay their eggs on the same beaches where they hatched years before. Most often they do this under the cover of night, a remarkable sight.

Once the eggs are laid and buried, mom returns to the sea, and the hatchlings face survival to adulthood on their own. So many things, including human actions, are a threat to newborn turtles. Driving on the beach is discouraged for this reason.

TortugAruba asks that observers report, but do not disturb, a female laying her eggs. The area will be cordoned off to protect the nest and monitored during the two-month gestational period. Volunteers maintain a vigil for when the young turtles emerge, helping them make it to the sea safely.

Certain island resorts, such as Bucuti & Tara Beach Resort and Amsterdam Beach Resort, have made great strides in the past five years to become green certified, the former even being cited as "a champion" by Green Globe International. Visitors can help encourage all resorts to go green by selecting green-certified resorts.

Volunteer Programs

ARUBA REEF CARE PROJECT

What began as an underwater reef cleaning effort by some young diving enthusiasts is now the long-standing **Aruba Reef Care Project** (297/740-0797, castroperez@gmail.com), which polices both the shore and marine environment. Volunteers sign up with a number of dive operators to use either scuba or snorkeling gear while cleaning under the water, as hundreds of others take to all the island beaches to remove refuse. (This event took place over the July 4 weekend for more than a decade, but in 2012 the event moved to September.) Volunteers are rewarded with a festive party (this is Aruba, after all) and lunch afterward, plus a raffle for many great prizes donated by local concerns (dinners for two, weekend stays at resorts, and so on) and an attractive certificate.

COASTAL ZONE CLEAN-UP

Since 2002, the Aruba Hotel and Tourism Association (AHATA) Environmental Committee has conducted its **Coastal Zone Clean-Up** (297/582-2607, vanessa@ahata.com) in November. It also targets every beach and awards prizes for groups that collect the most refuse.

PROJECT AWARE

Every April, Red Sail Sports carries out **Project Aware** (297/586-1603, info@redsailaruba.com). Red Sail rewards its volunteers with a sailing cruise on one of its large catamarans to wind down after a morning of strenuous garbage collecting. The effort is on a smaller scale, focusing on a particular beach needing attention.

GARNIER ANNUAL BEACH CLEANUP

Aruba's newest effort, May's **Garnier Annual Beach Cleanup** (297/582-5672, lizayra.polak@curapharm.com) also does a "surgical strike" on certain beachfronts vulnerable to incoming tides that dump garbage tossed overboard by passing ships, mostly tankers. Certain beaches along the north coast need regular policing. The amount that can accumulate in a short time is alarming.

Plants and Animals

PLANTS

Trees

A combination of yearlong tropical temperatures and little rainfall produces a wild plant population leaning heavily toward thorny succulents, flowering plants, and trees. They sport an abundance of prickles from the microscopic to inches long as natural protection from roaming herbivores. Hiking trips into the Aruban countryside require care to avoid them.

Island trees are best known by their Papiamento names. **Kwihi** are prolific and valued for their wood. After these have been felled to build lots for houses, whole trunks often end up as arresting tables, maintaining their original configurations. Kwihi are practically weeds, germinating easily in the slightest bit of soil, with huge thorns to protect the young green plants. They finally grow into majestic shade trees.

Watapana, or **divi** trees *(Caesalpinia coriaria),* almost resemble what artists try to accomplish with bonsai when full grown; the continual northeast wind bends and carves them to lean over in dramatic, gnarled formations. Common advice for those who decide to go out exploring the outback on their own and eventually get lost: Just follow the direction the divi trees point and you will always end up back in Oranjestad.

Another tree that is abundant and green year-round is the aptly named **Crown of Thorns** *(Acacia tortuosa),* called *hubada* by islanders; it is good to give these a wide berth. They produce an appealing yellow ball of a flower, but keep their long, painful spikes even when full grown.

Vacationers fortunate to be visiting in May or June might be rewarded with the rare sight of the **kibrahacha** *(Tabebuia billbergii),* commonly known as yellow poui, in bloom. This only happens for a few days a year and, during that time, only when there have been some showers, which will trigger a flurried attempt at seeding and pollinating. The normal foliage of the hills around Arikok National Park or the Hooiberg turns into a riot of brilliant yellow blooms, which will disappear in less than a week. The tree gets its local name from the extreme hardness of the wood; it literally translates as "break the hatchet" (*kibra* means "break" and *hacha* means "hatchet").

Fruits

A number of regional wild fruit trees are scattered across the landscape, producing an impressive harvest in wetter years. **Sea grape** *(Coccoloba swartzii)* are a sweet snack and provide welcome shade alongside many beaches. The **West Indian cherry** *(Malpighia emarginata),* locally known as *chimarucu,* is sometimes sold in the markets. Cultivated in gardens or growing wild are ***kenepa*** *(Melicoccus bijugatus),* also known as "Spanish lime." This is a regional tree that produces clusters of green-skinned fruit the size of a lychee. Inside is a large seed coated with a delicious pulp that is a beloved treat, eaten by sucking on the seed; a tasty and nonfattening way to stop smoking!

Aruba has an endless variety of cactus and prickly flowers growing wild or cultivated, not the least of which is aloe vera. The most common endemic varieties are the towering *cadushi,* better known as **candle cactus** *(Stenocereus griseus).* It produces a deep red, tasty fruit, attracting birds who manage to avoid the proliferation of thorns and are able to spread the seeds.

Showing off a very delicate yellow flower

divi trees on Eagle Beach

The Aruban Orchid

Aruba does have a specific native strain of the orchid *Brassavola nodosa*. It originates in Venezuela, where it is referred to as *Dama de Noche* (Lady of the Night) because it emits a noticeably sweet, somewhat citrus scent from sunset to sunrise. Aruba has a cactus that had already claimed that name by producing beautiful white blooms only at dark. Local orchid aficionados refer to the Aruban strain of orchid as the far earthier *Puta Chiquito* (Little Prostitute).

During the 1940s, Esso executive Russ Ewing, who lived in the colony, harbored a passion for orchids. He produced a unique hybrid by cross-pollinating the hardy Aruban *Brassavola nodosa* with the Venezuelan *Encyclia cordigera*. The result was larger than both. He registered this new species with the Royal Horticultural Society of the United Kingdom as *Brassoepidendrum arubiana* on January 1, 1950. The common name is the "Aruba Good Friend."

Aruban orchid

The **Aruba Orchid Society** (sociedaddiorquidiaaruba@yahoo.com) has existed for almost 40 years and is very active. They recruit members and stimulate interest in cultivating orchids with regular shows. They have published some how-to books on growing orchids in Papiamento.

is the "tuna" or **prickly pear** *(Opuntia wentiana)*, which will also eventually produce a sweet fruit of many seeds. The comical *bushi*, or **Turk's cap cactus** *(Melocactus macracanthus)*, have brilliant neon-pink flowers sprouting from their white, spongy centers. These become tart, equally bright pink fruit, shaped like a small pepper to attract lizards and birds.

Flowers

Among the many wild flowering plants, one of the most noticeable is *Passiflora* or **passion flower**, known in Papiamento as *shoshoro*. The bulbous pods open into a delicate purple flower with green stigmata. It is a tenacious vine, often twining around other plants.

A garden left to grow naturally will eventually produce an abundance of typical dessert foliage, scrub, and cacti. Though brilliantly hued tropical flowers, such as dewdrops, azaleas, hibiscus, frangipani, flamboyan, and begonias, are imported, they are commonly seen decorating landscaped resort gardens and most homes. Recycling wastewater from septic tanks is a common practice to maintain these gardens.

ANIMALS

Insects

Since this is a tropical climate, insects of every type are found in abundance. Desert denizens such as scorpions and millipedes are common to the outlying areas, but have a distinct distaste for well-populated neighborhoods, and the chance of seeing one around a resort is highly unlikely.

During a 2003 study of the ABC islands (Aruba, Bonaire, and Curacao), 29 species of butterflies were collected on Aruba with **Lycaenidae, Pieridae,** and **Hesperiidae** being the most common families found. **Monarch butterflies** *(Danaus plexippus)* are seen everywhere, as milkweed, their chosen plant for laying their eggs, grows abundantly. Known as the athletes of the insect world, they travel thousands of miles, often "hitching" rides on boats at sea. It is likely that Aruba was a welcome rest stop along the way to South America, where they established a home. Most butterflies are a tasty treat for birds, but monarchs are foul and poisonous because of the caterpillars feeding on milkweed. They display their dramatic colors without fear of being eaten.

Birds

Aruba is an important rest stop and haven for many migrating species. Over the centuries, several have stayed and made Aruba their home. Two brilliantly colorful species common to Aruba are the native **Caribbean brown-throated parakeet,** or *prikichi,* and the **trupial.**

The **yellow oriole** is a cousin of the trupial, and within the ABC islands has earned the name *trupial kachù*. On Aruba it is better known as a *gonzalito.*

Aruba's more common predatory birds, **eagles, falcons,** and **hawks,** are best known by their charming local names such as *caracara, falki,* and *kini kini.*

Common to the Caribbean is the **tropical mockingbird** *(chuchubi).* This dramatically marked gray bird nests on rooftops and ferociously defends its home against all intruders. It wakes the neighborhood with its beautiful song. The **bananaquit,** a bold, tiny bird that loves sweets, is called *barica geil,* meaning "yellow belly" for obvious reasons.

The **brown pelican** is common to all three ABC islands, but researchers find Aruba is where these pelicans breed. During breeding season the hind neck plumage turns dark, reddish-brown. It remains white during other times or in the winter.

Wetlands are home to herons, egrets, cormorants, and ducks of various species. The yellow feet of the **snowy egret** has earned it the name "The Lady with the Golden Slippers," which helps to differentiate it from a great egret.

Though **flamingos** are usually associated with Bonaire, a thriving flock can be found on the Flamingo Beach of Renaissance Island. They are very accommodating about posing for photographs. The characteristic deep salmon color is a result of their diet of a particular brine shrimp. They also eat small marine snails and the larvae of pesky flies and mosquitoes, making them a worthwhile creature to preserve and protect, not only for their beauty.

Reptiles

As one would expect from a desert climate, the island is home to a wide variety of lizards *(lagadishi),* from tiny geckos to iguanas of all sizes. It is not uncommon to find birds and lizards gathered at the edges of outdoor restaurants ready for crumbs and bits of fruit or bread tossed their way.

Iguanas *(Iguana iguana)* are plentiful and can be seen around hotel gardens, particularly rock formations. While adolescent they

Aruba's National Bird

An endemic species of the American burrowing owl, **the shoco,** was declared Aruba's National Symbol in 2011. Studies have shown that of the three ABC islands (Aruba, Bonaire, and Curacao), Aruba is the only one graced with this amusing, tiny creature. Their large, golden eyes are a particularly beautiful, distinctive feature.

A pair will usually be found protecting their hole in the ground nest. When they anticipate the possibility of being disturbed, one will fly off to draw attention away from the nest.

As ground-dwelling birds, their habitats are extremely vulnerable to boa constrictors and the ill effects of bulldozing and construction. Bird protection lobbyists hope that national symbol status will provide the impetus for laws protecting their nests.

maintain a brilliant jade green hue. As they grow, they begin to develop the characteristic striped tail. Eventually, they fade to dusky, camouflage colors.

The **Aruban whiptail lizard** *(Cnemidophorus arubensis)* or *kododo blauw* is an endemic species named for the striking aqua coloration shown by the mature male; females and the young are varying shades of brown.

Visitors to Arikok National Park will see a display of the **cascabel** *(Crotalus durissus unicolor),* Aruba's endemic and endangered rattlesnake, and the santanero, the Aruban **cat-eyed snake** *(Leptodeira bakeri).* Only the cascabel is venomous and rarely seen outside of the wilds. The **santanero** can be found anywhere, even in domestic gardens, but is absolutely harmless; both snakes help to control vermin.

INVASIVE BOA CONSTRICTORS

Aside from Aruban companies finally promoting recycling, an aspect of another environmental issue is being looked upon as an opportunity. A predator threatening indigenous mammals and birdlife is the boa constrictor. How it was introduced into the Aruban landscape is a matter for debate. Many point to the practice of buying the snakes as an interesting pet while young, than letting them go into the wild. It is also proposed that the very young boas were nestled among bunches of bananas and other fruit brought into the island by small boats from Venezuela.

However they arrived, their intrusive presence was noticed around 1990 as they began consuming not only vermin but threatened native species of birds, rabbits, lizards, and, on rare occasions, pet cats and dogs. Herpetologist Andrew Odum from the Toledo Zoological Society has taken a particular interest in the impact on the native cascabel. The largest boa constrictor found on Aruba to date measures 2.9 meters (nearly 10 ft. long).

Boa constrictors give birth to up to 64 young snakes at any time; they are immediately viable and out hunting for food. Their preferred method is to wait in ambush for their prey, which they crush and kill. They can be found on the ground, under bushes, in trees, and on cacti. A scientific team from Texas did an extensive study as to how they are impacting the local wildlife.

The snakes are found mostly in Arikok National Park and in rural areas; one section of Arikok is reserved for the study of the snake

a green iguana

and its habits. A Boa Task Force headed by Arikok National Park biologist and director Diego Marquez began a training program for the general populace, conducting regularly scheduled boa hunts on weekends. Perhaps 100 boas were caught at a time, but the task force assumes that for every boa found there are at least another four in the bush. To continue to tackle this problem, Arikok National Park acquired sponsors and placed bounties on boas.

In 2011, **Arte Sano Studios** (297/733-5232, artesano@setarnet.aw) opened a workshop producing various accessories made from boa skin. Each item is handcrafted and unique. This new industry is also a social project, teaching a trade and rehabilitating delinquent young islanders. The project is heartily endorsed by both Aruba Bird Conservation and the Boa Task Force, turning a liability into an asset by establishing an industry of singular, fine-quality products made in Aruba, while diversifying the economy. They expect to produce two limited collections annually.

Marinelife

The island's tropical marine environment is an important asset, with extensive reefs in depths from less than a meter to over 60 meters (2-200 ft.). They are populated with countless species of brilliant tropical fish and colorful corals, providing breathtaking experiences for thousands of vacationers annually. Colorful angelfish, triggerfish, wrasses, and parrotfish, of all varieties and hue, are in the water. Fortunately, there is no manufacturing despoiling these waters with toxic runoff.

Aruba also appears to have a minimal population of dangerous predatory fish, and shark attacks are unheard of. Barracuda are plentiful, but their fierce appearance and fictional media have imbued them with an undeserved ferocious reputation.

Divers and snorkelers should be mindful that they are much larger than any fish life they will encounter. Actually, humans are the largest and most dangerous predator around. Most fish will dart away at your approach, except in the few areas where they have become accustomed to being protected and fed. Spearfishing is illegal in Aruba, and any equipment for this pastime will be confiscated at customs.

INVASIVE LIONFISH

The influx of nonnative species, like lionfish, threaten indigenous animals: Lionfish are a challenge to every island from the Bahamas, south. They began showing up in Aruban waters around 2010. Speculation places their invasion as a result of the destruction done by Hurricane Andrew in 1992; lionfish began being spotted soon after in waters around Florida, then the Bahamas. It is suggested they escaped into the wild after homes where they were kept in aquariums were destroyed and flooded. Some lionfish hunters are firmly convinced that they were introduced by people releasing them into the wild when they became too big and troublesome to care for; they are an aggressive species that will consume every other fish in a tank.

Lionfish are native to the Indo-Pacific and Red Sea, where a natural form of control has developed. Predators such as large groupers and certain sharks consume them with regularity. The fish also do not reproduce as often or develop as quickly in their natural habitat as they do in the Caribbean's warmer waters. Their fins are distinctive, containing highly venomous spines, so there are few fish that will feed on them. They can extend the spines and stick in the throat of any fish attempting to eat them.

Lionfish are extremely prolific and ravenous, deadly predators. They have been observed literally vacuuming schools of smaller fish into their large maws, which extend for this purpose. They also hunt in packs, cooperating to drive their prey toward the waiting jaws of the larger, dominant lionfish.

Though stunningly beautiful, they are a real pest, reproducing in regional waters at an alarming rate, 2,000,000 eggs annually. Their devouring the many fish that play an important role in the delicate reef environment has serious ramifications. Within a year, they can strip a reef area of nearly 80 percent of its small fish population. A number of these feed on the algae which grows on coral and are necessary for keeping the reef healthy; lionfish disrupt this entire marine cycle, potentially causing the reef to die.

Various solutions have been initiated to deal with the issue, including fishing tournaments directed specifically at lionfish. Diving operations are encouraged to hunt them whenever spotted in the water or to notify the agency charged with their control. There is a group called "Lionfish Hunters" that regularly hunts them and provides instruction on how to do it properly. Island restaurants are even adding lionfish to their menus.

Special events conducted by the local fishing organization, Centro di Pisca Hadicurari, and the Aruba Marine Park Foundation, teach consumers how to clean and prepare lionfish for the table. They are quite tasty, despite the paltry return of edible flesh proportional to their size. It took no time for islanders to imbue lionfish soup with the magical properties of such expensive medications as Viagra, a greatly desired effect long attributed to the meat of the iguana. Perhaps now lionfish can prove useful and give that endangered species a respite from poachers seeking to liven up their weekends.

Mammals

Most mammals that are actually indigenous to the island are small desert creatures such as rodents, very tiny hares (some fit in the bowl of a standard soup spoon), and quite a few bats, found mostly but not exclusively in the caves at the eastern end of the island. The last are being closely monitored to insure that their population remains constant, as they perform the vital role of feeding on annoying insects and pollinating fruit plants. None of the bats are rabid; rabies does not exist on Aruba.

Aruba also has a marine mammal population of dolphins and the occasional whale pod passing by on their migratory patterns. There is an organization dedicated to monitoring and protecting them: the **Aruba Marine Mammal Foundation** (http://arubadolphins.wordpress.com) founded in 1998.

Aruba has a notable population of undomesticated donkeys and goats. These are remnants of a time when they were brought to the island for breeding and allowed to roam freely; they are not really native species. It is not unusual when touring Arikok National Park and other undeveloped areas to suddenly come face to face with a family of donkeys or goats living in the wild.

History

Perhaps the fact that conquistadors did not detect any rich minerals, sparing Aruba from their unwanted attention, contributes to its peaceful history. Aruba's lack of value to Spanish conquistadors earned it the label "Islas Inutiles" (Useless Islands) along with Curacao and Bonaire, so records of its encounter by Europeans are somewhat sketchy. Alonso de Ojeda is credited with first spotting Curacao, and it is presumed Aruba and Bonaire, around 1499, describing them as "*islas adyacentes a la costa firme*" (islands adjacent to the mainland). Ojeda returned to Spain in June of 1501 to be appointed governor over the coastal regions of Coquibacoa and Guajira, with the "Adjacent Islands" under his administration. It appears Aruba also earned the title "Isle of the Giants," which is interesting because unearthed remains of Aruba's indigenous people reveal they were quite short by modern standards.

Historians are unsure of the actual true origins of the modern name Aruba; the discovery of gold in 1824 fuels speculation that it is an adaptation of the Spanish word for gold, *oro.* Some assert it means "Island of Shells." The lack of documentation regarding the early history of the island makes it difficult to know for certain.

EARLY HISTORY

Caquetio Indians and the Spanish Rule

The fortunes of the ABC islands (Aruba, Bonaire, Curacao) were always tied to their proximity to the mainland, whether under the rule of the local Amerindian caciques (chieftains) or the Spanish. The Paraguaná Peninsula east of Lake Maracaibo was a seat of power for the caciques, and during the 1500s the fate of Aruba remained closely related to what is now known as Venezuela.

A small community of Amerindians, a subgroup of the peaceful Arawak people called Caquetio, lived nomadic lives, establishing small villages along the coast and in the caves at the island's south end. It was important to be able to harvest food from the sea. Over 300 of their pictographs and a few petroglyphs (rock carvings as opposed to paintings) can still be seen. The indigenous population was eventually enslaved by the Spanish, and by 1515 nearly all were transported to Hispaniola to work in the mines.

Juan Martinez De Ampues was appointed administrator of the ABC islands in 1525. Under his (relatively) benevolent administration, an agreement was made with the supreme Amerindian chieftain of Coro, called Manaure, residing in Paraguaná. This allowed the Caquetios to return to the islands and awarded them protected status; in a sense, Aruba became a reservation.

De Ampues declared slave hunting of Amerindians illegal on the ABC islands; his intentions, however, were far from altruistic. The treaty with the Manaure was that in exchange for protection, the chieftain would capture new slaves from other tribes to be sent to the mines.

Eventually, to settle his enormous debt, Charles V of Spain awarded the trade rights to the region to the Welsers, a German banking family. Their 30-year administration ending in 1559 proved particularly harsh for the indigenous people of the peninsula, prompting them to flee to the nearby islands.

Beginning in 1529, Aruba was set up as a *rancho.* It was one great pasture for roaming goats, pigs, cows, sheep, horses, and donkeys. Most Amerindians left on the island tended the herds. This has spurred speculation as to the original flora of the island, as compared to the cacti that dominates today.

Introduction of Christianity

It was during the mid 1500s that the conversion of the Caquetios to Catholicism by missionaries began in earnest. Archaeologists have unearthed a number of remains in a communal gravesite discovered in 2002. The skeletons have all been identified as Amerindian, but the burial style is a mix of Caquetio traditions and those uniquely identifiable as Christian. Other artifacts confirm the graves dating from this period. The mixture of cultures indicates the conversion process had not yet fully taken hold, with sacred Amerindian practices still a part of the burial ritual.

Aruba's first Christian church, the Alto Vista Chapel, was built in 1750 on what was sacred ground to the Caquetios. Spaniard Padre Domingo Antonio Silvestre led the mission to bring the sparse native population into the fold of Catholicism.

The Dutch Conquer Aruba

Aruba's defining relationship to the Netherlands was established during the Eighty Years' War for Independence between the Dutch Republic and Spain (1568-1648). It prompted the Dutch to conquer Spanish and Portuguese colonies in the Caribbean, with direct Dutch trade beginning around 1593.

Merchants in Holland were eager to establish a Dutch trading company similar to the highly profitable Dutch East India franchise. Dutch trade in the area was restricted by a treaty until 1621. When the treaty expired, a group called the Heren XIX (19 Gentlemen) actively sought private investors to open trade routes. Encouraged by the Dutch Republic, they founded the West Indian Company (WIC). Many were interested in this high-risk enterprise, which included substantial financial assistance from the government.

Dutch trade in the region was also another method for Holland to interfere with their Spanish enemies, a desirable offshoot of any enterprise. They also wished to "free the natives" from religious oppression, which was a fundamental motivation behind the war. Holland defeated Spanish forces in Curacao in 1634, taking possession of all three islands.

Despite the involvement of the Dutch in the slave trade from Africa, the native population of the ABC islands was treated equally under Dutch law as colonists. It was prohibited to enslave Amerindians. Despite being equal under the law, documents prove it was not so in practice. Discrimination made life harsh for the Amerindian population.

The advent of the Napoleonic Wars resulted in Aruba falling under control of England between 1799 and 1802, and again from 1804 until 1816. Very little is written about this period, and the effect on island culture or tradition is undetectable. Aruba soon reverted back to Dutch control.

Slavery

It was long believed that since Aruba did not have the extensive agriculture and plantations of other islands, as well as being sparsely populated, slave labor of imported Africans was not practiced among the colonists. Careful investigation by a new generation of historians has disproved this. Historical documents reveal an estimated 10 percent of the population during the late 1700s and early 1800s were household slaves, usually maids, nannies, cooks, gardeners, and handymen. They were fortunate to have a more lenient and closer relationship with their owners and families, and it is believed they were better treated than field hands. Aruba did not experience a slave revolt such as Curacao, home of the notorious slave markets, did in 1795. By declaration of the king of the Netherlands, all slaves were freed throughout the kingdom and its territories in 1863. Records show Aruba had almost 500 slaves living on the island at the time.

Settlement on Aruba in the 1700s

Actual settlement in Aruba was forbidden until at least 1750. There was concern about the security of the area and Curacao, an important port and commercial center, if there was overdevelopment and population on its sister islands. Only a few personnel of the West Indian Company (WIC), including the lieutenant governor, his entourage and slaves, plus about 20 soldiers, occupied the island. Aruba's being virtually ignored by administrators encouraged smuggling, as Aruba was a tax-free port, as well as a hideout for privateers and pirates, or "Zeerovers."

Aruba's isolation ended when Mozes Maduro, a Sephardic Jew originally from Portugal, was granted land and became the first non-Amerindian settler. The WIC deployed a system of land tenure, with land leased in exchange for various services or fees, but WIC continued to own the land.

Settlers coming to Aruba from around 1780 began changing the makeup of the population. According to Jan Hartog's history of Aruba, a report from the early 1800s counts the population of the island as comprised of 1,732 inhabitants. Of this, 564 were the original indigenous inhabitants, 584 freed "colored people," and 37 free "black people," along with 133 "colored slaves" and 203 "black slaves," with less than 100 European colonists. Accounts from the 1800s by an unknown Dutchman described the islands as quite unsuitable for agriculture and basically useless. Even then, however, it states that "Arubans displayed great pride and love for their island, despite the barren, infertile soil."

Decline of Amerindian Population

As the colonial influence grew, the native

Amerindian population and culture declined. The death of Aruba's last full-blooded native Amerindian, Nicolass Payklaas, is reported to have been in 1843. Based on the accounts of colonial Aruba by historian Father van Koolwijk, the end of the Amerindian historic period is pinpointed by scholars as 1860. Aruba's colonial era is defined from 1724 until 1924, with the establishment of the oil refineries. The departure of Esso and the first closing of the San Nicolas refinery coincide with Aruba's independence from the five other islands of the Netherlands Antilles.

STATUS APARTE: ARUBAN INDEPENDENCE

Aruba's achievement of independence from the other five islands of the Netherlands Antilles, while remaining an autonomously ruled entity within the Dutch Kingdom, is an inspiring success story. It was achieved without bloodshed or violent revolt, setting an example for other islands. Indeed, it is the Aruban model that paved the way for the same status for Curacao and San Maarten in 2010. The other islands of the Netherlands Antilles, Bonaire, Eustatius, and Saba, now called the BES islands, chose to become Dutch municipalities. Their status is more closely related to Holland than before.

The AVP and PPA

The concept of Status Aparte starts with the story of Jan Hendrik "Henny" Eman, founder of the Arubaanse Volkspartij political party (AVP). He planted and nurtured the seed of decentralization. He organized a petition to separate from the Colony of Curacao. Getting signatures was a monumental task in prewar Aruba, often carried out by a donkey cart traveling from home to home. The 2,147 signatures confirmed that Eman had obtained the majority support for this movement.

It was Eman's son, Albert "Shon" Eman, who first presented Aruba's formal proposal to Queen Juliana on March 18, 1948. This was during roundtable talks with Suriname and the other Dutch islands at The Hague in Holland. The crown "took it under advisement."

These talks resulted in the Constitution of the Netherlands Antilles enacted in February 1951. On March 3, 1951, the Island Regulation of the Netherlands Antilles was issued by royal decree. Eventually, this spurred Arubans even more to seek independence from the other islands, as it was frustrating to have Aruba's economic and developmental reins in the hands of Curacao politicos.

Particularly dissatisfied by this turn of events was Juan "Juancho" Irausquin, a member of the AVP along with its founder, Henny Eman. Irausquin went on to establish the Partido Patriotico Arubano political party (PPA) and to build Aruba's first major resort in Palm Beach, the Royal Caribbean.

Henny Eman died in 1957 and his son "Shon" Eman took over leadership of the AVP. The PPA began to acquire some influence until Irausquin's death in 1962. "Shon" Eman died in 1967 and the influence of both parties waned with the founding of MEP by Gilberto Francois "Betico" Croes.

Betico Croes and the Path to Independence

The ascendancy of Betico Croes in Aruba's political arena began in 1967. He was originally a part of the AVP, but began his own political party, Moviemento di Electoral di Pueblo (MEP), while taking up the banner of autonomy. He is credited with actually assigning the formal name of Status Aparte, making national identity and self-determination a priority. It was during the 1960s and 1970s, with the decline of the refinery, when Aruba began to focus more on tourism. Tourism would soon become the principal pillar of the economy. The desire to construct more hotels and acquire additional airlift was again hampered by controls from Curacao.

Aruba's acquisition of Status Aparte was not entirely without incident. The month described as Agustus Scur (Dark August) in 1977 was marked by civil disobedience and

Monuments to "The Liberators"

GILBERTO FRANCOIS "BETICO" CROES

Gilberto Francois "Betico" Croes is considered by many the last best instrument in the establishment of Aruba's right to self-rule within the Dutch Kingdom, or Status Aparte. Originally a member of Arubaanse Volkspartij (AVP), he founded the Moviemento di Electoral di Pueblo (MEP) in 1971. As party leader he became the principal negotiator and facilitator of Aruba's independence from the Netherlands Antilles, earning him the informal title of "El Liberatador."

Plaza Gilberto Francois "Betico" Croes is one block inland from Plaza Las Americas, the huge rotunda marking the eastern end of Oranjestad. Standing directly behind the Cas di Cultura is a statue of Aruba's beloved statesman, holding the nation's flag high over his head.

Betico Croes relentlessly pursued Status Aparte while strongly promoting the concept of Aruban national pride. In 1976 he advocated and expedited the creation and adoption of an Aruban flag and national anthem.

Despite his pivotal roll in the negotiations resulting in Aruban autonomy, Betico and his party did not earn the majority during Aruba's first independent elections. The title of Aruba's first prime minister was denied him.

The eve of Aruba's official independence from the Netherlands Antilles, December 31, 1985, saw instead the inauguration Jan Hendrik "Henny" Eman to that post. On his way to the ceremony, Croes was gravely injured in a traffic accident. He stayed in a coma for 11 months and then passed away on November 26, 1986. After dedicating the last 15 years of his life to Aruba's Status Aparte, he never actually witnessed the realization of that goal. His birth date, January 25, was declared a national holiday.

SIMÓN BOLÍVAR

The statue of Betico Croes gazes upon what is the largest and unquestionably most impressive monument in Oranjestad. Directly across the street from his plaza, Simón Bolívar majestically salutes his admirers from his rearing stallion in the Plaza Bolivariana.

"The Great Liberator" of Latin America is immortalized in a striking sculpture donated by Aruba's expatriate population from Venezuela, Colombia, Peru, Bolivia, Ecuador, and Panama. It is here that Venezuelan and Colombian consuls welcome fellow compatriots and island dignitaries to observe their respective independence days of July 5 and July 20.

July 5, 1811, was when Venezuelan independence was first called for by a revolutionary congress and, in 1813, Bolívar took up the cause instigated by Francisco de Miranda in 1810. Miranda died in exile in 1816. After leading the war for independence through many bloody battles, Bolívar finally ousted the Spanish colonists in the famous Battle of Carabobo on June 24, 1821.

Bolívar also dedicated his life to fighting for the independence of Colombia, Peru, Ecuador, and Panama. Eventually, he founded the nation of Bolivia.

Bolívar died in Cartagena, Colombia in 1830, after a life devoted to achieving freedom from Spanish control for most of Latin America. He was buried in Colombia, but in 1942, after years of petitioning, Venezuela finally received his remains with great pomp. He now lies in state at the National Pantheon in Caracas.

protest marches. Work stoppages by ELMAR, which regulates and distributes electricity, brought business to a standstill. Lights were out for several nights during the summer months as a show of solidarity and a wish for Holland to respond to the will of the people. Those who were children and witnessed these events describe it as "exciting, adventurous times."

Betico Croes led the highly successful talks with Holland in 1981 and 1982, which resulted in an agreement for Aruban self-rule under Dutch supervision for the first 10 years. The date set for it to be enacted was January

1, 1986, with Aruba to be fully independent from Holland in 1996.

Surprisingly, elections in 1985 resulted in Henny Eman, son of Albert, and leader of the AVP, becoming Aruba's first prime minister. It was during his administration that Aruba's independence from Holland was renegotiated. Aruba remains an independent part of the Dutch Kingdom, and islanders maintain their Dutch citizenship and passports. Coalition administrations consisting largely of AVP party members dominated the government until 2001, when MEP won a clear majority of seats in parliament. MEP, headed by Nelson Oduber, held sway until the 2009 elections, with Oduber occupying the office of prime minister. Michel Godfried Eman, the younger brother of Henny, became prime minister when the AVP party won a record 11 parliamentary seats in 2009. They remain in power after winning 12 seats in 2013. The next elections will be in September of 2017.

ECONOMIC DEVELOPMENT

Gold and Phosphate

Aruba's economic elite during colonial times established their fortunes through shipping and importing necessary goods. Others eked out a living farming, fishing, and by breeding horses and selling what livestock they could. Change came when 12-year-old Willem Rasmijn discovered gold in 1824 while herding his father's sheep along the north coast. As with all the New World, the crown had sent surveyors to search for precious minerals nearly a century before on all the ABC islands, but nothing of consequence was found. The gold at Rooi Fluit started a gold rush, increasing the population and facilitating the official designation of Oranjestad as the capital of Aruba. Some argue Aruba's first capital was Savaneta on the south side, as this was the headquarters of the Dutch marine commander, and it is where their camp is still located today.

Everyone who could afford a pickax went looking for gold, but regulations were in place to control its sale to the government at fixed prices. This naturally encouraged many attempts to smuggle gold to more lucrative markets. Finally the government prohibited free prospecting, choosing to award mineral rights to the highest bidder. The initial rush died down after about five years, but new veins found in 1854 revived interest in the economic development of the island. Gold mining rights passed from one company to another until they finally settled with the Aruba Island Gold Mining Company of London.

The discovery of phosphate during the early 19th century provided another economic stimulus for the island. Aruba Island Gold Mining Company of London demanded the harvest rights, claiming it already had exclusive rights for the extraction of minerals. The courts denied the suit, and rights went to the Aruba Island Phosphate Company Ltd. It did not fare very well, and eventually evolved into the Aruba Phosphaat Maatschappij.

The establishment of gold and phosphate industries stimulated immigration to Aruba and settlement in areas such as San Nicolas, which had been virtually ignored until then. This is where the phosphate works were established. In 1833, Aruba had a population of 2,476, which increased to 8,065 by 1893.

The collapse of the gold and phosphate industries reduced immigration to Aruba to a trickle, with an increase of only 1,000 people by 1923. However, Aruba's fortunes changed radically with the inception of the Lago Oil Refinery.

Aloe Vera

The cultivation and processing of aloe also contributed to prosperity and an influx of population in the 1800s. Introduced to the island in 1840, aloe vera thrived in Aruba's arid climate to produce a high-quality extract, which was in great demand.

The aloe industry truly became profitable in 1890 when Cornelius Eman founded Aruba Aloe Balm. At one point, nearly two-thirds of the island's agricultural production was dedicated to aloe. Aruba became the world's number one exporter of aloe products. World interest waned in the early 1950s, and Aruban production and export dropped dramatically.

New methods of manufacture and a renewed interest in the natural healing properties of aloe prompted Louis Posner to acquire the factory and fields in Hato in 2000. He replaced the old plant with a modern, attractive facility that accepts visitors for tours and provides a history of the industry.

Refinery Era

No island historian would deny that the opening of the Lago Refinery was a defining moment in Aruba's history. It brought employment, prosperity, and technology, resulting in a noticeably higher standard of living and education than in other nations in the region.

ARUBA'S FORGOTTEN REFINERY

There were actually *two* refineries opening at almost the same time. Lago was preceded by two years by a collaboration of British Petroleum and Royal Dutch Shell. First to begin production was Arends Petroleum Maatschappij, better known by the English translation of *Arend*—Eagle Oil Company. This was located on the western outskirts of Oranjestad, where an exclusive gated and guarded community was constructed for the management.

Eagle Oil Company occupied a vast expanse of land, from what is now Bubali, where the company's medical facility was housed at Quinta Del Carmen, to the turbo rotunda now situated at the far west border of Oranjestad. It extended about a quarter mile inland. Within its borders were a social club, tennis club, private golf course, and private train lines to transport construction materials. A pier was built for the tankers where the Tamarijn Beach Resort now stands. Oranjestad Harbor had not yet been dredged and refitted for large ships. The pier was demolished in 1974.

The end of WWII reduced demand for the Eagle Refinery product, as it did not produce jet fuel. It closed its doors in 1954. The majority of employees were relocated to Shell's Curacao refinery. The land was sold back to the Aruban government, with the housing purchased by islanders to become an upscale community. The beach areas were zoned for tourism.

THE SAN NICOLAS REFINERY

The discovery of oil in Lake Maracaibo, Venezuela, in 1918 would herald a complete change of lifestyle and standards for Arubans. The Venezuelan dictator Juan Vicente Gomez purposely generated great interest in U.S. and European oil companies to relieve the country's extreme debt. He spurred development of the industry by granting concessions and selling oil very cheaply. Those days are long gone.

An impediment to development was that it was simply not possible to fill the large oceangoing tankers with crude at Maracaibo. Smaller ships called lake tankers could be used, and a more suitable transshipment station was sought where the loads of the smaller tankers could be transferred to huge oceangoing vessels. In 1924, Captain Robert Rogers of the British Equatorial Oil Company began scouting out a site for such a terminal. Originally he had Curacao in mind, but the Dutch government was not cooperative about competition for its Shell refinery.

Powerful U.S. oil companies were wielding a strong influence in the region at the time. They were reluctant to build refineries in Latin America because of the constant political turmoil. Aruba attracted their attention for its stable government and close proximity to the source. During negotiations, Gomez also pressured the Dutch government to concede to the construction of a facility.

Although San Nicolas harbor would require dredging and preparation at great cost to accommodate the big ships, the existing infrastructure from the phosphate industry made it very attractive to Captain Rogers. A few savvy local businesspeople were also involved in convincing him of the wisdom of a facility on Aruba. They pointed out the advantage of Aruba being even closer to Maracaibo than Curacao, whose port was already well occupied from the Shell refinery. Rogers was convinced that the money saved with the shorter distance for the lake tankers easily justified the expense of creating the deep-water harbor at San Nicolas.

Within a year of the contracts being signed, British Equatorial Oil was purchased by Canadian Lago Oil & Transport. The original idea transshipment terminal took off into a full-blown refinery during the planning stages. Lago Oil & Petroleum Company Limited began operations in January 1929, under General Manager Lloyd G. Smith.

The construction of the first refinery already radically affected Aruba's economy. The refineries were providing jobs locally and bringing in workers from around the world. Their operation required certain skills not found among islanders. Once construction was completed, the need for new skills and personnel resulted in an increase in island population of 7,000 new residents originating from 56 countries. In 1945, only 32 percent of the employees at the refinery were native born.

Eventually, the refinery was taken over by Rockefeller's Standard Oil of New Jersey, which became Esso, then Exxon. The refinery and adjacent residences continued to be referred to as "Lago" and "Lago Colony"—a name still used to this day.

It was the influx of immigrants and near doubling of Aruba's population that prompted the construction of one of the first modern, large-capacity water desalination plants in the world. It was accompanied by a complex and efficient clean water distribution system. Experts and engineers traveling through the region assert these advances in production and distribution to every home and business as a key element in the higher standard of living enjoyed by Arubans over many other Caribbean nations.

WAR STORIES OF ARUBA'S FAMOUS SHIPWRECKS

The **Antilla** was a German cargo ship, one of three along with the **Heidelberg** and **Troja** moored in the neutral waters of the Aruban coast, but believed to be used to supply U-boats. Curacao harbor also saw German ships hiding out from British destroyers before Holland was invaded in May of 1940, ending their policy of strict neutrality.

German sailors were well aware that their homeland was going to invade Holland and were given orders to either make a run for it or scuttle their ships. The *Heidelberg* and *Troja* managed to escape Aruba's waters but were unable to break through the British blockade and scuttled far out at sea, while *Antilla* returned to anchor when it encountered a British destroyer just outside the three-mile limit. Seven others were captured in Curacao. When Germany invaded, island authorities attempted to board the *Antilla* at night and claim her, but the captain refused to lower the gangway. The machine gun backup on shore was unable to sight the ship in the dead of night, so they came back at first light, which gave the ship's Captain Ferdinand Schmidt time to prepare.

Rather than turn her over, he ordered the sea cocks opened, which flooded the ship, while the rest of the crew set fires in many of the cabins. *Antilla* eventually listed to port and sank in 60 feet of water around 750 yards off the coast of Malmok. It became a haven for sealife and a favorite dive and snorkel spot since it can easily be seen without scuba gear. Its large, open compartments allow scuba divers the thrill of an actual wreck penetration with no risk. The captain and crew surrendered and were placed in a temporary internment camp on Bonaire, then transported to Jamaica in July of 1940 to a POW camp maintained by the British for the remainder of WWII.

Pedernales was an Italian oil tanker under British registry, which was anchored off the harbor in San Nicolas on February 17, 1942, when it was torpedoed by a German submarine, U-156, along with the ***Oranjestad.*** The latter sank in very deep waters off the south side; in doing so, it became the first tanker sunk in the Western Hemisphere during WWII. This was part of a concerted effort by Axis powers to cripple Allied fuel supply routes deploying seven German and Italian submarines attacking tankers and refineries on February 16, 1942. U-156 fortunately had a malfunction of its long-range gun, so it was unable to do damage to the Eagle refinery. The same night, two other Lago tankers, the *San Nicolas* and *Tia Juana,* were torpedoed 40 kilometers (25 miles) southwest of Punta Macolla in the Gulf of Venezuela by U-502. Four days later a torpedo ended up on Eagle Beach in an attempt to blow up the refinery, and a team of four Dutch soldiers died trying to defuse it. The final death toll from crew members on the tankers was 47. This event prompted a greater U.S. military presence on Aruba for the remainder of the war.

The *Pedernales* was towed to dry dock where the bow and aft sections were removed and transported to a U.S. shipping yard, joined with a new midsection and put back into use; it was finally retired in 1959. What remained of the wreck offshore was used by troops stationed on Aruba for target practice. Some of the giant unexploded ordinance can still be seen under the water.

Because of Aruba's highly strategic position in the war effort, it was officially under British protection for two years during the war. Troops from England and the United States were stationed on the island to protect the refinery from the German wolf pack, the submarines continually attempting to sink tankers and destroy the refineries.

The end of WWII signaled the gradual decline of the refinery's place in the island's economy. Automation resulted in a drastic reduction in personnel. Eventually, in the final decades, only around 700 employees staffed the refinery. A number of peripheral companies cropped up around San Nicolas, working as subcontractors to perform repairs and maintenance.

Farsighted island leaders, entrepreneurs, and legislators had already turned their attention to Status Aparte and tourism as priorities for Aruba to advance and prosper.

TOURISM TAKES OVER

Nearly simultaneous with the realization of Status Aparte came the closing of Lago Refinery. It was seemingly abandoned overnight. The 60-year contracts for crude oil from Venezuela had expired. During the interim, oil concerns and Venezuela had constructed numerous refineries. There was really no great need to transport the oil to an outside facility. Added to that the refinery was getting old, and the costs of improvements were not conducive to continuing operations.

By this time, tourism had quite a foothold on Aruba, with several large resorts already standing in Palm Beach and timeshares proliferating like proverbial bunnies. The first major resort, the Aruba Caribbean, now the Hilton Caribbean, was built by Juancho Irausquin, a definitive force in the development of Aruba's tourism industry, and opened in 1959. Prior to that, Chaven Neme, who had built the first tourist hotel in Oranjestad, had opened the tiny Basi Ruti Resort in Palm Beach—its first—where the Playa Linda Resort was erected 1985.

By 1980, quite a few large resorts had altered the Palm Beach coastline. Visionary developers such as Ike Cohen, a Holocaust survivor from Holland, and Wally Wiggins, a New York lawyer, founded the Manchebo Beach Resort and Divi Hotel, respectively. These established the concept of the "low-rise" at Manchebo Beach. In the late 1970s, Sun Development opened the first timeshare on Aruba in that area, heralding a highly successful industry which catered to a core of dedicated vacationers returning annually. Statistics have shown timeshare owners account for close to 40 percent of Aruba's annual visitors.

Island leaders saw tourism as Aruba's future. They offered very attractive conditions to developers. These are criticized now, as

What is a Lagoite?

From 1925 until 1986, Aruba, and specifically San Nicolas, was host to what was to become the world's largest refinery during WWII, operating under Esso, then Exxon, as the Lago Refinery. Adjacent to the refinery was "The Colony," a facility for the refinery executives. It was an elite and fully equipped community with its own hospital, school, social center, restaurant, bowling alley, and bachelors' quarters as well as elegant homes for the married executives with families.

Many of the executives lived on Aruba for decades; many children were born and raised in this uniquely multicultural community, graduating from the school. They came to call themselves Lagoites. Despite the years that have passed since the refinery closed and the employees and their families scattered to all corners of the globe, they maintain a healthy interest in Aruba and a great nostalgia for what many consider absolute paradise and the gift of growing up in such singular circumstances. Families originated from all around the world; a multitude of languages were spoken and cultures shared, along with that of the Aruban people.

Lagoites have recounted much of their history on a dedicated website: www.lago-colony.com. Input and scrapbooks from children of the 800 executives who resided on Aruba within the colony at some point in its 60-year history have evolved into a rich tapestry of island life during its key developmental years. This was a fantasy existence for these privileged children, with stunning blue seas, beautiful beaches, a richly social and connected community with constant access to wonderful water activities and nature. It was an innocent time, when the arrival of the first jet on the island was a spectacular landmark event.

guarantees signed by the government cost Aruba millions on the failed plans. Huge projects were begun at the southern and northern ends of Palm Beach at nearly the same time; each experienced shortages of labor and materials. The numerous delays, rather symptomatic of the region, resulted in three unfinished projects declaring bankruptcy.

Despite this, Aruba's reliable climate, political stability, and the reputation of Arubans as famously cooperative and hospitable people attracted developers and the attention of important hospitality franchises. The Marriott chain was rewarded for acquiring and completing one failed project by opening the most successful resort in its stable. This prompted the chain to reclaim another failed project, which became the Marriott Ocean Club, and to construct the Surf Club, both timeshare operations. A Ritz-Carlton opened its doors on the north side of the Marriott in November of 2014.

Ever practical, Cohen and Wiggins also realized the numerous small resorts operating on shoestring budgets could not afford to market individually. They formed a cooperative that was to become the Aruba Hotel and Tourism Association (AHATA). It is one of the most successful public-private collaborations in the region, working closely with Aruba's official tourism marketing entity, the Aruba Tourism Authority (ATA). The combined efforts of several knowledgeable businesspeople and legislators provided the marketing brain trust and will to see this fledgling industry become the principal pillar of the island economy that it is today.

THE REFINERY IN THE 21ST CENTURY

There is a footnote to the refinery's continuing role in Aruba's economic well-being. A number of businesses came and went since the departure of Exxon, interspersed with periods when it remained idle. Valero Corporation of Texas finally took over the facility from Coastal Oil in 2004. Valero initially invested hundreds of millions of dollars in modernizing the refinery, but circumstances resulted in stoppage of production in July of 2009.

This was two months prior to a crucial national election resulting in a complete change of Aruba's political landscape. All employees were kept on salary, and not long after, Valero and the new government announced a meeting of minds on the reopening of the refinery. It recommenced operations in early 2011. The continuing rise of crude oil prices precipitated the announcement of a number of closings of Valero refineries around the United States and the world. The Aruban facility was included, which finally came to pass in March 2012. Employees were kept on salary while a solution was sought or a buyer found.

In September of 2012, Valero announced the refinery would shut down entirely, and only serve as a transshipment station, downsizing the workforce by 90 percent. This finally came to pass in April of 2014. Ironically, the facility now fulfills the function originally planned for it.

Government and Economy

GOVERNMENT

The Parliament and Ministries

Aruba is an autonomously ruled entity within the Dutch Kingdom. Arubans are considered Dutch citizens and carry Dutch passports. The government is comprised of a 21-seat Parliament, with elections taking place every four years, one year after U.S. presidential elections. There are a president and vice president of Parliament, positions occupied by elected officials.

For a political party to be in power, it must capture an 11-seat majority or form a coalition among a few parties to hold a majority. The individual heading the dominant party of the coalition assumes the title of prime minister and appoints a cabinet of ministers.

The government deploys various ministries to administer important aspects of island operations. Presently, Aruba has ministers of tourism, transport, labor, immigration, environment, infrastructure, public health, sport, technology, finance, utilities, social affairs, economic affairs, culture, education, and justice, who are selected from those who have been elected to Parliament. Aruba also has ministers-plenipotentiary to Holland and the United States, which are appointed positions and serve as ambassadors to these countries. The common practice is for the elected officials comprising the cabinet to have a number of ministries under their command; often they are interrelated, supporting each other with legislation and policies.

Dutch Representation

The island maintains strong ties with Holland. Despite a distinctly Caribbean-Latin culture, the official language of schools, business contracts, regulations, legislation, and official government notifications is Dutch.

The Dutch royal monarch's official representative on Aruba is the governor, an appointed position lasting six years. They may serve a maximum of two terms. His Excellency, Governor Fredis Refunjol, took office in May of 2004 and is serving the second of two terms, due to expire in 2016. It is the governor who ratifies national ordinances and resolutions. Among his many duties, he alone awards decorations in the name of the monarchy, signs off on passports and visas, and considers extradition requests. His presence is required at all official functions that are related to Holland. He is charged with the swearing in of dignitaries such as ministers, members of the Common Court of Justice and the public prosecutor, as well as the Advisory Council, General Audit Office, and the Central Bank of Aruba. The following is stated on the governor's official website (www.kabga.aw.en): "The Governor is inviolable, immune, and carries out his powers as a national organ under the responsibility of the

Ministers of Aruba, who, in their turn, are accountable to the Parliament of Aruba."

Until April 27, 2013, Aruba counted Queen Beatrix as its monarch, preceded by her mother Queen Juliana and grandmother Queen Wilhelmina. On this date, Queen Beatrix abdicated the throne in favor of her eldest son, HRM Willem-Alexander, the first male monarch the Dutch Kingdom has had in place since 1890.

The Judiciary, Foreign Affairs, and Defense

Holland still has jurisdiction in certain fields: The judiciary is one, partly to maintain impartiality. Judges and prosecutors are appointed within the Dutch system. Foreign affairs also fall under its control. If Holland signs a treaty with foreign entities, Aruba is bound by it. Aruban administrators do have the power to negotiate agreements for the island, which may not directly affect Holland. Thirdly, Holland is charged with Aruba's national protection, maintaining a division of the Royal Dutch Marines at the camp in Savaneta. Aruba has a subordinate branch of service at the camp, the ArubaMil.

Dutch Immigration to Aruba

For many decades, there were strictures against unfettered Dutch immigration to the island, which have been eased over the past few years. Much of this had to do with older Dutch laws to prevent miscreants from escaping to the colonies after committing crimes or accumulating debt in Holland. However, it is a stated policy that jobs should first go to a qualified Aruban before issuing approval for bringing in someone from outside the country to fill the position. Individuals wishing to retire on the island must be able to prove they are financially independent, with no need to work.

ECONOMY

Aruba's economy is a free-enterprise system with entrepreneurship and fair trade heavily encouraged. Tourism is acknowledged as the primary pillar of the economy, accounting for 55 percent of the island's GDP. It provides employment for 65 percent of the population.

Though tourism can be a volatile industry affected by global events, aside from small setbacks from the world financial crash of 2008 and the destruction of the World Trade Center, Aruba's tourism has seen steady growth since it achieved Status Aparte. In December of 2012, the Reina Beatrix International Airport welcomed its millionth paying passenger, and cruise ship tourism broke records during that year for their number of passengers. Statistics show Aruba welcomes over 1.5 million visitors annually.

Aruba's government is mindful that dependence on tourism alone is not in the best interest of the economy and is always seeking methods to diversify. In 2012, a contract was signed with Repsol, a Spanish energy development conglomerate. The terms allow seismic exploration for natural gas reserves in the territorial waters north of the island, with Repsol accepting all costs for developing a rig if a viable resource is discovered.

In May of 2013, Aruba hosted an international "Europe Meets the Americas" Conference, the purpose being to implement a plan for the island to become a liaison and business hub between the European Union and Latin America and Caribbean region. It is believed that Aruba's unique multicultural makeup can provide the meeting of minds between two very different cultures, and that this can be developed into another economic pillar for the island.

It is acknowledged that Aruba is highly dependent on the import of goods. Agriculture is encouraged, and the Santa Rosa Center of Agriculture and Animal Husbandry and Fisheries has begun a regular program instructing and encouraging islanders to grow and harvest their own food. A very small commercial agricultural industry has been established, using unique methods of desert reclamation and aquaculture.

Some small manufacturing exists on the island, such as Office Systems, which is the local and regional manufacturer and distributor for Dauphin, a famed European brand of office furniture. Freezone Aruba has proved innovative in providing not only product storage but also services, increasing Aruba's export statistics over 2012.

Generally, the standard of living is high for the region, with salaries averaging around $22,000 annually and retirement pensions also among the highest found in the Caribbean. The cost of consumer goods is relatively high due to import duties and shipping costs. Aruba is also one of the most highly taxed nations in the world.

The most recent Fitch rating for Aruba's economy is "stable," as of April 2015. The Fitch Report states, "The Stable Outlook reflects Fitch's view that upside and downside risks to the rating are evenly balanced."

People and Culture

The description "One Happy Island" is apt. It is a small island where the inhabitants understand the need to get along. The past and its legacy are treasured, while at the same time, Arubans look to the future, treating sustainability as a paramount concern. Arubans have enormous pride in their island and their sense of community is strong.

The most beloved time of year for most Arubans is during Carnival, when weeks of revelry consume the island's attention. Festivities on Aruba are frequent and instigated for the simplest of reasons. The majority of Arubans have an appreciation for their good fortune to live on the island and continue celebrating life.

Arubans are also very proactive, with strong community concerns. Service organizations such as Rotary, Kiwanis, Women's Club, Lion's Club, and Quota, to name a few, play a strong role in community events. Visiting members of organizations like Rotary are welcome to sit in on the meetings.

Aruba has over 1,000 registered foundations, many of these established in only the last decade. It is the nature of islanders, when presented with a situation that needs attention, to recruit, organize, and educate the uninformed.

POPULATION

Aruba participated in the 2010 UNESCO worldwide census. The Central Bureau of Statistics (CBS) reports from the results a population of 106,000+ officially registered residents, of which over 35 percent are immigrants. Many have been nationalized and received their Dutch passports. According to the CBS, there are 90 distinct ethnic or national groups inhabiting this little rock quite harmoniously.

Aruba has substantial East Indian, Filipino, and Chinese populations. They have integrated well into the community while maintaining many aspects of their native cultures. Each group has some sort of community organization to continue traditions among the second generation born on the island. They are the Aruba Indian Association (IAA), United Filipino Community of Aruba (UFILCOA), and the Chinese Center where classes are taught in the language and culture. The center is located in Bubali, next to the Super Food complex.

The important celebrations of these groups have been integrated into Aruban life; IAA organizes a community event for Diwali. The honorary consul of the Philippines to Aruba and UFILCOA conduct a protocol event annually at Wilhelmina Park for Filipino Independence Day. Aruba's prime minister and important dignitaries usually attend. The Lion Dance, authentically performed by the Chinese community, is a welcome part of many island celebrations. Every year, the congregation of Temple Beth Israel conducts a community First Seder for Passover. Jewish vacationers are welcome and regularly participate.

During a visit of the royal family in October of 2011, reigning monarch HRM Queen Beatrix was accompanied by then Dutch Crown Prince HRH Willem-Alexander and Crown Princess HRH Maxima, who then became king and queen in 2013. They were treated to the first official event at Aruba's Plaza Turismo in Oranjestad. It was comprised of authentic performances by a dozen of Aruba's various ethnic or national groups, with offerings of native food and specialized beverages. Informative displays regarding each group's culture and history were part of the event. It was a vibrant demonstration of pride in the multicultural nature of island society. Aside from these groups, there were authentic cultural programs by expatriates from Portugal, the Dominican Republic, Venezuela, and Colombia.

RELIGION

The Spanish influence is still evident with the majority of the island being Catholic, and each district has a large church. The Dutch Protestant Church is well established, with a landmark building in Oranjestad.

There is also a synagogue, Temple Beth Israel, erected in 1962, at Adrian Lacle Boulevard 2. The Jewish cemetery in Oranjestad has historic headstones dating back centuries. The present congregation is perhaps 35 families.

San Nicolas has a large Anglican church, and there a few Methodist and Baptist institutions on the island. Evangelicalism has had a strong influence on the community over the past 20 years. A number of Evangelical ministries have cropped up in all sorts of venues, with too many storefront churches to count.

EDUCATION

Attending school is compulsory for island children ages 5-15. Elementary schools encompass kindergarten through sixth grade. English and Spanish become a part of the curriculum of local schools from fifth grade on. Upon completion of sixth grade students are filtered into academic or vocational schools. This is based on an IQ test administered in sixth grade, their grades, and observances by their teachers and principals.

Island children begin learning Dutch in kindergarten, if they do not already use it in the home. Many of the island's schools are under the authority of a Catholic school

King Willem-Alexander and Queen Maxima enjoy a visit with Aruban children.

association, SKOA, or are Protestant affiliated. Aruba has two private schools without affiliation, the Skagel, which is strictly Dutch in use of language, and the International School of Aruba (ISA), taught in English, but with a distinctly multicultural flavor to the student body. ISA deploys the Montessori method in the younger grades. It provides education from kindergarten to the equivalent of 12th grade.

Exceptional students may immediately qualify for Brugclasse (Bridge Class), a trial, introductory year testing their performance and ability to progress on to the higher levels of learning. Diplomas are called degrees. Attaining a HAVO degree is the equivalent of a U.S. high school diploma, thus qualifying for university. The VWO program is accelerated learning for the particularly gifted and determined. It is very academically demanding. Typically, VWO students in their freshman year at U.S. universities report finding they are already at a sophomore level of college education, or beyond.

Students graduating from elementary school who are not yet ready for an accelerated program of academics are directed towards MAVO, a four-year school. Graduates can go on to acquire their HAVO or VWO degrees. They may also elect to take professional training courses at EPI, Educativo Professional Intermedio.

EPI consists of four faculties which award an associate degree in technology, business administration, social work, or tourism and hospitality management. The last faculty of the EPI is also the center for the renowned Aruba Culinary School, where graduates receive certification from the American Culinary Federation. This school accepts students from around the world.

EPI also receives students from Aruba's Educativo Basico Professional (EPB) who have gone through four years or more of dedicated

Why *Himno y Bandera*?

Aruba's **National Day** is March 18, often referred to as ***Himno y Bandera*—Anthem and Flag Day.** It is a celebration of the establishment of Aruba's self-identity, 10 years before actual autonomy was achieved. It marks the day Aruba's official flag and national anthem were first introduced.

Before to the introduction of Aruba's own flag, a contest was held with a general invitation to all islanders to submit designs for the nation's symbol. There were more than 700 entries.

The desired concept was a simple but distinctive flag, representative of the island both culturally and physically, but easily recognizable from a distance. Typical to many flags, the symbols of stripes and stars were included in the designs and many Arubans felt the sun was important to Aruba's lifestyle and history.

The color most commonly suggested was blue, representing the clear sky and sea. Other highly popular colors were yellow to represent sunlight; white for Aruba's unique beaches; and red, symbolizing sunsets, the island's clay soil, progress, or the blood of Arubans, though none was actually shed in acquiring autonomy.

A bold and unique four-pointed star, something unheard of for flags before, was settled upon as the primary symbol. It was felt that the four points represented Aruba's four main languages: Papiamento, English, Dutch, and Spanish. While the yellow stripes, sometimes attributed to the discovery of gold that first initiated island posterity, symbolized Aruba's movement to the future and independence.

"Aruba Dushi Tera" ("Sweet Land Aruba") was first known as a popular and patriotic song composed by Juan Chabaya "Padu" Lampe and Rufo Wever, more than 20 years earlier. It was immediately considered for the honor. A few couplets were added to the end by the founder of the Instituto di Cultura, composer and musician Lio Booi, before it was first performed as Aruba's national song, accompanying the raising of the flag.

vocational training. EPB classes are divided into three levels of academic accomplishment, with only the top level qualified to go on to EPI. Students can work their way up the ladder of scholastic achievement from the lowest to highest level, but that is rare.

After completing four years of the lesser levels of EPB, graduates may decide to join the workforce in apprentice positions in mechanics, electrical repair, woodworking, or as beauticians and caregivers. EPB also has a highly acclaimed school of culinary training, where many of the students continue to the EPI culinary school to become certified chefs. The HORECA (HOtel, REstaurant, CAfé) program also trains youngsters for the tourism and food industry as waitstaff, bartenders, and restaurant management.

For almost 20 years Aruba has had an institution of higher learning, the University of Aruba, but with a limited curriculum awarding only law and accounting degrees. Most students travel abroad for advanced degrees, primarily in Holland, the United States, or Latin America. In the past 10 years the university has expanded its fields of studies, and faculties now include hospitality and tourism management, accounting, financing and marketing, arts and sciences (similar to liberal arts), and law. Graduates earn a bachelor's degree. The **University of Aruba** (www.ua.aw) readily accepts students from abroad and most will find tuition is considerably less than U.S. schools.

NOTABLE ARUBANS

Aruba has its heroes and heroines, personages who have contributed greatly to the island's advancements in education, sports, culture, and technology. Among them are some who have received worldwide attention, aside from regional recognition for their achievements.

Juan Chabaya "Padu" Lampe

Best known for his musical compositions, Juan Chabaya "Padu" Lampe was the coauthor with Rufo Wever of Aruba's national anthem, "Aruba Dushi Tera." He is truly a Renaissance man as a painter, musician, composer, and author. Padu made his living as a representative of ALM airlines and contributed to the island's culture not for profit, but purely out of love of the arts. His work required that he travel extensively, and he was an unofficial ambassador of Aruba, performing to appreciative audiences and establishing good will, wherever his work took him. His enormous, diverse body of work and influence on the island population earned him the popular title of "Father of Culture."

Never charging for musical performances, his presence was considered to elevate any event. Padu gave many concerts in Venezuela, where he finally began recording LPs in the 1960s. Some won Golden Piano awards, the equivalent of a Grammy. "Padu Del Caribe" was his recording name, and he still has a very loyal following in the region.

Born in 1910, he earned his nickname in honor of his *Padu*, his grandfather and namesake, who had died the same week he was born. His mother called him *Padushi* ("Sweet Little Grandfather"); the nickname stuck, and later shortened to Padu.

Padu began his love affair with the arts as a painter. While he was just a teenager, one of his works was selected to be shown at the 1939 World's Fair in New York as an example of Caribbean art. He authored metaphysical treatises in English, titled "The 3rd Element" and "Harmoniology—The Art and Science of Living in Harmony with the Universal Laws." They were published in 1960 and 1978, respectively.

"Sir" Dr. Edward Cheung

Passing along the Sasaki Highway on the way to a Palm Beach resort, many may spot the Dr. Edward Cheung Center for Innovation and wonder about its namesake. When he was still a relatively young man, this native son actually sent Aruba into space!

Born and raised on Aruba by immigrant parents, Dr. Cheung went on to obtain his PhD in electrical engineering, specializing in robotics, from Yale, with a scholarship from

Phillips and NASA. He joined the NASA team and in 1995 was assigned to the Hubble Space Telescope (HST) maintenance project.

His work with NASA particularly electrified his homeland when HST experienced a failure in the NICMOS cooling system that threatened to send it crashing to earth. When it became clear that a substitute system was problematic, Dr. Cheung and his team had three months to devise a solution. It was named ASCS/NCS Relay Unit Breaker Assembly, or ARUBA box. Its installation during a 2002 mission saved the HST. It can be seen in photos taken during space missions, attached to the outside of the Hubble; the word "ARUBA" is very clear.

Dr. Cheung's was one of the voices heard during broadcasts of the final mission to the telescope, when they installed his invention, the Wide Field Camera III. This revolutionary equipment is delivering images of space never possible before to scientists. Dr. Cheung was also part of the team present for the last manned space mission of NASA, working the "Tweet Tent" at Kennedy Space Center during the blastoff.

Dr. Cheung now heads a new division at Goddard Space Center, devising robotic means of in-space repair of satellites. The new technology extends their use and saves tens of millions of dollars in prematurely replacing equipment.

During his annual visits to his family in Aruba, Dr. Cheung has made it a regular practice to give free lectures about space and the HST. It is his stated goal to inspire young Arubans to consider careers in science and to continue their education to the highest levels.

In 2010, NASA was proud to report that its principal engineer was dubbed a Knight in the Order of the Netherlands Lion. This is the highest honor the monarchy bestows on a civilian subject, and it is a rare occurrence. His colleagues at NASA affectionately refer to him as "Sir Ed," though the actual title of "Sir" is not an affectation of being dubbed a knight within the Dutch system.

Sarah-Quita Offringa

An exemplary role model for island youth is Sarah-Quita Offringa, the reigning Professional Windsurfing Association's (PWA) Women's Freestyle Windsurfing World Champion since 2008. At the time she won her first world championship title she had just turned 17, setting a new world record for the youngest champion ever.

Sarah-Quita, "the girl with big hair,"

Sarah-Quita Offringa

turned the windsurfing world around when she burst upon the professional scene, going pro at the age of 12. At 15, she won her first gold medal, also setting a new PWA record for the youngest to do so.

Since claiming the freestyle title, she has never lost a single competition heat or elimination round. In 2011, she was also crowned Women's World Champion in Slalom, proving to be a double-threat on the water. For the remarkable achievement of earning two world champion titles in a single year, she was selected as a contender for the ISAF Rolex World Sailor of the Year Award.

Though the life of a sports champion offers fame and travel, Sarah-Quita is acutely aware of her position as a role model for young Arubans. She always put her studies first and foremost, and in 2014, she obtained her bachelor's degree in science and innovation at the University of Utrecht, Holland.

Before going for her master's, she decided to show the windsurfing world her true capabilities. Not only did she successfully maintain her status as freestyle champion in both 2014 and 2015, she also won the Slalom title in 2015 for the second time, and placed third worldwide in wave sailing. Her ultimate goal is to be the first triple crown winner for the sport's three major international competitions.

Sarah-Quita is such an important figure in the sport that her 2015 windsurfing pilgrimage around the world has been made into a documentary by French filmmaker Julian Robbinet. It is titled *Cabaibusha,* which means bushy hair in Papiamento, after her iconic profile.

THE ARTS

Regional Music and Traditions

During national holidays, Carnival, and the end of the year seasonal celebrations, Arubans put their idiosyncratic cultural traditions on display. European and regional influences that comprise what is considered authentically Aruban can best be observed in the festive music and dance performances. Ties to **Holland and Dutch traditions** are evident in the celebration of **King's Day,** and at the end of the year, when **Sinterklaas** comes to visit. Families look forward to *oliebollen,* a typically Dutch holiday treat, and fireworks on **New Year's Eve.**

The approach of Christmas means the manifestation of ***gaita*** singing groups performing regularly at dozens of public events and private parties. *Gaita* actually originates from Maracaibo in the Zulia State of Venezuela. It is very lively, upbeat music. *Gaita* groups usually consist of 8-12 female singers, accompanied by native instruments, such as a *cuarto,* a small guitar, and *tambora,* the goatskin drums.

The end of the year is also the time for **Dande,** traditionally performed by wandering minstrels. Dande has a distinctive, repetitive chorus; the lyrics change to personalize the song to each household visited. Dande minstrels come with hat in hand, for each family member to ritualistically drop in a little *propina* for luck.

Just before the end of the year is the annual Dande competition to crown a new king or queen. It starts in the early evening, and there are so many bands, and the songs are so long (with each one sounding *exactly* the same, except for slight variations in lyrics), it doesn't end until dawn. Those who make it through this marathon musical event are truly devoted to the art form.

Carnival time produces three extremely important musical competitions: the Roadmarch (Soca) Contest, the Calypso (Caiso) Contest, and the crowning of a Tumba king or queen. These entail several nights of concert competitions, as winners are declared in three age groups: child, youth, and adult. Costumes are an important part of the event, as well as the quality of performance and the suitability of the piece, which must be an original composition.

The winning song of the adult Roadmarch contest will be the official theme for that year's Carnival season, performed endlessly during parades and events. This is selected by judges as the best piece to inspire participants and spectators to dance along. It is usually a classic example of Afro-Caribbean polyphonic music, making it impossible to resist shaking the hips and guaranteed to start shoulders twitching. A second song, likely more popular with the public than the judges, will also be heard just as frequently. This is dubbed the "Road Jam," an unofficial winner, as no one will ever completely agree with the judges' decision.

Tumba is the island's music most steeped in the roots of slavery and African culture, brought to Aruba and Curacao in the 1700s. It has evolved to incorporate more Latin harmonics in recent times. **Calypso** is a traditional regional music originating from Trinidad and Tobago. Songs are not only judged for their musicality, but also for their lyrics and pithy social commentary. They are usually quite humorous and topical, wry observances of human behavior based on events of the previous year.

Beyond these, islanders consider the pieces derived from more **classic European music** such as waltzes, *danzas,* and mazurkas, typical of their culture. Most folkloric dance is performed to such pieces, usually composed by well-respected artists such as Juan Chabaya "Padu" Lampe and Rufo Wever (coauthors of Aruba's national anthem, an excellent example), and Lio Booi, founder of the Aruba Institute of Culture, who also contributed to the national song.

Steelpan is another musical art form integrated into island culture, which arrived with the great migration prompted by the opening of the refinery. The Connor family is particularly noted for this, and Lee and Nico Connor carry on a tradition promulgated by their father over 50 years ago, which continues with a new generation. Steelpan music is regularly heard at many events, and there are concerts dedicated to it at least once a year. It is an integral part of the Bon Bini and Carubbian festivals.

Aruba has been described as "an island of dancers," by some. Every weekend several bands perform around the island, often giving free concerts. At nearly any party or gala, the dance floor will be full, particularly when the band plays merengue. Islanders dance with complete abandon during Carnival and such events.

Performing Arts

Aruba has many centers for performing arts and concerts, and a number of galleries. **Cas di Cultura** (Vondellaan 2, 297/582-1010, www.casdicultura.aw), meaning "House of Culture," is where most dance recitals and classic concerts are staged. Located on the large traffic circle at the east end of Oranjestad, it has been Aruba's theatrical and cultural center since 1958, and is booked nearly every weekend for some sort of recital or play. It also has an exhibition room for art and educational or commemorative expositions. The main auditorium seats over 400.

Holiday time on Aruba can include indulging the family in the seasonal favorite *The Nutcracker* staged and choreographed by former star of the Bolshoi and New York Ballet companies, and creative director of the New Jersey Ballet, Leonid Kozlov (www.dancearuba.com and www.leonidkozlov.com). A part-time resident of Aruba, he has brought Tchaikovsky's fairy-tale classic to the island as a new holiday tradition. Performances run twice over the holiday week at the Cas di Cultura.

Private studios offer dance lessons and conduct recitals annually. Visual artists are regularly featured in shows and in a few galleries. The Cas di Cultura is home to the Rufo Wever School of Music, occupying one side of the building, and the Da Vinci Academy, dedicated to classical piano, on the other. Aruba is also home to several highly respected jazz musicians, many of whom teach at the Rufo Wever School. They are producing a new generation of music students who are enthusiastic about interpretive music.

Internationally known performers are brought in annually for the weeklong Aruba International Piano Festival in June and the Caribbean Sea Jazz Festival over Columbus

Day weekend. These are just two isolated international events; at least once a month some international talent is imported to perform.

It is perhaps in the continuing tradition of original music created for Carnival where that which can truly be called Aruban originates. Many of these fine, self-trained musicians and composers are producing the distinctive, complex, polyphonic works that are close to the hearts of islanders.

Literary and Visual Arts

UNOCA (Stadionweg 21, 297/583-5681, www.unocaruba.org, 8:30am-noon and 1:30pm-5pm Mon.-Fri.) is a foundation dedicated to the promotion and development of all the literary, visual, and performing arts. It funds publication of books, both poetry and prose, usually in Papiamento; dance recitals; art expositions; and other projects that elevate the cultural awareness of the community. The offices double as a permanent exhibit hall for local artwork, and it also sells many of the publications it has helped publish.

There is a long-established, active community producing work in several mediums. A number of foundations are dedicated to promoting education and interest among youth. Traditional painters and primitive style held sway for years, and their work is revered. Current schools of art, however, lean much more toward the abstract, the impressionistic, and particularly, the avant-garde.

Island hotels and restaurants support this community by displaying works of art on their premises, where they are offered for sale.

Essentials

Getting There

AIR

Reina Beatrix International Airport (Reina Beatrix Airport z/n, 297/524-2424, www.airportaruba.com) is the official and only air entry to Aruba, whether by commercial or private flights. Visitors will be pleasantly surprised by Aruba's large, comfortable air terminal. It is not typical of most island facilities. New arrivals are greeted by air-conditioned halls, decorated with artistic environments where local artists have created a stimulating introduction to Aruban culture. A graceful sculpture garden bids visitors farewell, as they wait in line to pass through port control to depart.

The airport has a diverse and attractive arcade of shops and restaurants for departing passengers. The arrivals area also offers some duty-free shops where discounted liquor and cigarettes can be purchased before officially stepping on Aruban soil. Those who take advantage of this should be mindful of the limits, which are two cartons of cigarettes and two liters of liquor for personal use. There is a separate terminal for private flights at the south end of the airport. It is staffed by separate Aruban immigration and ICE officials. It is modern and comfortable with several amenities.

There are several options to get from the airport to your accommodation. While major resorts do not provide shuttle service to and from the airport, there are several car rental agencies directly across from the arrivals exit, and taxis are lined up in the nearest lane to the terminals. Taxis are the most common form of transport to your hotel. Cab fare ranges $22-40 one-way, depending on whether you are staying in Oranjestad or one of the farther Palm Beach resorts.

Commercial Airlines

The Ministry of Tourism and Transportation has authorized two regional companies, the Aruban **Insel Air Aruba** (Reina Beatrix International Airport, 855/493-6004, 297/582-1200, www.fly-inselair.com) and **Aruba Airlines** (Cumena 69, 297/5823-8300, www.arubaairlines.com), to provide direct access to Aruba from the United States. Formerly only providing regional service, they have acquired jumbo jets for direct round-trip service to cities such as Boston, Ft. Lauderdale, and Orlando. Insel Air Aruba now provides daily round-trip service to and from Miami. Suriname Airlines can also make a Miami connection from other points across the United States and Canada.

On weekends there are additional flights to Aruba from the commercial carriers as well as several charter services from the United States and Toronto. Veteran travelers know the best prices and most relaxing travel will usually be on weekdays. Weekend planes sometimes have to wait on the tarmac for a gate to deplane passengers, particularly during the peak arrival time of mid-afternoon. All ticket offices for commercial U.S. and Canadian airlines are within Reina Beatrix International Airport. The following are U.S. and other commercial airlines that fly to Aruba daily:

- American Airlines: 297/582-2700, www.aa.com
- Delta: 297/588-5623, www.delta.com
- JetBlue: 297/588-5977, www.jetblue.com
- U.S. Airways: 800/622-1015, www.usairways.com
- Copa Air (via Panama City): 297/525-2672, www.copair.com

Previous: Bucuti Yacht Club provides berths for visiting yachts; Tiara Air Aruba is the island's endorsed logo airline.

Aruba's First Airport

An airport was in the planning stages when the first tourist flight arrived on Aruba, a tri-engine Fokker in September of 1934. It had to land in a field in Savaneta. The airport was ready to receive flights by the following January, with the first from Curacao setting down on January 19. During the first year of operation, 2,659 passengers were transported between the two islands.

The first air-traffic control tower went into operation in 1937. Aruba's importance to Allied fuel supplies during WWII brought expansion and some modernization, initiating the construction of a new terminal. It opened in 1950, and was called the Dakota Airport until 1955. On October 22, it was rechristened Princess Beatrix Airport, with her father, HRH Prince Bernhard presiding over the ceremony. The old terminal was converted into a fire station, so fire trucks could always be close at hand.

Two years later, preparations began for the extension of the runways in anticipation of large commercial jets bringing vacationers to Aruba. In 1964, the first two jets to arrive were from Pan Am. One year later, ground was broken for another terminal; it was inaugurated in 1972. When HRM Juliana abdicated the throne on April 30, 1980, and her daughter was crowned, the airport then became Reina Beatrix International Airport. Airport management was privatized and entered into a strategic cooperative agreement with Schiphol International in Amsterdam in 2004. This assured its profitable management as well as adherence to international safety standards.

The enormous expansion and modernization of the present facility was begun in 2000 and completed in 2003. This added an entirely new terminal for non-U.S. departures and an enlargement of the gate areas. They are configured to provide a complete division of arriving and departing passengers for increased safety and control, as well as smoothing the flow.

- United Airlines: 800/864-8331, www.united.com

Commercial flight schedules change from one season to the next; new carriers are continually establishing airlifts and opening gateway cities. The best source for current airline information for regularly scheduled flights is the airport's official website.

Since it is so far south in the Caribbean, one might expect that airfares to Aruba would be higher in comparison to other destinations, but the difference is surprisingly marginal, particularly during the off-season. **American Airlines,** one of the first to begin regular service to Aruba in the 1960s, has two direct flights from its Miami hub daily, servicing feeder flights from all points in the United States. A weekend flight from Miami can range from as little as $227 in economy class to $526 in business during the off-season, depending on availability. High-season tickets can go for as little as $279 for super economy class on the weekends. Peak holiday rates, such as Christmas, run as high $1,000 or more for economy.

Aruba's most frequent carrier is now **JetBlue,** with daily direct flights from New York and Boston. You can pay as little as $506 for a no-frills flight on weekdays during the high season, or $614 round-trip from Boston, which includes all taxes and airport fees. The exception is a departure tax of $37.50, which will be collected at the ticket counter when checking in for a returning flight to the United States. This is a common practice throughout the Caribbean and Latin America.

SEA

Cruise Ships

Cruising "high season" usually begins in November with as many as four to five megaships arriving at the centrally located Oranjestad Harbor two or three days a week. This tapers off in April. Immigration procedures for arriving passengers are handled by cruise officials on the boat, so passengers can disembark and simply walk into town.

Arrival by sea is under the administration of the **Aruba Ports Authority** (L. G. Smith Blvd. 23, 297/582-6633, control tower direct

297/582-1740, www.arubaports.com, 24 hours daily). The most current schedule of all ships set to call in Aruba, with dates and times, can be found on the website, usually no more than one season in advance. The cruise ship schedules are quite fluid from one year to the next. It is best to check the APA website to find the time of travel that interests you.

A local agent for cruise companies stopping in Aruba is **S.E.L. Maduro & Sons** (Rockefellerstraat 1, 297/528-2343, 8am-noon and 1pm-5pm Mon.-Fri.), which can book passage with Aruba as the embarkation point.

Cruise lines with Aruba on their itineraries include **Royal Caribbean** (www.royalcaribbean.com), offering one-week tours departing from Puerto Rico. **Holland American Line** (www.hollandamerica.com) runs two-week to one-month excursions from Ft. Lauderdale or San Diego. **Carnival** (www.carnival.com) departs from Ft. Lauderdale and Puerto Rico regularly. **Celebrity** (www.celebritycruises.com) has two-week charters departing from Ft. Lauderdale, as does **Princess Cruises** (www.princess.com), which also has two-week and one-month excursions embarking from Los Angeles and Vancouver, Canada.

Private Yacht

Aruba's immigration and customs regulations for yachts are somewhat different than most Caribbean islands. Arriving vessels must first report to the clearing center, formerly in Baracadera Harbor on the south side of the island. As of April of 2015, however, Barcadera has been undergoing a complete renovation to become the island's container harbor. Oranjestad Harbor is now the clearing point for immigrations and customs. Northwest entrance to Oranjestad Harbor is 12° 31' 070° 04' W, southeast entrance is 12° 30.3' N 070° 02.' The port control should be hailed on channel 16 at least half an hour before entry; the duty officer will likely switch to channel 11 or 14 once contact has been made. Be prepared with all documentation when authorities board your vessel; all hands must remain on board until this process is completed. This will be done at the second basin, to the west of the long cruise ship dock, which is called Hans Dock. It is located to port at 12° 31.285' N 70° 02.709' W.

After clearing customs and immigration, boats can proceed to their registered berths. Visas for the other islands of the Dutch

Many cruise ships come into Oranjestad Harbor during high season.

Caribbean are not valid for Aruba; a separate visa must be obtained. Pleasure yachts no less than 14 meters moored in Aruban waters, or registered at a slip, are immediately eligible to extend their stay and harbor managers recommend they do so. They must be able to show proof of ownership of the boat.

Since October 1, 2012, a regulation requiring the boat itself to be declared to customs came into effect. Customs declaration forms can be downloaded from the APA website in English, Dutch, and Spanish, along with an immigration form. If the yacht stays in Aruban waters no more than 180 days, then a temporary import permit must be acquired; this does not require a deposit. If it stays longer, up to one year, a temporary import permit must be applied for with payment of a deposit (or a bank guarantee) for the value of the duties on the yacht. Any stay longer than a year will categorize the yacht as an import and duties must be paid. Once a temporary permit has expired, the yacht must leave Aruban waters for no less than 15 days before another permit can be obtained.

Aruba Ports Authority charges a port fee for yachts tied up to docks. These fees are additional to the private slip fee. Rates are $10 per hour 8am-4pm, $15 per hour 4pm-8am, and $20 per hour on weekends and holidays. A uniformed harbor security officer collects this, in cash, while boats are tied up at the slip.

Principal harbors accepting visiting yachts are Renaissance Marina, adjacent to Oranjestad Harbor, and Bucuti and Varadero Yacht Clubs, behind the airport and next to each other. Offshore protected anchorages are, from west to east, beginning north of the Palm Beach resorts: Arashi, Malmok, Eagle Beach, Surfside, Bucuti, Spanish Lagoon, Savaneta, and Roger's Beach. VHF channels deployed by the APA are 16 and 1.

Ship Chandlers

Within the Seaport Marketplace, adjacent to Renaissance Marina, **East Wind Marine Services** (L. G. Smith Blvd. 5, 297/588-0260, ewms@renaissancemarina.com, 8am-6pm Mon.-Sat.) handles the marina business. The shop provides nautical maps for the entire world, can arrange for parts and repairs, and has a diverse inventory for boaters, anglers, and casual water activities.

The exclusive agent for authentic Evinrude parts on Aruba is **Salas Marine** (Bushiri 37, 297/593-4706, john@slasamarine.com, 9am-noon and 2pm-6pm Mon.-Fri., 10am-2pm Sat.). It also carries a selection of boat accessories, but no paint. If Salas Marine does not have a part in stock, it will take about one week to obtain it. Salas Marine is not far from the harbor, on a dirt road behind the complex of large supermarkets on the west end of Oranjestad.

Getting Around

Not a very large island, Aruba is thoughtfully outfitted with connecting roads, most of which eventually intersect into a single route, the 1A, stretching from the far eastern tip to the very western point. The road parallels the southern shore, often bordering the beachfront. If traveling from the major resorts to the airport, Oranjestad, San Nicolas, or the California Lighthouse, stay on the road to arrive at most destinations. There are a few major roads that will connect to it that transect the island. Beyond these major routes, explorers will find many streets are sand or dirt roads. Once beyond the city limits or main thoroughfares, addresses are by area and building number, and most streets do not have a title. Principal areas with street addresses are Oranjestad, with its outlying neighborhoods of Ponton, Dakota, and Eagle. Beyond the capital, other urban centers, such as Santa Cruz and San Nicolas, also have named streets.

Road Signs and Regulations

Islanders are very patient with tourists on the road who are unfamiliar with the road signs and traffic laws. They know tourists will be driving rental cars, which have license plates that start with a "V" for *Verhuur,* Dutch for "rental." They expect visitors to drive slowly in their confusion to figure out where they need to turn, and are quite understanding and helpful.

Aruba uses standard international road signs. Drivers need to take note of some signs in particular. A solid red circle with a white slash means **do not enter,** and if ignored, motorists will find they are going the wrong way on a one-way street. Oranjestad in particular has several narrow, one-way streets.

A round blue sign with a white arrow indicates traffic is **one way,** and the driver must follow the direction indicated. This can also be seen as a square, which informs the driver they are traveling in the right direction on a one-way street.

An upside down white triangle, outlined in yellow, is a **yield** sign; a white diamond outlined in yellow indicates you are on a main thoroughfare and have **right-of-way** at upcoming intersections. If there are three parallel black slashes through the sign, it is warning that the road status has changed. At the upcoming intersection you **forfeit right-of-way.** There should be a yield or stop sign at the intersection.

A **no-passing zone** will be indicated by a picture of a red car on the left of a black car. Drivers should take note of any sign with red symbols as an indication of a prohibition of some kind.

The Department of Public Works and Ministry of Infrastructure have not quite mastered the art of clearly understood road signs, but they are improving. When venturing into rural areas, you will find that maps indicate some sort of road where there is little more than a well-beaten path. This makes getting around beyond the main roads confusing.

Most major destinations and resort areas are easily reached along a few principal roads, as are several sights. Exploring the Aruban outback is another matter entirely, where landmarks are a matter of interpretation. Islanders, who are quite familiar with their surroundings, are notoriously deficient in giving good directions. It is a common practice for them to hop in their car, or change their personal itinerary, to lead visitors to the destination.

CAR

After exiting the airport, visitors can find several car rental agencies directly across from the arrivals exit. Cars rented at the airport have a 10 percent surcharge added on to the regular rental rates; however, this charge is likely equal to or less than the round-trip cab fare to and from most resorts.

Several resorts host car rental agency desks, and others can be found close by. Car rental rates are quite reasonable; third-party liability insurance is included in the rental rate as required by law, though there is normally a $150 deductible. There are 38 car rental agencies on Aruba, many with affiliations that will be familiar. Several are associated with reliable European or Latin agencies. All must conform to stated business and safety regulations, but prices can vary. Daily rates for a compact car start at $30. The lowest rate for a weekly rental is $145 for a subcompact, which includes unlimited mileage. Every manner of driver's license is accepted.

Driving on Aruba

Traffic flows on the right-hand side of the road, the same as the United States and Canada. Speed limits are posted regularly. Top speed on a highway is 80 kilometers per hour (50 mph); in town, 40 kilometers per hour (25 mph); and in "suburban" areas, 60 kilometers per hour (37 mph).

Urban areas and busy streets are populated

Parking in Oranjestad

Arubus, Aruba's mass transit system, has established paid parking in the town of Oranjestad, the island's principal cultural and daytime shopping center. The system is in effect Monday through Saturday from 7:00am until 7:00pm. Those dining after 7:00pm or visiting the town on Sunday need not be concerned.

Paid parking spots are marked with numbers and pay stations are scattered frequently around the principal parking areas. Cost is 1 Aruban Florin (57 cents U.S.) per 45 minutes; cost decreases by 30 percent beyond a one hour purchase. Machines will only accept local 1 florin pieces, not American money, so come prepared. They are computerized, so just follow the cues, which are in English, for entering your spot number.

Paid parking extends through all the side streets surrounding L.G. Smith Boulevard and the Caya Betico Croes, where most shops are located. It begins at Columbiastraat on the eastern end of the town and extends through the service roads on the western side until the traffic light at the Sasaki/Sun Plaza intersection. Parking spots marked in yellow are reserved by business owners in town for their employees.

Cars occupying a space beyond their time will have a lock placed on the tires. The overtime fine for less than half an hour is $43. After half an hour, the car will be towed, and it is $100 to retrieve it from the impound. All parking fees and fines support Arubus and the mass transit system. If you plan to spend a day in town, you might want to consider experiencing Aruba's clean, well-kept busses, which offer frequent service to Oranjestad from all the main resort areas.

with zebra walks for pedestrians. Traffic regulations demand that motorists stop for a person standing on the black and white striped crossings. If making your way around town on foot, look for these walks. Use zebra walks to cross the street, rather than braving traffic in unauthorized areas.

International road signs are used. A chart of these signs is usually provided with the map from rental agencies, so take the time to get acquainted with them. There are few traffic lights on the island, but those at the more important intersections on the divided Sasaki Highway can be confusing. It is important when stopped for drivers to *take note of the light directly on the near side of the road, not across the highway.* A green light on an island in the middle of the Sasaki Highway is to allow highway traffic to turn left. It is *not* an indication for traffic at intersections to cross the highway. Look to the near light to the right or left to see if it is safe to feed or cross the highway. At no time is a right turn allowed on a red light.

To ease bottlenecks, roundabouts have replaced traffic lights at most intersections; plans are to eventually phase out all traffic lights completely. Those entering the circle are always required to yield to cars already on the circle. When stopping at a four-way intersection, motorists must yield to the car on the right; it is of no consequence which car arrived first. If you have not spotted a traffic sign indicating right-of-way at a major intersection and are confused, look at the marks painted on the road. Arrows pointing at you indicate you must yield to the intersecting street. Boxes painted where you are stopped mean you have the right-of-way. Left-turning traffic must always give way to oncoming traffic, until the way is clear. Passing on the left at intersections is forbidden. Make sure your turn indicator is on.

Aruba has quite a few cars and trucks for such a small island, most of which seem concentrated in Oranjestad's main thoroughfares. Traffic is usually stop and go for a half mile along L. G. Smith Boulevard fronting the cruise terminal, especially when several ships are in port, or during typical commuter hours in the morning and late afternoon.

BICYCLE

Biking to various tourist sites has become quite popular over the past decade; a number of operators conduct tours. These areas are usually not so crowded with cars, and bikers can travel safely. Caution is recommended if you are planning to bike into downtown Oranjestad; the streets are narrow and crowded, with no bike paths and little room to maneuver. Portions of J. E. Irausquin Boulevard and L. G. Smith Boulevard north of Palm Beach have been designated as official bike paths. These areas are painted blue and provide bikers with a legally protected route from Oranjestad to Malmok. The shorefront from Governor's Bay to the Reina Beatrix International Airport has been remodeled to provide safe biking and jogging tracks completely away from traffic.

Pablito's Bike Rental (L. G. Smith Blvd. 234, 297/587-8665, $15/day) is conveniently located for Eagle Beach visitors and provides an easy way to get to town and shops. You will find it on the short road adjacent to Screaming Eagle restaurant, leading to Pearl Residences. **Velocity Beach Bike Rental** (Irausquin Blvd z/n, 297/592-1670, 8:30am-4:30pm daily, $15/day) services the Palm Beach area and has brand-new bikes and mountain bikes, including a tandem. It offers a special bargain for weekly rentals: if you rent for seven days, you only pay for five.

MOTORCYCLES, MOPEDS, AND ATVS

Motorcycles are a common form of transport, but mopeds are rarely seen in regular traffic anymore. Generally, 4x4s, UTVs, and sturdier vehicles providing better sun protection have become the general preference. Mopeds are still available for rental and are good for short hops to closer sights However, if you are planning a full day of traveling around the island, it is recommended you look for a vehicle that allows you to get a break from Aruba's intense sun.

On the western outskirts of Oranjestad is the **Big Twin Harley-Davidson** dealership (L. G. Smith Blvd. 106, 866/978-6525 or 297/586-8220, www.harleydavidson-aruba.com, 9am-5:30pm Mon.-Sat., $140-175 half-day rentals $175-200 full-day rentals), easily spotted by the HOGs lined up in front. Two on a bike is allowed. **George's Cycle Rental** (L. G. Smith Blvd. 124, 297/593-2202, www.georgecycles.com, 9am-5pm daily, mopeds $40-50/day, Yamaha motorcycles $70-100/day, ATVs $120-200/day) is on the highway just at the western side of Oranjestad and has a variety of vehicles for rent, from tiny mopeds to ATVs with automatic transmission and hardtop shade canopies. Special discounts are available for longer-term rentals of 3 or 4 days. Resort pickup and drop-off plus helmets are part of the service.

BUS

Arubus (Weststraat 13, 297/588-0617, www.arubus.com, 5:40am-11:20pm Mon.-Fri., modified schedule on weekends, $2.25) is the official mass transit system. Buses are new, clean, and comfortable. The L10 route runs between Oranjestad and Palm Beach, past all resorts, passing through Manchebo Beach and Eagle Beach along J. E. Irausquin Boulevard. It runs a round-trip route from the Oranjestad Bus Terminal daily, nearly every 10 minutes during the day. Frequency is reduced to 20-30 minutes or more between buses after 6pm and on Sunday. A complete schedule can be found on the website. There are clearly marked bus stops, with shelters at many, along J. E. Irausquin Boulevard. They are small yellow sign stations in front of each resort and by the hospital, which is on the route.

In 2012 a "Smartcard" system was introduced. This is for residents only. Cash is still accepted for infrequent users and visitors. Another innovation was the introduction of official minivans for less frequently used routes and off-hours. There is also a system of privately owned minibuses that pick up the slack during night hours when Arubus service is more sporadic. They are strictly controlled by the Ministry of Transport and clearly marked, charging no more than

Arubus. They are perfectly legitimate to use if they come along first, rather than waiting for what looks like a more official bus.

TAXI

Because major resorts do not provide shuttle service to and from the airport, taxis are the most common transport to your hotel upon arrival. Cabs will be lined up at the airport to take arrivals without tour bus transfers to their respective resorts. The airport even has a special rest station for cabbies, and the nearest lane to the terminals is reserved for taxi pickup and drop-off. Taxi drivers are happy to give you their card so they can be summoned for further service, if required.

Every resort has a taxi stand at the entrance; hotel staff calls the dispatcher if one is not immediately available. Licensed cabs are clearly marked, but they do not use meters. The Ministry of Transport sets the rates. Ask hotel personnel at the front desk to see the rate chart; they should have it on hand.

Cabdrivers charge extra for luggage, on Sunday, and after midnight. Taxis in Aruba are rather pricey: the average rate from the Marriott to Playa Linda (if you don't feel like doing the 10-minute walk along the beach) is $6; some might ask $9. Markets will be happy to call you a cab after grocery shopping. A complete list of official taxi rates can be downloaded from www.aruba.com.

Taxis have display lights on their hoods or dashboards, but they do not turn on or off when occupied or empty. It is always worth trying to flag down a cab if you need one. It is not their usual procedure, but islanders are adaptable when need be. Don't be disheartened if they don't stop; they likely have a fare already. If you are in town and looking for a cab, there is a taxi stand at the entrance of either section of the Renaissance Resort. An empty cab is always waiting there.

Taxi Dispatch Services

When you need a cab and one is not in sight, try calling **Aruba's Transfer Tour Taxi** (Pos Abao 41, 297/583-6988), **Diamond Taxi Service** (Salinja Cerca 27 A, 297/587-2300), or **Taxi Address Service** (J. E. Irausquin Blvd. 228 F, 297/588-0035). All resorts have a taxi stand, usually well populated around the dinner hours. If not, the front desk or concierge personnel will be happy to call taxi dispatcher.

Gas Stations

Aruba has two chains of gas stations, Valero and Texaco, for a total of nine outlets. The

A free tram takes passengers from the cruise terminal to Oranjestad's main sights and shopping.

island is not that large, and they are in sufficient numbers to avoid running out of gas. Self-service pumps do not take credit cards. Motorists must first go into the station to inform the cashier of the amount of gas required and pay. Prices are in Arubian florins, but stations happily take U.S. currency and traveler's checks in denominations of no greater than $20. The exchange rate is 1.75 Arubian florins to dollars. U.S. and Canadian credit and bank cards are accepted; a valid photo ID is required.

TRAM

Aruba has a tram that departs in front of the cruise terminal and takes visitors to downtown Oranjestad along the Caya G. F. Betico Croes. There are eight stops along the route, with attractive shaded tram stations at key locations for sightseeing and shopping. The tram operates 10am-4pm Monday-Saturday. It runs on solar power and has a hydraulic lift for passengers in wheelchairs. The service is free.

Part of the Green Aruba program, it is an electric tram powered by solar energy. The purpose is to reduce auto traffic through town and carbon emissions, as well as provide a pleasant service for visitors and residents.

Visas and Officialdom

Until a few years ago, travel to Aruba required only proof of citizenship; a certified birth certificate was sufficient. Regulations were passed by the United States and Canada making it mandatory for all traveling internationally to acquire a passport. Aruba, as an independent Dutch territory, is a signatory to agreements between NATO countries with an understanding that visitors from the United States or Canada do not require any special visa for travel to the island, but a valid passport is required. Aruban Immigration officers require a return ticket to be shown before approving entry. Aruba has installed the newest technology in reading passports. Though, when processing large planes filled to capacity, the new technology may slow the process of passing through immigration. It has proven quite valuable in detecting bogus passports, so it is a necessary inconvenience.

Foreign nationals residing in the United States or Canada without passports issued by these countries must be able to show valid residence permits to local immigration upon entry and departure.

Aruba does not have restrictions on traveling with foodstuffs or live animals, though it is a good idea to have a certificate showing a pet is free of rabies, as rabies does not exist on the island. The importation and trafficking in exotic and endangered animals is strictly forbidden.

For traveling by cruise ship, immigration protocols are usually handled by officers from the cruise lines, and passengers returning to the terminal after a day of touring or a visit to town need only show a personal, government-issued photo ID, such as a driver's license, and the pass received when departing the ship.

According to immigration regulations, officers at entry points may request that a tourist be able to prove to the satisfaction of the officer they have valid reservations for an accommodation in Aruba (e.g., hotel or apartment) or they own property—a home, condominium, apartment, timeshare apartment, or a pleasure yacht moored in Aruban waters no less than 14 meters (26 ft.) in size.

An immigration officer can also demand that a traveler show sufficient funds to carry through the determined stay on the island, or has the sponsorship of a relative, friend, or employer living on Aruba, who can provide this guarantee.

Aruba is one of the rare vacation destinations to have a division of the **U.S.**

Department of Immigration and Customs Enforcement (ICE; Reina Beatrix Airport Z/N, 297/588-7720, www.ice.gov) within its borders. This does not affect arriving passengers. However, upon returning to the United States, travelers will pass through U.S. customs and immigration on Aruba, prior to their flight. This expedites matters when arriving back in the United States, tired after a day of travel. U.S. residents need only pick up their luggage and head home. This does mean passing through two immigration checkpoints at the end of a stay. The Aruban immigration process upon departure is perfunctory; it is wise to allow time for the double process when heading for the airport. Customs declarations are made prior to entering the gate area.

CUSTOMS REGULATIONS

Personal clothing and belongings are not charged duty upon entering Aruba, nor are electronics, computers, or cameras. Individuals over 18 are allowed to bring in one-fifth (2 liters) of liquor and 200 cigarettes, 50 cigars, and 250 grams of tobacco.

Cats and dogs from most countries are allowed if accompanied by valid rabies and health certificates from a veterinarian. Pets from South and Central America, Cuba, Haiti, and the Dominican Republic are not allowed.

Conduct and Customs

The extreme mix of Aruba's population over the past two decades has caused social behavior to evolve from what used to be. Being a predominantly Catholic island, and somewhat conservative, the attitude of residents is tempered with tolerance for visitors and the understanding they do not know island ways. The multilingual talent of the Aruban people is famous. Though most are fluent in English, particularly those working in tourism, they appreciate an effort to pick up a word or two of the local language. A genuine interest by visitors to understand island customs and traditions will be warmly welcomed and evoke enthusiastic responses to queries.

ETIQUETTE

Arubans are very polite people and appreciate good manners. Before stating one's business, a sincere *Bon dia* (Good day) will always bring a smile and similar response, with the mind-set to be of help in any way possible. After midday the greeting is *Bon tardi,* and once the sun has set, *Bon nochi. Por Fabor* and *Danki* (Please and thank you) are noticed and appreciated, not just said without thought or response.

Shopkeepers and restaurant owners may stay politely quiet when a customer enters wearing only a bathing suit, perhaps under the sheerest of cover-ups, but they are not really comfortable with skimpy attire. Arubans are accustomed to tourists wearing shorts and T-shirts around the town, but beachwear is not considered proper while walking through Oranjestad or beyond the resorts.

Somehow this extreme politeness is suspended once they are behind the wheel of a car on the highway or need a parking spot. Islanders will park anywhere—on sidewalks and other places that would amaze—but they do try to respect and not block driveways most of the time. During Carnival and special events, anything goes. They are very good about allowing traffic to filter during commuter-hour snarls in town, or where there is roadwork; again, their innate courteousness comes into play.

CONCEPTS OF TIME

As with much of the Caribbean and Latin America, punctuality on Aruba is highly subjective. Being influenced by Dutch timeliness and dealing daily with American expectations has generally improved the Aruban attitude. Visitors do need to learn patience as most things are done at island pace. If planning a day tour, be sure to allow plenty of time for breakfast or select buffet style if you wish to be ready by pickup time. Dinners will usually be leisurely, but that is the purpose of such a vacation, is it not?

Tips for Travelers

WHAT TO PACK

Aruba is decidedly casual. Typical resort wear will easily see visitors through the week. Fancy dresses and sports jackets are not required. Visitors may wish to bring some sweaters or blazers, as air-conditioned restaurants can get chilly, as can nights, when walking about in Aruba's gusty trade winds.

Sunny days of intense tropical strength require a goodly supply of sunblock. Sunglasses are always needed. A spare pair of prescription glasses is advised, but contact lenses can be easily replaced. During the fall rainy season it is a good idea to pack some mosquito repellent, particularly if you plan to do much dining alfresco. The electric current is the same as the United States; no special adapters are required. Roaming charges on cell phones can be outrageous. Phones can be rented for far less. It is not necessary to change money for local currency. U.S. dollars, traveler's checks, and credit cards are readily accepted everywhere.

TRAVELERS WITH DISABILITIES

Aruba still has a ways to go to be completely wheelchair-friendly, but they are industriously working toward this. Oranjestad is getting a face-lift wherever you look, with the needs of pedestrians and those with disabilities integrated into the plans. An ambulance dispatch station has been set up at Playa Linda Resort, centrally located to all of Palm Beach. A few businesses offer transportation in vans set up to board individuals in wheelchairs.

Lite Life Medicab

Before arrival, travelers with wheelchairs can arrange for **Lite Life Medicab** (Hooiberg-Kavel, 297/585-9764, U.S. number 786/955-8829, info@litelifemedicab@com, 6am-9pm daily, $80 round-trip from airport) for transport to and from their hotel, or wherever needed. The company has several vehicles. Some deploy hydraulic lifts and have room for multiple wheelchairs with additional attendant seating; others are smaller vans with ramps.

Posada Clinic Aruba

Individuals requiring dialysis during their stay can set up appointments with **Posada Clinic Aruba** (L. G. Smith Blvd. 14, 297/582-9477, posadaaruba@gmail.com, 7am-7pm Mon.-Sat.) in Oranjestad. Visiting patients are very positive about the cleanliness of the facility and the capable staff, whom they describe as exceptionally friendly and accommodating. Each of the 13 dialysis stations has its own cable television. Staff members serve snacks and refreshments during sessions. It is located right across from the Surfside Marina Hotel and very easy to find.

Aruba Happy Wheels

Special wheelchairs designed to enter the water and travel on sand are rented out by **Aruba Happy Wheels** (Palm Beach 472, 297/568-4787, adaptedhappywheels@hotmail.com, $40 for 24 hours). A fold-up platform may also be rented to allow wheelchair access on difficult surfaces. They will deliver the equipment to resorts and offer discounts for long-term rentals.

A Fantasy Wedding on Aruba

Destination weddings are in. The advantages are numerous (including some financial ones). A winter wedding can be conducted outdoors with clear skies, comfortable temperatures, and no coats.

For the legal ceremony, Aruba's Town Hall is picturesque with a beautiful interior. Government staffers perform the ceremonies with grace and emotional fervor. Formal papers must be submitted at least one month prior to the nuptials, in Dutch. This is where the assistance of local wedding planners is vital. They will translate the required forms, which are requested of the prospective bride and groom. Forms must be accompanied by:

- Birth certificate with the names of BOTH parents and an embossed Apostille Seal
- Copy of passport/picture ID
- Divorce Certificate with Apostille Seal OR Final Decree of Divorce with Apostille
- Death Certificate with Apostille Seal (if applicable)
- Letter of Intent to Marry
- U.S./Canada Negative Statement of Marriage or Affidavit of Single Status; must include Apostille Seal

Begin collecting the documents at least six months prior to the planned wedding date. Two witnesses must be present for the ceremony. (The wedding planner can provide them if necessary.)

If conducting only a spiritual ceremony on the beach, a proof of marriage is required. Ministers need to see a certified copy of the wedding certificate. Several nondenominational ministers perform touching ceremonies in any location of your choice. **Diane Keijzer** (www.dianekeijzer.com) does a fine job. The Catholic Church will not perform destination weddings because of the required spiritual preparation.

Every major resort on Aruba has a dedicated wedding planner. Their services are available only if you are using the resort's facilities. Veteran independent wedding planners include:

- **Aruba Fairy Tale Weddings** (297/593-0045, www.arubafairytales.com)
- **Aruba Weddings by Bonny** (297/730-0350, www.arubaweddingsbybonny.com)
- **Cayena Weddings** (973/460-0284 or 212/292-4221, www.cayenaweddings.com)
- **Ceremonies & Celebrations in Aruba** (321/473-3856, candcaruba@yahoo.com)

A renewal of vows does not require the abovementioned paperwork.

Aruba.com has a separate wedding section and a bridal registry, http://bridal.aruba.com, where friends and family can purchase gifts for newlyweds honeymooning on Aruba. Spa days, sailing cruises or tours, flowers, and romantic dinners can be purchased in advance to give as wedding gifts. Newlyweds-to-be should investigate the **One Happy Honeymoon** perks offered in cooperation with local resorts.

GAY AND LESBIAN TRAVELERS

Aruba has an active and open gay and lesbian community, and islanders are quite nonchalant about visitors' sexual orientation. There are some Caribbean islands where sodomy and homosexuality are capital crimes, but Aruba has no such discrimination.

There are frequent gay and lesbian cruises that include Aruba among their ports of call; all visitors are welcome.

TRAVELING WITH CHILDREN

Traveling with children, no matter the destination, presents some distinctive considerations and precautions. Aruba is, moreover, surrounded by the sea, which is adjacent to most resorts, along with on-site swimming pools, so water safety for children is paramount. Aruba's beaches do not have lifeguards stationed along the shores, so parents must be vigilant.

Utmost precaution with the tropical sun on young skin is also a priority. Better than continually annoying a squirming child to reapply sunblock, keep a supply of old T-shirts for them to wear in the water, and dry ones on hand to change into afterwards.

The excitement of travel and the constant activity, along with tropical temperatures, usually result in overtired, cranky youngsters. Keep this in mind when making dinner plans. Aruba has many family-oriented eateries that provide children's menus.

If a child appears to be ill, medical service can be accessed 24 hours a day. Resort staff will assist in calling the doctor on duty and arranging a consultation. There are always at least two drugstores on the island providing off-hours service to fill prescriptions.

Aruba is, generally, a very family-friendly island. Children are welcome and respected, and most resorts provide a wealth of activities to keep them engaged throughout the day. They also have a roster of vetted babysitters, and parents can dine out with peace of mind. Sensitive to the needs of families, the Aruba Tourism Authority (ATA) has devised the **One Cool Family** program. It is effective June 1-September 30 for kids ages 12 and under. Save cash on dining and accommodations by signing up through the website (www.aruba.com). Then present your One Cool Family ID when reserving with participating vendors.

WOMEN TRAVELING ALONE

Despite some notoriety and misconceptions, female visitors experience no more unpleasant encounters or attention than they would at home, and likely far less. Making safe and smart decisions about new acquaintances in bars or on the beach shouldn't change under the influences of a tropical moon and a romantic destination.

Female tourists are welcome at various clubs and nightspots; the opportunity to mix and mingle with locals is plentiful. Islanders are quite accustomed to women traveling on their own. However, it is advised not to leave an unfinished drink in a crowded club. Finish it before going off to the bathroom or dance floor. If it was left unattended for some time, leave it and order a new drink.

Incidents of women being bothered while walking unattended at night are rare to nonexistent, but being alert or avoiding such situations is always advisable. Larger hotels post security guards day and night to discourage intruders. Several overt and hidden security cameras are installed at all major resorts and along popular walkways. Stay in well-lit, populated areas.

Health and Safety

SUN PROTECTION

Aruba is only 12° north of the equator. Those who have traveled to the tropics know that the sun here has to be taken very seriously. "I never burn" are famous last words for those hiding out in their rooms for a major portion of their vacation. Common sense and the wealth of information available about skin damage from the sun have resulted in most visitors being smart about exposure and protection. Unfortunately, sunbathers who don't see any color blooming after a few days panic at the thought of not having a tan to show off on their return. Dermatologists know you don't get a great tan in three days, but a surprising number try for and expect it.

Aruba's Pure Water

Aruba began the process of producing sweet water from the sea in 1931, at one point boasting the world's largest plant. Wells and cisterns were originally deployed to obtain fresh water. **Water-en Energiebedrijf Aruba N.V.,** or **WEB,** is Aruba's water and power-producing plant, located at Balashi. Hence the term "Balashi Cocktail," meaning a drink of cold tap water.

Aruba's plant still ranks among the top 10 water desalination plants in the world. Executive engineers at WEB are credited with innovations in the field that have revolutionized the industry.

Frequent visitors often declare the water straight from the tap "the best in the world," a refreshing relief from the heavy chlorination to which most are accustomed. This has been purposefully planned by WEB engineers to insure it is exceptionally clean and refreshing for drinking and bathing. It is also very soft, so less shampoo or soap is required to work up a good lather.

Until 2008, Aruba deployed the unique practice of running the distilled seawater over coral to imbue it with phosphorus and manganese to enliven what would otherwise be flat and tasteless, while providing necessary minerals for the body.

Originally, a steam method of distillation was deployed, but in 2008 WEB opened its first sea water reverse osmosis (SWRO) plant, which is far more energy efficient. Steam plants are steadily being retired as more SWRO plants are brought online. The first produces 44,000 metric tons daily, more than enough to meet Aruba's average daily demand. In July of 2012, a new plant with a capacity of 24,000 metric tons began operation. Combined, they make WEB the largest freshwater producer in the Caribbean.

There is great debate about the strength of sun protection people should wear. Without a good base tan, SPF 15 should be considered the minimum strength to use. Limit sun exposure the first few days, and take a break during the peak midday hours.

Areas that many forget to cover, which are quite sensitive, include behind the ears, the back of the neck, and particularly the tops of feet and the instep, which tend to be turned to the sun and get maximum exposure. Commonly, while lying around the beach, everyone likes to break up the day with a relaxing walk along the shoreline. The gentle waves lap over their feet, insidiously washing away sun protection. It is necessary to reapply after a bit of exercise.

Even if you are not actually sunbathing, but just walking around town or touring, sun exposure is no less fierce and protection should be worn. Use sunblock or wear shirts that cover the shoulders.

Children require special attention; particularly if they are constantly in and out of the water. This will wash off any protection. Often kids are impatient and reapplying lotion constantly is a tedious chore. It is a good idea to have a few old T-shirts they can wear in the water to protect tender young shoulders, and a hat for that vulnerable back of the neck. Keep some dry shirts for them to change into when resting and playing on shore. Hair braiding on the beach is very popular, and makes hair easy to care for. However, this exposes the scalp, and strong sunblock should be applied between the rows of braids.

ALCOHOL

Aruba's many fine restaurants entice visitors to indulge in exceptional, often rich meals, every night. The beach bars, happy hours, and exotic cocktails that taste like desserts encourage the overconsumption of alcohol. This is often at levels to which most are unaccustomed. A few days of this, and it is not surprising that many visitors are afflicted with seriously upset digestion, or worse. Don't blame the local water.

Alcohol also dehydrates, contributing to possible heatstroke or heat exhaustion. Periodically, take a break on both food and alcohol overconsumption. Even on vacation, perhaps even more so, moderation in all things is wise. Drink plenty of water, juices, or nonalcoholic beverages.

DENGUE FEVER

Despite Aruba being a desert island, it does get rainfall, particularly in autumn—the rainy season for the region. Showers mean standing water, and standing water means mosquitoes. Usually the island's strong winds keep them to a minimum, but during the late fall and early winter, mosquitoes and dengue fever can be an issue. The rest of the Caribbean, which receives far more rainfall year-round, reports much greater numbers for dengue fever, but it should not be discounted on Aruba. The amount of rainfall over the season is a significant factor in dengue statistics.

Dengue virus is carried by the Aedes aegypti mosquito, which requires clean water, not dirty, in which to lay their eggs. The mosquito has very distinctive white striping on its legs. Standing puddles are not breeding grounds for the Aedes aegypti, but any sort of container in which rainwater can pool provides a place for them to lay their eggs. This is another reason why controlling litter is so important.

There are four strains of dengue. Each strain can produce a general malaise, similar to flu, but with distinctive symptoms. Dengue symptoms can include severe headache; pain around the eyes, back, and joints; high fever; a rash; and possibly nausea and diarrhea. Depending on the strain, symptoms can be minor to severe. It is a virus, so antibiotics are useless.

A single bout of dengue can be highly unpleasant, but is not fatal, unless, like for the flu, other chronic conditions are present. Once a person is infected with a particular strain, antibodies are manufactured in the system, and the individual will be immune to that strain for life. If bitten by a mosquito carrying a different strain, then the reaction of the two in the body can be catastrophic. Dengue often mimics flu symptoms, so do not dismiss being ill. Go see a local doctor, as they will also arrange for blood tests to confirm if infected with dengue.

Aruba's Department of Health and Office of Communicable Diseases pays very close attention to this situation. Inspectors travel from house to house and business premises searching for breeding grounds. Homeowners and landlords are warned and citations issued for noncompliance in correcting conditions favorable for mosquitoes. Each year, in the fall, they mount an information and prevention campaign.

Bush Medicine

On the islands, a deep-rooted (yes, pun intended) reliance on natural, homegrown remedies is rampant, even among the most erudite and educated islanders. Every drugstore has a shelf of herbs. The leaves and roots are for steeping to produce fresh, holistic teas. These are not in commercial packaging, but fresh, individual baggies, with a label sometimes describing their purpose. It's best to ask the pharmacist how to use the various items. Freshly processed lotions and potions are also sold; some have to be made to order and kept refrigerated, such as *Lotio Alba,* a mild, natural remedy for heat rash.

Most residents cultivate a few aloe plants in their garden, cutting a piece of leaf to apply the fresh juice to burns. Many believe the beneficial property of the plant goes well beyond the dermis, and will drink the juices mixed with water. It takes quite some determination and a healthy dose of honey to make this even remotely palatable. Others even nibble on the gelatinous meat inside the leaves, also hard to imagine for anyone familiar with the malodorous species that grows on Aruba.

HOSPITALS AND EMERGENCY SERVICES

Aruba has a doctor on duty outside of normal office hours. They will conduct examinations and treatment at the **Dr. Horacio E. Oduber Hospital** (Dr. Horacio E. Oduber Hospital Blvd. 1, 297/527-4000, www.arubahospital.com, 24 hours daily). A number of resorts have a local doctor they work with regularly, who will come to the resort and make "house calls" or accept visitors at their office. Inquire with the front desk. If the resort does not have a doctor, staff will advise you or call an ambulance if needed. Emergency room service at the hospital is $316 for examination and diagnosis; X-rays and other testing are extra.

Emergency services for visitors must be paid for in cash or by credit card. The hospital or doctor will not accept U.S. or foreign coverage. Receipts will be issued for insurance claims once you return home. The same procedure is in place for a regular policy or a travel insurance policy.

Aruba's hospital is a clean, modern facility, continually being renovated and improved. They can perform MRIs, CAT scans, and other tests. In 2010 the hospital acquired a hyperbaric chamber. As of 2015, it is undergoing a total renovation and refurbishment that will double the number of beds, modernize the wards, and add several new diagnostic tools and specialized treatment facilities.

Emergency Hotline

To further expedite emergency service for all visitors and residents, Aruba established a 911 number for a 24-hour hotline. Responders dispatch police, the fire department, or ambulances to a location, as needed.

PHARMACIES

Prescriptions must be filled and paid for at a pharmacy or *botica*. If at night or on Sunday, prescriptions will be at the venue on duty. Pharmacies on Aruba are open 8am-8pm Monday-Saturday. Two pharmacies remain open on Sunday, holidays, and after-hours. There will be one servicing each side of the island, with the bridge at Spaanslagoen the dividing line. They change on a rotating basis. The *botica* on duty will be posted in newspapers and in the window of all pharmacies. The information can also be obtained by calling the hospital.

The following pharmacies are close to the resort areas. All pharmacy hours are 8am-8pm Monday-Saturday.

- **Oranjestad: Botica Kibrahacha** (Havenstraat 30, 297/583-4908), directly behind the Royal Plaza Mall
- **Eagle and Manchebo Beach: Botica di Servicio Eagle** (Caya Punto Brabo 17, 297/587-9011), next to the Dr. Horacio E. Oduber Hospital
- **Palm Beach, Malmok, and Noord: Botica Santa Anna** (Noord 41B, 297/586-2020), right next to Caribbean Palm Villas Resort
- **Santa Cruz, Paradera, and Piedra Plat: Botica Santa Cruz** (Santa Cruz 54 A, 297/585-8776), on the corner across from Mundo Nobo Supermarket

CRIME

According to statistics and the CIA Factbook, Aruba is one of the safest destinations in the Caribbean. Incidents of wallets and handbags forgotten at a store or market but returned intact are common. However, there is no place in the world that is utterly crime-free.

Petty Theft

As in any vacation destination, petty theft by a few active miscreants can be an issue. Thieves know that vacationers have extra cash, traveler's checks, cameras, and other valuable electronics or jewelry.

Safes and Deposit Boxes

Safes and deposit boxes are provided by nearly all accommodations. This is the place for passports and extra monies, credit cards, and bank cards. The purchase of a watertight "beach box" for cash, a credit card, or small valuables is a minor but worthwhile investment that can be worn in the water. Do not leave a bag with your watch and wallet unattended on the beach when taking a swim; this is simple common sense.

Car Theft

If you are driving around the island in an open car, such as a jeep, and parking in an isolated spot to take a swim, do not leave valuables in the car. Even a closed car should be kept in sight; it is always possible to break a window and open the trunk. Wear a waist pack or small backpack for exploring the caves and Arikok National Park. Individuals who victimize tourists know the places where they are most likely to leave valuables and cash behind. Carry very little and find methods, such as watertight carriers or simply sealing them in a few plastic bags, to foil ill intentions while you frolic in the water. The same applies while sitting on the beach of your resort. Do not leave a beach bag filled with valuables behind. Take with you only what you need and keep it in a watertight container you can wear in the water. It is difficult for police to make a case after the fact, unless specific items are recovered and there is definitive forensic evidence.

Car theft was on the rise for a few years, particularly of the most common rental cars. The KPA (Korps Politie Aruba, www.kparuba.com) created a specialized task force and in 2010 arrested over 25 individuals in a theft and chop shop ring, which has relieved the situation to a great degree.

Information and Services

STRAY DOGS AND CATS

It is unfortunate, but the practice of neutering domestic animals has not taken hold sufficiently to control the unwanted dog and cat population of Aruba. Some will take the animals to be euthanized. Others may drop animals somewhere in the hopes that a kind person will adopt them or that they will fend for themselves. This is a state of mind prevalent throughout the Caribbean and Latin America. Most islands do not have a collection service to take the unwanted dogs off the streets, despite tourists finding it distressing to see them hungry or injured. Visitors need not fear that they may be rabid, as rabies does not exist on Aruba.

Cas Animal Foundation

Aruba's first no-kill animal refuge is the ultimate goal of **Cas Animal Foundation** (hotline 297/742-8732). Founder Kirsten Arndt has converted three homes into a temporary facility, while fundraising to build a proper center.

Cas Animal conducts various fundraising and awareness-raising events during the year. The Divi Links hosts a golf tournament at the end of September. Dog owners are invited to invent costumes and show off their four-legged friends during the annual Carnival Doggy Pawrade. Cas Animal maintains an Animal Ambulance to pick up strays. The foundation also welcomes donations. They can be in the form of paying veterinary bills or providing bags of dog food; anything is helpful.

Another primary objective of Cas Animal is to facilitate the adoption of local mixed breeds by tourists. Quite often, one of Aruba's sweet and intelligent strays will capture the heart of a sympathetic tourist. Arndt will assist in any way possible in obtaining inspection and treatment for the dog from a qualified vet, allowing it to pass U.S. standards for importation. She will also assist in acquiring a carrier and arranging transport. Vacationers returning to the United States or Canada with an Aruban dog or cat is a far more common occurrence than most imagine. The pets adapt well to their new environment.

ELECTRICITY

Adapters for electrical appliances and devices are not required for travelers from the United States and Canada. Aruba uses the same 110-120 volts AC (60 cycle). European appliances will require adapters, but it is likely that hotels can provide them. If not, they are readily available at home or hardware stores. Some facilities may not have an outlet that handles a three-pronged plug, but adapters for that situation are also on hand. It is advisable to notify your resort of your requirements before arrival to ensure they have an adapter reserved for your use.

Aruba is far less prone to power outages than in the past. Aruba's power plant, WEB, has greatly increased its output and efficiency of production, though a lightning storm could result in a loss of current. It is advisable to unplug all appliances or devices, as the surge when the power comes back on has been known to burn out anything from laptops to refrigerator motors.

BANKS, MONEY, AND FOREIGN EXCHANGE

The official currency of the island is **Arubian florins,** officially expressed in writing as **AWG.** The term "guilders" may also be heard among locals, this is similar to saying "bucks" instead of dollars. The official exchange rate at banks is 1.77 florins to $1. This can vary on the street from 1.75-1.80, depending on the shop; it is completely arbitrary. Supermarkets usually exchange at 1.75, where prices are strictly in florins. Jewelry stores will most often exchange at 1.80, though prices are marked in dollars.

Aruba has four important banks. One is in Oranjestad, and the other branches are strategically located in Palm Beach, conveniently close to some of the resorts. They are all only a short walk heading away from the water, past the Sasaki Highway.

It is not necessary to change money from U.S. dollars to Arubian florins. Stores and restaurants readily accept dollars, traveler's checks, and U.S. and Canadian credit cards. A valid photo I.D. will be required when using credit or bank cards and traveler's checks at shops and markets. ATMs accepting MasterCard, Visa Cirrus, and Visa Plus for cash withdrawals or advances are located in every mall, casino, gas station, and major grocery store.

Caribbean Mercantile Bank

Caribbean Mercantile Bank (CMB; Caya G. F. Croes 53, Palm Beach 4-B, 297/522-3000, www.cmbnv.com, 8am-4pm Mon.-Fri.) is a subsidiary of Maduro & Curiel Bank of Curacao, which is affiliated with The Bank of Nova Scotia. The Palm Beach branch is midway between the Sasaki Highway and Santa Ana Church on the principal Palm Beach road.

Royal Bank of Canada

RBC (Italiestraat 36, 297/523-3100, www.rbtt.com, 8am-4pm Mon.-Fri.), the Caribbean chain of the Royal Bank of Canada, has taken over RBTT, a widespread regional institution. The main headquarters is very close to all Manchebo resorts, on the Sasaki Highway.

Aruba Bank

Aruba's first bank, **Aruba Bank** (Camacuri 12, 297/527-7777, www.arubabank.com, 8am-4pm Mon.-Fri.) is affiliated with the regional Orco Group. The headquarters is near the airport, but there is a branch in Hato, which is quite close to the Eagle/Manchebo Beach resorts.

Banco di Caribe

Aruba's fourth major bank, **Banco di Caribe** (Vondellaan 31, 297/523-2000, www.bancodicaribe.com, 8am-4pm Mon.-Fri.) has many ATMs around the island, but no branches beyond the Oranjestad headquarters.

COMMUNICATIONS

Internet and Long-Distance Calls

Calling the United States from hotels can be an expensive and often time-consuming affair. Guests often have to wait for the hotel operator to make the connection and pass it through to their rooms. There are several "Call Home" phone stations to be found around shopping centers and near resorts. These only require the swipe of a credit card, but they automatically charge $15, even when there is no answer.

Roaming charges on cell phones from home can often be outrageous. Aruba cell phone systems work on charging only for calls made, with users not charged for calls received. Renting a cell can prove an economical alternative for keeping in touch.

SETAR

Aruba's national telecommunication company, **SETAR** (Palm Beach z/n, 297/525-1000, http://setar.aw, 9am-5:30pm Mon.-Sat.) is the company that installs all landlines. It has a branch in Palm Beach where long-distance calls can be made at minimal rates. It is located right next to Amazonia restaurant. Phones are outside the shop and available at all hours. An adjacent vending machine dispenses phone cards (the phone cards are needed for making calls). The main headquarters is on the outskirts of Oranjestad.

SETAR also maintains a cell phone rental kiosk in the arrivals hall of the Reina Beatrix International Airport (9am-11am and noon-6pm Mon.-Sat.) to arrange mobile service immediately upon arrival.

INTERNET SERVICES

Islanders take pride in being technologically savvy and Internet-wise; social networking is very popular on Aruba. Almost all resorts and guesthouses have Wi-Fi, a majority of them for free. Major resorts offer in-house communications stations for guests to check their email and chat with the folks back home.

Most laptops and tablets do not necessarily connect to the Internet once beyond the server at your resort. Some resorts charge for Wi-Fi or only allow for one device. Many visitors complain about the quality of connection as well, particularly when using more than one device. Long-term vacationers at timeshare resorts have found **MIO** (Caya G. F. Betico Croes 222, 168/600-0077, http://mioaruba.com, 9am-5:30pm Mon.-Sat., $40 for device, $40 for bandwidth) offers a viable solution. USB plug and play modems provide speedy Internet connections anyplace without long-term contracts and are very moderately priced. The MiFi wireless device provides fast, reliable service to up to five devices simultaneously. Bandwidth can be purchased in monthly packages starting at 4GB.

MEDIA

Newspapers

Aruba is an island with a highly literate population that likes to keep informed. Despite the ascendancy of web-based news, it has several printed papers in each of the four predominant languages. The English paper is *Aruba Today*. It presents various aspects of world and local news and can be found distributed for free at hotels, supermarkets, fast-food franchises, and various other locations every morning.

ARUBA TODAY

Aruba Today (Weststraat 22, 297/582-7800, Mon.-Sat., free) places more of a focus on international news, with a few local pages dedicated to superficial events. On Mondays, they feature an international version of *The New York Times* in an additional section.

ARUBA HERALD

Another paper only found online is the ***Aruba Herald*** (297/583-2424, http://arubaherald.com), with a diversity of local news. They cover every aspect of island life that makes the Papiamento papers, from domestic disputes to lost dogs. International coverage is generally reserved to politics and top headlines.

Tourist Magazines

An inordinate number of annual tourist publications in English provide information on restaurants, services, and island happenings. They can be found freely distributed at supermarkets, hotel lobbies, restaurants, and stores. Hotels provide a hard copy of *Aruba Nights* in every room. The bible of Aruba's Carnival—*Bacchanal*—is printed in both English and Papiamento.

The English magazines available are:

- *Aruba Experience*
- *Aruba Nights*
- *Bacchanal*
- *Destination Aruba*
- *I Love Aruba*
- *Island Gourmet*
- *Island Temptations*

Radio and Television

Aruba has 18 FM radio stations and 3 AM stations. There are three island-based TV stations: **TeleAruba,** channel 13; **ATV,** channel 15; and **TOP TV,** channel 22; with two Venezuelan stations, picked up on channels 10 and 12. Television and radio programming is consistently in Papiamento and Spanish, with some Dutch newscasts. ATV (channel 15) has an English Lifestyle and News program for local events at 7:15pm Monday-Friday, with commentator Yentl Lieuw. All resorts are connected to SETAR Cable or have satellite dishes to carry U.S. programming and sporting events, as do most bars and lounges.

Easy 97.9 FM radio plays a nice mix of soft listening music from the United States and the Caribbean. Commentary is practically nonexistent. It is relatively commercial-free and broadcasts 24 hours daily. **Hits 100** radio station at **100.9 FM** targets the 35+ audience with Billboard hits from the 1980s and 1990s. Other radio stations are geared to the cultural tastes of the region.

WEIGHTS AND MEASURES

Aruba uses the international metric system in all things. Fresh meats, produce, and baked goods are measured by kilo when purchased by weight. An ounce measure in metric is one-tenth of a kilo, a bit less then a quarter of a pound in English and American measurements.

A kilo is 2.2 U.S. pounds. A liter is 3.3 quarts, or less than a gallon. Prices on gas pumps in Aruba are per liter of gasoline, and it is quite expensive.

Distance and speed postings on roads are in kilometers.

Resources

Papiamento Phrasebook

Islanders' fluency in English leaves little need to use Papiamento in tourist venues. It is rare to find someone working at resorts, restaurants, or shops who does not speak and understand English well.

Still when patronizing native restaurants or shops, a few phrases can be helpful, and sometimes necessary. Anyone with a good working knowledge of Spanish will also do well in these circumstances, as it is more often used by those who don't know any English. This may be because of a media orientation and input from the more southern latitudes.

PRONUNCIATION GUIDE

Papiamento combines elements from Spanish, Portuguese, Dutch, and also English, with even the occasional French, such as *petit pois* for peas. Emphasis is frequently placed on the last syllable of a word, but keep in mind that a shift in emphasis can actually change the meaning of a word, morphing it from a verb to adjective for instance.

Consonants

Only a few consonants differ from standard English pronunciation

dj as in "join"—"djispi" is a precocious child; "djucu," a good luck charm

g can be normal, as in "go," but is frequently soft "h" as in "hello"

j is a "y" sound, as in "year"; June and July are "Yuni" and "Yuli"

ñ is a "ny" sound, as in the Spanish words such as "señor" or "aña"

zj is a soft "j," such as "zjilea" (jelly), but rarely seen

Vowels

Standard vowel pronunciation is very different. The long vowels of English never come up.

a as in "papa"

e as in "they"

i as in "police"

o as in "blow"

u as in "dude"

u as in "buck"

The influence of Dutch can be seen in the oft-used *IJ,* the Dutch way of writing *Y* as in "ray." An example is *Tamarijn,* with the final syllable pronounced "rain."

TERMS OF ADDRESS

I *mi* or *Ami* (Example: "*Mi ta bai*"—"I am going"; "Who gets this?"—"*Ami.*")

You *bo* or *Abo* (Example: "*Undo bo ta biba?*"—"Where do you live?"; "Who do you love?"—"*Abo*")

he or she *e*

us or we *nos*

they *nan* (Also added to the end of words to make them plural as in *mucha* for "child" and *muchanan* for "children.")

IMPORTANT GREETINGS AND RESPONSES

Good Day *Bon Dia* (Bon DEE-A)

Good Afternoon *Bon Tardi* (Bon TAR-dee)

Good Evening, Good Night *Bon Nochi* (Bon NO-chee)

How are you? *Con ta Bai?* (literally translates as "How does it go?")
Everything is good? *Tur cos ta bon?*
Yes, good, thank you. *Si, bon, danki.*
Good enough; ok. *Basta Bon.*
Welcome. *Bon Bini.*
Please. *Por Fabor.*
Thank you. *Danki.*
Goodbye. *Ayo.*

USEFUL PHRASES

It is a pleasure to meet you. *Ta un plaser di conocebo.*
Until next time. *Te otro biaha.*
Have a nice day *Pasa un bon dia.*
What time is it? *Cuant'or tin?*
I don't understand you. *Mi no ta comprende bo.*
Do you speak English? *Bo por papia Ingles?*
My name is... *Mi nomber ta...*
What is your name? *Con jamabo?*
How much? *Cuanto ta?*
How do you say...? *Con bo ta bisa...?*
Excuse me. *Despensa.*
I love you. *Mi stimabo.*
Help! *Yudami!*
Fire! *Candela!*
Merry Christmas and Happy New Year *Bon Pasco y Bon Aña.*
Happy Birthday *Cumpleaño Felis*
Congratulations *Pabien* or *Bon Suerte*
anthem and flag *himno y bandera*

Suggested Reading

DESCRIPTIONS AND TRAVEL

Bäcker, Jennifer, and Wodl, Josefa, photographers. *Wings Over Aruba.* Aruba: Wings Global Media, 2011. The ultimate coffee table photography book of Aruba is very big, very bright, with new aerial angles of the prettiest places.

Bertsch, Werner. *Aruba Tropical Moods of the Caribbean.* Oranjestad: DeWit/Van Dorp, 2008. Another picture book by Bertsch, focused on the colors of Carnival.

Bertsch, Werner, and Croes, Charles. *Aruba, I am your Island.* Aruba: Self-published, 2012. A lovely picture book from Werner Bertsch, combined with the reflective prose and poetry of Charles Croes, well-known as the storyteller of Aruba forums, comes in a plain paperback or a handsome sleeve for gift giving.

Bertsch, Werner, and Hiller, Linda. *Aruba Picture Book.* Oranjestad: DeWit/Van Dorp, 2011. Bertsch loves photographing Aruba. This collection of his charming shots with captions by Hiller is a smaller, budget-priced paperback.

Boland, Matt (author), and Kock, Eva. *Aruba Tips for Travelers.* N.p.: Vitae Publishing, 2005. This compiles a longtime resident's folksy bits of advice on what to expect when vacationing on Aruba. He clarifies all those new and funny things that make visitors scratch their heads in confusion.

Knevel, Theo. *Aruba, Ariba.* Aruba: ATA Publishing, 2011. Stunning aerial photography will inspire anyone to take a helicopter tour. It provides a very interesting perspective.

Night, Sam. *Aruba: Including its History, the Alto Visto Chapel, the Ayo Rock Formations, the Quadriki Caves, Fort Zoutman, and More.* N.p.: Earth Eyes Travel Guides, 2012. Culled from Wikipedia articles and images under Creative Commons licensing, this guide gathers popular subjects within one portable resource.

HISTORY

Bongers, Evert. *Creating One Happy Island.* N.p.: Self-published, 2009. Put out in commemoration of the 50th anniversary of the opening of the Aruba Caribbean Resort—considered the defining moment when tourism became a pillar of the island's economy—this compendium of a few island writers showcases the visionary personalities that established Aruba as a vacation giant in the Caribbean.

Dijkhoff, Raymundo, A.C.F., and Linville, Marlene S. *The Marine Shell Heritage.* Oranjestad: Aruba Archaeological Museum Press, 2004. The head of the museum's Scientific Department has edited essays on shore areas and a society dependent on marine animals, particularly mollusks. Shells were used for everything from building to decoration and money.

Hartog, Dr. Johannes. *Aruba Picture Book. A Short History of Aruba.* Oranjestad: DeWit/Van Dorp, 2003. A very short history, indeed. Dr. Hartog, historian and archaeologist, was one of the first to initiate digs and investigate the island's Amerindian population. The book focuses on their time occupying the island.

Kock, Adolf (Dufi). *The Story of the German Freighter E.S. Antilla.* N.p.: Self-published, 2012. A longtime friend and chronicler of Lagoite culture and life at the colony recalls WWII. This is a very detailed description of the dramatic events leading up to the sinking of the *Antilla.*

Ridderstaat, Jorge R. *The Lago Story.* Aruba: Cha Aruba, 2008. A visually beautiful and thorough accounting of Aruba's economic history prepares the reader by first painting a picture of the island's initial development for mining gold and phosphate. It passes through the years when the refinery was in its prime, WWII, and then the decline of its influence and the growth of tourism.

van der Klooster, Olga, with Bakker, Michel. *Monument Guide Aruba.* Amsterdam/Aruba: Kit Publishers/Charuba Foundation, 2013. An attractive guide to a majority of Aruba's many landmark buildings. Each page is dedicated to one of the 127 structures profiled, with beautiful color plates and a detailed history of the landmark, frequently including the effort undertaken to save it from demolition. The front and back covers fold out to provide detailed maps of Oranjestad and San Nicolas, respectively. Eight lovely postcards for sending or framing are at the back of the book.

Versteeg, Aad H., and Rostain, Stephen. *Archeology of Aruba—The Tanki Flip Site.* Oranjestad: Aruba Archaeological Museum Press, 1997. This book profiles Aruba's first major archaeological dig and the revelations it contained.

Versteeg, Aad H., and Ruiz, Arminda C. *Reconstruction in Brasilwood Island—The Archeology & Landscape of Indian Aruba.* Oranjestad: Aruba Archaeological Museum Press, 1995. NAMA administrators and archaeologist Versteeg delve into the significance of artifacts.

NATURE

De Boer, Bart, with Newton, Eric, and Restall, Robin. *Birds of Aruba, Curacao, and Bonaire.* Princeton, N.J.: Princeton Field Guides, 2012. This is the first comprehensive field guide to the birds of the region. This compact and portable book contains close to 1,000 color illustrations on 71 color plates, helping to identify the more than 200 species that inhabit the three islands.

Roll, Barbara. *Explorer's Guide to Aruba.* Beckenham, UK: Loft Publishing, 2010. The author's charming way of introducing Aruba and its endemic animals to children, with highly entertaining artwork and prose.

MISCELLANEOUS

Croes, Robetico. *Anatomy of Demand in International Tourism: The case of Aruba.* Saarbrücken, Germany: Lap Lambert Academic Publishing, 2010. This is a must-read for tourism executives from Aruba's former Minister of Tourism, who now holds a chair at the UCF School of Hospitality Management. He examines the dynamics of a small island and the impact of international tourism, based on statistics from an extended study.

Fenzi-Thayer Sargent, Jewell. *This is the Way We Cook!* Oranjestad: DeWit/Van Dorp, 1971. Already in its 14th printing, this is a compendium of recipes from the outstanding cooks of Aruba, Bonaire, Curacao, Saba, St. Eustatius, and San Maarten, for those who wish to try their hand at preparing some of the regional cuisine.

Viana, Carlos. *Prescriptions from Paradise.* Merritt Island, Fl.: Healing Spirit Press, 2012. Viana, a holistic healer and certified in Chinese medicine, presents a compilation of more than 10 years of health columns. The easy-to-understand entries are organized from A to Z. His years of practice have resulted in some quite surprising insights. This book is the winner of the 2012 International Book Award in Alternative Medicine from USA Book News.

Internet Resources

GENERAL INFORMATION

Aruba Online

www.arubatourism.com

This is one of the earliest Aruba websites. It has been around since 1992, founded by a frequent visitor to the island. The site includes information and visitor reviews with links to websites. This is an impartial, basic site. It is left to the visitors to rate and comment on services. Home of a long-established and popular Aruba forum, an excellent resource for current information and input, the site also provides a booking engine for lodging through Travelocity and has webcams set up in various locations around Aruba.

Official Tourism Website of Aruba

www.aruba.com

Aruba's official website is very conscientious about providing complete information on every aspect of island life. It has booking engines for room reservations, activities, and dining out. There is a bridal registry allowing family and friends to purchase excursions, romantic dinners, and shopping as gifts for newlyweds honeymooning on Aruba. Newly married couples can also take advantage of the "One Happy Honeymoon" special discounts on lodging, dining, and activities. Other packages include "One Happy Family."

"The Official Aruba Travel Guide," a downloadable app for smartphones available on the website, has several features for planning activities. Users can review and rate attractions and services, and even upload the information to social media later when back within an Internet service area. A GPS locator provides directions to sites and amenities.

A very busy forum section is an excellent place to pose queries and obtain firsthand advice.

VisitAruba

www.visitaruba.com

This extremely thorough venue is one of Aruba's longest established websites, in operation since 1997. It maintains impartiality, but offers reviews by users and a busy forum. Frequent and first-time visitors are welcome to file trip reports, which can be highly informative.

Find a complete schedule of island events,

including all Carnival events, posted here. The site strives to stay topical and up to date, including useful links to restaurants, car rentals, current weather reports. Visitors can purchase a VisitAruba discount card for $13.95. This does not include postage or delivery to your resort on arrival, which can be arranged for a $3.95 fee. Cardholders get discounts from over 100 island vendors for shopping, dining, accommodations, car rentals, and other activities.

U.S. GOVERNMENT SITES

Centers for Disease Control and Prevention

wwwnc.cdc.gov/travel/destinations/aruba.htm

Full and current information regarding any health issues on Aruba are posted here. Though minimal, it will inform on recommended shots and medicines.

CIA Factbook Aruba

www.cia.gov/library/publications/the-world-factbook/geos/aa.html

The go-to guide for statistical information on every aspect of Aruba: Factual and impartial, it lists everything from geographic details to the number of Internet subscribers.

U.S. Department of Agriculture

www.aphis.usda.gov

Listed here is exactly what is and isn't allowed to be brought back to the U.S. from Aruba, including live animals, plants, and foodstuffs, and why. It explains what diseases, fungi, or parasites are problems in certain areas and what to watch out for.

U.S. Department of State

www.state.gov/r/pa/ei/bgn/22491.htm

Find official U.S. State Department policies and news about Aruba.

U.S. Travel and Customs Regulations

www.cbp.gov/xp/cgov/travel/vacation/kbyg

Find a complete description of all taxable purchases, allowances, and exemptions, plus explanation of duties charged when bringing home purchases over allowances.

ARUBA GOVERNMENT AGENCIES

Aruba Airport Authority

www.airportaruba.com

This complete guide to the Reina Beatrix International Airport includes arrival times, amenities, clearing customs, and the latest notice of restricted items and luggage allowances.

Aruba Department of Foreign Affairs

www.arubaforeignaffairs.com/afa/home.do

An interesting site for travelers to learn about consular affairs and Aruba's international treaty partners, it provides information about all the various international organizations with which Aruba is aligned. Anyone interested in the extent of Aruba's international relations will find the information here.

Aruba Ports Authority

www.arubaports.com

This website offers a complete listing of all cruise schedules and port information including shore safety regulations and communications, cargo services, and cruise statistics.

Arubus

http://arubus.com

The official website of Aruba's mass transit system features complete bus schedules to every route on the island.

Central Bureau of Statistics

www.cbs.aw/cbs/home.do

The Central Bureau of Statistics posts complete statistics on every aspect of island life. This is where the CIA Factbook gets its figures.

DIMAS in English
www.aruba.com/sigma/Entry_Req-Eng.pdf
Find full information on entry requirements for visiting Aruba, as well as residency requirements and permit procedures, with downloadable forms, from Aruba's immigration site.

Government of Aruba
www.overheid.aw
The official site of the government of Aruba is in Dutch, but Google can translate it to English. Every aspect of government authority is explained, and current government news is posted. The translation is somewhat stilted, but informative.

Governor of Aruba
www.kabga.aw
This site explains the position and duties of the queen's appointed representative in Aruba.

Korps Politie Aruba
www.kparuba.com
The official site of Aruba's Police Department shares a history of the service, the location of its various branches and districts, and travel advisories.

BUSINESS

Department of Economic Affairs
www.arubaeconomicaffairs.aw
Details of exactly what it takes to do business in Aruba, like investing, economic reports, acquiring a business license, economic relations, and Aruba's Freezone, are explained in downloadable forms for applying for business and investment permits.

WEATHER

Departmento Meterologico Aruba
www.meteo.aw
Aruba's official site for all weather warning and forecasts provides five-day forecasts, alerts, and live weather maps, in English, Dutch, and Papiamento.

RECREATION

Arikok National Park
www.arubanationalpark.org
Everything you want to know about Arikok National Park is here: maps, hiking trails, park news, and information about island flora and fauna.

Aruba Cruising Guide
www.aruba-cruisingguide.com
This is one of the best sources of need-to-know facts and advice for private yachts. Run by sailors for sailors, it has everything from bottom clearances and how to handle harbor entries to the best places for supplies and repairs. Find downloadable forms for customs and immigration especially for yachts.

IGFA International Billfishing Tournament
www.igfaoffshorechampionship.com
This world series of fishing tournaments for fanatical anglers is conducted at various locations throughout the year. Bucuti and Varadero Yacht Clubs host a qualifying event every October. Only the big fish, marlin and sailfish, qualify, with a strict catch-and-release policy; no fish are taken. This site has detailed information and sign-up forms.

TRAVEL

Cruise Critic
www.cruisecritic.com
This is the most complete site for finding and booking cruises with Aruba as a port of call.

REAL ESTATE

Casnan.com
http://casnan.com/realestate
Every real estate agent on Aruba and their listings are consolidated into this site. View houses, condos, and apartment sales and rentals on the island via agents, without the need to jump around from one website to the next.

VBRO Vacation Rentals for Aruba
www.vrbo.com/vacation-rentals/caribbean/aruba

This is one of the most complete listings to be found anywhere for direct owner to renter arrangements for condominiums, houses, apartments, or timeshares on Aruba. Both sides save on commissions paid to intermediaries.

ISLAND LIFE

The Bent Page
http://bentpage.net

Novelist Daniel Putkowski is a part-time resident of Aruba. He has written three novels set on the island and keeps readers current on island happenings on his blog, punctuated with nice photography and the occasional video. His thoughts take him anywhere and everywhere. There is an entire section dedicated to videos of driving directions.

Lago Colony
www.lago-colony.com

This is an active site where a dedicated group interacts. They have the unusual bond of having been born or raised in the Lago Colony during the Esso/Exxon heyday. Posters share recollections, old photos, and current news. Interesting stories and discussions bring alive this important time in Aruba's history.

Temple Beth Israel Aruba
http://bethisrael-aruba.blogspot.com

Visitors curious about Aruba's synagogue, wishing to attend services while on vacation, or curious about a destination bar or bat mitzvah should visit this site.

Index

D

E

F

GH

IJK

L

M

N

OP

QR

S

T

UVWXYZ

Also Available

MOON ARUBA
Avalon Travel
An imprint of Perseus Books
A Hachette Book Group company
1700 Fourth Street
Berkeley, CA 94710, USA
www.moon.com

Editor: Rachel Feldman
Series Manager: Kathryn Ettinger
Copy Editor: Ashley Benning
Graphics Coordinator: Elizabeth Jang
Production Coordinator: Elizabeth Jang
Cover Design: Faceout Studios, Charles Brock
Interior Design: Domini Dragoone
Moon Logo: Tim McGrath
Map Editor: Kat Bennett
Cartographers: Karin Dahl, Chris Henrick
Indexer: Greg Jewett

ISBN-13: 978-1-63121-377-9
ISSN: 2331-5202

Printing History
1st Edition — 2014
2nd Edition — October 2016
5 4 3 2 1

Front cover photo: flamingos on Renaissance Island © George Oze / Alamy

Back cover photo: Carnival pageantry © Rosalie Klein

All photos © Rosalie Klein, except the following: page 13 (lower left) © skdesign/123rf.com; page 16 © Ritu Jethani/123rf.com; page 18 © Gail Johnson | Dreamstime.com; page 21 © Ritu Jethani/123rf.com; page 33 © Christian Offenberg/123rf.com; page 43 © Kjersti Joergensen | Dreamstime.com; page 83 © Ritu Jethani/123rf.com; page 143 © Emotionart | Dreamstime.com; page 151 © Darryl Brooks | Dreamstime.com; page 189 (bottom) © Renato Galindo/123rf.com; page 197 © David Smith/123rf.com; page 200 © Chris and Allison Bickum/123rf.com

Printed in Canada by Friesens

KEEPING CURRENT

If you have a favorite gem you'd like to see included in the next edition, or see anything that needs updating, clarification, or correction, please drop us a line. Send your comments via email to feedback@moon.com, or use the address above.

MAP SYMBOLS

Expressway
Primary Road
Secondary Road
Unpaved Road
Feature Trail
Other Trail
Ferry
Pedestrian Walkway
Stairs

City/Town
State Capital
National Capital
Point of Interest
Accommodation
Restaurant/Bar
Other Location
Campground

Airport
Airfield
Mountain
Unique Natural Feature
Waterfall
Park
Trailhead
Skiing Area

Golf Course
Parking Area
Archaeological Site
Church
Gas Station
Glacier
Mangrove
Reef
Swamp

CONVERSION TABLES

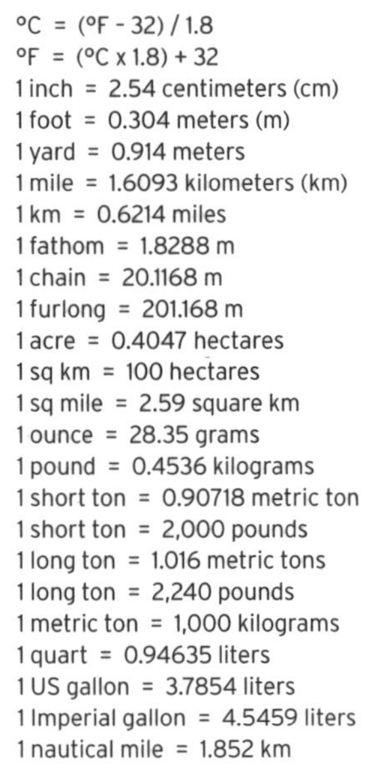

°C = (°F - 32) / 1.8
°F = (°C x 1.8) + 32
1 inch = 2.54 centimeters (cm)
1 foot = 0.304 meters (m)
1 yard = 0.914 meters
1 mile = 1.6093 kilometers (km)
1 km = 0.6214 miles
1 fathom = 1.8288 m
1 chain = 20.1168 m
1 furlong = 201.168 m
1 acre = 0.4047 hectares
1 sq km = 100 hectares
1 sq mile = 2.59 square km
1 ounce = 28.35 grams
1 pound = 0.4536 kilograms
1 short ton = 0.90718 metric ton
1 short ton = 2,000 pounds
1 long ton = 1.016 metric tons
1 long ton = 2,240 pounds
1 metric ton = 1,000 kilograms
1 quart = 0.94635 liters
1 US gallon = 3.7854 liters
1 Imperial gallon = 4.5459 liters
1 nautical mile = 1.852 km

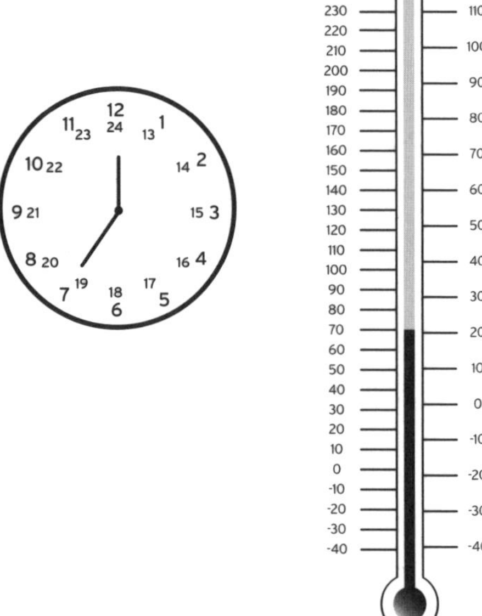

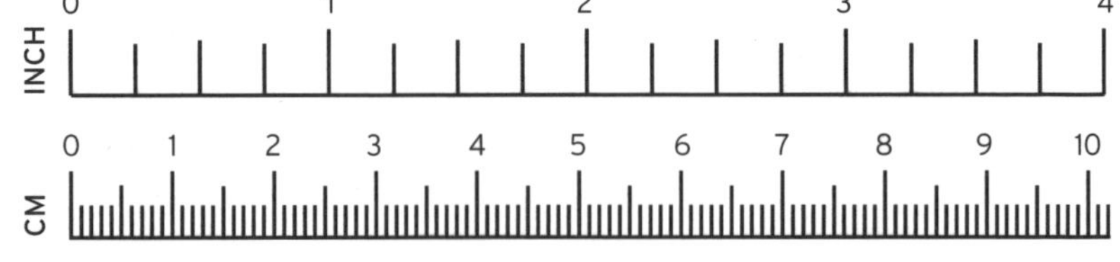